Advance Praise

"Professors Pandey and Pestonjee have produced an authoritative book on stress in the workpl ce. While most stress theories originate in Western countries, this book i ased on research, conducted in India, and was written by prominent n scholars, working in a variety of academic and business organizations I am convinced that this volume will become an essential handbook of workplace stress-related research in India and will be a useful reference source for researchers and HR and HRD practitioners. As one of the rare non-Western volumes, written on this subject, the book will also be of interest to scholars doing international and comparative research on work and human resource management and development."

—**Alexand e Ardichvili, PhD, Professor, University of Minnesota, USA, and Editor-in-Chief,** *Human Resource Development International*

"This book addresse, a powerful issue that spans two centuries and offers four blended strengths. First, the essence of the stress response and its origins circa 1915 are capr ed concisely in the neuropsychology of stress. Second, the most salient ele ents of occupational stress and work–family conflict are pulled to the fore in two well-organized sections of nicely focused chapters. The critical gender issues are isolated into one chapter. Third, the emerging positive aspects of stress and its experience are brought to the fore with two strong chapters. Stress does well more than cause damage. Fourth, the under considered connection of stress to spirituality and within context, in this case India, are nicely explored. All and all, an excellent volume with the right balance in the correct context."

—**James Campbell (Jim) Quick, Distinguished Professor of Leadership & Organizational Behavior, John and Judy Goolsby – Jacqualyn A. Fouse Endowed Chair, Goolsby Leadership Academy, College of Business, The University of Texas at Arlington, USA**

"Pestonjee and Pandey provide a thoughtful and relevant insight into the complex issue of occupational stress within the Indian context. The text is a valuable resource for both researchers and people managers for its coverage of both traditional stress issues such as the impact of job demands, control and support upon employee health, and for a discussion of emerging issues such as flourishing at work."

—Professor Paula Brough, Director, Social & Organisational Psychology Research Unit (SOPRU), School of Applied Psychology, Mt Gravatt Campus, Griffith University, Australia

"This compendium is well structured with an introduction to the foundations of stress in the environment that we are in followed by papers in the occupational area stress which is a major component of stress in today's globalised world. I am sure that the judiciously selected papers in the compendium will enrich the reader and also contribute to the understanding of stress for an ardent student, researcher and all of us who are always interested in uncovering the 'enigma' of stress. I must congratulate Dr D. M. Pestonjee and Dr Satish Pandey for this excellent endeavor and wish them all the best in their continued contribution to the field of stress and stress management."

—Professor (Dr) Krishna Moorthy, Dean, L & T Institute of Project Management, Gujarat, India

Stress

and Work

Stress
and **Work**

Perspectives on Understanding
and Managing Stress

Edited by

D. M. Pestonjee
Satish Pandey

⑤SAGE | Response Business Books

www.sagepublications.com

Los Angeles • London • New Delhi • Singapore • Washington DC

First published in 2013 by

SAGE Response
B1/I-1 Mohan Cooperative Industrial Area
Mathura Road, New Delhi 110 044, India

SAGE Publications Inc
2455 Teller Road
Thousand Oaks, California 91320, USA

SAGE Publications Ltd
1 Oliver's Yard, 55 City Road
London EC1Y 1SP, United Kingdom

SAGE Publications Asia-Pacific Pte Ltd
33 Pekin Street
#02-01 Far East Square
Singapore 048763

Published by Vivek Mehra for SAGE Publications India Pvt Ltd, typeset in 11/13 Adobe Garamond Pro by Diligent Typesetter and printed at Saurabh Printers Pvt Ltd.

Library of Congress Cataloging-in-Publication Data

Stress and work: perspectives on understading and managing stress/edited by D.M. Pestonjee and Satish Pandey.
    p. cm.
  Includes bibliographical references and index.
  1. Job stress. 2. Stress (Psychology) 3. Work–Psychological aspects. 4. Stress management. I. Pestonjee, D. M., 1939- II. Pandey, Satish C.
  HF5548.85.S752   158.7'2–dc23   2013   2012049736

ISBN: 978-81-321-1088-0 (PB)

The SAGE Team: Sachin Sharma, Punita Kaur Mann, and Nand Kumar Jha

Dedicated to

Late Professor Udai Pareek

Who inspired by his words and deeds generations of scholars

Thank you for choosing a SAGE product! If you have any comment, observation or feedback, I would like to personally hear from you. Please write to me at <u>contactceo@sagepub.in</u>

—Vivek Mehra, Managing Director and CEO,
SAGE Publications India Pvt Ltd, New Delhi

Bulk Sales

SAGE India offers special discounts for purchase of books in bulk. We also make available special imprints and excerpts from our books on demand.

For orders and enquiries, write to us at

Marketing Department
SAGE Publications India Pvt Ltd
B1/I-1, Mohan Cooperative Industrial Area
Mathura Road, Post Bag 7
New Delhi 110044, India
E-mail us at <u>marketing@sagepub.in</u>

Get to know more about SAGE, be invited to SAGE events, get on our mailing list. Write today to <u>marketing@sagepub.in</u>

This book is also available as an e-book.

————&❦—————

Contents

List of Tables and Figures

Tables

Figures

Figures

Foreword

During the 1980s, the West embraced the "Enterprise Culture," then came the global recession, and out of this downturn, we had an increase in international competition with cross-national mergers, joint ventures, and major restructurings within organizations. Throughout the West, and in the emerging economies (e.g., India, China, Brazil, and Russia), we had a period of accelerated growth for over a decade and a half, until the crash at the end of 2007 (Bowles & Cooper, 2012). Now we are entering an era of differential development, with the US and Europe in recession or very slow growth, and the emerging economies accelerating, but still adversely affected by the economic troubles in the Eurozone and in the US. These developments have meant, in many countries, a substantial personal cost for managers and employees, as they attempt to cope with the massive changes that are taking place, whether in declining economies or growing ones (Weinberg & Cooper, 2012). This cost is captured by a single word, "stress." Indeed, "stress" has found as firm a place in our modern vocabularies as "apps," "call centers," and "social media." We toss the term around casually to describe a wide range of health behaviors and illnesses resulting from our hectic work and private lives. "I really feel stressed," someone says to describe a vague, yet often acute sense of unhappiness. "She's under a lot of stress," we say when trying to understand a colleague's irritability or aggressive behavior. "It's a high-stress job," someone says awarding an odd sort of prestige to his/her job. But for those whose ability to cope with the day-to-day excessive work pressures—the long hours at work, the difficult relationships, and blocked careers—the concept of stress is no longer a casual one, it translates into pain and distress.

But the reality of stress in the workplace has now become a bottom-line issue, costing companies, public sector bodies, and the health services of countries a great deal of money. In the UK alone, the cost of stress and mental ill-health in the workplace was estimated at £25.9b in 2008, resulting in absenteeism, presenteeism (people turning up to work even when ill but contributing little added value to their products or services), and labor turnover (Cooper et al., 2009). Indeed, as jobs become more insecure in this global recession, we are beginning to see the costs of presenteeism soar, as people come to work earlier and stay later to show commitment, so that they are not the next tranche of employees to be let go. In a recent report of the European Agency for Safety and Health, which was based on a poll of over 35,000 workers in 36 European countries, they sought to establish the level of perceived job-related stress in each country, and whether this was likely to increase over the next 5 years. The findings make grim reading, as 77% of respondents from the 36 countries said they thought job-related stress would increase over the next 5 years, with only 7% saying they thought it would decrease. This perception was Europe-wide, with most countries showing high levels of stress now and the prediction of more to come in the future. This is not surprising, given the downsizings of most public and private sector workers in most European countries hit by the recession or little growth, with fewer people doing more work, feeling more insecure, and being managed more autocratically. In terms of this last point, the Chartered Management Institute, the professional body of managers in the UK, in their Quality of Working Life survey (Worrall & Cooper, 2012) found, among a cohort of 20,000 managers in 2012, that the most common management styles were bureaucratic (45%), reactive (33%), and authoritarian (30%). The empowering and engaging management style was in the minority. It was found that all of these dominant management styles had a negative impact on motivation, health, well-being, and productivity.

So how can we manage stress at work in these difficult times? Cartwright & Cooper (2011) suggest a three-pronged approach: primary, secondary, and tertiary prevention. *Primary prevention* is concerned with modifying or eliminating the sources of stress inherent in the work environment, so reducing the negative impact on the individual. This is achieved by doing stress or well-being audits, using standardized measures like ASSET (Faragher et al., 2004), and then when diagnosing specific problems, dealing directly with them. *Secondary prevention* is developing the skills of the individual through training and other educative activities to deal with the stresses and strains in their work lives. This might include time management, resilience training, learning to prioritize work, etc. And finally, *tertiary prevention* is concerned with the treatment, rehabilitation, and recovery process of individuals who have suffered from stress. This might include employee assistance programs or other counseling techniques, financial and legal support for problems, re-training in a new skill, etc.

In the end, we are all interested, as is this impressive book, in helping people cope with the excessive pressures of the workplace. Our role as occupational and health psychologists is to enhance well-being in the workplace. As Robert Kennedy said in a speech in 1968 when he was on the campaign trail:

> Too much and for too long, we seemed to have surrendered personal excellence and community values in the mere accumulation of material things. Our Gross National Product, now is over $800b a year—but that GNP—if we judge the USA by that—that GNP counts air pollution and cigarette advertising, and the ambulances to clear our highways of carnage. It counts special locks for our doors and the jails for the people who break them. It counts the destruction of the redwood and the loss of our natural wonder in chaotic sprawl. It counts napalm and counts nuclear warheads and armoured cars for the police to fight the riots in our cities ... yet the Gross National Product does not allow for the health of our children, the quality of their education or the joy of their play. It does not include the beauty of our poetry or the strength of our marriages, the intelligence of our public debate or the integrity of our public officials. It measures neither our wit nor our courage, neither our wisdom nor our learning, neither our compassion nor our devotion to our country, it measures everything in short, except that which makes life worthwhile.

And this is our challenge for the years to come.

Cary L. Cooper, CBE
Distinguished Professor of Organizational Psychology and Health
Lancaster University Management School
England

Chair of the Academy of Social Sciences
President of British Association of Counseling and Psychotherapy
President of RELATE

References

Bowles, D. & Cooper, C.L. (2012). *The high engagement culture: Balancing me and we.* Basingstoke,UK: Palgrave Macmillan.

Cartwright, S. & Cooper, C.L. (2011). *Innovations in stress and health.* Basingstoke,UK: Palgrave Macmillan.

Cooper, C.L., et al. (2009). *Mental capital and wellbeing.* Oxford: Wiley-Blackwell.

Faragher, E.B., et al. (2004). A shortened stress evaluation tool (ASSET). *Stress and Health,* 20, 189–201.

Weinberg, A. & Cooper, C.L. (2012). *Stress in turbulent times.* Basingstoke, UK: Palgrave Macmillan.

Worrall, L. & Cooper, C.L. (2012). *The quality of working life 2012: Managers' wellbeing, motivation and productivity.* London: Chartered Management Institute.

Preface

Human life has been full of struggle since ancient times. To survive for their identity amongst various species created by the Almighty, human beings started to evolve as civilized society, and civilizations continued to grow. Some civilizations could not survive with changes happening around them. The struggle has not ended even today and modern human society has continued to advance. We have evolved from a hunting society to an agrarian one, then came the industrial revolution, followed by information technology revolution, which shaped our society into a knowledge society. It has also changed the functioning of organizations and world of work for human beings. Earlier, we used to hunt for fulfilling our basic needs, then we started growing food through agriculture and small industries took birth. Later in the 19th century, industrial revolution gave birth to units of mass production, called factories. All these changes shaped the ways human beings used to work in organized forms. Our organizations today are in totally different shape than those of the last century; but one thing has not changed—human beings still need organizations to earn their livelihood and satisfy social needs. People could be part of organizations as employees, partners, or entrepreneurs but they need organizations to survive.

The survival need could be termed as a major force behind the struggle of human beings to search for right kind of work. This is equally important for an unskilled, uneducated worker as well as highly educated and tech-savvy professional. Hence, world of work cannot be considered "smooth" for anyone; rather, it is full of stresses. If we look into a developing country like India, we are facing problems of being the second largest population in the world and increasing urbanization, which is leading to expansion of cities and migration of people from one corner of the country to other corners. Our cities have become bigger and overcrowded, civic amenities are in shambles, distances and commuting create havoc on personal and social well-being. An individual's continuous struggle for survival has forced psychologists, sociologists, anthropologists, economists, and other social scientists to study the phenomenon of stress in context of work. Initially borrowed from natural and physical sciences, this term "stress" has become perhaps the most "lovable" term for social scientists to study interaction between individuals and organizations in the world of work. Since the first book of Hans Selye, *The Stress of Life*, was published in 1956, a number of research papers, popular articles, and books have been published on the topics of stress and stress management. There is no dearth of bestseller books in the market on teaching techniques of stress management.

There has been a felt need amongst researchers and academicians for a research-focused compendium of knowledge which could be helpful to new researchers in understanding the field of stress management from multiple perspectives and contribute to develop their own theoretical framework of stress research. There were few books published in the past with focus on contemporary research in the field of stress management, including the famous seminal work of Professor D. M. Pestonjee, *Stress and Coping: The Indian Experience*, which was first published by SAGE Publications, New Delhi, in 1992, then, second edition came in 1999. Some selected Indian titles are:

- *Studies in Organizational Role Stress and Coping*: D. M. Pestonjee and Udai Pareek (Eds), Rawat Publications, Jaipur, 1997.
- *Studies in Stress and Its Management*: D. M. Pestonjee, Udai Pareek and Rita Agrawal (Eds), Oxford & IBH, New Delhi, 1999.
- *Psychological Perspectives on Stress and Health*: Girishwar Mishra (Ed.), Concept Publishing Company, New Delhi, 1999.
- *Recent Trends in Human Stress Management*: Akbar Husain and Mohammad Ilyas Khan (Eds), Global Vision Publishing House, New Delhi, 2006.

The present volume contains both theoretical papers and empirical studies focused on various issues related to stress and work especially in the Indian context. We believe that the present volume will provide sufficient research literature reflecting on different theoretical perspectives and empirical findings relevant to different occupational settings at one place. We hope that the present volume will be helpful to new as well as experienced researchers in enriching their knowledge and identifying new issues for future research.

This volume could not have been possible without collaborative efforts and support of academicians and researchers who joined hands with us in this project. Our contributors worked very hard with us for making this effort successful. People revised their drafts several times for improving quality of the content in their papers in line with feedback given by the editors. We got support from academicians and researchers working with premier institutes and universities including National Institute of Mental Health and Neurosciences (NIMHANS, Bangalore), Defence Institute of Psychological Research (DIPR, Delhi), Xavier's Institute of Management (XIMB, Bhubaneswar), Management Development Institute (MDI, Gurgaon), Mudra Institute of Communications Ahmedabad (MICA), Delhi University, Aligarh Muslim University, Bangalore University, and also two institutions from USA: Syracuse University, New York, and Saint Mary's College, Notre Dame, Indiana.

We are very thankful to our colleagues at School of Petroleum Management, Pandit Deendayal Petroleum University, Gandhinagar, for their continuous encouragement, support, and appreciation of our dream project. We are also very grateful to Professor Bhavesh Patel, Former Director, School of Petroleum Management, PDPU for his continuous support during his tenure. We would also like to acknowledge the help, encouragement, critical appraisal, and support received from Professor N. R. Dave, Educational Advisor, PDPU, Gandhinagar.

We are extremely grateful to Professor Paritosh Banik, Director-General, PDPU for his continuous support and encouragement to us. We are very thankful to Pandit Deendayal Petroleum University, Gandhinagar, for sponsoring this project through a research grant. We are also thankful to SAGE Publications for their commitment and support to publish this volume. Without support of these two major stakeholders, this dream could not have come true.

A very special "Thank You" to Professor Cary L. Cooper, Distinguished Professor of Organizational Psychology and Health, Lancaster University Management School, Lancaster, UK, for the "Foreword" he has so graciously wrote for the volume.

Last but not the least, we also would like to express our gratitude to our family members who continuously supported and encouraged us.

D. M. Pestonjee
Satish Pandey

October 18, 2012

1

Introduction

D. M. Pestonjee and Satish Pandey

New World of Work

For a person who belongs to the current civilized society, the world of work has changed quite a lot in the last few decades of the 20th century and especially in the first decade of the 21st century. Stable and rapid growth of large organizations in the 20th century ensured a secure and long-term employment to individuals; though there were phases of economic ups and downs at different intervals, the overall work life of an individual was relatively stable. In the 20th century, be it work itself or workplace, things were quite organized and well defined for individuals and social systems including organizations.

The rapid growth of information technology and new communication technologies has changed human life dramatically. Individuals and organizations are bewildered with the growth of virtual world and its invasion in their lives. Work is no longer limited to one's physical workspace but it rather extends to a virtual workspace where many people can connect with each other and work together to achieve common goals. Internet and mobile communication became an inevitable part of life of an individual belonging to the modern civil society. First e-mail, and then social networking applications like Facebook, Orkut, Myspace, Twitter changed the ways of Internet communication. These changes also impacted on the way organizations used to communicate and connect with individuals—their employees, customers, or other stakeholders. The modern world of work is more dynamic and complex than ever before. Organizations can also no longer afford to work as large bureaucracies, but rather they need to be more adaptive and resilient to the changed business environment. The first decade of the 21st century has seen fall of many giants in the recession of 2008; whereas many small Davids challenged existing Goliaths and defeated them in their fields. Future organizations need to understand and manage the following factors effectively if they wish to survive and achieve excellence in their respective domains. The modern world of work has to take cognizance of the following important characteristics of organizations:

1. *Uncertainty*: The external environment of future organizations will be full of uncertainty and very volatile. Traditional approaches of devising strategies will not be effective anymore and managers will need to think differently for new business models relevant for different markets across the globe.

2. *Complexity*: Future organizations will be more complex systems than ever before. They would be designed around multiple business processes/models and targeting different markets in different regions. There could be numerous interdependent subsystems working with numerous external systems. Both external and internal boundaries will become blurred and permeable. Though organizations will be flatter, but ambiguity and multiplicity of organizational roles of individuals and departments/work groups/teams will be making organizational systems more complex.

3. *Speed*: For future organizations, time could be perhaps the most precious resource to control. High uncertainty and complexity will force organizations to shorten their long-term plan and they will need to work with a very fast pace to achieve their targets. Organizations need to review and revise their goals, objectives, and plans very frequently. Strategies designed today may not remain effective by the time they are implemented.

4. *Technology*: Efficient technology will be the key to success for future organizations and it has to be continuously evolving, real-time, relevant, and key to innovation. New technologies will drastically bring down costs and make decision-making more efficient. Only organizations investing in R&D for technology innovation will be able to survive and achieve excellence. Organizations need to invest more money on developing and using clean technologies for achieving energy efficiency, doing less damage to the environment, and making human life better.

5. *Virtual Workspace*: In the present century, geography and physics both need to be reinterpreted. Distances have shrunk and the term "global" has acquired a new significance. Work teams can be far apart and may focus on achieving their goals while operating in different geographical locales with different time-zones. Till recent past, when we talked of "teams," we thought of individuals who are in close proximity with

each other, but not anymore. Future organizations will have more virtual space than physical one. Organizations could be hiring highly competent and talented professionals across the globe to achieve their targets. New communication technologies, e.g., cloud computing will make virtual workspace more cost effective in comparison to traditional physical workspaces. Most of core business processes would be done online by several virtual teams together.

6. *Hyperspecialization*: As future organizations will be more adaptive to their environment, many jobs which are dominating today's job market will be extinct in future or could only be of archival value. Future organizations will be driven by hyperspecialized jobs which could be very complex but designed around very specific processes or outputs (Malone, Laubacher & Johns, 2011). Hyperspecialized jobs will demand multiplicity of tasks, skills, and knowledge of special domains. Hyperspecialized jobs will achieve improvements in quality, speed, and cost. Possibly a future hyperspecialized job would merge many interrelated jobs of today and eliminate them in future.

7. *Cultural Diversity*: Since workspace is becoming "virtual," a necessary concomitant is diversity of cultures within a given team. The geographical spread of the organization and various operations which they perform at various locations imply cultural diversity. Organizations need to frame "culturally sensitive" HR policies for effective handling of cross-cultural issues at culturally diverse workplaces. Issues related to minorities, gender, and special groups, e.g., people with disabilities, need to be given special attention in HR policies of the organizations.

8. *Communication*: To manage uncertainty and complexity effectively, in the era of mergers, acquisitions, and alliances, organizations will need to design better internal and external communication strategies with various stakeholders. Collaborative interorganizational relationships with other organizations will be a strong determinant of success of any organization.

All the above factors have macro-level impact on organizations, e.g., restructuring of business operations, downsizing of workforce, or closing down of specific business units which will have ultimate impact on individuals in terms of their employment, workplace behavior, and personal life. In future, people would be continuously striving to maintain their employability rather than securing their current employment. This will put tremendous stress on individuals and organizations, as organizations too need to work hard for attracting and retaining "talented employees" with them, whereas individuals would be working hard for sustainable career growth in their organizations.

We also need to consider that individuals, families, and organizations create a society. When organizations hire individuals to work for them, they are not just hiring a skilled professional to do a specific job but a family with human needs. In future, organizations need to be more sensitive and humane for effective management of human affairs. Organizations need to focus on issues like work–life balance, gender issues, social support issues, and emotional issues for improving quality of life and well-being of individuals. We would like to highlight some of these issues:

1. *Gender Issues*: The composition of working population has been subject to change during the past few decades. Increasing proportion of women employees in the workforce across industries and occupational sectors has raised the need for special attention to address gender issues at workplaces. Organizations need to be more "sensitive" toward gender issues in their policy, especially with regard to sexual harassment, fair career opportunities to competent professionals irrespective of gender, and fair treatment of women employees on work and performance.

2. *Work–Life Balance*: The social fabric of the society is under tremendous tension and has started showing the signs of "wear and tear." With better-qualified, younger professionals entering in the employment markets combined with concepts of gender equality, things are going to be tough for the future managers. Gender roles are probably going to be the most important issue of concern for the society in general and organizations in particular. And as we all see, the IQ is having a toll on the EQ.

3. *Changing Legal Environment*: Organizations need to work under legal framework of the country where they operate. At the macro-level, legal issues are potential sources of stress for organizations as social systems. Stress in a social system percolates to individuals who are members of the system. As a sovereign country, we have had our own constitution to govern our destinies for over six decades now. It is fascinating to see how the constitutional provisions have been modified time and again to suite the external realities, e.g., UN policies, international laws related to business, and governance. In future, we have to align our regulations and laws with international legal norms, e.g., labor laws, intellectual properties, cyber laws, international climate change agreements, to name a few. In future, organizations need to be more sensitive toward the impact of their legal compliance on their employees, clients, and customers.

4. *Social Structure and Support Systems*: It has been a social aphorism that the worst of the stress can be managed if we have the best of the support system! Not true anymore. Our support system, like the traditional family bonds and traditional parent–child or grandparents–grandchild linkages are getting weaker day-by-day. With long-term organizational commitment, people could develop long-term friendships. The Gen-Y does not believe in staying with the same organization long enough to develop socially meaningful relationships. In the absence of adequate support systems, the chances of break-ups and break-downs increase manifold.

5. *Mental Health Issues*: With so much changing so fast in our social environment, technology environment, and organizational environment, we cannot think of the "poor individual" going unscathed. Naturally, mental health issues are becoming more and more pronounced as the century progresses. "Keeping up with the Jonasis" has been known to the previous generations; it is time now to learn to "keep up with oneself." There is a strong argument in the contention that stress research, especially in the organizational context, is actually represented by the interface between HRM practitioners and clinical psychologists.

To manage all these factors effectively, adaptive organizations need to build a collaborative culture which should drive their stakeholders toward continuous learning and excellence. Organizations need to design more dynamic work systems and organizational roles for individuals and teams. We need to treat "work" or "work systems" not as sources of distress but "positive stress"; and focus of "work and work systems" should not be on reducing, preventing, or eliminating distress but to enhance positive orientation of challenging work as positive stress. "Positive stress in work environment" can be understood in the form of a metaphor, when we imagine a surfer surfing on sea waves, a skier skiing on snow-covered hills, many musicians playing melodies together, or skydivers forming different formations in the sky though they are for a very short period in the sky. In this example, all of them (surfer, skier, musicians, and skydivers) are working because of the force of positive stress. Collaboration is meant to play on mutual strengths together, not competing strengths in friction with each other.

Some recent researches on happiness have indicated that happy employees collaborate among themselves, with customers and clients more effectively and thrive together to achieve excellence. Thriving employees are highly energized, and they know how to avoid burnout (Spreitzer & Porath, 2012). Spreitzer &

Porath (2012) identified two most important components of thriving—the first one is *vitality*, which means the sense of being alive, passionate, and exciting; the second one is *learning*, which indicates growth that comes through gaining new knowledge. Enhancing vitality and continuous learning are good enough to create positive stress and reduce burnout.

Collaboration also requires effective role systems within organizations which allow employees to craft and modify their work roles as they grow on their career path in the organization. In their proposed model of positive work role behavior, Griffin, Neal, & Parker (2007) identified three most important factors of determining positive work role behaviors—proficiency, adaptivity, and proactivity—and how an employee's work role behaviors at individual level, as team member, and as organizational member influence individual work performance, team performance, and organizational effectiveness overall. To build innovation-focused work culture, organizations need to encourage collaboration at every level and develop self-evolving role systems.

This volume includes 14 chapters covering various issues related to stress in context of work. Some chapters reflect on different theoretical perspectives (philosophical, neuropsychological) of stress, coping, health, and well-being. Some of the chapters present empirical studies on testing of different models of stress, e.g., work–family conflict, job demands–control–support, organizational role stress, role-focused burnout, learned helplessness–role stress relationship, naming a few. There are some chapters in this volume which have attempted to cover a wide range of issues, e.g., gender issues, methodological issues, and special context like military environment. This volume consists of four sections focused on different aspects of stress and work—occupational stress and burnout, work–life balance and stress, positive management of stress, and stress and spirituality. Two chapters, "The Neuropsychology of Stress" and "Methodological Issues in Stress Research: Challenges, Concerns, and Directions" could not be classified under any section, hence we kept these chapters independent.

The chapter on "The Neuropsychology of Stress" by Jamuna Rajeswaran and Cathlyn N. Bennett reflects on neuropsychological perspective of stress. In this chapter, the authors have discussed on implications of neuroscience research on studying cognitive and emotional aspects of stress and coping. The authors have also discussed on how neurofeedback training could be effectively used in relaxation training and stress management interventions. There is enormous scope for applications of social neuroscience approach in stress research and in future, we need more collaborative researches involving neurologists, psychologists, and other social scientists to explore neuroscience of stress, coping, health, and well-being.

Section-I, "Occupational Stress and Burnout," covers various issues ranging from stress in extreme conditions (military setting), perceived organizational role stress to executive burnout.

The chapter on "Learned Helplessness and Organizational Role Stress" by Fakir M. Sahoo, examined relationship of perceived learned helplessness, attributional styles of managers with perceived organizational role stress in context of managers working in different organizations located in costal Odisha. The results supported the prediction that personal helplessness is significantly related to role stress while universal helplessness is unrelated to role stress. Personal helplessness is also found positively associated with negative attributional styles. There was negative association between personal helplessness and satisfaction. No significant differences were observed between male and female managers on various role stress factors except role stagnation, role expectations conflict, self-role distance, and role ambiguity. Male managers reported higher role stagnation and role expectations conflict, whereas female managers reported higher self-role distance and role ambiguity. The findings of the study may have implications in the context of enhancing workplace learning and designing better role systems by controlling personal learned helplessness and attributional styles.

The chapter on "Role Stress among Varied Occupational Groups" by Parvaiz Talib and Irfana Rashid presents a comparative analysis of perceived organizational role stress among four different occupational groups—private sector companies, public sector companies, government organizations, and university employees. The trends observed in this study clearly indicate dominance of role erosion and inter-role distance as dominant stressors across all the four occupational groups. Though all four occupational groups have different work environments and their own complexities, dominance of role erosion and inter-role distance stressors indicates increasing feelings of job insecurity and work–family conflict in employees' daily work life. These findings also indicate that now people are more concerned about their long-term career growth within the organization or chosen occupation, meaningful professional development, ensuring employability security rather than employment security, and balancing their work and family life. The authors also suggested some intervention remedies for improving role systems in different occupational sectors, viz., private, public, government, and universities.

The chapter on "Executive Burnout: Prediction and Prevention through HR Interventions" by Radha R. Sharma reflects on research gaps on burnout research in Indian and global contexts. She argued that construct of burnout as initially defined on the basis of researches conducted on human service occupations (e.g., nurses, teachers, social workers, etc.) is not perceived in the same way in manufacturing and other industries. The findings of the chapter present an empirical account on personality and role-related determinants of executive burnout in managers of manufacturing and service industries in Indian context. The chapter suggests some HR interventions for preventing or mitigating executive burnout for greater competitiveness and employee well-being. The findings of this study may also be considered as validity measures for widely used "organizational role stress model" (Pareek, 1983).

In the chapter, "Stress in Extreme Conditions: A Military Perspective," Updesh Kumar, Vijay Parkash, and Manas K. Mandal reflect on psychological impact of extreme work conditions in armed forces and how combat soldiers and other professionals who work in those extreme situations, cope with those stressful situations. Deployments in counter-insurgency and low-intensity conflict areas, high altitude, and extreme temperatures in glaciers and deserts are the potential stressors for soldiers on land; whereas, extreme temperature and noise in cockpits, and high speed are few major stressors in military aviation. Repetitive surroundings, social confinement, extreme hydrostatic pressure, and danger from invisible enemy adversely impact the well-being of naval personnel and submariners. They also reflect on the psychological impact of extreme military conditions on soldiers working on global peacekeeping missions and internal security operations, e.g., anti-terrorists operations and rescue operations in natural or man-made disasters. The chapter also proposes remedial measures for designing stress management interventions relevant to military forces. We believe that though the chapter is focused on military settings, its findings and reflections could provide sound theoretical foundations for conducting stress research on similar occupations where people have to work under extremely risky work conditions, e.g., firefighters, police, and paramilitary forces, to name a few.

Section II, "Work–Family Conflict and Stress," predominantly covers issues related to work–family conflict, work–life balance, and gender issues in organizations. The chapters in this section reflect on how work–family conflict and gender issues influence individuals' perception of work stress in organizations and make impact on the work–life balance. The chapter on "Work–Family Conflict in India: Test of a Causal Model" by Ujvala Rajadhyaksha and Kamala Ramadoss presents a critical examination of work–family conflict model by Frone, Yardley, & Markle (1997) in the Indian context. The chapter adopted "etic" approach to discuss work–family conflict model in the Indian context. The sample for this study comprises 405 white-collar men and women employees from health, education, finance, and manufacturing industries located in two prominent Indian industrial cities, Mumbai and Bangalore. Data tested via structural equation modeling provided a very poor fit for the original model; but modified models demonstrated improved fit. The findings indicate that social support was positively, rather than negatively, related to demands and negative outcomes in both work and family domains; and work demands was negatively, rather than positively, related to negative family and work outcomes. The findings of this study have shown contrary patterns in comparison to North American or Western work context. The findings also indicate toward development of "culturally appropriate" models for explaining work–family conflict in non-Western cultures. The findings also indicate possibility of emerging market for childcare, household chores maintenance, and eldercare facilities in a developing country like India in future, similar to the developed countries.

The chapter on "Work Stress, Work–family Conflict and Health: A Multilevel Perspective" by Kamala Ramadoss critically examines Karasek's Demand–Control–Support model from a multilevel perspective in the context of Indian IT services industry. The study was conducted on 774 employees of 54 organizations located in western and southern India. The findings indicated that job demand and work–family conflict at the individual level were significantly related to health and the direction of the relationship was negative. At the organizational level, organizations differed significantly from each other in how supportive they were of their employee's work and family issues. The study also supports this argument that low job demands and low work-family conflict at the individual level and support at the organizational level significantly improve employee's health. The study suggests that ITeS companies in developing countries like India need to adopt culturally sensitive practices that can help in reducing stress and burnout, e.g., frequent workshops focused on yoga, meditation, art and lining, etc., on regular basis (not once/twice in a year).

The chapter on "Gender Issues in Work and Stress" by Shubhra P. Gaur and Shikha S. Jain presents an overview of gender theories in the context of work and stress. With increasing proportion of female employees in organizations across different sectors, gender issues have become critical for researchers, policy-makers, and industry practitioners. The chapter reflects on perceptual differences between genders on work-related stressors and coping behavior patterns across different occupational groups. The chapter also addresses important issues related to work and stress in the context of dual career families. The authors also recommend for bringing gender inclusivity in designing workplace stress management interventions. The authors have also raised concerns over the lack of sufficient comparative statistics on gender-related parameters of work in terms of sector-wise, occupation-wise, and hierarchy-wise distribution which could be useful for government policy-makers, industry practitioners, and researchers.

Section-III, "Positive Stress Management," focuses on coping with stress in positive context. The chapter on "Coping with Stress" by Paulomi Sudhir and Arathi Taksal presents an overview of different theories and models of coping behavior. It discusses on different types of coping strategies, various psychometric measures of coping, different kinds of psychotherapeutic and counseling techniques for improving proactive coping, and coping-focused workplace interventions. The chapter also reflects on future research directions in the context of stress–coping relationship and coping-focused workplace interventions.

The chapter on "Flourishing at Work" by Seema Mehrotra and Ravikesh Tripathi presents a valuable discussion on positive perspective of stress and work. Influence of positive psychology school has motivated many researchers in India to shift focus of research from "distress" to "positive stress." This chapter argues that flourishing (feeling good in general usage) has not yet been defined theoretically as psychological construct and has not attracted enough attention of researchers working on organizational behavior issues. They presented a valuable account of researches done on psychological and social well-being and examined their relevance in work settings. The chapter presents a strong theoretical framework for understanding and defining "flourishing" as psychological constructs and reflects on future research prospects aimed at designing effective stress management interventions focused on enhancement of "flourishing at work," not on "reduction or prevention of distress at work."

Section-IV, "Stress and Spirituality," focuses on spiritual context of stress. Spirituality has not only been considered a buffer to counter stressful situations in life but it also provides psychological strength to fight with stress. The chapters included in this section narrate and discuss various philosophies, e.g., Buddhism, Vedic philosophy, Yoga, Bhagavad Gita, etc. The chapter on "Existential Rhythm, Spiritual Synergy and Spiritual Immunity: Spiritual Approaches to Stress Management" by Husain reflects on Indian philosophical perspective on spirituality, psychoneuroimmunology, existential rhythm, stress, and health. The chapter also discusses on how existential rhythm affects mind–body relationship and relationship of human beings with their environment, and ultimately contributes to perception of stress and proneness of diseases. He also argued that effective control of spiritual energy in daily routine could be very helpful in enhancing psychoneuroimmunology among human beings at personal, interpersonal, and social levels.

In the chapter on "Managing Constructive and Destructive Emotions: Indian Psycho-spiritual Perspective" by Sinha, the author presented a wonderful comparison of West-originated psychological theories of emotions with a new psychological theory of emotions based on Rasa-Guna theory as mentioned in ancient Indian Sanskrit texts, Bharat's *Natyasastra* and Bhagavad Gita, a holy text. The Rasa-Guna (R-G) theory of emotions reflects on interpretation of positive and negative emotions in Indian culture and how these emotions make impact on consciousness and personality of individuals and society. The author also explains how arousal of constructive (positive) and deconstructive (negative) emotions is associated with our food habits, daily lifestyle, and our worldview. The author further argued that we can manage constructive and deconstructive emotions very effectively by following wisdom of our sages, as narrated in ancient texts, in our daily lifestyle. At the end, the author also suggested that for Indian organizations, stress management interventions based on R-G theory could be more effective in emotional management of employees and help individuals and organizations in improving quality of work-life and achieving work–life balance.

The chapter on "Vipassana Meditation Reduces Stress and Strain—An Empirical Study" by Gopalakrishna not only presents an empirical study on the impact of Vipassana meditation on work stress and strain, but also reflects on a theoretical perspective of stress management based on the principles of Buddhism. The findings of this study suggest that Vipassana meditation has positive impact on personal effectiveness, interpersonal effectiveness, and professional effectiveness of managers. The findings also suggest implications of Vipassana meditation in designing stress management interventions, team-building training programs, and organization development interventions. Similar findings have been reported by Adhia et al. (2010) on positive impact of yoga training on reducing stress and strain at workplaces. We need more experimental studies in future on the testing of Indian meditation techniques in stress reduction and improvement of personal effectiveness and positive behavior.

The chapter on "Methodological Issues in Stress Research: Challenges, Concerns, and Directions" by Satish Pandey, Shubhra P. Gaur, and D. M. Pestonjee critically examines various methodological issues related to stress research. In this chapter, the authors attempt to critically discuss paradigm shifts in stress research in last few decades, different research approaches being used by researchers, new emerging issues in stress research, and directions for future research. Some major issues discussed are: quantitative vs. qualitative approach; cross-sectional vs. longitudinal studies; positive vs. negative orientation of stress research; unit of analysis in stress research—individual, group, or organization; self-reported vs. physiological measures; indigenous vs. western "imported" models of stress; cultural issues in stress research; and quality of stress research in developing countries. The authors suggested various directions for future research on theoretical research, adopting advanced research designs and appropriate methods, measurement of stress and coping variables, developing multidimensional and contextual models for explaining stress and coping behavior patterns, and relevance of stress research to organizations in the context of the changed work environment of 21st century.

In the Epilogue, "The Road Ahead," the editors commented on common themes emerging from the contributions in the volume. The editors also reflect on the future of stress research in light of those common themes, especially in a culturally diverse country like India. We are passing through a phase of rapid transitions in almost all walks of life. Technology is impacting on social and personal well-being like never before. Hence, we need to relook into the phenomenon of stress from different angles and adopt multiple approaches for any research on it.

References

Adhia, H. N. & Mahadevan, B. (2010). Impact of adoption of yoga way of life on the reduction of job burnout of managers. *Vikalpa, 35*(2), 21–33.

Frone, M.R., Yardley, J.K., & Markel, K.S. (1997), Developing and testing an integrative model of the work–family interface. *Journal of Vocational Behavior, 50,* 145–67.

Griffin, M.A., Neal, A., & Parker, S.K. (2007). A new model of work role performance: positive behavior in uncertain and independent contexts. *Academy of Management Review, 50*(2), 327–47.

Malone, T.M., Laubacher, R.J., & Johns, T. (2011). The age of hyperspecialization. *Harvard Business Review* (South Asia), July–August, *89*(7/8), 46–55.

Pareek, U. (1983). Organizational role stress. In L.D. Goodstein and J.W. Pfeiffer (Eds), *The 1983 annual for facilitators, trainers and consultants*. San Diego, California: University Associates.

Spreitzer, G. & Porath, C. (2012). Creating sustainable performance. *Harvard Business Review* (South Asia), January–February, *90*(1/2), 85–91.

2

The Neuropsychology of Stress

Jamuna Rajeswaran and Cathlyn N. Bennett

Abstract

"Stress" appears to be the watchword of the day. A stressor is any factor that disturbs homeostasis, which can be in the form of increased mental or physical disturbances. Stress responses are generally categorized as a physiological response, a behavioral response, an emotional response and a cognitive response which emphasize the importance of subjective perception. The brain plays a vital role in mediating our response to stress. Some studies have shown that there are neurochemical, electrical, and electrophysiological changes in the brain during stress. The stress response mediated by cortisol decreases neuronal growth factors, thereby hampering neuronal plasticity. The stress response has been known to adversely affect neuropsychological and cognitive function, which in turn has a bearing on activities of daily living. The traditional methods of coping with stress include relaxation techniques such as Progressive Muscle Relaxation, Self-hypnosis, Autogenic Training, Meditation, and Biofeedback-assisted Relaxation. In recent years, EEG Neurofeedback, a state of the art technology, has been implemented not only to induce relaxation but also to augment other associated cognitive functions and improve quality of life.

Keywords: neuropsychology, cognitive functions, neurogenesis, EEG neurofeedback, cognitive appraisal

Acknowledgments

We thank Dr Rita Christopher, Professor and Head, Department of Neurochemistry, NIMHANS for her valuable contribution.

Introduction

Deliberations on stress can be formally traced back to Selye's conceptualization of the General Adaptation Syndrome in the 1930s. Since then the debates have progressed and currently "Stress" appears to be the watchword of the day. There is an exorbitant investment into researching it, into understanding the mechanisms by which it works, the effects that it has on people and into discovering means of coping with it. Stress has been attributed with a pervasive non-ethereal quality that creeps its icy invisible fingers into every nook, thereby sparing none. It is, therefore, these qualities of stress coupled with the current lifestyle that demands that everything be done faster without compromising on efficiency, which has made "stress" extremely popular in today's parlance. Stress, then, has derived for itself an exceedingly negative connotation and is constantly depicted as a horrendous monster lurking behind the darkness.

Historically speaking, however, stress was never intended to be portrayed merely as a negative, blood drawing, and unhealthy entity. The conceptualization of Selye's General Adaption Syndrome itself attempts to elucidate the functional aspects of stress which, when experienced excessively over prolonged periods of time, can well have deleterious consequences.

STRESS—A DEFINITION

To begin to discuss stress and then in the context of neuropsychology, one must first understand it in its entirety. To make a beginning, one generally starts with a definition. What makes things difficult is not the lack of a definition but the lack of the specificity of one. Stress has been previously defined as a "real or interpreted threat to the physiological or psychological integrity of an individual that results in physiological and/or behavioural responses" (McEwen, 2000). Stress, therefore, is widely understood to have two important components, i.e., a stressor and a stress response.

TYPES OF STRESSORS

A stressor is any factor that disturbs homeostasis which can be in the form of increased mental or physical disturbances. It may be purely physical, for instance an injury or trauma, noise, extreme temperatures, and so on. Stressors may also be psychological or psychosocial such as uncertainty, significant life events, time pressure, interpersonal difficulties, etc. Or they may be a combination of several factors.

STRESS RESPONSES

> *Stress is not what happens to us. It's our response to what happens. And response is something we can choose.*
>
> — *Maureen Killoran (2012)*

Stress responses are generally categorized as a physiological response, a behavioral response, an emotional response, and a cognitive response which emphasizes the importance of subjective perception.

THE PHYSIOLOGICAL RESPONSE OF STRESS

The physiological response of stress refers to the physical changes that one experiences during times of stress. All of us are familiar with the bodily sensations associated with stress. Popular descriptions such as "butterflies in the stomach" have become part of contemporary language. Some experience nausea before stressful situations, while others battle to quieten a racing heart. Some begin to perspire while others feel their throat grow dry and parched.

In defining stress as a physiological response, one is automatically drawn into a discussion of the Hypothalamic-pituitary-adrenal axis (HPA axis) and elevated cortisol. The hypothalamus in times of need is known to produce corticotrophin releasing factor (CRF) which in turn triggers the Pituitary gland to produce Adrenocorticotropic hormone, which subsequently stimulates the adrenal gland to produce cortisol. Increased levels of cortisol have been traditionally associated with higher levels of stress and increased autonomic nervous system activity. Elevated levels of cortisol, in turn, inhibit the hypothalamus from further escalating the stress response through a feedback mechanism. However, the picture is far from simple and albeit hazy. There appears to be three basic regulatory disorders of the HPA axis:

1. The first reflects a problem in the feedback mechanism of cortisol to the preliminary areas of the HPA axis. Generally, once cortisol is elevated in blood plasma over a prolonged period of time, the hypothalamus is

stimulated to alter its manner of functioning leading to the ultimate decrease of plasma cortisol levels. However, when this inhibition does not occur in the prescribed fashion, cortisol levels remain elevated. This clinical picture is typically seen in Cushing's syndrome as well as in psychiatric depression.

2. The second disorder refers to low cortisol levels in the plasma which reflect a lack of response to the stimulation of the HPA axis. Generally, stimulation of the HPA axis acutely produces increase in plasma cortisol levels. However, on some occasions this stimulation fails to achieve the natural succession of rising cortisol levels even on artificial stimulation. This type of dysfunction is typically seen in individuals who are suffering from Chronic Fatigue Syndrome, and perhaps even those with Fibromyalgia.

3. The third type of regulatory disturbance is reflected in fluctuating levels of cortisol. Plasma levels are found to be low in the rest state and disproportionately high in the face of specific triggers. This type of disturbance is typically seen in individuals with Posttraumatic Stress Disorder.

Figure 2.1 HPA Axis in Stress

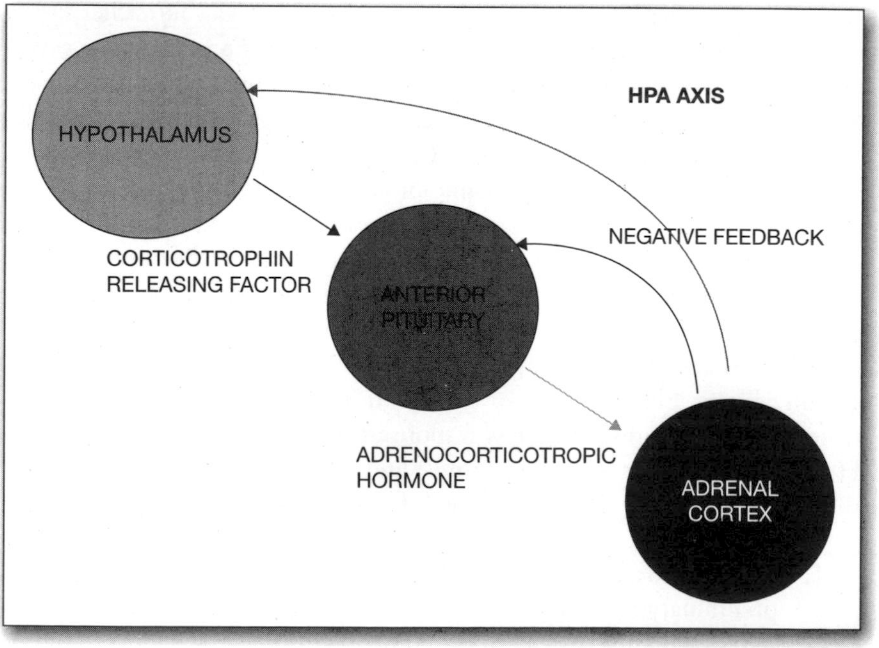

Source: Authors.

THE BEHAVIORAL RESPONSE OF STRESS

Behavioral response occurring due to stress is well established. Stress can be exhibited based on three potential factors; namely novelty, uncertainty, and the absence or loss of control.

1. Novelty refers to the difficulties that a person encounters when faced with a potentially incomprehensible situation, where there are few if any familiar elements.
2. Uncertainty refers to the difficulties that the individual may face considering the nature of instability in the object that is causing the distress. For instance, through the process of classical conditioning, a warning signal before administration of an electric shock serves as a fear producing stimulus. Similarly, a signal that is not followed by a shock signifies safety. However, in uncertain situations, where the signal does not consistently signify potency of a particular situation, the picture becomes less clear. In such cases, the individual may resort to active avoidance (where they deliberately learn to avoid the fear producing stimulus by moving completely out of the situation) or they may resort to passive avoidance (where they remain in the given situation but refuse to come into contact with the potential threat).
3. The individual may also respond based on the amount of control they have over a given situation—the lesser the control, the greater is the sense of helplessness.

THE COGNITIVE RESPONSE OF STRESS

> Adopting the right attitude can convert a negative stress into a positive one.
> —Hans Selye (n.d.)

The way we think has often been linked to the way we react to stress. "Psyching" ourselves into not feeling stress has been incorporated into our learning from childhood. "Think positive," "Say to yourself that you can do it," and "If you think you can, you really can" are phrases that we are all familiar with. Cognition, of course, plays a vital role in one's response to a stressor. The importance of cognition can be traced right back to Freud in 1926 where he described the defenses of Intellectualization, Rationalization and even Denial as mechanisms to reduce anxiety.

Steckler (2005) has elucidated various cognitive mechanisms that are associated with the stress response. When attempting to cope with a given stressor, an individual makes use of two general means of coping, i.e., the Defensive Avoidance (where the stressor is avoided) or Defensive Approach (which involves risk assessment and behavioral inhibition). The value attributed to the defensive distance is dependent on the physical and temporal distance of the stressor and the individual, and the subjective perception of the stress.

Naturally, it also becomes important to discuss the role of appraisal and anticipation in this context. Not only must one evaluate the defensive distance between the subject and the stressor, but one must also understand the subject's appraisal of the nature of the stressor. Does (s)he perceive it as merely inconveniencing, moderately threatening, or completely overwhelming? Also, studies on rats have indicated that the anticipation of an aversive stimulus (such as an electric shock) can result in a stress response that far exceeds the actual experience of the stressor. It is also important here to describe the role of perceived control. Now, perceived control must be differentiated from behavioral control, as an individual may perceive a situation as uncontrollable even though (s)he has the ability to control it. Learned helplessness is a phenomenon in which the individual is unable to control a situation although (s)he has the resources to do so.

A closely allied concept is that of learning. By learning one may refer both to classical as well as operant responses. From the classical conditioning viewpoint, any cue that precedes the occurrence of the stressor by way of association becomes a potent representation of the stressor itself and may induce an emotional fear response. From the operant conditioning perspective, an individual learns a behavioral pattern that alters the frequency of occurrence of the stressor. In this context, it becomes important to discriminate between escape and avoidance learning. In escape learning, the individual comes in contact with the stressor, i.e., the aversive stimulus has to occur before the response. In avoidance, the individual learns to avoid the occurrence of the stressor. In this case, if the learning is successful the stressor is rarely or never encountered. This type of learning is, however, also resistant to extinction.

The Brain Basis of Stress

> *Every stress leaves an indelible scar, and the organism pays for its survival after a stressful situation by becoming a little older.*
>
> *— Hans Selye (n.d.)*

The brain is considered to be one of the most fascinating organs of the human body, whose organization and working has not been completely understood to this day. The brain as well is not exempted from the effects of stress. The brain also plays a vital role in mediating our response to stress.

Generally, most sensory modalities are processed through two pathways. The more direct reflex like pathway is referred to as pathway A, where most of the processing occurs—in the spinal cord, brain stem, and hypothalamus.

SENSORY PERCEPTION

Somatosensory impulses from the skin and viscera are first transmitted to the dorsal horn neurons of the spinal cord. Information about the body's relative position is also transmitted to the spinal cord. These impulses are then transmitted to the brain stem and thalamus for higher level processing. Nocioceptive information may also enter through the dorsal horn leading to adrenocorticotropic hormone release, thereby affecting the neuroendocrine motor neurons in the hypothalamic paraventricular nucleus. However, the picture about these pathways is far from clear. Information from the cranial nerves related to the visual, gustatory, vestibular, and somatosensory aspects reach the brain stem. Information regarding the internal environment of the body as well is processed in the brain stem which is conveyed to the nucleus of the solitary tract through the vagus nerve. This information is then sent to areas in the forebrain such as the hypothalamic paraventricular nucleus and the telencephalon which affect the HPA axis. All exterosensory information, except for olfaction, enters the thalamus before being processed by the amy gdala and the cerebral cortex.

MOTOR PATHWAYS

The motor areas involved also include the spinal cord and brain stem as well as the hypothalamus. The behavioral stress responses are mediated by alpha motor neurons in the ventral horn. The intermediolateral column in the thoracic and upper lumbar spinal cord is found to be responsible for the release of adrenaline through the stimulation of the adrenal medulla through the sympathetic preganglionic neurons. The preganglionic neurons of the brain stem as well are responsible for visceral stress responses. The medial parvicellular area of the paraventricular nucleus of the hypothalamus contains corticotrophin releasing hormone neurons, which stimulate the release of corticotrophin hormone and vasopressin. This in turn stimulates the release of adrenocorticotropic hormone in the anterior pituitary gland. The paraventricular nucleus and supraoptic nucleus contain magnocellular neurons that stimulate release of vasopressin and oxytocin.

The hypothalamus is also associated with the motivation of behavior. Therefore, inhibition of certain responses such as feeding and reproduction are clearly reflective of the inhibitory responses associated with stress. Also the presence of the suprachiasmatic nucleus of the hypothalamus, which regulates the circadian rhythm, has well defined implications for the nature of stress responses.

Graeff in 1994 has described a defense system by which increasingly more brain areas will be associated with more complex defense patterns. According to this system, the point of entry includes the Periaqueductal grey matter which is responsible for undirected escape including the fight flight or freezing response. At a higher level of processing comes the medial hypothalamus which mediates directed escape. The amygdala is associated with simple active avoidance and the cingulate cortex with more complex avoidance. This system has been extended by Gray and McNaughton (2000) who propose that the periaqueductal gray, the medial hypothalamus, the amygdala, and anterior cingulate cortex are associated with defensive avoidance, whereas the defensive approach is mediated by the septal-hippocampal system and the posterior cingulated. They also propose that the posterior cingulate cortex is associated with innate anxiety plans, whereas the prefrontal cortex is associated with acquired anxiety plans and involve working memory and motor programming functions.

Innate anxiety plans are more beneficial than those involving higher cognitive functions under certain circumstances. Research indicates that noradrenaline release increases in the prefrontal cortex during times of stress. It is hypothesized that this increase leads to activation of the post synaptic alpha 1 adrenoreceptors which lead to a decrease in prefrontal function. While this contributes to rapid means of responding thereby aiding survival, the same stress can impair working memory due to the effect of alpha 1 adrenoreceptors in prefrontal function. The effects have been found to decrease with the infusion of alpha 1 adrenoreceptor antagonist in the prefrontal function. Also found to be of some importance is the change in the dopaminergic system on contact with stressors.

The role of the septohippocampal system, of course, cannot be minimized. The septohippocampal system plays an important role in conflict resolution and values or shifts the bias towards affectively negative information. This acts as an integral part of the behavioral defense system proposed by Gray and McNaughton (2000). Generally, this system is known for its role in risk assessment. The hippocampal cholinergic and monoaminergic pathways, therefore, may well explain this bias.

It also becomes important here to discuss the role of the amygdala. The amygdala plays a vital role in emotional conditioning, particularly that which is related to fear. Information from the thalamus is sent to the central nucleus of the amygdala through the lateral nucleus of the amygdala. Information from the lateral nucleus may travel through a direct route or an indirect route (through the basolateral amygdaloid nucleus) to the central nucleus. The basolateral amygdala appears to control the central nucleus, which in turn affects hypothalamic and brainstem function leading to increases in adrenaline and cortisol. The central nucleus also has pathways involving the periaqueductal gray mediating the freezing response and the pontine nucleus mediating the fear potentiated startle. Therefore, it can be seen that the central nucleus is associated with processing of stimulus specific fear. More complex information is found to be mediated by the bed nucleus of the stria terminalis.

The basolateral nucleus, thus, plays an important role in assessing the affective value of a stressor as associated with a conditioned stimulus. This is then relayed to frontal and cingulate cortices as well as the striatum. From the striatum it appears to be relayed to the core of the nucleus accumbens. Dopamine is therefore increased in the core of the nucleus accumbens on exposure to conditioned stimuli and is found to increase in the shell of the nucleus accumbens on exposure to unconditioned stimuli. The activity in the shell allows an individual to switch from a primary state to a situationally appropriate one such as from feeding to fleeing.

At a molecular level, recent studies at the Max Planck Institute of Psychiatry have implicated the protein DRR1 (down-regulated in renal cell carcinoma 1) which plays a role in synapse formation and affects nerve cell outgrowth. They have demonstrated that by increasing DRR1 in mice, improved communication has been observed among the neurons and subsequently enhancement in learning (Schmidt et al., 2011).

STRESS AND NEUROGENESIS

Most of the neurons of the dentate gyrus among rodents are known to be produced during the first two post natal weeks. This period is generally known as the stress hyporesponsive period where rat pups are known to produce a diminished response to stressors. However, it is found that when male rats are exposed to the odor of unfamiliar adult males (natural predators of rat pups), there is an increased level of corticosterone. During the hyporesponsive period, this phenomenon is generally followed by substantial diminution in growth and proliferation of granule cell precursors of the developing dentate gyrus. This change occurs within 24 hours of exposure. Adult rats, which are exposed to the odors of natural predators, exhibit increase in corticosterone levels in the serum as well as a characteristic electrophysiological response in the dentate gyrus. This is accompanied by a decrease in growth of the cells of the dentate gyrus.

Throughout life it is noticed that proliferation of granule cells and amount of circulating levels of adrenal steroids are negatively correlated. Evidence indicates that this relationship is achieved through the excitatory pathways affecting the NMDA (N-methyl-D-aspartate) receptors. In fact, studies indicate that growth and proliferation of granule cell precursors and production of granule cells in adult rats and tree shrews were found to increase on the administration of NMDA receptors antagonists.

Brain-derived neurotrophic factor (BDNF) is a homodimeric protein that has been found to be highly conserved in function as well as during evolution (Gotz, Raulf, & Schartl, 1992). BDNF is known to function as a target-derived survival and differentiation factor for neuronal subpopulations in prenatal stages (Snider, 1994). BDNF has been found to largely play a functional role in the adult nervous system. Both long- and short-term effects of BDNF have been established (McAllister, Katz, & Lo, 1999). BDNF is known to act as an effective excitatory neurotransmitter leading to rapid depolarization of postsynaptic neurons, even at very low concentrations (Hartmann, Heumann, & Lessmann, 2001). BDNF also generates long-lasting changes in synaptic plasticity, neurotransmitter, and neuropeptide production and excitability (Carter et al., 2002). BDNF signaling at synapses improves both neuronal plasticity and long-term potentiation (LTP), which enables learning and memory through synaptic strengthening. Also, long-term developmental phenomena like neuronal survival, migration, and differentiation are mediated by BDNF through its ability to enhance activity dependent refinement of synaptic architecture and brain regions that are majorly involved in executive functions. Since BDNF is capable of crossing the blood–brain barrier bidirectionally, a major part of circulating BDNF may arise from neurons and glial cells of the central nervous system (Poduslo & Curran, 1996).

Glucocorticoids are regulators of adult neurogenesis (Sapolsky, 1999). Administration of high levels of corticosterone has been shown to decrease cell division in the adult rat hippocampus. Stress down regulates cell growth in the dentate gyrus and eventually neuronal development in the adult rat dentate gyrus. The effects of glucocorticoids on cell genesis appear to be affected through a downstream effect on BDNF. Zhou, Zhang, & Zhang (2000) demonstrated that BDNF gene expression and protein translation in the hippocampus, along with other neurotrophins, is significantly inhibited on exposure to glucocorticoids. In a further study by Schaaf, de Kloet, & Vreugdenhil (2000), it was noted that between four and six hours after administration of high dose cortisol a decrease in BDNF protein was observed, while an *in vitro* study by Nitta et al. (1999) demonstrated that the BDNF protein content of cultured hippocampal cells was diminished by the application of cortisol. Physiological responses to stress, likely to be mediated by cortisol, are therefore sufficient to regulate BDNF protein. Moreover, numerous findings link stress-relieving activities such as learning, exposure to a new yet benign environment, and exercise propagates an enhancement of neurogenesis.

Cognitive Functions Associated with Stress

Studies regarding the effect of stress on cognitive processes such as attention appear to be albeit mixed at first glance. Individuals with Post Traumatic Stress Disorder often report problems with concentration and memory (Vasterling et al., 1998). Studies by Chajut and Daniel (2003) discuss three important theories of social cognition discussing performance under stress. According to the first theory, i.e., the attention view, the reduction of utilization of task-irrelevant attributes help to improve the selectivity to task relevant attributes. According to the capacity–resource approach, the presence of stress utilizes attentional resources. Therefore, selective attention is attributed only to chronically accessible information. The third hypothesis, i.e., the ironic process theory, also states that selective attention fails under stress. However, it also states that task-irrelevant information becomes hyper accessible. Several experiments quoted by the research appear to favor the attention view indicating that selective attention indeed increases in times of stress.

The controversy remains unresolved for other cognitive functions apart from attention in that Vedhara et al. (2000) report increased perceived stress under circumstances of acute stress such as exam time. However, this was accompanied with decrease in salivary cortisol as compared with a non-stress period (i.e., non-examination time). Accompanying this depression of cortisol levels was an elevation of short-term memory, impairment of attention and the primacy effect, and no significant influence on auditory verbal working memory. Some studies confirm Easterbrooke's cue utilization theory which maintains that emotion and/or stress depletes the individual's attention, causing them to focus only on main events or the central theme without wasting resources on the peripheral themes.

The effects of stress are also translated to decision-making. In a study by Keinan (1987), it was found that exposure to stress—both controllable and uncontrollable forms—increased the individual's tendency to offer a solution before scanning through all possible alternatives in a systematic manner.

Christian and Loftus have also demonstrated that when the same story is presented with or without emotional loading; central events are remembered better in stories with emotional loading and peripheral details in those with neutral inclinations. Memory for emotional words is also found to be better at delayed recall rather than immediate recall. Research also indicates that while stress affects production of new granule cells, it inadvertently affects hippocampal dependent learning through the effect of corticosterone. The effects as early as the early embryonic development may well have long-lasting deleterious effects on the developing brain.

These apparently conflicting results demonstrate the relatively complex relationship between the experience of stress and its cognitive outcome. Some studies demonstrate the improvement of cognitive functions while others imply their deterioration. These varied findings, however, can be put into perspective when using the framework that this chapter originally begins with. That is, stress has an adaptive function and is not merely a tyrannical, harsh entity. According to the Yerkes–Dodson law, performance can actually improve with an optimum amount of stress. It is only in the face of excessive and chronic stress that the outcomes prove to be maladaptive. Therefore, it may be safe

Figure 2.2   Stages of Responses to Stress

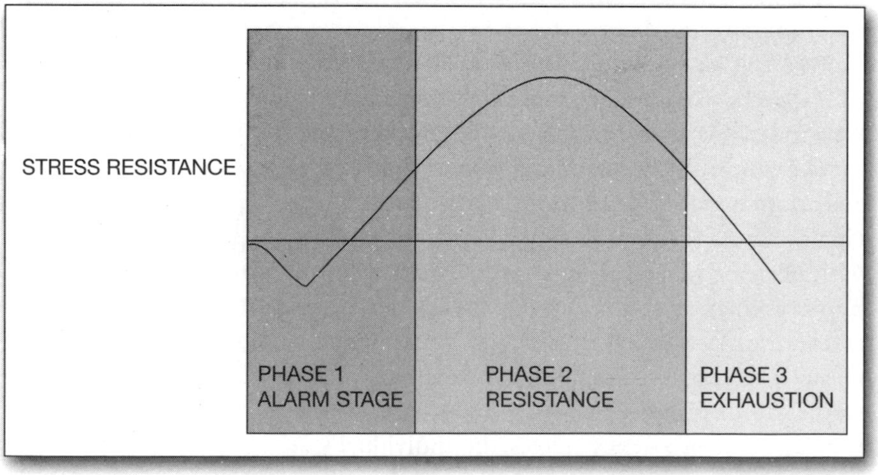

Source: Authors.

to say that in understanding the relationship between stress and cognitive functioning one must first determine the level of stress. Unfortunately there are difficulties in quantifying this level, as stress is dependent on several factors and is strongly based on subjective perception rather than something that is purely objective and tangible.

Coping and Treatment Methods

> *Rest is not idleness, and to lie sometimes on the grass under trees on a summer's day, listening to the murmur of the water, or watching the clouds float across the sky, is by no means a waste of time.*
>
> *—J. Lubbock (2012)*

Relaxation techniques commonly used include Progressive Muscle relaxation, Self-hypnosis, Autogenic Training, Meditation, and Biofeedback assisted relaxation.

THE ROLE OF COGNITIVE APPRAISAL

The concept of cognitive appraisals put forth by Lazarus and Folkman in 1984 essentially describe two processes. The first describes our initial appraisal of the stressor or the situation associated with stress. When one's initial appraisal is unfavorable, then it is likely that the given situation is perceived as stressful. On the contrary if the situation is perceived as a challenge, then the chances are that the stressor is perceived as less stressful. The second process has a direct bearing on our mechanisms of coping with stress. Once a situation has been perceived as stressful, then our appraisal of resources that would help us cope with stress would influence the manner in which we manage the stress. Appraisal, therefore, can be positive or negative.

RECENT ADVANCES IN THE FIELD OF RELAXATION TRAINING

Electroencephalography (EEG) Neurofeedback is a fairly recently developed state of art technology. EEG Neurofeedback is used to modify amplitude, frequency, and even coherency of one's own brain waves using operant conditioning methods (Thatcher et al., 1999).

EEG Neurofeedback training alters the electrical activity in the brain. This in turn affects the way an individual feels and responds to others. Some individuals have greater difficulty in relaxing after a difficult and stressful day. Their brains have more trouble in recuperating from stressful incidents. Generally, when the eyes are closed, there is an enhancement of alpha wave activity which is believed to be instrumental in the recuperation of the brain. When this fails to occur, the exhaustion can lead to a host of psycho-neuro-immunological complications. EEG Neurofeedback training—particularly alpha-theta training—modifies brain activity, thereby making the brain more receptive to a relaxation response and helping the individual to live a healthier and well balanced life.

EEG Neurofeedback has been used in normal individuals to improve peak performance in athletes, in academic performance and for stress relief. Olympic gold medalist Abhinav Bindra had regular training using neuro-feedback to enhance focused attention and to reduce stress which affected his performance.

EEG Neurofeedback has also been used in several clinical conditions including alcoholism and traumatic brain injury. In a study by Thmas, Rajan, & Murthy (2010), it was found that relapse rates among alcoholics were found to be reduced following alpha-theta training. It was hypothesized that the mechanism of change includes reduced levels of anxiety which in turn decreases stress levels. This was concurred by Reddy, Rajan, Bagavathula, & Kandavel (2009) who report that memory and learning improvement is seen after Neu-rofeedback intervention in Traumatic Brain Injury following reinforcement of alpha wave activity.

A study by Nowlis & Kamiya (1970) showed that by increasing alpha levels, relaxation increases. The effect of alpha-theta training aiming to increase relaxation is less clear. Egner, Strawson, & Gruzelier (2002) demonstrated that alpha-theta training works to increase the relaxation level. This was evident in within session theta/alpha increments.

These findings were also corroborated by those of Batty et al. (2006). Three types of methods known to increase relaxation were used, i.e., EEG Neurofeedback, Progressive Muscle Relaxation, and Self-hypnosis. All three groups showed an increased hypnotic susceptibility, probably reflecting a high level of relaxation. However, alpha-theta training was not more effective than the other relaxation paradigms. Alpha-theta training is also used for therapeutic purposes. Especially the Peniston & Kulkosky (1991) brain wave neurotherapy (PKBNT) showed to be effective in the treatment of alcoholics and Post Traumatic Stress Disorder. Patients suffering from these disorders showed a significant improvement in their disease pattern, when compared with controls that were not treated with the PKBNT. In comparison with traditional medical treatment paradigm, those who underwent PKBNT had reduced dosage of medication and were less likely to relapse at a 30-month follow-up. Other anxiety disorders are also treated with Neurofeedback training. Results of these studies showed that alpha increases, and most of the time, anxiety scores dropped. Thus, EEG Neurofeedback can help in initiating a relaxed state, but it is not completely clear whether it is more effective than other relaxation methods.

Conclusion

We are drawing towards a world that demands easy answers and quick solutions. Our search for happiness is leading us towards a world that is racing against time, a world that is fast changing and a world that believes that true success lies in accomplishment. It is no wonder that stress has become an important aspect of human life or that the latest search for a panacea is one that lies in preventing stress. In our race to find meaning and joy in life, have we forgotten what it is to simply live?

It can be safely stated that stress has serious implications on brain functioning. Deliberations on stress and neuropsychology are at their infancy. While some pathways of the influence of stress on the brain are fairly tangible, others are sketchier. Further research is required to understand the neurochemical and neurophysiological bases of stress and their relevance to specific aspects of cognitive functions. Needless to say that the relationship between stress and the brain is a significant one. The understanding of this relationship has important consequences for the practice of neuropsychology not only in a clinical population, but also in enhancing optimum functioning of human behavior.

So,

> *Take your seat on the shore. Listen to the ancient voice in the waves. Taste the salt of life on your tongue. Run your fingers through the eternal sand. Breathe deeply. If you find yourself worrying about your cell phone and emails, if you find yourself feeling guilty that you should be doing "something important," breathe deeply again. And again. Breathe deeply until every fabric of your being is reminded that this, being here, is your top priority. This is peace. This is wisdom. The work is a means to living, but this is the living.*
>
> *—Brian Vaszily (n.d.)*

Future Directions

With technological advancement and lifestyle changes, the working conditions of the individual has changed radically. This being the scenario, efforts at modifying stress variables, either individually or situationally, should be undertaken. Future research can focus on understanding the interplay between personality and genetic vulnerability and their influence on the brain mediation of stress. Research on EEG Neurofeedback can be undertaken at workplaces to induce relaxation and subsequently to improve work performance. Functional magnetic resonance imaging studies can also be undertaken in order to further develop our understanding of the brain response to stress and its ramifications.

References

Batty, M.J., Bonnington, S., Tang, B.K., Hawken, M.B., & Gruzelier, J.H. (2006). Relaxation strategies and enhancement of hypnotic susceptibility: EEG neurofeedback, progressive muscle relaxation and self-hypnosis. *Brain Res Bull*, *71*(1–3), 83–90.

Carter A.R., Chen C., Schwartz P.M., & Segal R.A. (2002). Brain-derived neurotrophic factor modulates cerebellar plasticity and synaptic ultrastructure. *J. Neurosci.*, *22*(4), 1316–27.

Chajut, E., & Daniel, A. (2003). Selective attention improves under stress: Implications for theories of social cognition. *Journal of Personality and Social Psychology*, *85*(2), 231–48.

Christianson, E.F., Hoffman H., & Loftus, G.R. (1991) Eye fixations and memory for emotional events. *Journal of Experimental Psychology: Learning, Memory and Cognition*, *17*(4), 693–701.

Egner, T., Strawson, E., & Gruzelier, J.H. (2002). EEG signature and phenomenology of alpha/theta neurofeedback training versus mock feedback. *Appl Psychophysiology Biofeedback*, *27*(4), 261–70.

Gotz R., Raulf F., & Schartl M. (1992). Brain-derived neurotrophic factor is more highly conserved in structure and function than nerve growth factor during vertebrate evolution. *J. Neurochem*, *59*(2), 432–42.

Gray, J.A., & McNaughton, N. (2000). The neuropsychology of anxiety: An enquiry into the functions of the septo-hippocampal system. Oxford, UK: Oxford University Press.

Hartmann M., Heumann R., & Lessmann V. (2001). Synaptic secretion of BDNF after high frequency stimulation of glutamatergic synapses. *EMBO J.*, *20*(21), 5887–97.

Keinan, G. (1987). Decision making under stress: Scanning of alternatives under controllable and uncontrollable threats. *Journal of Personality and Social Psychology*, *52*(3), 639–44.

Killoran, M. (2012). Maureen Killoran quotes. Retrieved from: http://www.searchquotes. com/quotation/Stress_is_not_what_happens_to_us._It%27s_our_response_to_what_happens_and_response_is_something_we_can/278975/ (accessed on December 2012).

Lazarus, R.S. & Folkman, S. (1984). *Stress, appraisal and coping*. New York: Springer Publishing Company.

Lubbock, J. (2012). In goodreads. Retrieved from: http://www.goodreads.com/author/quotes/415473.John_Lubbock (accessed on December 2012).

McAllister A.K., Katz L.C., & Lo D.C. (1999). Neurotrophins and synaptic plasticity. *Annu. Rev. Neurosci.*, *22*, 295–318.

McEwen, B.S. (2000). Stress, definitions and concepts of. *Encyclopedia of Stress* (Volume 3, pp. 508–09). San Diego: Academic Press.

Nitta, A., Ohmiya, M., Sometani, A., Itoh, M., Nomoto, H., Furukawa, Y., & Furukawa, S. (1999). Brain-derived neurotrophic factor prevents neuronal cell death induced by corticosterone. *J Neurosci Res*, *57*, 227–35.

Nowlis, D.P. & Kamiya, J. (1970). The control of electroencephalographic alpha rhythms through auditory feedback and the associated mental activity. *Psychophysiology*, *6*(4), 476–84.

Orne, T.M. & Whitehouse, W.G. (2000). Relaxation techniques. *Encyclopedia of Stress* (Volume 1, pp. 296–99). San Diego: Academic Press.

Peniston, E.G. & Kulkosky, P.J. (1991). Alpha-theta brainwave neuro-feedback for vietnam veterans with combat related post-traumatic stress disorder. *Medical Psychotherapy*, *4*, 47–60.

Poduslo, J.F. & Curran, G.L. (1996). Permeability at the blood–brain and blood–nerve barriers of the neurotrophic factors: NGF, CNTF, NT-3, BDNF. *Brain Res. Mol. Brain Res.*, *36*(2), 280–86.

Reddy R., Rajan, J., Bagarathula, I., & Kandaver T. (2009). Neurofeedback training to enhance learning and memory with patient with traumatic brain injury: A single case study. *International Journal of Psychosocial Rehabilitation*, 14(1), 21–28.

Sapolsky, R. (1999). Glucocorticoids, stress, and their adverse neurological effects–Relevance to aging. *Exp Gerontol, 34*, 721–32.

Schaaf, M., de Kloet, E., & Vreugdenhil, E. (2000). Corticosterone effects on BDNF expression in the hippocampus - Implications for memory formation. *Stress, 3*, 201–08.

Schmidt M., Schülke, Jan-Philip, Liebl, Claudia, Stiess, Michael, Avrabos, Charilaos, Bock Jörg et al. (2011). Tumor suppressor down-regulated in renal cell carcinoma 1 (DRR1) is a stress-induced actin bundling factor that modulates synaptic efficacy and cognition. *Proceedings of the National Academy of Sciences of the United States of America*. Retrieved from the advance online publication (doi: 10.1073/pnas.1103318108).

Seyle, H. (n.d.). Hans Selye quote. In Izquotes. Retrieved from: http://izquotes.com/quote/167028 (accessed December 2012).

———. (n.d.). Hans Selye quote. In Izquotes. Retrieved from: http://izquotes.com/quote/167030 (accessed December 2012).

Snider W.D. (1994). Functions of the neurotrophins during nervous system development: What the knockouts are teaching us. *Cell, 77*(5), 627–38.

Steckler, T. (2005). The neuropsychology of stress. In T. Steckler, N.H. Kalin, & J.M.H.M. Reul (Eds), *Handbook of Stress and the Brain* (Part I). New York: Elsevier.

Thomas, S., Ranjan J., & Murthy, P. (2010). Neurofeedback training in alcohol dependent syndrome. Unpublished Ph.D thesis, NIMHANS, Bangalore.

Tanapat, P. & Gould, E. (2000). Neurogenesis. *Encyclopedia of Stress* (Volume 3, pp. 31–37). San Diego: Academic Press.

Thatcher, R.W., Moore, N., John, E.R., Duffy, F., Hughes, J., & Krieger, M. (1999). QEEG and traumatic brain injury: Rebuttal of the American Academy of Neurology 1997 Report by the EEG and Clinical Neuroscience Society. *Clinical EEG, 30*(3), 94–98.

Vasterling, J., Brailey, K., Constans, J.I., & Sutker, P.B. (1998). Attention and memory dysfunction in posttraumatic stress disorder. *Neuropsychology*, *12*(1), 125–33.

Vaszily, B. (n.d.). In Wordpress. Retrieved from http://centralpacific.wordpress.com/20/12/10/17/xoxo-21 (accessed December 2012).

Vedhara, K., Hyde, J., Gilchrist, I.D., Tytherleigh, M., & Plummer, S. (2000). Acute stress, memory, attention and cortisol. *Psychoneuroendocrinology*, *25*, 535–49.

Zhou, J., Zhang F., Zhang Y. (2000). Corticosterone inhibits generation of long-term potentiation in rat hippocampal slice—Involvement of brain-derived neurotrophic factor. *Brain Res*, *885*, 182–91.

Section-I

OCCUPATIONAL STRESS AND BURNOUT

3

Learned Helplessness and Organizational Role Stress

Fakir Mohan Sahoo

Abstract

The study examined the relationship between learned helplessness and organizational role stress. The participants in the study were 220 managers in organizations of coastal Odisha. The questionnaire involved personal helplessness, universal helplessness, noncontingency, satisfaction, motivational deficits, attributional styles, and organizational role stress. The results supported the prediction that personal helplessness is significantly related to role stress while universal helplessness is unrelated to role stress. Personal helplessness was significantly related to noncontingency and motivational deficit. There was negative association between personal helplessness and satisfaction. There was no sex difference with respect to overall role stress. The findings were explained in the light of current understanding of the construct of helplessness. The implications of the study in terms of attenuating personal helplessness were indicated.

Keywords: personal helplessness, universal helplessness, attributional styles, organizational role stress

Introduction

The core concern in the understanding and management of stress has now shifted to the study of intervening variables. What are the factors that prevent rejuvenating the body and mind? This fundamental question has been approached from several perspectives. Although we have not yet examined the entire spectrum of intervening variables, the empirical investigations employing a variety of approaches are likely to generate a converging answer in the future.

Of several approaches adopted towards the understanding and management of stress, the construct of learned helplessness appears to be a robust construct, especially in a system where resource constraints constitute an inescapable parameter of the environment (Sahoo, 2002). The construct of learned helplessness, although derived from an experimental tradition, has gone beyond its original confines of space and time. Viewed as an integrative construct, it has been applied to a wide variety of situations and behaviors. In the context of stress experience, its implication as an intervening variable offers a nomological network, linking antecedents and consequences.

A Theoretical Framework of Learned Helplessness, Attributional Style, and Stress

Stress experience can best be conceptualized within the framework of learned helplessness. The phrase "learned helplessness" was employed by Overmier & Seligman (1967) and Seligman & Maier (1967) to describe the debilitated escape–avoidance responses of dogs exposed to uncontrollable shocks in the laboratory.

In the typical animal experiments, rats learn to jump to the safe side of the platform when such animals are placed in the unsafe side which is electrically charged. During 1960s, M. E. P. Seligman and his colleagues in the University of Pennsylvania got curious to investigate the effects of noncontingent conditions. Both sides of the platform were charged rendering the entire setting as inescapable. The exposure of animals to this uncontrollable situation led the animal find out escape routes initially but later found that there was no escape. Following a prolonged exposure, the animal exhibited learned helplessness in the sense that the organism did not learn to escape to the safe compartment even if it was made safe.

Thus, learned helplessness is a reaction to conditions of uncontrollability resulting from the perception and/or learning that responses and outcomes are independent. Once induced, helplessness deficits are manifest in three interrelated areas of functioning—cognitive, affective, and motivational. The cognitive deficits are manifest in terms of associational deficiencies; organisms fail to learn the association between new stimulus and response. The acquisition of skills is made impossible. Second, organisms display depressed affects. A depressed posture sets in following the experience of uncontrollability. Third, there is retarded initiation of responses. The organisms learn that all attempts to solve a problem are exercises in futility.

While the initial studies were confined to specific animals such as rats and dogs, subsequent investigations documented helplessness syndrome across a wide variety of animals. In the context of human beings, a fourth deficit came to the fore. It was shown that humans experience self-esteem loss following their exposure to uncontrollability.

The typical learned helplessness experiment involves a triadic design. In this arrangement, the first group of subjects is exposed to uncontrollable events. A second group yoked to the first group is exposed to controllable events of same intensity or duration, while the third group is not exposed to such events. The comparison of "give-up" responses during this test phase demonstrates helplessness phenomenon; the phenomenon predicts that the first group would not be able to control the event, whereas the other two groups would be able to control.

Hiroto's (1974) study is a typical illustration of human helplessness experiment. A group of college students were exposed to loud controllable noises which they could terminate by pressing a bottom four times. Another group of college students were exposed to uncontrollable noise that terminated independently of their responses. A third group of subjects were not exposed to the event. Later, all the three groups were tested on a hand-shuttle box where noise control was possible. Subjects were asked to terminate noise. Subjects exposed to controllable noise or no noise could terminate the noise whereas subjects exposed to uncontrollable noise failed.

However, exposure to uncontrollable events is not sufficient to produce helplessness deficits. While experiencing uncontrollability, the organism must come to expect that responses and outcomes are independent. Thus, the expectancy that responses and outcomes are unrelated is a very crucial factor in the induction of helplessness deficits.

The other important feature of helplessness syndrome is the cross-situational consistency. Helplessness in one specific domain may get generalized to other task domains. For instance, helplessness is induced by exposing subjects to uncontrollable loud noise condition. Following the experience of uncontrollability in such instrumental domain, subjects may be tested on a cognitive task such as mathematical problem solving. The impaired performance in this cognitive domain is indicative of helplessness deficit. Similarly, helplessness induced by exposing subjects to unsolvable mathematical problems may lead to the debilitated performance on controllable loud noise.

ATTRIBUTIONAL ANALYSIS

While the original learned helplessness theory provided a framework of understanding cognitive, affective, and motivational deficits as a result of the expectation of response–outcome independence, its critical examination revealed an important inadequacy. Supposing that a number of individuals are exposed to similar levels of uncontrollability, does it guarantee the induction of same magnitude of helplessness? Empirical studies indicate that individuals exposed to similar magnitude of uncontrollability exhibit dissimilar intensities of helplessness. How can we explain individual difference in learned helplessness?

In an attempt to resolve this problem of individual difference, Abramson, Seligman, and Teasdale (1978) used the attributional dimensions. It was posited that individuals encountering uncontrollable situations ask themselves three fundamental questions. These three questions are:

1. Who is responsible for the bad event?
2. How pervasive is its effects?
3. How long would it stay?

Every person is presumed to have a characteristic way of responding to these questions. The style of response determines the helplessness pattern.

It is possible that individuals may attribute the causality to internal factors. On the contrary, they may explain the events in terms of the role of other individuals or outside factors (external attributions). Similarly they may feel that the event would pervade into all aspects of their life (global attribution) or they feel that the effects would be limited to specific domains of their life (specific attribution). Furthermore, some people may believe that the negative events would continue forever (stable attribution), while others believe that the events would be short-lived (unstable attribution). Thus, attributional styles, also called explanatory styles, may assume magnitudes along three dimensions.

In attributional version of the theory of learned helplessness, internal, global, and stable factors for explaining negative (bad) events are considered maladaptive; they constitute the risk factors for the induction of helplessness deficits (Peterson & Seligman, 1984). It is observed that the attributional version brings to the fore a number of implications.

First, the attribution of internality predicts the type of helplessness to be induced. With internal attribution, the individual is likely to experience *personal helplessness*. On the contrary, external attributions denote the unresponsiveness of external environment, the individual experiences *universal or shared helplessness*. The distinction between internal and external attribution also explains the degree of self-esteem loss experienced by helpless individuals. Why should individuals blame themselves for failures if causal agents are outsiders? Accordingly, people with internal explanatory style experience guilt and self-blame and they show depressed affect. The degree of self-esteem loss is proportional to the internality of attribution.

The attributions of globality explain the pervasiveness of helplessness syndrome. With global attributions for explaining negative events, persons transfer their helplessness to new situations. For instance, a person may encounter a negative event in the form of an accident of losing a hand. With global attributions, the person believes that his or her life is doomed; nothing can be done. For such a person, helplessness spills over to many domains of his/her life. In similar situations, another person may use specific attribution and prevent generalization. It may generate the belief that the person can do many useful things by using several of his/her limbs, although the use of hand is not possible. Similarly, persons may limit the effect of the negative to a specific domain (i.e., work domain), whereas individuals with global explanatory style generalize from work to family domain. This generality of helplessness deficit is postulated to be proportional to globality of attribution.

Finally, the attribution of stability explicates the chronicity of helplessness. When people use stable explanatory styles for explaining bad events, they consider uncontrollable happening as permanent. Consequently helplessness deficits persist over time. On the contrary, people with unstable attributions regard bad events as passing clouds. For them, deficits are short-lived. The degree of chronicity is correlated with the magnitude of stability of attribution.

HELPLESSNESS AND STRESS

The generality of a construct is reflected in the range and diversity of its application. Over the decades, helplessness has been extended to a wide variety of application domains such as depression, disease susceptibility, ageing problems, coping difficulties, work inefficiency, academic impairment, and health-related issues (Sahoo, 2002).

While the relationship between helplessness and coping difficulties has been documented in a general way, the examination of association between helplessness and organizational role stress deserves scientific scrutiny. There are two important reasons for such an investigation. First, as indicated earlier, helplessness takes two possible forms. A person may experience personal helplessness; such a person has the feeling that he/she himself/herself is helpless while others are not. In contrast, another person may experience universal or shared helplessness; he/she feels that many people including him/her are helpless. It is plausible that people with personal helplessness are likely to be more adversely affected than are people with universal helplessness. This hypothesis has been supported (Sahoo & Tripathy, 1990).

Second, the issue of cultural relevance demands a close examination of the relation between helplessness and role stress. It is a common observation that people in India are susceptible to induction of universal helplessness. Because of collectivist nature of Indian society, there is a great deal of carry-over from family socialization to work socialization. Consequently, the investigation of the linkage between helplessness and organizational role stress in the context of personal–universal taxonomy is a seminal one.

ATTRIBUTIONAL STYLE AND ROLE STRESS

Peterson and Seligman (1984) have provided convincing support with respect to the role of causal explanation as a risk factor for depression and other affective disorders. They have shown that prisoners' faulty attributional style dimensions indicate increasing trends as they spend more and more time in prison. Conversely, faulty attributional dimension scores show decreasing tendencies as the clients spend more time in psychotherapeutic sessions. (Peterson & Seligman, 1984).

These findings implicate the role of attributional styles in work-related stress. The newer therapeutic approach of positive psychology has basically used a process of retraining attributional styles. This essentially involves a type of self-management (Snyder & Lopez, 2007). The initial stage of this approach is to gather information about the attributional styles including faulty cognitions and the level of discomfort.

In the second stage of attributional retraining, the client learns to explain stressful events in terms of external, unstable, and specific terms. Since this form of optimism therapy (Seligman, 2002) has worked effectively in reducing stress, it is expected that the framework of attribution would be relevant in the context of role stress.

In addition to learned optimism therapy, some attention has presently been given to implementing what has been called "hope therapy" in one-on-one settings. In a series of group sessions, people are given the opportunity of discussing the negative consequences of faulty attribution and positive outcomes of adaptive attributions. These experimental learning is found to produce positive impacts (Snyder & Lopez, 2007)

The present study is empirically geared to delineate the nomological network of helplessness syndrome and to examine the correlation between helplessness and organizational role stress. In view of the consideration that Pareek and Purohit's (2010) Organizational Role Stress Instrument offers an effective operationalization of the construct domains, this ORS is included in the framework of empirical testing.

Method

SAMPLE

There were 220 professionals (in the managerial rank) randomly sampled from organizations in the coastal districts of Odisha. There were 150 males and 70 females. Participants were in the age group of 23 to 38 years (Mean = 30.7, SD = 3.1). Almost all of them were in the upper-middle income group. All were graduates belonging to engineering and non-engineering streams.

MEASURES

The measures included standardized tests: Measure of Employees' Helplessness, Attributional Style Questionnaire, and Organizational Role Stress Scale.

MEASURE OF EMPLOYEES' HELPLESSNESS

Drawing on Kanungo's Students' Helplessness Questionnaire, Kanungo and Sahoo (1988) developed and validated a Measure of Employees' Helplessness. The reliability and validity of the measure has been reported elsewhere (Sahoo, 1991). Test includes a measure of helplessness (both personal and universal), non-contingency, satisfaction and motivational deficit. The measure used in the present study consists of three parts. The first part of the scale measures helplessness on a Likert type scale. There are 12 items in this part. Again each item is divided into two segments 'a' and 'b' asking information about participants' personal helplessness and universal helplessness, respectively. For instance, in 'a' there are sentences like "As an employee, I feel totally in control/totally helpless." This sentence is clearly indicative of individual's feeling about himself. Likewise, in 'b' the following type of sentences occur: "I think that other employees in my organization feel that they are totally in control/totally helpless." The statement reveals the feeling of the participant regarding his feeling towards the extent of helplessness of his co-workers concerning a similar working situation. Responses to these types of situations are indicative of the extent of universal helplessness.

All these items are given and a six-point scale against each sentence. There are six numerals, each indicating the variation of the degree of helplessness. The number '0' and '5' are two extremes indicating full confidence possessed by the participants regarding himself and also of his co-workers in handling different problems of working situations, on the one hand, and the feeling of his utter helplessness in perceiving himself and his co-workers when they are faced with any problematic situation, on the other. Other numbers 1, 2, 3, 4 are indicative of increasing feeling of helplessness that is experienced by the individual about himself and others in between these two extremes.

In part 2 of the measure, some items are given and by the side of each item, four alternatives are indicated like "strongly agree, agree, disagree, and strongly disagree." The participant chooses one of the categories of responses to report his reaction to each item. Twenty-two items are included in this part. Items 1 to 11 in this part measure non-contingency variables and rest measures satisfaction variables. Item numbers 16, 18, 20, and 22 measure motivational deficit variable.

The third and the last part of the measure seeks personal information about the participants on gender, income, age, experience, working hours, etc. The knowledge about these personal factors is very important in studying the relations among variables.

The psychometric characteristics of this scale has been reported elsewhere (Sahoo, 1991). The internal consistency of the personal and universal learned helplessness measure is very high. The Cronbach's coefficient 'α' (alpha) values of 0.85 and 0.83 were obtained for personal and universal helplessness scales, respectively. These coefficients are sufficiently high to justify the conclusion that both the personal and universal learned helplessness scales are reliable. Similarly the Cronbach's coefficient 'α' for the non-contingency part was 0.79. The value of 0.81 and 0.74 were obtained for the satisfaction and motivational deficit scales, respectively. In sum, measures of high internal consistency offer satisfactory level of reliability for their further use in research.

ATTRIBUTIONAL STYLE QUESTIONNAIRE (ASQ)

This is a 24-item forced choice questionnaire developed and validated by Sahoo (2000). Each item presents a hypothetical good or bad event. Each event is followed by two explanations, which vary in one of the dimensions while keeping the other two constant. Eight events pertain to each of the three dimensions. Half refers to good events while the other half refers to bad events. An example of an item from ASQ is given here:

You received appreciation for a project
A. I am smart
B. I am good in the area the project was in

The ASQ is scored by assigning a '1' to each internal or stable or global response, and a '0' to each external or unstable or specific explanation. Scales are formed by summing these scores across the appropriate questions for each of the three dimensions, separately for good items and for bad items. Scores for each of the scales range from 0 to 8. In addition, a composite score for all negative items is computed by summing scale scores across internality, stability, and globality. Similarly, a composite score for all positive items is also computed.

ORGANIZATIONAL ROLE STRESS (ORS)

Organizational Role Stress Questionnaire developed by Pareek and Purohit (2010) is an oft-used standardized test. This contains 50 simple statements relating to several aspects of role stress in organization. Respondents are asked to indicate their agreement/disagreement on a five-point Likert type of responses. The responses range from 'never' ('0') to very frequent or almost always ('4'). The dimensions represented include: inter-role distance, role stagnation, role expectancy, role erosion, role overload, role isolation, personal inadequacy, self-role distance, role ambiguity, and resource inadequacy. Each dimension is represented by five items. Apart from generating a score one each of the ten dimensions, an average score is computed for overall role stress.

The psychometric properties of this questionnaire have been reported elsewhere (Pareek & Purohit, 2010). More specifically, the robustness of this test in Indian sociocultural setting is highly satisfactory.

PROCEDURE

Participants were individually contacted at their workplace; measures were administered to each of them individually. The participant was asked to respond to each item according to instructions indicated in the text booklet. It was clearly indicated to each participant that there was no correct or incorrect answer. Care was also taken to assure them that their responses would remain confidential and would be used only for research.

Results

The analysis is first geared to examine the predicted pattern of relationship amongst studied variables. As shown in Table 3.1, the patterns of association amongst dimensions are shown for male and female managers separately. Personal helplessness and universal helplessness are significantly associated: $r(148)=.13$, $p<.05$ for males and $r(68)=.28$, $p<.01$ for females (see Table 3.1). As expected, personal helplessness is significantly associated with non-contingency while universal helpless is unrelated to non-contingency. The trend towards positive correlation between personal helplessness and motivational deficit and negative association between personal helplessness and satisfaction, shown through correlation values, do not reach the level of statistical significance. In sum, personal helplessness if found to be positively related to universal helplessness, non-contingency, and motivational deficits and negatively associated with satisfaction. Universal helplessness is found to be unrelated to non-contingency, motivational deficit, and satisfaction.

As has been indicated earlier, attributional factors of internality, stability, and globality for explaining negative events are considered to be risk factors for helplessness syndrome. As shown in Table 3.1, these factors are found to be significantly intercorrelated. More importantly, these factors as well as the composite attributional score (for explaining negative events) are positively related to personal helplessness. In the group of male managers, the correlation between personal helplessness and internality is highly significant: $r(148) = .17$, $p < .01$. Similarly, in the group of female managers, the association between personal helplessness and internality factor for explaining bad event is significant: $r(68)=.31$, $p < .05$. Interestingly, such factors are not significantly associated with universal helplessness.

Attributional factors of internality, stability, and globality for explaining positive events are considered adaptive. However, the results reveal non-significant relationship with personal helplessness and universal helplessness. Of course, there is a trend in the expected negative direction when relationship between personal helplessness and composite attribution for explaining positive events is considered ($p < .10$).

Table 3.1 Descriptive, Statistics, Correlation, and Differences between Male and Female Managers on Studied Variables

Variables	1	2	3	4	5	6	7	8	9	10	11	12	13
1. Personal helplessness		.28*	.27*	-.25	.20	-.07	-.08	-.03	-.11	.31*	.27*	.29*	.29*
2. Universal helplessness	.13*		.06	.02	.06	-.03	-.01	-.01	-.08	.03	.05	.12	.13
3. Noncontingency	.14*	.05		-.29*	.37**	-.01	-.19	-.19	-.29*	.37**	.39**	.39**	.39**
4. Satisfaction	-.11	.04	-.14*		-.39**	.09	.21	.08	.31*	-.10	-.28*	-.14	-.29*
5. Motivational deficit	.10	.09	.19**	-.17**		-.03	-.03	.28*	-.06	.05	.11	.28*	.28*
Positive Events													
6. Internality	-.09	-.07	-.08	.05	-.01		.39*	.27*	.31*	-.31*	-.27*	-.29*	-.31*
7. Stability	-.08	-.06	-.11	.11	-.04	.27**		.31**	.35**	-.34*	-.29*	-.28*	-.34*
8. Globality	-.06	-.04	-.10	.09	-.06	.31**	.37**		.37*	-.40**	-.31*	-.28*	-.40**
9. Composite	-.11	-.09	-.13*	.12*	-.09	.34**	.39**	.35**		.13	-.30*	-.31*	-.28*
Negative Events													
10. Internality	.17**	.05	.18**	-.11	.08	-.13**	-.16**	-.13*	-.11		-.31*	.31*	.41**
11. Stability	.15*	.06	.21**	-.12*	.10	-.12*	-.13*	-.12*	-.12*	.20**		.39**	.35**
12. Globality	.14*	.08	.24**	-.09	.13*	-.17**	-.12*	-.17**	-.13*	.27**	24**		.39**
13. Composite	.19**	.10	.30**	-.16**	.15*	-.29**	-.24	-.22**	-.16**	.39*	.38**	.37**	

(Table 3.1 Continued)

(Table 3.1 Continued)

Variables	1	2	3	4	5	6	7	8	9	10	11	12	13
Males (n = 150)													
M	28.32	34.73	27.36	16.37	7.31	1.91	2.90	2.83	8.01	1.93	2.34	2.67	8.31
SD	4.10	3.91	3.47	3.41	1.87	0.73	0.65	0.67	1.34	0.33	0.47	0.83	1.11
Females (n = 70)													
M	27.92	37.23	28.41	19.70	6.39	2.87	2.84	2.60	9.44	2.47	3.31	2.94	10.53
SD	3.94	4.05	2.94	2.97	1.69	0.69	0.47	0.53	1.73	0.91	0.67	0.74	1.67
t-value	0.67	0.92	0.83	4.35**	0.53	4.53**	0.53	0.41	0.93	1.99*	1.29	0.89	1.39

Source: Author.

Note: Diagonal correlations (= 1) are omitted. Correlations above the diagonal are for females and below the diagonal are for males.

*p < .05.

**p < .01.

A major thrust of the personal investigation is to examine the association between helplessness and role stress. As shown in Table 3.2, an interesting pattern is revealed. In both the groups of male and female managers, personal helplessness is significantly related to almost all types of role stress. In the group of male managers, it has significant association with each of the role stressors excepting Role Expectations Conflict and role isolation. In the context of these two, there is a trend in the direction of positive association, though the correlation values do not reach the level of statistical significance (p < .10). The association between personal helplessness and overall role stress is highly significant: $r(148)=.16$, p < .0 (see Table 3.2).

In the group of female managers, the pattern is similar. Significant associations between personal helplessness and role stressors are shown with respect to all cases excepting role erosion and resource inadequacy. However, trends in the direction of positive association are shown for these two cases even though correlation values do not reach the level of statistical significance (p<.10).

Table 3.2	Product Moment Correlation Coefficients between Role Stress and Helplessness			
	Males (n = 150)		Females (n = 70)	
	Personal Helplessness	Universal Helplessness	Personal Helplessness	Universal Helplessness
1. Inter role distance	.12*	.09	.29*	.11
2. Role stagnation	.17**	.06	.37**	.13
3. Role Expectations Conflict	.10	-.05	.28*	.05
4. Role erosion	.13*	.08	.21	.04
5. Role overload	.16*	.10	.27*	.10
6. Role isolation	.11	.05	.22	.08
7. Personal inadequacy	.21**	.09	.31*	.05
8. Self-role distance	.24**	.10	.34*	.12
9. Role ambiguity	.15*	.11	.29*	.13
10. Resource Inadequacy	.13*	.08	.14	.09
11. Overall role stress	.16**	.11	.37**	.13

Source: Author.
Notes: *p < .05.
**p < .01.

In contrast, the relationship between universal helplessness and role stressors is found to be non-significant for both the groups of male and female managers. This is in harmony with the expectation. Table 3.3 depicts sex differences on dimensions of role stress. It is shown that female managers experience greater self-role distance than male managers (M = 14.9 and 10.3, respectively). Similarly, female managers report greater role ambiguity than male managers (M = 16.4 and 12.9, respectively). However, male managers report greater role stagnation and role expectations conflict than female managers. There is no sex difference with respect to overall role stress.

It is also interesting to observe that male and female managers do not differ significantly with respects of dimensions of learned helplessness (see Table 3.1). However, female managers indicate greater satisfaction than male managers (M=19.70 and 10.37, respectively). In addition, female managers indicate greater internality in explaining positive events compared to male managers. However, female managers reveal greater internality in explaining negative events than male managers.

Table 3.3 Mean Organizational Role Stress Scores of Participants

| | Males (n = 150) | | Females (n = 70) | | |
Variables	Mean	SD	Mean	SD	t-Value
Inter role distance	12.7	1.9	11.9	1.8	0.67
Role stagnation	14.5	1.7	10.7	1.5	2.11*
Role Expectations Conflict	15.8	1.3	10.9	1.7	3.81**
Role erosion	14.8	0.9	14.2	0.8	0.57
Role overload	16.7	1.4	15.9	1.4	0.87
Role isolation	15.6	1.6	16.3	1.8	0.89
Personal inadequacy	14.9	1.3	15.2	0.9	0.54
Self-role distance	10.3	1.4	14.9	1.2	1.98*
Role ambiguity	12.9	0.9	16.4	0.8	2.93**
Resource Inadequacy	10.5	1.9	11.5	1.7	0.87
Overall role stress	12.7	1.5	11.3	1.9	0.94

Source: Author.
Notes: *p < .05.
**p < .01.

Taken together, personal helplessness is significantly associated with various dimensions of role stress. In contrast, universal helplessness is unrelated to organizational role stress. Personal helplessness is positively associated with non-contingent beliefs and motivational deficits while it is negatively related to satisfaction. There is no overall sex difference with respect to organizational role stress. Female managers exhibit greater self-role distance and role ambiguity whereas male managers show greater role stagnation and role expectations conflict.

Discussion

The objective of the present investigation was to examine the relationship between learned helplessness and organizational role stress. The other purpose was to evaluate the pattern of association amongst facets of helplessness. The findings offer several interesting conclusions.

From a theoretical perspective, the construct of helplessness has been applied to a number of domains such as personality, health, cognition, and education. However, its application to the organizational setting is a challenging task. This is possible only when an effective operationalization of the construct of employees' helplessness is available. The measure of employees' helplessness used in the present investigation offers the possibility of examining a seminal proposition concerning personal helplessness vis-à-vis universal helplessness.

The construct nature of personal helplessness predicts that it is related to dimensions of role stress. The findings of the study clearly support such a prediction. In contrast, universal helplessness is found to be unrelated to role stress. This is consistent with an earlier finding that personal helplessness is significantly related to depression while universal helplessness is unrelated to an individual's depression (Sahoo, 2002).

A basic element of this finding relates to cultural relevance. In Indian sociocultural system, a greater proportion of individuals feel that many people in their environment are helpless. This perception of others' uncontrollability helps to combat depression. This is also found in the context of role stress. Various forms of role stress are significantly associated with personal helplessness, whereas these are unrelated to universal helplessness.

On the basis of this robust finding, intervention programs need to be geared towards the reduction of "personal helplessness." An effective way of reducing personal helplessness and boosting perception of controllability involves Bandura's (1997) concept of self-efficacy. In recent years, a bulk of empirical studies has documented the positive effects of efficacy building measures.

In addition, the role of attributional styles has to be stressed. Since the past studies (Garber and Seligman, 1980; Sahoo, 2002) have evinced the role of internality, globality, and stability (in explaining negative events) as risk factors in helplessness (Peterson and Seligman, 1984), reattribution training is suggested as a process of remediation. Employees who habitually tend to explain negative events in terms of internal factors need to be trained to explain such events in terms of external factors. Individuals who tend to explain negative events in terms of stable factors ought to be trained in the direction of developing habits to explain bad events using unstable factors. Similarly individuals tending to explain bad events using global factors must be trained to use more of specific factors. In sum, attempts to change people's internal, stable, and global attribution to external, unstable, and specific attribution in explaining negative events are likely to reduce helplessness and thereby attenuate role stress.

The issue of sex difference does not appear to be crucial in the context of the present investigation. The participants of the present study are skilled personnel. There is not much sex difference. However, a few differences are revealed. Female managers have shown greater satisfaction and greater internality for explaining both positive events and negative events. It is conjectured that women report greater work satisfaction possibly because of their perception that they have been working against a number of odds. The multiple demands placed on them in our society may be a factor of enhanced self-evaluation.

The other finding concerning females' greater internality (for explaining both positive and negative events) is explainable in terms of gender studies. The literature on gender role has shown that females have a greater range of affect experience compared to their male counterparts (Sahoo, 2004). As a result, women are more vulnerable to depression and self-blame while, at the same time, they have greater capacity to experience joy. This explains as to why they tend to use maladaptive attribution of internality to explain negative events and positive attribution of internality to explain positive events.

The observation that female managers experience greater self-role distance and role ambiguity and male managers report greater role stagnation and role expectation is conceivable in the light of gender-linked socialization in our sociocultural system.

Finally, it is important to recognize that a construct acquires explanatory strength in the light of its cultural appropriateness. It is asserted that the network of helplessness construct offers such a promising possibility in the context of many organizational behaviors including role stress. Research efforts to further such explanation are likely to generate desirable dividends.

Conclusion, Implications, and Limitations

A major *conclusion* of the present study involves the identification and rectification of faulty cognitions. In the context of reattribution training, Seligman (1991) has persuasively argued the importance of disputation method. Once faulty attributional styles (internal, stable, and global styles for explaining bad events) are indentified, it is possible to offer convincing arguments in favor of adaptive attributions (external, unstable, and specific styles for explaining stressful events).

Such reattribution training can be offered in the form of one-to-one counseling. Alternatively, group settings may be arranged and the clients may learn the usefulness of adaptive attributions.

However, the intervention strategy needs to focus on the *saliency* of particular attributional dimension. It appears that the factor of stability–instability is of greater significance in some organizations, whereas the factor of globality–specificity is relatively more important in certain other types of organizations. A *limitation* of the present study is the uncritical generalization regarding organizations as a whole. Yet, research acumen demands specification of attributional dimensions in relation to particular organization type. For example, employees experiencing techno stress may exhibit characteristically different weightages of faulty attribution vis-à-vis employees of traditional industrial sectors. Future studies need to be addressed for generating fine-grained information.

References

Abramson, L.Y., Seligman, M.E.P., & Teasdale, J. (1978). Learned helplessness in humans: Critique and reformulation. *Journal of Abnormal Psychology, 87,* 49–74.

Bandura, A. (1997). *Self-efficacy.* New York: Free Press.

Garber, J. & Seligman, M.E.P. (1980). *Human helplessness.* New York: Academic Press.

Hiroto, D.S. (1974). Locus of control and learned helplessness. *Journal of Experimental Psychology, 102,* 187–93.

Kanungo, R.N. & Sahoo, F.M. (1988). *Employees' helplessness questionnaire.* Unpublished report, Psychology Department, Utkal University, Bhubaneswar, India.

Overmier, J.B. & Seligman, M.E.P. (1967). Effects of inescapable shock upon subsequent escape and avoidant learning. *Journal of Comparative and Physiological Psychology, 63,* 28–33.

Pareek, U. & Purohit, S. (2010). *Training instruments in HRD and OD.* (Third edition). New Delhi: Tata McGraw Hill.

Peterson, C & Seligman, M.E.P. (1984). Casual explanation as a risk factor for depression: Theory and evidence. *Psychological Review, 91,* 347–74.

Sahoo, F.M. (1990). Learned helplessness in industrial employees: A study of non-contingency, satisfaction and motivational deficits. *Psychological Studies, 35*(2), 79–87.

Sahoo, F.M. (1991). Learned helplessness in organizations. *Management and Labor Studies*, *16*(1), 1–10.

———— (2000). *Attributional style questionnaire*. Unpublished report, Psychology Department, Utkal University, Bhubaneswar, India.

———— (2002). *Dynamics of human helplessness*. New Delhi: Concept.

———— (2004). *Sex roles in transition*. New Delhi: Kalpazam.

Seligman, M.E.P. (1991). *Learned optimism*. New York: Knopf.

———— (2002). *Authentic happiness*. New York: Free Press.

Seligman, M.E.P. & Maier, S.F. (1967). Failure to escape traumatic shock. *Journal of Experimental Psychology*, *74*, 1–9.

Snyder, C.R. & Lopez, S.L. (2007) (Eds). *Positive psychology*. New Delhi: SAGE.

4

Role Stress among Varied Occupational Groups

Parvaiz Talib and Irfana Rashid

Abstract

Organizational role systems have been considered as potential sources of stress for individuals in organizational settings. The present study aims at understanding the phenomenon of organizational role stress among four occupational groups, viz., private, government, public, and university. This study aims at investigating the difference in the nature and quantum of role stress amongst these occupational groups and their sub-groups. Organizational Role Stress (ORS) developed by Pareek (1983a) was used in the study. The original English language version along with Hindi translated version (developed by the authors) was administered on 540 participants. Findings of the study revealed that private sector is the most stressed group amongst all the four occupational groups while university sector reported lowest level of stress. The three occupational groups, viz., private, government, and university sector differ significantly in stress patterns. However, significant differences were not observed across hierarchical levels of public sector. Measures have been proposed to deal with the different stressors. This study reported some common stressors. Yet there are differences in the nature of stress in each group.

Keywords: organizational role stress, coping strategies, private sector, public sector, government employees, university employees

Introduction

Research work over the past 20 years has shown that workplace stress has undesirable consequences, both for the health and safety of individuals and for the well-being of their organizations. Workplace stress has been related to organization's problems such as managerial ineffectiveness (Srivastava, 2009), poor job performance, turnover, absenteeism, accidents, and errors (William et al., 2001).

The experience of workplace stress across different occupational groups has been of extensive research. This chapter outlines the experience of role stress in various occupational groups, viz., private, public, government, and university sectors. The organizational role stress (ORS) scale (Pareek, 1983a) was used to measure 10 role stresses. The stress experienced by different occupation types and job roles has been explored in many research papers with a number of occupations being described as experiencing above average levels of stress; for example, bank employees (Sharma and Devi, 2011; Kumar and Dileep, 2006; Rajeshwari, 1992), police personnel (Talib, 2001), healthcare (Cooper et al., 1999), ambulance services (Young and Cooper, 1999), nurses and social workers (Kahn, 1993), teachers (Travers and Cooper, 1993), and industrial sales persons (Behrman and William, 1984). Researchers have also demonstrated the direct and indirect costs of stress (Matteson and Ivancevich, 1987). According to Kalia (2002), an estimate of the World Health Organization (WHO) Global Burden of Disease Survey showed that mental health disease, including stress-related disorders, would be the second leading cause of disabilities by the year 2020. A survey in 2007 by Associated Chamber of Commerce and Industry of India also reported that work-related stress and mental fatigue is affecting the Indian employees (www.assocham.org). The four occupational groups included in the present study cover the major chunk of organized employment in India. So choosing these occupational groups for the present study was considered a relevant idea.

Literature Review

A number of studies have been undertaken in India that investigated the problem of role stress (Table 4.1). The pioneer of such studies in India is Professor. Udai Pareek. The ORS scale consisting of 50 items, developed and conceptualized by him, is widely used instrument for investigating the problem of role stress in varied occupational settings.

After reviewing the available literature (Table 4.1), need for conducting the present study was felt in order to explore the contradictory findings in case of public and private sector employees. The authors also aimed to explore the consistency in findings (Role Overload as a potent stressor) in case of

	Occupational	
Authors	Groups Studied	Main Findings
Bhaskar (1986)	Police officers and Constables	Factors intrinsic to job at workplace were most dominant whereas organizational culture and climates were least dominant in role stress in both the groups.
Jasmine (1987)	Public and Private sector blue-collar employees	Public sector employees scored more on role stress than private sector employees.
Sharma (1987)	Managers and Supervisors of Public and Private Pharmaceutical organizations	Private sector employees scored higher on role stress than public sector, except for Role Stagnation (RS).
Rees & Cooper (1992)	Healthcare and non-healthcare workers	Healthcare workers showed significantly higher levels of stress in workplace.
Samanta & Singh (1993)	Industrial workers in public and private sectors	Total physical and mental distresses were significantly high.
Jagdish (1994)	University sector	Staff below senior lecturer level reported more job stress than other staff.
Walter & John (1994)	Academic Department Chairpersons (Higher Education)	Work overload followed by compliance to rules and regulations were the potent stressors.
Mishra (1996)	Male and Female teachers	Female teachers were more stressed than male teachers.
Pareek & Mehta, (1997)	Female gazetted officers, Female bank employees, Female teachers	Gazetted officers showed significantly higher stress levels, followed by bank employees. Teachers were the least scoring group.
Pandey (1998)	Public sector Organizations	High degree of tough mindedness and emotional tendencies lead to high degree of role stress.
Pandey (2003)	Advertising professionals in India	Among three functional groups, media professional scored higher on role stress than executives creative and account management executives.

Table 4.1 Summary of Stress-related Studies across Various Occupational Groups

(Table 4.1 Continued)

(Table 4.1 Continued)

Authors	Occupational Groups Studied	Main Findings
Aziz (2004)	Women in Indian Information technology sector	IT professional women scored significantly higher on Role Stress.
Nilufaret et al., (2009)	University Staff	Role Overload emerged as a potent stressor.
Sharma & Devi (2011)	Private and Public sector bank employees	Public sector bank employees were found to be more stressful than private sector bank employees.
Manzoor et al. (2011)	University faculty	Role stress among University employees was found to be on lower side (except Role Overload) and scores on job satisfaction were on higher side.

university employees. The present study also aimed to investigate the trend of role stress across government sector employees, viz., gazetted officers, teachers, and other groups in government setting.

The Study

OBJECTIVES AND HYPOTHESIS

In line with the previous researches conducted across various occupational groups, the study aims at:

1. Investigating the difference in the nature and quantum of organizational role stress among four occupational groups, namely, private sector, government sector, public sector, and university sector.
2. Investigating the difference in the nature and quantum of organizational role stress among various sub-groups of private sector.
3. Investigating the difference in the nature and quantum of organizational role stress among various sub-groups of government sector.

4. Investigating the difference in the nature and quantum of organizational role stress among various sub-groups of public sector.
5. Investigating the difference in the nature and quantum of organizational role stress among various sub-groups of university sector.

On the basis of objectives of the study, the following null hypotheses have been formulated.

Ho1: There is no difference in the nature and quantum of organizational role stress amongst four occupational groups.

Ho2: There is no difference in the nature and quantum of organizational role stress amongst various sub-groups of private sector.

Ho3: There is no difference in the nature and quantum of organizational role stress amongst various sub-groups of government sector.

Ho4: There is no difference in the nature and quantum of organizational role stress amongst various sub-groups of public sector.

Ho5: There is no difference in the nature and quantum of organizational role stress amongst sub-groups of university sector.

Method

The present study aims to understand the phenomenon of stress among four occupational groups, namely, private sector, public sector, government sector, and university sector.

MEASURES

Organizational Role Stress (ORS) scale developed by Pareek (1983a) was used to measure respondent's "role stress" in an organization. The original version (English language) as well as the Hindi version, translated by the researcher in his doctoral study (Talib, 1999), was administered among the respondents. This scale measures respondent's quantum of stress in terms of total ORS score. It also measures intensity of ten role stressors contributing to total ORS score.

RELIABILITY OF THE TEST

The ORS scale has high level of reliability and validity as ascertained by Professor Udai Pareek. Retest reliability of scale also has acceptable reliability value. Sen (1982) used ORS on the sample of 500 bank employees and retest reliability coefficient were found for total role stress (0.73) and for the dimensions of role stress SRD (0.45), IRD (0.58), RS (0.63), RA (0.65), RO (0.53), RE (0.37), RI (0.58).

SCORING

The ORS scale is 5-point Likert type rating scale (0 to 4), having the scoring pattern as follows:

— A score of '0' was assigned to an item if the respondent never or rarely felt that way.
— A score of '1' was assigned to an item if the respondent occasionally felt that way.
— A score of '2' was assigned to an item if the respondent sometimes felt that way.
— A score of '3' was assigned to an item if the respondent frequently felt that way.
— A score of '4' was assigned to an item if the respondent very frequently or always felt that way.

As there are five statements for each role stress dimension, range of scores on each of stressors may vary from a minimum of 0 to a maximum of 20 and the cumulative ORS score may range from 0 to 200.

SAMPLE

The study covers 546 respondents from four occupational groups, viz., private, public, government, and university sector. Respondents have been selected on the basis of purposive judgmental sample. The sample covered various hierarchical levels, i.e., lower, middle, and top positions. The number and percentage of respondents is presented in Table 4.2:

Table 4.2	Sample Size	

Sectors	Sample Size (n)	Percentage
Private	205	37.54
Government	128	23.44
Public	131	24.00
University	82	15.00
TOTAL	**546**	**100**

Data Analysis and Results

STATISTICAL ANALYSIS

This study used mean and standard deviation (SD) to analyze pattern of stress in varied occupational groups. Significance of difference was calculated using t-test to see whether the sectors differ significantly on the level of stress experienced by these groups. Each occupational group was analyzed in terms of ten role stressors, too. On the basis of researcher's personal judgment, sub-sectors were identified amongst the four occupational groups to observe the impact of role stress and find out the difference within these sub-sectors. This helped carry out stressor-wise comparison. Analysis of variance (ANOVA) was used to ascertain difference when more than two groups were compared. Further, t-test was used to find the significance of difference on ORS amongst the sub-groups of each sector.

RESULTS

Analysis of data reveals that private sector is the most stressed group among all the four groups, followed by the government sector. The level of stress in the university and public sector is comparatively less (Table 4.3).

In order to ascertain the significance of difference amongst these four occupational groups, analysis of variance (ANOVA) was calculated. F-ratio for these four occupational groups was found to be 8.07, indicating a very high level of difference in the intensity of stress across four occupational groups. As shown in the Table 4.3, private sector emerges as the most stressed group.

Table 4.3 Summary ORS Scores among Four Occupational Groups

Stressors	Public Sector N=132		Pvt. Sector N=205		Govt. Sector N=128		Univ. Sector N=82		F-ratio	P-value
	Mean	SD	Mean	SD	Mean	SD	Mean	SD		
IRD	7.25	5.00	7.67	4.81	7.66	4.73	7.34	4.75	0.27	N. Sig
RS	5.62	4.63	7.29	4.53	6.30	4.92	5.13	4.03	5.90	0.01
REC	4.44	3.75	5.57	4.03	5.10	4.13	5.24	3.82	2.17	N. Sig
RE	8.09	3.91	7.68	3.81	8.65	4.77	6.81	4.22	3.57	0.01
RO	4.25	3.95	5.80	4.64	5.09	5.02	5.25	4.18	3.17	0.05
RI	6.21	3.50	6.62	3.60	7.08	4.69	5.63	3.30	2.70	0.05
PI	6.33	4.73	6.71	4.14	5.00	4.74	4.70	4.39	6.29	0.01
SRD	5.65	4.06	6.14	3.90	6.11	4.84	4.64	3.70	2.89	0.05
RA	3.44	3.58	4.38	4.29	4.36	4.48	2.58	2.98	5.06	0.01
RIn	5.78	4.10	6.70	4.33	7.60	5.16	5.82	3.84	4.58	0.01
ORS	57.11	28.83	64.59	31.15	63.01	35.44	45.85	24.11	8.07	0.01

The higher level of stress in the private sector is understandable. Private sector is witnessing a period of swift changes in the wake of trends towards liberalization and globalization. Thus pressure to perform has increased manifold. These factors explain high *Role Erosion* scores in the private sector. Stressors that have contributed to relatively high stress in private sector are *IRD, RS,* and *RE* (7.67, 7.29 and 7.68, respectively). Respondents in the government sector have maximum scores on *Role Erosion* amongst all occupational groups.

Role Erosion indicates a feeling of responsibility without power. It indicates that employees in the government sector suffer from a feeling of loss of importance and thus suffer from high *Role Erosion*. The *Role Erosion* score is high in the public sector (8.09) also. This along with *Inter Role Distance* (7.25) and *Personal Inadequacy* (6.33) are important source of stress in public sector. In the university sector, *Inter Role Distance* and *Role Erosion* are the two noteworthy stressors.

STRESSOR-WISE ANALYSIS ACROSS FOUR OCCUPATIONAL GROUPS

1. *Inter-Role Distance*: All the four sectors are uniformly stressed on this count. That is why significant difference has not been observed among (F=0.27) four occupational groups on this count. SD values of IRD across four occupational groups indicate that there is a wide variation of this stressor among these sectors.
2. *Role Stagnation*: Emerges as significant stressor in the private sector, only and a high F value (5.90) indicates that there are significant differences among four occupational groups on this count.
3. *Role Expectation Conflict*: Does not emerge as significant stressors in any of the occupational groups and significant differences have not been observed in four occupational groups on this count.
4. *Role Erosion*: Emerges as a very potent stressor in at least three occupational groups, viz., private sector, public sector, and government sector. Role Erosion scores for the university sector is comparatively low. It has been found significantly different for these four occupational groups (F = 3.57) at .01 level of significance.
5. *Role Overload*: Does not show very high figure in these four occupational groups. A significant feature of the finding with respect to Role Overload is a very high SD value. In government sector, it is almost equal to the mean score. This indicates that although, overall, it does not emerge as potent stressor but for some of the respondents, this is contributing to a high level of stress. It seems that a selected few

employees are shouldering most of the work-related responsibilities. They are making up for the inefficiencies of their fellow employees.

6. *Role Isolation*: Emerges as important stressor in the government sector. A high SD value of 4.69 in government sector on this count indicates a lack of coordination and a feeling of being isolated from others amongst at least some of these respondents.

7. *Personal Inadequacy*: Maximum scores on this count have been obtained amongst the respondents in private sector. In rest of the sectors, scores on this count are on the lower side. However, high SD values on this stressor indicate that some of the employees are feeling extremely stressed because of perceived feeling of inadequacy. Significant difference has been observed on this count as well (F = 6.29, sig. at .0003).

8. *Self-role Distance*: Higher scores have been observed in private sector and government sector only. Significant difference has been observed on these stressors as well with F ratio of 2.89, significant at .05.

9. *Role Ambiguity*: The scores of the respondents on this count are on the lower side indicating the fact that this is not important stressor for any of the occupational groups.

10. *Resource Inadequacy*: Emerges as the most important stressor for the government sector. This indicates a mismatch between the expectation of the stakeholders and the resources available for meeting those expectations.

In all significant differences have been observed on the total ORS scores in these four occupational groups and this difference is significant for as many as eight stressors out of ten. *Thus, our first null hypothesis (Ho1) that there is no difference in the nature and quantum of organizational role stress amongst various occupational groups is rejected.*

A significant feature of the findings discussed above is high standard deviation scores across all occupational groups. Standard deviation measures the dispersion of data around the mean. A high standard deviation indicates that there is wide variation in level of stress experienced by the respondents across these occupational groups. This suggests that some respondents feel more stressed than others. To understand the nature of stress among respondents, the data was further analyzed and the respondents were placed in the four varying levels of stress, starting from low stress group to very high stress group. The distribution of stress in each quartile is given in Table 4.4.

Respondent's score on one stressor may vary range from 0 to 20. Thus the average of this scale would be 10. Any score above it would indicate relatively

Table 4.4 Classification of Different Levels of Role Stress

Level of Stress	Role Stress Factors	Total ORS Score
Low	0–5	0–50
Low Medium	6–10	51–100
High Medium	11–15	101–150
High	16–20	151–200

high level of stress and any score below would indicate rather low level of stress. Thus all the respondents having a score of 11 and above would fall in the group of high stress category. Within that, those who have scores of 16 and above would be experiencing enormously high level of stress.

As stated earlier, out of four occupational groups, private sector has emerged as most stressed group. In private sector, 14% of the respondents are experiencing high level of stress. This figure in the government sector is above 18% indicating that the significant numbers of respondents are suffering from high level of stress.

Table 4.5 Classification of Respondents as per Varying Levels of Stress

Stressors	Stress Interval	Govermnent No.	%	University No.	%	Private No.	%	Public No.	%
IRD	0 to 5	47	37	33	40	70	34	58	44
	6 to 10	50	39	30	37	77	38	41	31
	11 to 15	22	17	13	16	44	21	23	17
	16 to 20	09	07	06	07	14	07	10	08
RS	0 to 5	66	52	45	55	74	36	75	57
	6 to 10	32	25	31	38	82	40	33	25
	11 to 15	25	20	04	05	39	19	19	14
	16 to 20	04	04	02	02	10	05	05	04
REC	0 to 5	77	60	47	57	112	55	90	68
	6 to 10	35	27	27	33	66	32	32	24
	11 to l5	14	11	07	09	26	13	07	05
	16 to 20	02	02	01	01	01	02	03	02

(Table 4.5 Continued)

(Table 4.5 Continued)

Stressors	Stress Interval	Goverment No.	%	University No.	%	Private No.	%	Public No.	%
RE	0 to 5	31	24	36	44	64	31	29	22
	6 to 10	49	38	29	35	94	46	69	52
	11 to 15	39	30	14	17	42	20	30	24
	16 to 20	09	07	03	04	05	02	04	03
RO	0 to 5	82	64	49	60	110	54	88	67
	6 to 10	25	20	22	27	58	28	32	24
	11 to 15	14	11	09	11	32	16	10	08
	16 to 20	07	05	02	02	05	02	02	02
RI	0 to 5	56	44	41	50	91	44	58	44
	6 to 10	40	31	36	44	73	36	59	45
	11 to 15	25	20	04	05	40	20	40	11
	16 to 20	07	05	01	01	01	00	01	01
PI	0 to 5	79	62	49	60	80	39	67	51
	6 to 10	29	23	20	24	90	44	41	31
	11 to 15	17	13	12	15	31	15	19	14
	16 to 20	03	02	01	01	04	02	05	04
SRD	0 to 5	66	52	54	66	95	46	73	55
	6 to 10	38	30	19	23	83	40	41	31
	11 to 15	19	15	08	10	24	12	15	11
	16 to 20	05	04	01	01	03	01	03	02
RA	0 to 5	93	73	69	84	140	68	101	77
	6 to 10	18	14	09	11	43	21	22	17
	11 to 15	12	09	02	02	19	09	09	07
	16 to 20	05	04	00	00	06	03	05	04
RIn	0 to 5	50	39	38	46	93	45	67	51
	6 to 10	42	33	32	39	73	36	50	38
	11 to 15	26	20	12	15	33	16	10	08
	16 to 20	10	08	00	00	06	03	05	04
ORS	0 to 50	54	**42.18**	42	**51.21**	81	**39.52**	61	**46.21**
	51 to 100	5.1	**39.84**	33	**40.24**	96	**46.82**	62	**46.96**
	101 to 150	22	**17.18**	07	**8.53**	28	**13.65**	08	**6.06**
	151 to 200	01	**0.78**	00.00	**00.00**	00.00	**00.00**	01	**0.75**

Let us probe the factors contributing to this state of affairs. *Inter-Role Distance, Role Erosion,* and *Role Isolation* account for the major sources of stress amongst all occupational groups, especially private sector and government sector. As many as 28% of the respondents (21% medium high and 7% in very high) are experiencing *Inter-Role Distance* in the private sector. This suggests that they are unable to negotiate and balance successfully the demands of their organizational and non-organizational roles. This implies that the job responsibilities are taking a toll of their family and social life. The situation is not very different in the government sector on this stressor. As 24% of the respondents (17% in medium high and 7% in very high) feel stressed on account of *Inter-Role Distance,* it may be argued that percentage wise this figure is not high. But we have to look at data beyond numbers. If 31 respondents are experiencing *Inter-Role Distance,* we need to take note of it.

Role Erosion is also another powerful stressor. This factor seems to be playing a very prominent role in the government sector as 37% of the respondents (30% in medium high and 7% in very high) are experiencing *Role Erosion.* This feeling of loss of power has serious implications for the morale of employees. This issue needs probing. This feeling of loss of power might be because of growing outside interference in the governmental work. This has serious implication for the morale of the employees in the government sector.

Sector-wise Analysis

1. **Private Sector**

   Private sector emerges as most stressed group. It has a mean Organizational Role Stress value of 64.59 with SD 31.15. Three stressors emerge prominently in this occupational group namely *Role Erosion* (7.68), *Inter Role Distance* (7.67) and *Role Stagnation* (7.29). High SD values indicate that some of these respondents are experiencing rather higher level of stress (Table 4.6).

   In order to understand the nature of stress in the private sector, the data was analyzed as per various sub-groups. The researcher exercised judgment to identify relevant sub-groups in the private sector. In order to study the nature of stress in private sector the data was divided in two groups, namely manufacturing and service sector. Employees in manufacturing sector are experiencing greater amount of stress than employees of service sector (Table 4.6). This difference is significant at 0.01. *Thus, second null hypothesis (Ho2) that there is no difference in the nature and quantum of organizational role stress amongst various sub-groups*

Table 4.6 Results of Stress (Private Sector)

Stressors	Private (Manufacturing + Services)		Manufacturing N=156		Services N=49		t-Value df=203	p-Value
	Mean	SD	Mean	SD	Mean	SD		
IRD	7.67	4.81	7.91	4.97	6.91	4.21	1.26	Non Sig
RS	7.29	4.53	8.01	4.54	4.97	3.68	4.25	.01
REC	5.57	4.03	6.14	4.05	3.75	3.41	3.72	.01
RE	7.68	3.81	8.17	3.87	6.14	3.18	2.33	.01
RO	5.80	4.64	6.24	4.70	4.38	4.15	2.47	.05
RI	6.62	3.60	7.01	3.66	5.38	3.12	2.80	.01
PI	6.71	4.14	7.21	4.15	5.12	3.71	3.14	.01
SRD	6.14	3.90	6.67	3.84	4.44	3.61	3.59	.01
RA	4.38	4.29	4.91	4.50	2.69	3.02	3.22	.01
RIn	6.70	4.33	7.17	4.37	5.18	3.68	2.86	.01
ORS	64.59	31.15	69.49	31.38	49.02	24.85	4.17	.001

of private sector is rejected. Most significant difference in these two groups has been observed on Role Stagnation (t=4.25). Manufacturing sector experienced greater amount of Role Stagnation stress.

In fact, difference has been observed in these two groups on all stressors except *Inter Role Distance.* Both these groups have almost identical level of stress on Inter Role Distance. Employees of manufacturing sector are experiencing significantly high amount of stress than employees of service sector on rest of the stressors.

2. **Government Sector**

In this study government sector emerges as the second most stressed group with a Mean ORS value of 63.01. The SD for this group is also high (35.4) indicating a wide variation in the level of stress amongst respondents. As pointed out earlier in Table 4.5, 18% of the respondents are found experiencing either medium–high or very high stress in government sector. The reality of stress in the government sector is presented in Table 4.7.

The stressors that emerge important in government sector are *Role Erosion, Inter Role Distance,* and *Resource Inadequacy.* As many as 24%

| **Table 4.7** | Results of Stress in Government Employees |

Stressors	Govt. Sector (central + state govt.)		Central Govt. N=50		State Govt. N=78		t-Value df = 203	p-Value
	Mean	SD	Mean	SD	Mean	SD		
IRD	7.66	4.73	8.90	5.35	6.87	4.14	2.40	.05
RS	6.30	4.92	7.26	5.14	5.67	4.72	1.77	Non Sig
REC	5.10	4.13	6.36	4.06	4.31	4.01	2.81	.01
RE	8.65	4.77	8.98	4.74	8.45	4.82	0.61	Non Sig
RO	5.09	5.02	6.28	5.54	4.33	4.54	2.17	.05
RI	7.08	4.69	7.60	4.87	6.76	4.58	0.99	Non Sig
PI	5.00	4.74	6.06	4.95	4.33	4.53	2.02	.05
SRD	6.11	4.84	7.06	4.60	6.76	4.93	1.77	Non Sig
RA	4.36	4.48	5.36	4.94	4.33	4.08	2.02	.05
RIn	7.60	5.16	8.42	5.29	5.51	5.05	1.42	Non Sig
ORS	63.01	35.44	72.28	36.07	3.73	33.95	2.41	.05

of the respondents are experiencing high Inter Role Distance. This figure for Role Erosion is even more at 37%. However the percentage of respondents falling in medium high or high stress category is 30% and 7%, respectively. Another stressor that emerges important in this analysis is Resource Inadequacy as among 28% of the respondents has contributed to high level of stress.

Respondents were divided into two groups, viz., Central government and state government employees (Table 4.7). Most significant difference among these two groups has been observed on *Role Expectation Conflict*. Differences have been observed in these two groups with respect to four other stressors also, namely, *Inter-Role Distance, Role Overload, Personal Inadequacy,* and *Role Ambiguity*. The difference is significant for overall ORS score also. Central government employees reported higher ORS score than state government employees (significant at 0.05). *Thus, the third null hypothesis (Ho3) stating that there is no difference in the nature and quantum of organizational role stress amongst various sub-groups of government sector is not accepted.*

3. Public Sector

Public sector emerges as the third most stressed group in this study. The mean ORS score for this sector is 57.11 with a S.D value of 28.83. The most significant stressor causing stress in this occupational group is Role Erosion (mean value of 8.10). Along with that Inter Role Distance also causes occupational stress (mean value 7.26) (Table 4.8)

Another significant stressor for this occupational group is *Personal Inadequacy*. This stressor also records a high SD value vis-à-vis mean (i.e., 4.73 on a mean value of 6.33). At least 18% of the respondents have a perceived feeling of inadequacy in terms of their skills and knowledge base. Another cause of concern among public sector employees is *Role Isolation* with a mean value of 6.22. A high SD value of 3.5 on this count, too, indicates that some employees in this occupational group are feeling more *Role Isolation* stress than others.

The analysis of score across hierarchical groups in the public sector does not reveal any significant difference in the lower and middle management groups (Table 4.8). *Thus, null hypothesis (Ho4) stating that there is no difference in the nature and quantum of organizational role stress amongst various sub groups of public sector is accepted.*

Table 4.8 Summary Results of Public Sector

Stressors	Results of Public Sector		Lower Management N=70		Middle Management N=62		t-Value df = 130	p-Value
	Mean	SD	Mean	SD	Mean	SD		
IRD	7.26	5.00	7.86	5.34	6.58	4.55	1.46	Non Sig
RS	5.63	4.63	5.84	4.92	5.39	4.32	0.56	Non Sig
REC	4.45	3.75	4.11	3.82	4.82	3.66	1.08	Non Sig
RE	8.10	3.91	8.27	4.10	7.90	3.71	0.53	Non Sig
RO	4.25	3.95	4.54	3.88	3.92	4.05	0.90	Non Sig
RI	6.22	3.50	6.70	3.61	5.68	3.32	1.68	Non Sig
PI	6.33	4.73	7.39	5.18	5.15	3.89	2.78	.01
SRD	5.65	4.06	6.11	4.42	5.13	3.59	1.39	Non Sig
RA	3.45	3.58	3.51	3.76	3.37	3.39	0.22	Non Sig
RIn	5.78	4.10	6.03	4.18	5.50	4.04	0.73	Non Sig
ORS	57.11	28.83	**60.37**	28.67	**53.44**	28.80	1.38	Non Sig

4. **University Sector**

Out of the four occupational groups covered in this study, university sector emerges as the least stressed group. The Mean ORS Score for university sector is only 45.85 (Table 4.9)

Still a relatively high SD score (24.11) indicates that some employees in the university sector are more stressed than their fellow employees. To understand this, it is important to assess the number of employees falling in the medium high and high stress category. In terms of overall ORS score, just seven employees figure in the medium high stress category. However, some stressors contribute more to the stress among university employees. *Inter-Role Distance* and *Role Erosion* appear as potent stressors as 23% and 21% of employees are severely afflicted by these stressors respectively. *Personal Inadequacy* also accounts for medium high or very high stress among 16% of respondents.

It is important to understand the differences among various relevant sub-groups of this sector. The most important differences observed have been amongst academic (Deans, Chairpersons, and Principals) and administrative heads (persons holding non-teaching higher positions).

Table 4.9 Summary Results of University Sector

Stressors	Univ. sector (Adm. + Academic)		Administrative Heads N=48		Academic Heads N = 34		t-Value df = 80	p-Value
	Mean	SD	Mean	SD	Mean	SD		
IRD	7.34	4.75	8.91	4.89	5.11	3.54	3.85	.01
RS	5.13	4.03	6.10	4.14	3.76	3.49	2.68	.01
REC	5.24	3.82	5.79	4.13	4.47	3.24	1.55	Non Sig
RE	6.81	4.22	7.70	4.16	5.55	4.03	2.33	.05
RO	5.25	4.18	6.27	4.41	3.82	3.41	2.70	.01
RI	5.63	3.30	6.12	3.39	4.94	3.09	1.61	Non Sig
PI	4.70	4.39	6.31	4.44	2.44	3.18	4.34	.01
SRD	4.64	3.70	5.85	3.97	2.94	2.46	3.78	.01
RA	2.58	2.98	3.33	3.47	1.52	1.65	2.80	.01
RIn	5.82	3.84	5.72	3.98	5.97	3.69	0.27	Non Sig
ORS	45.85	24.11	62.14	28.62	40.55	19.40	3.81	.01

The stressors on which significant differences have been observed in these two groups are: *Inter-Role Distance, Role Stagnation, Role Erosion, Role Overload, Personal Inadequacy, Self-Role Distance,* and *Role Ambiguity.* Within this, the level of stress is especially high for administrative heads on Inter Role Distance and Role Erosion (mean value 8.91 and 7.70, respectively).

The nature of stress in the university sector is different for these two groups. Administrative heads are part of the non-teaching staff of university. The teaching staff of university shoulders additional administrative responsibilities as academic heads. The findings of this study indicate that the nature of stress in these two groups differ markedly. Administrative heads are significantly more stressed than the academic heads (ORS scores 62.14 vis-à-vis 40.55). The difference is significant at 0.01 level. *Thus, our last null hypothesis (Ho5) stating that there is no difference in the nature and quantum of organizational role stress amongst various sub-groups of university sector is rejected.*

Discussion

	Hypothesis	*Status*
Ho1	No difference in the nature and quantum of ORS among four occupational groups, namely, private, government, public, and university.	Rejected
Ho2	No difference in the nature and quantum of ORS amongst various sub-groups of private sector.	Rejected
Ho3	No difference in the nature and quantum of ORS amongst various sub-groups of government sector.	Rejected
Ho4	No difference in the nature and quantum of ORS amongst various sub-groups of public sector.	Failed to reject
Ho5	No difference in the nature and quantum of ORS amongst various sub-groups of university sector.	Rejected

1. **Private sector**
   The findings of the present study indicate that private sector has emerged as the most stressed group. Previous researches (Sharma, 1987; Malik, 2011) also found private sector as the most stressed group. However, there are contrary findings as well, e.g., Jasmine (1987) and Sharma and Devi (2011) found low scores of role stress in private sector.

In the present study, *Inter-Role Distance* and *Role Erosion* have emerged as key stressors. The employees in private sector are expected to perform consistently at higher levels with longer working hours and reduced support staff. This leaves the employees with very little time for family, social, and religious duties, resulting in Inter Role Distance. Also in private sector, there is a need in competition with each passing day. It gives role occupants a feeling of Role Erosion.

In the present study, the data were analyzed as per the sub-groups, i.e., manufacturing and services sector. Manufacturing group has emerged far more stressed than respondents in the services sector. A striking thing observed in the context of employees of manufacturing sector is the lack of team spirit, especially the relationship of trust amongst seniors and juniors. The junior level employees find the attitude of their seniors non-cooperative. High level of Role Expectation Conflict has also been observed amongst these employees, reflecting conflicting expectations towards their roles. This, too, has created a situation of discomfort amongst the employees. Another reason for scoring more on stress amongst manufacturing sector may be that the services have witnessed far greater growth than manufacturing. Therefore, employees who are part of the old economy may be feeling left out. They might be feeling stuck in a sector that is witnessing less growth, giving rise to a feeling of Role Stagnation.

2. Government sector

Government sector employees has emerged as the second most stressed group in the present study. This is in line with the findings of another study (Pareek and Mehta, 1997), where the gazetted officers emerged as the most stressed group.

The findings of the study revealed that *Role Erosion, Resource Inadequacy* and *Inter-Role Distance* are potent stressors in government sector employees. The feeling of Role Erosion in government sector may be due to the routine nature of work. The role occupants have to perform almost the same duty every day. They want to come out of the routine nature of their work and take challenging responsibilities. An interesting finding in the study was that there was an implicit race among various hierarchical levels to get ahead and score over a fellow colleague anyhow. This may create in them a feeling that some functions which he would like to perform are being performed by some other roles leading to Role Erosion. Feeling of Resource Inadequacy was more prevalent in higher officials. This may be because the work of officers and higher level employees is more challenging and difficult. To perform these duties effectively, they feel inadequacy of requisite facilities like financial resources and modern equipment for advanced technical work.

Government employees were divided into two sub-groups, i.e., Central and state government employees. The findings of the study revealed that Central government officials are far more stressed than their state government counterparts. Role Expectation Conflict was the key stressor for this group. It might be so that the nature of demands of various tasks related to responsibilities for Central government employees are more. They are, therefore, experiencing greater conflict with regard to expectations of various role senders.

3. Public sector

Public sector emerged as the third most stressed group in this study. The study revealed that public sector is less stressed than private sector. This is contrary with the findings of other studies (Jasmine, 1987; Sharma and Devi 2011). In these studies, public sector employees scored more on role stress than private sector employees.

The reality of public sector is somewhat similar to that of government sector. *Role Erosion* and *Inter Role Distance* have emerged as key stressor for this group also. The high scores on Role Erosion in this sector exhibit a feeling that their ability is not utilized fully in comparison to their counterparts in private sector. In private sector the employees share more responsibilities and grow faster in their job. While as there seems a mismatch between the requirements of job and ability of employees in public sector. Inter Role Distance, in a way, is even more noteworthy than Role Erosion because of the high SD values (i.e., 5 on a mean score of 7.25). This indicates that there is a wide variation in the level of stress being experienced by the respondents on this count. As has been noted earlier that as many as 25% respondents fall in the high and very high stress category, this is a serious cause of concern for this occupational group.

Public sector employees were divided into two hierarchical groups, i.e., lower and middle management. Overall respondents in the lower management group appear more stressed. However, this difference is insignificant on total ORS score as also for most of the stressors. However, one stressor, *Personal Inadequacy*, is a point of concern for lower management group. They have reported significantly higher score than the middle management group. It indicates that there is an urge among respondents in the lower management group to upgrade their skill base. It seems that, there are no conscious efforts to arrange training programs for this group of employees. This is a serious cause of concern for this sector, as these respondents are now called upon to compete in a more open environment.

4. **University sector**

    The university sector has reported overall lower levels of stress vis-à-vis other occupational groups. This finding is supported by many previous studies (Jagdish, 1994; Nilufar et al., 2009; Manzur et al., 2011; Walter and John, 1994). In all these studies, *Role Overload* emerged as a potent stressor in university employees. Contrary to this, the findings of the present study revealed that *Inter-Role Distance* and *Role Erosion* are potent stressors in university employees.

    Respondents in this group were divided into two sub-groups, viz., administrative and academic heads. Administrative heads (the non-teaching staff) has reported relatively higher level of stress in comparison to academic heads. When an individual occupies more than one role, there may be a conflict between the roles he occupies and familial roles. In the present study, it was found that the teaching staff of university shoulders additional responsibilities as academic heads. Long and Porter (1984) pointed out that psychological consequences of role accumulation depends on the nature of particular role and on the number of roles occupied. This may be the reason that teaching staff in university suffers from *Inter Role Distance*. In non-teaching staff, scores of Inter Role Distance are also on higher side. This may be because the demands of their job. They have to take care of all the non-teaching functions, which are more in number. This may leave them with less time for familial responsibilities. Role Erosion was also on the higher side. This may be because of the competition among colleagues for moving ahead. They may feel like taking more responsibilities than their colleagues to prove their worth and move ahead in a race.

LIMITATIONS OF THE STUDY

1. Cooperation of respondents was a serious problem. Respondents were doubtful about the utility of the study. Many respondents felt that such studies hardly result in betterment of their lot in India. They were also doubtful whether their senior officers would go through their responses.

2. Although the Original English version of Organizational Role Stress (ORS) scale was administered with Hindi-translated version for facilitating effective comprehension of items in the questionnaire but some respondents reported difficulties in understanding of the content of the questionnaire.

3. Being a large-scale study, field investigators were employed to collect the data. Although uniform guidelines were provided, but a field investigator's ability to respond to queries of the respondents might have influenced respondents' understanding of the content of the questionnaires.

IMPLICATIONS OF THE STUDY

In the study, high scores were found on *Inter Role Distance, Role Erosion, Role Stagnation, Resource Inadequacy,* and *Role Isolation.* Following recommendations for organizations are suggested, in line with the findings of the present study:

Table 4.10 Recommendations for Organizational-level Stress Management Strategies

Potent Stressor	Sectors	Recommendations
Inter Role Distance (IRD)	Private, Government, Public, University	a) Spouse Involvement program may be introduced. b) Platform for social activities may be set. c) Childcare facilities at workplace may be provided for female employees. d) Flexible work options may be given to employees so that they may be able to work for a fixed number of hours spread as per convenience.
Role Erosion (RE)	Private, Government, Public and University	a) *Job design*: Before allotting any specific task to an employee, organizations should try to match the skills of the employee with the job requirements. Then judiciously allocate the work. b) *Redefining tasks*: Monitoring work performance and providing employees with challenging tasks who show good results.

(Table 4.10 Continued)

(Table 4.10 Continued)

Potent Stressor	Sectors	Recommendations
Role Stagnation (RS)	Private, Government	a) Effective and performance appraisal systems may be introduced. b) Attractive system of promotions and rewards for good work.
Resource Inadequacy (RIn)	Government sector	a) Technology advancement equipment may be provided. b) Necessary information for the job and sufficient financial resources may be provided.
Role Isolation (RI)	Government and Public sector	a) Introduction of measures to create a feeling of togetherness. b) Training programs for team building be provided. c) Providing opportunities to open channels of communication.

Conclusion

The findings of the study indicate that all the four occupational groups, viz., private, government, public, and university sector, differ in the nature and quantum of organizational role stress. Private sectors emerged as the most stressed group followed by government sector and public sector. University sectors was found to be the least stressed group. An important finding of the study was that all the four occupational groups scored high on Inter role distance. This indicates that the employees in these sectors are unable to negotiate and balance successfully the demands of their organizational and non-organizational roles. Job responsibilities are taking a toll of their family and social life. Organizational interventions, e.g., spouse involvement programs can be of help to cope with this stressor. Another stressor which showed high figures amongst all the groups was role erosion. This implies that employees suffer from a feeling of loss of importance. Stress management needs to address this concern as well.

Scope for Future Research

Future research could usefully incorporate stress management strategies for these occupational groups, both at individual and organizational level. Further, analysis of the impact of role stress on physiological and behavioral performance and other organizational outcomes can be carried out.

References

Ahsan, N., Abdullah, Z., Fie, G.Y.D., & Alam, S.S. (2009). A study of job stress on job satisfaction among university staff in Malaysia: Empirical study. *European Journal of Social Sciences, 8*(1), 121–31.

Behrman, D.H. & William, P. Jr. (1984). A role stress model of the performance and satisfaction of industrial salespersons. *Journal of Marketing, 48,* 9–21.

Bhaskar, S. (1986). Investigation into relation between job stress and personality factors among police officers and constables. Unpublished Ph.D. thesis, University of Delhi, Delhi.

Jagdish, D.K. (1994). Job stressors and their effects on physical health, emotional health, and job satisfaction in a university. *Journal of Educational Administration, 32*(1), 59–78.

Jasmine, R. (1987). A comparative study of private and public sector blue-collar employees on job-related stress. Unpublished M.Phil dissertation, Calicut University, Calicut.

Kahn, W.A. (1993). Caring for the caregivers: Patterns of organizational caregiving. *Administrative Science Quarterly, 38*(4), 539–64.

Kalia, M. (2002). Assessing the economic impact of stress-the modern day hidden epidemic. *Metabolism, 51* (6 [Suppl 1]), 49–53.

Kumar, D.M. (2006). A study on job stress of nationalized and non-nationalized bank employees. Retrieved from: http://www.indianmba.com/Faculty Column.

Malik, N. (2011). A study on occupational stress experienced by private and public bank employees in Quetta city. *African Journal of Business Management, 5*(8), 3063–70.

Manzoor, M.U., Usman. M., & Naseem, M.A. (2011). A study of job stress and job satisfaction among university faculty in Lahore, Pakistan. *Global Journal of Management and Business Research, 11*(9), 13–16.

Mishra, P.K. (1996). Motivational climate, role stress and coping strategies of air traffic controllers. Unpublished Ph.D thesis, University of Delhi, Delhi.

Mohsin, A. (2004). Role stress among women in the Indian information technology sector. *Women in Management Review, 19*(7), 356–63.

Pandey, S.C. (1998). A study of relationship between personality dimensions and organizational role stress in a public sector organization. *Indian Journal of Industrial Relations, 33*(4), 506–16.

——— (2003). Work stress in advertising professionals of India: A HRD perspective. *Human Resource Development in Asia: National Policy Perspectives, 16,* 1–8. Bangkok, Thailand: National Institute of Development Administration.

Pareek, U. (1983a). *Role stress scale: ORS scale booklet, answer sheet, and manual.* Ahmedabad: Navin Publications.

——— (1983b). *Organizational role pics (o) booklet, answer sheet, and manual.* Ahmedabad: Navin Publications.

Pareek, A. and Mehta, M. (1997). Role stress among working women. In D.M. Pestonjee and U. Pareek (Eds), *Studies in organisational role stress and coping.* Jaipur/New Delhi: Rawat Publications.

Pestonjee, D.M (1992). *Stress and coping: The Indian experience.* New Delhi: SAGE Publications.

Pestonjee, D.M (1999). *Stress and coping: The Indian experience* (Second edition). New Delhi: SAGE Publications.

Rajeshwari, T.R. (1992). Employee stress: A study with reference to bank employees. *Indian Journal of Industrial Relations, 27*(4), 419–29.

Rees, D.W & Cooper, C.K. (1992). Occupational stress in health service workers in the U.K. *Stress Medicine, 8*(2), 79–90.

Samanta, C.R. & Singh, A. (1993). Distress and job performance of industrial workers. *Indian Journal of Psychiatry, 35*(2), 119–21.

Sen, P.C. (1982). Personal and organizational correlates of role stress and coping strategies in some public sector banks. Ph.D. thesis in Management, Gujarat.

Sharma, T. (1987). Differential effects of organizational climates on job satisfaction, sense of participation, alienation and role stress. Unpublished Ph.D thesis, Gujarat University, Ahmedabad.

Sharma, J. & Devi, A. (2011). Role stress among employees: An empirical study of commercial banks. *Gurukul Business Review, 7*(4), 53–61.

Srivastava, S. (2009). Locus of control as a moderator for relationship between organizational role stress and managerial effectiveness. *Journal of Business Perspective, 13*(4), 49–61.

Talib, P. (2001). Stress afflicting police personnel. *The Indian Police Journal, XLVIII*(4), 77–84.

Travers, C.J. & Cooper, C.L. (1993). Mental health, job satisfaction and occupational stress among UK teachers. *Work and Stress, 7*(3), 203–19.

Walter, H.G. & John, S.B. (1994). Sources of stress for academic department chairpersons. *Journal of Educational Administration, 32*(1), 79–94.

Young, K.M. and Cooper, C.L. (1999). Change in stress outcomes following an industrial dispute in the ambulance service: A longitudinal study. *Health Services Management Review, 12*, 51–62.

5

Executive Burnout: Prediction and Prevention through HR Interventions

Radha R. Sharma

Abstract

This research bridges the knowledge gap by empirically determining the causes of *Executive Burnout* at the middle level of management from manufacturing and service industry in India. The construct of executive burnout was evolved in the industrial context by Sharma (2005) which has been found to be qualitatively different from 'burnout' developed on human service occupations (like nurses and teachers) and extended to non-service occupations (Maslach, 1993; Schaufeli et al., 1996); even cultural context has been found to make a difference.

The analysis reveals that executive burnout is caused by both personality and role-related factors. Further analyses have quantified the exact contribution of each of the personality and role-related factor in executive burnout. The paper suggests some HR interventions for preventing or mitigating executive burnout for greater competitiveness and employee well-being.

Keywords: executive burnout, Indian study on burnout in industry, mitigating stress and burnout, HR interventions for stress/burnout management

Introduction

Burnout is a typical stress syndrome which develops gradually in response to prolonged stress and mental and emotional strain (Sharma, 2006). Unable to cope with the increasing pressures and excessive demands, the employee gets pushed towards a state of exhaustion which is characterized by dissatisfaction, low energy levels, fatigue, inadequacy, depersonalization, and frustration resulting in a breakdown or burnout (Sharma, 2007). The cost of stress is high not only at individual level but also at organizational level resulting in reduced productivity, absenteeism, medical expenses, compensation claims, and health insurance (Quick et al., 2002). An International Social Survey of 15 countries revealed that 80% of employees in these countries had high occupational stress OECD (1999). Stress as the cause of job burnout is experienced by 25 to 40% of US workers (Stress Directions, 2007). This calls for strategic human resource management so that burnout could be prevented and employee well-being could be promoted. In order to adopt suitable HR measures, it is imperative to know what causes executive burnout. This chapter first examines the causes of burnout and later suggests strategic HR initiatives to mitigate executive burnout. Burnout does not occur suddenly and begins with small warning signals and most of the time one cannot pinpoint the exact cause.

Review of Researches

Researches in the area of burnout, mostly done in the Western context, have examined the role of a couple of variables which have been presented here.

PERSONAL EXPECTATIONS FROM THE JOB

The choice of occupation is rooted in one's own life experiences and every individual brings in a set of expectations to the job when he joins an organization. These are:(a) *achievement expectations* about what to accomplish in performing his job, which in the case of professionals, would be mainly inculcated while training for a professional qualification (Gold, 1995); and (b) *organizational expectations* about his job and profession as a member of that employing organization which would essentially be shaped by the organization itself during the time of recruitment (Wanous, 1973). Both *unmet expectations* and *shifts in expectations* influence the levels of burnout.

The former would be particularly true of the new recruit as was found with graduates entering a managerial career (Hall, 1976) and the greater the discrepancy between the initial expectations and the reality, the more debilitating will be the nature of stress experienced due to unmet expectations and this may lead to burnout (Wanous, 1973, 1976; Cordes & Dougherty, 1992). The risks of having very high and unreasonable expectations and the accompanying enthusiasm have been described as "first inflamed the out burned" (Schwanold et al. cited in Buhler and Land, 2003). In older employees, negative shifts in expectations occur and with experience they lower the expectations to reasonable levels (Cordes and Dougherty, 1992). Existential perspective has been used to explain the genesis of burnout from unmet high expectations (Pines, 1993). The professional who joins an occupation with very high expectations and idealism does so because it is through his work that he wishes to infuse his life with purpose and meaning. When he fails in that quest, it manifests itself as burnout.

ROLE EFFICACY AND ROLE CONFLICT

Sharma (2002) used Maslach's Burnout Inventory on middle level executives from public, private, and government organizations. Her analysis revealed role overload and self-role distance as critical determinants of burnout among Indian executives. The dimension of reduced personal accomplishment was not valid on the Indian sample implying that burnout does not result in reduced individual accomplishment. Role conflict has been found to cause absenteeism, job dissatisfaction, hypertension, and even burnout. The adverse effects of role conflict are pronounced in people who have the personality trait of rigidity. Role conflict and role ambiguity have been considered instrumental in preventing an employee from fulfilling the demands of a role effectively and causing severe stress. Both these factors have a moderate to high correlation with the different dimensions of job burnout (cf. Cordes and Dougherty, 1993; Maslach, Schaufeli, and Leiter, 2001).

High role conflict is prevalent in roles that exist at the boundary between departments of the organization or between the organization and the external world. Therefore, managers who often perform boundary-spanning functions, such as putting into action the policy demands of the senior management even while knowing the possible negative effect on the subordinates, are particularly prone to role conflict and its consequences (Sutherland and Cooper, 2000). People in market-oriented boundary-spanning positions such as those in sales and customer service are highly vulnerable to burnout as they face role conflict due to the often incompatible demands of the organization and the customers (Singh and Goolsby, 1994). This has been found to be true for even experienced product managers who are required to communicate across organizational and environmental boundaries (Lysonski, Singer, and Wilemon, 1988) and consequently feel torn between the competing demands of different work groups including management, coworkers, and customers (Harris and Lee, 2004) and end up suffering from burnout as a result of role conflict.

ROLE AMBIGUITY

The ambiguity arises because of lack of information about the scope of one's responsibilities. An employee can face role ambiguity when first inducted into a position or when changes are introduced in the organizational structure and processes (Ivancevich & Matteson, 1980). Kahn (1973) delineated two temporal elements of role ambiguity that could assist in addressing the issues of resultant stress and burnout—"present ambiguity" and "future prospects of ambiguity." Role ambiguity has been dealt with here refers to present ambiguity, whereas future prospects of ambiguity is subsumed under career development stress (Cooper & Marshall, 1978). The stress arising due to role ambiguity leads to job dissatisfaction, low self confidence and self-esteem, depression, and hypertension (Sutherland & Cooper, 2000).

Both role conflict and role ambiguity have been implicated in the etiology of job dissatisfaction across occupations (Sell, Brief, & Schuler, 1981) and psychological illness in public sector employees (Terry, Neilson, & Perchard, 1993). Studies have also shown that both these role problems can lead to emotional exhaustion and burnout (Burke & Greenglass, 1995; Lee and Ashforth, 1993; Manlove, 1994; Brookings et al., 1985; Jackson, Schwab & Schuler, 1986; Jackson, Turner, & Brief, 1987; Piero et al., 2001; Schaufeli & Buunk, 1996). Role conflict has been found to be related to irritation but role ambiguity is mainly related to anxiety (Dijkhuizen, 1980), and that role ambiguity, rather than role conflict, is a better predictor of job dissatisfaction and anxiety (Keenan & Newton, 1984). Another study revealed the existence of a negative relation between role ambiguity and job performance though this was moderated by job type and rating source, but no significant relation could be found between role conflict and job performance (Tubre & Collins, 1985).

TYPE A BEHAVIOR PATTERN

The typical features of Type A behavior pattern are excessive competitiveness and achievement orientation, preoccupation with work and deadlines, a chronic sense of time urgency manifested in a person's hurried overt behavior, control-orientation, and impatience which gets expressed as aggressive and hostile behavior. Type A behavior has been particularly linked to the exhaustion (Schaufeli & Enzmann, 1998; Maslach, Schaufeli, & Leiter, 2001). Moreover, the Type A behavior may itself ultimately lead to helplessness, hopelessness, and despair (Hallsten, 1993). Type A persons experience greater job stress when they feel that their level of control is low (Rhodewalt et al., 1991). Even in an insoluble situation, they indulge in self-blame for the failure when their attempts at control fail (Vingerhoets & Flohr, 1984). A study across 13 different companies revealed that Type A trait forces the individual to take more responsibility for others resulting in role overload and strong psychological strain (Winnubst et al., 1996). In another study, both Type A internals and externals were found to exhibit greater mental illness, it was the Type B externals who reported the existence of higher number of physical symptoms (Kirkcaldy, Cooper, & Furnham, 1999). The Type A individual can be a cause of serious stress for his colleagues and subordinates because of his need to control, inability to delegate work, and his propensity to demand too much from others (Sutherland & Cooper, 2000).

Burnout Models

Researches on burnout can be classified into two categories relating to: (a) stage model and (b) phase model. Cherniss (1980) has conceptualized burnout as a three-stage process involving job stress, strain, & defensive coping. It is a qualitative model which is viewed as a socio-psychological phenomenon marked by reduction in motivation & enthusiasm. It can be called *Transactional Process* model. According to Veninga & Spradley (1981) burnout occurs in five distinct stages: (a) Honeymoon stage (euphoria), (b) Fuel shorting stage (fatigue, inefficiency, and dissatisfaction), (c) Chronic symptom stage (physical and emotional symptoms), (d) Crisis stage (psycho-somatic disorders), and (e) Hitting the wall stage (total maladaptation). This model provides indications of the onset of burnout.

A longitudinal study on supervisors and managers by Lee & Ashforth (1993) reveals that it develops in phases. Model of Leiter & Maslach (1998) is a phase model which describes sequential development of the dimensions of emotional exhaustion, cynicism or depersonalization & reduced accomplishment. The model was refined by Maslach, Schaufeli, & Leiter (2001). Golembiewsky & Munzenriden (1988), in their phase model, view burnout in the form of a continuum of eight phases ranging from low to high. But his approach has been criticized for the lack of empirical support.

There are a few other models which have not received much empirical support. The existential model of Pines & Aronson (1988) views burnout as a unidimensional construct, marked by the feelings of low energy, emotional, and mental exhaustion. Meier (1983) conceptualized four elements of burnout, viz., reinforcement expectations, outcome expectations, efficacy expectations, and contextual processing. Smith (1986) proposed a model for athletes involving physiological, psychological, and behavioral aspects of stress and burnout which may not be valid for executives in organizations. Moore (2000) has conceptualized attributional model of work exhaustion wherein experiencing burnout by an individual at workplace depends on his perception of the attributed cause and attitudinal and behavioral reactions.

An Indian model of executive burnout has been developed by the author (Sharma, 2007) see Figure 5.1. The need for the Indian construct of burnout arose as the Western construct of burnout using Maslach Burnout Inventory (MBI, 1981) developed on people occupations (like nurses and teachers) and later extended to non-service occupations, when applied on the Indian sample of executives generated unexpected results. The dimension of diminished personal accomplishment was not valid on the Indian sample. Several dimensions—viz., ambiguity, dissatisfaction and powerlessness, inadequacy, and physical exhaustion, which were found empirically significant for executives in the Indian context—were not tested by MBI. Contrary to Maslach Burnout model these were high achieving executives who, in their incessant effort to achieve more and more, suffered from burnout rather than executives with low accomplishment.

Figure 5.1 An Indian Model of Executive Burnout

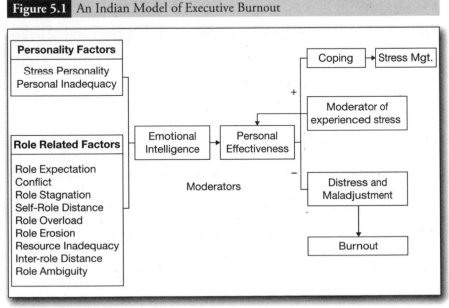

Source: Sharma (2007).

Based on empirical research on executives from Indian industry, the following definition of executive burnout has been derived:

Executive Burnout is marked by persistent feelings of inadequacy, ambiguity, dissatisfaction and powerlessness accompanied by behavioral manifestations of apathy and indifference; (depersonalization) and physical and emotional exhaustion.

—Sharma, 2005

Objectives

The empirically evolved construct of executive burnout by the author (Sharma, 2005) been has been adopted in the study. The lack of knowledge about determinants of executive burnout has provided impetus to undertake the present study to identify factors that cause executive burnout so that appropriate HR interventions could be introduced to prevent or mitigate executive burnout. The problem has been receiving increasing attention in print media in recent years in India which has gone for globalization about two decades ago. The present study is an effort to bridge this knowledge gap by empirically identifying the determinants of executive burnout in Indian industry. The specific objectives, the research envisages to study are as follows:

1. To identify personality related determinants of burnout among Indian executives.
2. To identify role-related antecedents (viz., inter role distance, role stagnation, role expectation, role erosion, role overload, role isolation, personal inadequacy, self-role distance, role ambiguity, and resource inadequacy) of executive burnout.
3. To quantify contribution of each predictor variable on Executive Burnout dimensions.
4. To suggest appropriate HR interventions to prevent or mitigate executive burnout and promote employee well-being

Hypotheses

The following hypotheses have been developed for testing:

- Hypothesis-1 (HO1): Type A personality and emotional intelligence are determinants of Executive Burnout among middle level executives.

- Hypothesis-2 (HO2): Executive Burnout is caused by role-related factors.

Operational Definitions of Variables

Independent Variables

A. *Stress personality (SP)*: Aggressive involvement in a chronic incessant struggle to achieve more and more in less and less time.

B. *Organizational Role Stress*

B1. *Inter-role distance (IRD)*: Conflict between organizational and non-organizational roles.

B2. *Role stagnation (RS)*: Feeling of being stuck in the same role with no opportunity for the furthering or progress of one's career.

B3. *Role expectation Conflict* (REC): Stress generated by different significant persons (superiors, subordinates, and peers).

B4. *Role erosion (RE)*: Feeling that some functions which should belong to one are transferred to or performed by some other role; or the credit for functions being performed by the role occupant goes to someone else.

B5. *Role overload (RO)*: Too many expectations from significant roles in the role set in quantitative and qualitative terms.

B6. *Role isolation (RI)*: Psychological distance between the occupant's role and other roles in the same role set.

B7. *Personal inadequacy (PI)*: Feeling of lack of necessary skills and training for effectively performing the functions expected from the role occupant.

B8. *Self-role distance (SRD)*: Stress arising out of a mismatch between the person's self-concept and his/her role.

B9. *Role ambiguity (RA)*: Lack of clarity about the expectations regarding the role due to lack of information or understanding.

B10. *Resource inadequacy (R.In)*: A feeling that a role occupant is not provided with adequate resources for performing the functions expected from his/her role.

C. *Emotional Intelligence*

C1. *Emotional Competence (EC)*: A learned capability that results in outstanding performance at work involving ability to handle emotional upsets, high self-esteem, tactful response to emotional stimuli and handling egoism.

C2.   *Emotional Maturity (EM)*: Behavioral pattern exhibited by the managers while dealing with inner self and the immediate environment. It includes self awareness, developing others, delaying gratification and adaptability and sensitivity.

C3.   *Emotional Sensitivity (ES)*: Characteristic of being peculiarly sensitive and understanding threshold of emotional arousal, empathy, improving interpersonal relations, and communicability of emotions.

DEPENDENT VARIABLES

D.   *Executive Burnout (Sharma Burnout Scale)*

D1.   *Inadequacy*: Feeling of insufficiency and inability to meet deadlines.

D2.   *Ambiguity*: Persistent lack of clarity about one's role and responsibilities.

D3.   *Dissatisfaction and Powerlessness*: Discontentment, lacking influencing ability, feeling of worthlessness, and depression.

D4.   *Depersonalization*: Indifference, apathy, and alienation from others.

D5.   *Physical and Emotional Exhaustion*: Manifestation of symptoms of loss of energy, fatigue, headache, anxiety, and irritability.

Method

SAMPLE AND SAMPLING FRAMEWORK

A sample of executives was drawn by stratified random sampling. It consisted of 300 middle level executives, 75 each from manufacturing and service industry representing public and private sector organizations in India. The management of the company was approached personally, with prior appointment, to brief them about the objectives and scope of the study and the value of their association with it. After explaining and answering queries, if any, the permission for data collection from their companies was sought. Random sampling method was used to identify executives from the list who would form part of the sample from a particular company. In the present sample executives belong to auto, oil and gas, power, electronics, chemical, steel, pharmaceutical companies in the manufacturing industry and banking, IT, engineering services, software, financial services, consulting, and marketing companies in the service industry from both public and private sectors from across the country.

Measures

Sharma Burnout Scale (SBS): The scale consisted of 28 items covering five dimensions of executive burnout, viz., (*a*) ambiguity, (*b*) dissatisfaction and powerlessness, (*c*) Inadequacy, (*d*) depersonalization, (*e*) physical and emotional exhaustion. Cronbach Alpha for the scale on the sample of the pilot study was found to be 0.85 ($p<.01$). In another study Cronbach Alpha for the test was found be 0.91 ($p<.01$). The concurrent validity of the SBS with MBI is 0.350 ($p<.01$) and on the two dimensions of Depersonalization and Emotional Exhaustion these are 0.418 and 0.280 which too are statistically significant ($p<.01$ level) (Sharma, 2007).

Although other research tools selected for research were standardized tests, yet their reliability was worked out on the sample of the study so that the data collected with the help of these tools are also reliable. The Cronbach alphas for various tests on the present sample have been *What's your Stress Personality?* (R. S. Eliot) 0.73; Organizational Role Stress Scale (Pareek) 0.92, and Emotional Intelligence Scale (Singh and Chadha) 0.67.

Results and Analysis

With a view to finding out determinants of burnout among senior and middle level executives in India, data were subjected to statistical analysis. The 14 independent variables involving role related factors, stress personality, and emotional intelligence were used as predictors in an attempt to identify a set of variables, which together, explain maximum variance in executive burnout (measured by Sharma Burnout Scale). This analysis was carried out with the help of correlation and multiple regression. Intercorrelations between 14 independent × 5 dependent variables are presented in Table 5.1.

Table 5.1 Basic Statistics and Intercorrelations

Independent Variables	Mean	SD	Ambiguity	Dissatisfaction and Powerlessness	Inadequacy	Depersonalization	Physical and Emotional Exhaustion	Total Burnout
Type A	2.02	0.31	0.496**	0.546**	0.493**	0.548**	0.318**	0.603**
Emotional(E) Competency	111.37	22.53	−0.150**	−0.072	0.493**	−0.128*	−0.134*	−0.158**
E-Sensitivity	52.82	13.89	0.038	0.002	0.548**	−0.051	−0.127*	−0.041
E-Maturity	51.25	10.34	−0.033	−0.063	0.318**	−0.108	−0.034	−0.085
EI (total)	71.65	12.55	−0.085	−0.065	0.603**	−0.139*	−0.153**	−0.146*
Inter Role Distance	1.42	0.92	0.264**	0.157**	0.381**	0.318**	0.257**	0.346**
Role Stagnation	1.14	0.76	0.434**	0.489**	0.427**	0.497**	0.251**	0.527**
Role Expectation Conflict	0.97	0.63	0.391**	0.473**	0.425**	0.520**	0.252**	0.517**
Role Erosion	1.50	0.77	0.196**	0.322**	0.169**	0.281**	0.207**	0.301**
Role Overload	0.95	0.77	0.215**	0.346**	0.361**	0.337**	0.160**	0.347**
Role isolation	1.08	0.64	0.346**	0.490**	0.355**	0.505**	0.234**	0.488**
Organizational Role Stress (T)	1.09	0.50	0.480**	0.574**	0.515**	0.613**	0.318**	0.627**

Notes: **p < .01; *p < .05.

Role of Type A (Stress Personality) in Executive Burnout

Executive Burnout (total) was correlated with all the 14 independent variables. Statistically significant correlations (p<.01) were found between all the dimensions of Executive Burnout and Stress Personality and 10 role-related factors. Further, statistically significant negative correlations were obtained between Emotional Competence and Burnout (total, ambiguity, depersonalization, and physical and emotional exhaustion). It is expected because emotional intelligence is a positive variable whereas executive burnout is a negative one. These correlations were subjected to multiple regression to identify predictors of executive burnout (total). The results indicate that Stress Personality explained 0.388 (39%) variance in total executive burnout. Research by Hallsten (1993) yields that Type A behavior leads to helplessness, hopelessness, and despair, i.e., burnout. Personality factors have been found to influence experienced stress, anxiety, and other occupational outcomes (Michie and Williams, 2003). Thus hypothesis-1 stands validated.

Contribution of Role Related Factors in Various Dimensions of Executive Burnout

In order to study, hypothesis-2 regarding the exact contribution of role-related factors in executive burnout hierarchical regression was employed. The analysis for identifying role related predictors of executive burnout (total) revealed that the three role-related factors together explain 28% of the variance. These are Role Expectation Conflict (0.219) + Role Stagnation (0.218) + Self-Role Distance (0.106). Emotional competence accounted for 2% of variation. The results of the study are supported by Pines and Aronson (1988) who found in their many workshops with managers that almost for all the managers, the most stressful aspects of their work corresponded very closely with their initial hopes and expectations regarding their role, status, autonomy, and the available resources that had been frustrated. In a study by Scott (2012), high rate of burnout was found among journalists as well with a moderate rate of exhaustion, a high rate of cynicism and a moderate rate of professional efficacy. Farahbakhsh (2011), in his study of job burnout and occupational factors in managers of governmental organizations in Iran, revealed that there was a relationship between job burnout (three dimensions of MBI) and the type and level of responsibility, service, and management experiences.

Table 5.2   Individual Contribution of Each Predictor of Executive Burnout (Total)

Predictors of Burnout Total	Zero order Co-relation	Adjusted R Square	Standardized Coefficients (B)eta	Individual Contribution
Stress Personality	0.627	0.365	0.388**	0.243
Role Expectation Conflict	0.517	0.466	0.219**	0.113
Role Stagnation	0.527	0.498	0.218**	0.115
Self-Role Distance	0.494	0.508	0.106**	0.052
Emotional Competence	–0.158	0.515	–0.093*	0.015

Notes: Total R Square = .538
**p < .01; *p < .05

Having found out the predictors of executive burnout (total), it was decided to take each dimension of it one by one and find out their predictors. These have been statistically tested and presented here.

DETERMINANTS OF AMBIGUITY: THE FIRST DIMENSION OF EXECUTIVE BURNOUT

With a view to identifying predictors of ambiguity among Indian executives as the first step, correlations were calculated between all the 14 independent variables with the dependent variable ambiguity. A perusal of Table 5.1 reveals that 11 variables involving stress personality and role-related variables are positively and significantly related to ambiguity whereas emotional competence has significant negative relationship. In order to identify predictors of ambiguity these correlations were subjected to stepwise multiple regression. The analysis reveals that on the dimension of ambiguity, contribution of stress personality is 16%, role stagnation 9%, emotional competence and personal inadequacy together 11%, and role expectation conflict only 6%. Emotional Intelligence and role overload play a negative role in ambiguity. Total variance explained is 47%. The results are substantiated by Scott who posited that unclear requirements, impossible requirements, big consequences of failure and poor communication contribute to employee burnout.

Table 5.3   Individual Contribution of Each Predictor of Ambiguity

Predictors of Ambiguity	Zero order Co-relation	Adjusted R Square	Standardized Coefficients (B)eta	Individual Contribution
Stress Personality	0.48	0.243	0.328**	0.158
Role Stagnation	0.434	0.304	0.208**	0.090
Personal Inadequacy	0.409	0.331	0.154**	0.063
Emotional Competence	−0.150	0.337	−0.318*	0.048
Emotional Intelligence (total)	−0.085	0.347	0.251*	−0.021
Role Expectation Conflict	0.391	0.353	0.162*	0.063
Role Overload	0.251	0.360	−0.111*	−0.028

Notes: Total R Square = .471
**p<.01; *p<.05

DETERMINANTS OF DISSATISFACTION AND POWERLESSNESS: THE SECOND DIMENSION OF EXECUTIVE BURNOUT

Another important dimension of executive burnout is Dissatisfaction and Powerlessness. For identifying predictors of this dependent variable, correlations were carried out between this variable and the 14 independent variables (Table 5.1). Results reveal high positive correlations between this variable and stress personality and 10 role-related variables. Further, multiple regression was deployed to explore its predictors. The hierarchical regression revealed seven predictors of dissatisfaction and powerlessness dimension of executive burnout, viz., *Stress Personality, Role Stagnation, Resource Inadequacy, Inter Role Distance, Role Expectation Conflict, Role Erosion,* and *Role Overload.* Of the seven predictors Stress Personality is the strongest predictor explaining 20% variance, followed by role-related factors contributing to 32% of variance. In the order of importance, these are: *Role Expectation Conflict, Resource Inadequacy, Role Stagnation, Role Erosion, and Role Overload.* While Stress Personality has emerged as the strongest single predictor, the contribution of Role related factors is higher, i.e., 32% variance.

| Table 5.4 | Individual Contribution of Each Predictor of Executive Burnout (Dissatisfaction and Powerlessness) |

Predictors of Dissatisfaction and Powerlessness	Zero order Co-relation	Adjusted R Square	Standardized Coefficients (B)eta	Individual Contribution
Stress Personality	0.574	0.295	0.347**	0.199
Role Stagnation	0.489	0.387	0.135**	0.066
Resource Inadequacy	0.458	0.412	0.166**	0.076
Inter Role Distance	0.157	0.425	−0.214**	−0.034
Role Expectation Conflict	0.473	0.435	0.180**	0.085
Role Erosion	0.322	0.448	0.148**	0.048
Role Overload	0.346	0.445	0.125**	0.043

Notes: Total R Square = 0.551
**$p < .01$; *$p < .05$

The findings are corroborated by researches by Buunk et al. (1998). According to them work underload and overload can result in negative emotions depending upon the discrepancy between the workload and the abilities and aspirations of the employee (Buunk et al., 1998). In an earlier study, Sharma (2002) found role overload and self-role distance to be predictors of burnout among Indian executives. While qualitative underload and qualitative overload both result in job dissatisfaction, the former is also associated with depression, irritation, and psychosomatic symptoms and the latter with tension and low self-esteem (ILO, 1986).

Determinants of Inadequacy: The Third Dimension of Burnout

Feeling of inadequacy has been found to be high among executives suffering from burnout. There is high positive relationship of *Inadequacy* with stress personality and the ten dimensions of Organizational Role Stress (Table 5.1). The correlations were put through multivariate analysis which revealed that there are five predictors of "Inadequacy." In this dimension of

Table 5.5	Individual Contribution of Each Predictor of Executive Burnout (Inadequacy)			
Predictors of Inadequacy	*Zero order Co-relation*	*Adjusted R Square*	*Standardized Coefficients (B)eta*	*Individual Contribution*
Stress Personality	0.515	0.244	0.309**	0.159
Role Expectation Conflict	0.425	0.316	0.126**	0.054
Inter Role Distance	0.381	0.344	0.180**	0.069
Role Stagnation	0.427	0.356	0.133**	0.057
Self Role Distance	0.361	0.366	0.118**	0.042

Notes: Total R Square = .381
**p < .01; *p < .05

Executive Burnout also Stress Personality is the most important predictor of Inadequacy explaining 16% of variation followed by Inter Role Distance, Role Stagnation, Role Expectation Conflict and Self Role Distance. Thus the contribution of personality and role-related factors for this dimension of burnout is 16% and 22% respectively. The total variance explained is 38%.

Inadequacy as a dimension of Executive burnout finds support in literature. Since people with poor self-esteem are ineffective in their interpersonal relationships, they are more likely to use depersonalization, and they are also more vulnerable to exhaustion in emotionally demanding situations (Janssen, Schaufeli, & Houkes, 1999; Rosse, Wayne-Boss, & Johnson, 1991).

DETERMINANTS OF DEPERSONALIZATION: THE FOURTH DIMENSION OF BURNOUT

Depersonalization is "detached concern" whereby a person distances himself from his work, clients, and others; consequently his behavior appears impersonal, cold, and aloof and distant. Relationship between Depersonalization and other variables has been studied with Pearson's correlation and have been reported in Table 5.1. These are significant (p < .01) for stress personality and 10 role-related factors and an expected negative relationship with

Table 5.6   Individual Contribution of Each Predictor of Depersonalization

Predictors of Depersonalization	Zero order Co-relation	Adjusted R Square	Standardized Coefficients (B)eta	Individual Contribution
Role Ambiguity	0.551	0.308	0.202**	0.111
Stress Personality	0.631	0.418	0.320**	0.202
Role Expectation Conflict	0.520	0.453	0.212**	0.110
Role Stagnation	0.497	0.463	0.137**	0.068

Notes: Total R Square = .491
**$p < .01$

all the dimensions of emotional intelligence. These correlations have been subjected to further analysis to identify a set of variables, which, together, could act as predictors of depersonalization. Analysis yields that the most important predictor for depersonalization, too, is stress personality. In order of their importance, other predictors are role ambiguity, role expectation conflict and role stagnation. Total variance explained is 49% of which role related factors explain 28% and stress personality explains 20% of the variance.

Other researches have also yielded similar results that it is especially Role Ambiguity that leads to executive burnout (Schaufeli and Buunk, 1996). Both Role Conflict and Role Ambiguity have been found to contribute to the etiology of job dissatisfaction across occupations (Sell, Brief, and Schuler, 1981) and psychological illness in public sector employees (Terry, Neilson, and Perchard, 1993). Studies (Burke and Greenglass, 1995; Lee and Ashforth, 1993; Manlove, 1994) reveal that both these role problems can lead to emotional exhaustion and burnout.

DETERMINANTS OF PHYSICAL AND EMOTIONAL EXHAUSTION: THE FIFTH DIMENSION OF EXECUTIVE BURNOUT

The extreme form of executive burnout—Physical and Emotional Exhaustion—reflects in various debilitating symptoms. Those who reach this stage of burnout suffer from sleep disturbance and depression, feel drained out, and often indulge in excessive consumption of alcohol, tobacco, or pills. High positive correlation (p<.01 level) has been obtained of this variable with stress personality and all the dimensions of organizational role stress (Table 5.1). As expected, Emotional Intelligence (EI) and its three dimensions have negative relationship with physical and emotional exhaustion. Statistically significant relationships (p<.05) have been found between EI (total), its dimensions of emotional competence and emotional sensitivity, and executive burnout represented by physical and emotional exhaustion. The correlations were regressed through multivariate analysis.

Results in Table 5.7 yield that there are three predictors of physical and emotional exhaustion, viz., stress personality, inter role distance and role erosion. In order to assess the exact contribution of each of these factors further analysis was carried out. The analysis revealed that stress personality explains 8% of the variance, followed by inter role distance (5%) and role erosion (3%).

The hypothesis that role-related factors are determinants of executive burnout has been substantiated by the analysis presented above. Cropanzano, Rupp, and Byrne (2003), based on their research, found that emotional exhaustion leads to negative consequences for both employees and employers. According to them emotional exhaustion would predict job performance, organizational citizenship behavior, and turnover intentions. It has been observed that organizations try to locate the problem of burnout in the individual and ignore the role of the organization in the etiology of executive burnout. But recognition of the work environment factors in the genesis of stress and burnout would help the organizations take a proactive role through integration of preventive measures into the organizational processes. These initiatives would help the employees cope effectively with unavoidable organizational stresses.

Table 5.7	Individual Contribution of Each Predictor of Physical and Emotional Exhaustion		
Predictors of Physical and Emotional Exhaustion	Zero order Co-relation	Standardized Coefficients (B)eta	Individual Contribution
Stress Personality	0.318	0.240**	0.076
Inter Role Distance	0.257	0.179**	0.046
Role Erosion	0.207	0.129**	0.027

Notes: Total R Square = .149
**p < .01

Role of HR Interventions

As stress personality, role expectation conflict, role stagnation, and self role distance have emerged as the determinants of executive burnout, the HR department needs to suitably design their HR processes and modify organizational policies where role stagnation, role expectation conflict, and role ambiguity can be taken care of. Counseling and mentoring can be helpful for employees with stress personality. Having presented the causes of burnout some HR interventions are recommended below to prevent and reduce incidence of executive burnout to promote employee well-being.

Burnout Audit

The most important step that can be adopted by an organization to prevent or effectively deal with executive burnout is organizational burnout audit. Once organization wide or critical department wide burnout audit is undertaken, it would help in identification of executives suffering from or prone to burnout so that effective steps could be undertaken to deal with them or prevent the same. Having identified burnout prone cases, Employee Assistance Program (EAP) can be introduced to help employees deal with their burnout proneness. Such a program provides a forum for outlet of stresses, emotions, job, or personal issues. Confidential counseling services are also provided as part of EAP which are beneficial. It is observed that organizations focus on physical ailment whereas the causes of many physical ailments are psychogenic. If this phenomenon does not receive adequate attention, the organization will not be able to tap the full potential of its human resource. Thus burnout audit is beneficial not only to the employees but also to the organization for optimum utilization of human potential for organizational productivity. Burnout audit can be undertaken once a year as part of employee check-up.

Person–Job Fit

Person–job fit refers to the match between the abilities of a person and the demands of a job or the desires of a person and attributes of a job (Edwards, 1991). In organizations some jobs are more stressful than others; similarly there are people equipped with better capabilities for handling stress than others. Considering the ability and skill requirement of a job, person–job fit has been the basis for employee selection (Werbel and Gilliand, 1999).

A more recent approach has been preparing competency framework for every position and matching that with employee's profile as an effective HR intervention. Behavioral dimensions are integral part of performance appraisal forms. Employees who exhibit high degree of stress, anxiety, inadequacy, and exhaustion in functional departments can be identified and referred to HR department for counseling or transfer to comparatively less stressful jobs thus taking care of role overload.

Developing HR capital that is in harmony with the organization's design and strategy is emerging as cornerstone of competitive advantage (Pfeffer, 1998). In India employees in high pressure oil exploration job in firms like Oil and Natural Gas Corporation (ONGC) have 15 days of posting on the rig in the middle of the sea and are given 15 days off to unwind. IT and ITes firms offer flexi time, time off, work from home to reduce stress among their employees. Recent trends observed in many Indian IT majors like Infosys and Tata Consulting Services that are expanding their operations abroad are "near shoring" or are acquiring software firms with their employees. In both the cases, a large number of people are hired locally who fit in the cultural demands of the job much better than natives who may have language barrier or may feel stress in trying to adopt to the foreign culture. Other firms can also do job analysis from the point of view of stress and adopt appropriate policy for person–position matching. This will reduce self role distance and role expectation conflict found as determinants of executive burnout in the study.

HUMAN CAPITAL DEVELOPMENT

Having identified the burnout prone cases through burnout audit, it would be important to equip them with skills of coping with burnout. Training and development can play a significant role in this regard for which learning and development needs of employees need to be identified periodically. There are specialized training programs which impart training in stress management techniques. There are also work-life balance programs which can be organized periodically. However, training should be imparted only by experts otherwise it could do more harm than good. It is to be noted that burnout prone or burnout cases are already experiencing tremendous stress; therefore, the training needs to be customized to meet their requirements lest they lose faith in training. In other words, training needs to be handled with care.

Role stagnation has emerged as one of the causes of executive burnout. Young employees do not like snail pace of growth of their career and look for learning and growth opportunities to optimize their potential. IT, telecom, airline, and hospitability sectors are in the growth phase and human potential development along with realistic expectations is very much needed. Therefore, charting out career path and meeting career and growth expectations of executives would be an important HR strategy to prevent and mitigate burnout among them.

EMPLOYEE-CENTRIC WORK CULTURE

In the spate of rapid modernization organizations have become work-centric consequently people have got reduced to replaceable components and have become peripheral to the organization. Supportive environment provides opportunity for performance of employees to peak which further fuels their motivation. Experience and research both support the fact that organizations where people are central to the organization are not only more prosperous but also have higher degree of organizational commitment, employee engagement, and employee well-being. Phillips (2006) found that coaching was the most effective part of the program in terms of its impact on motivation, performance, and commitment. The organization can leverage on strengths rather than focus on weaknesses. Executives can be encouraged to work with their unique strengths in their typical environments. A research by Chartered Management Institute (Blass, 2007) found that with overemphasis on weakness many people identified as talents had the feeling that they were underutilized. Kaplan & Kaiser (2006) report that a fair view of strengths enables people to avoid overplaying them and turning them into weakness. The recognition of the work environment factors in the genesis of stress and burnout would facilitate organizations take a proactive role through integration of preventive measures into the organizational processes. This would help the employees cope with/deal with or prevent burnout more effectively.

Conclusion

"Executive Burnout is marked by persistent feelings of inadequacy, ambiguity, dissatisfaction and powerlessness accompanied by behavioral manifestations of apathy and indifference; (depersonalization) and physical and emotional exhaustion" (Sharma, 2005). Stress personality has been found to be the most important determinant of burnout among executives which explains 24% of the variance. The second most important predictor of burnout is role stagnation followed by role expectation conflict and self role distance. The three role-related factors together explain 28% of the variance in executive burnout. Each dimension of burnout has its own determinants which also have been quantified for more sophisticated individualized HR intervention. The HR interventions discussed above can be adopted to prevent executive burnout and promote employee well-being.

The study generates new knowledge about the phenomenon of executive burnout and makes significant contribution to the causes of executive burnout. This knowledge would help the organizations in recruitment, selection, promotion, and training and development. Executives prone to burnout can be identified and suitable interventions be provided to prevent executive burnout which has become a major problem in the context of globalization and economic meltdown.

References

Blass, E. (2007). *Talent management: Maximizing talent for business performance.* Chartered Management Institute Report, November.

Brookings, J.B., Bolton, B., Brown, C.E., & McEvoy, A. (1985). Self-reported job burnout among female human service professionals. *Journal of Occupational Behavior, 6,* 143–50.

Bühler, K.E. & Land, T. (2003). Burnout and personality in intensive care: An empirical study. *Hospital Topics, 81* (4), 5–12.

Burke, R.J. & Greenglass, E.R. (1995). A longitudinal examination of the Cherniss model of psychological burnout. *Social Science and Medicine, 40*(10), 1357–63.

Buunk, B.P., Jonge, de Jan, Ybema, J.F., & Wolff, C.J. de. (1998). Psychosocial aspects of occupational stress. In P.J.D. Drenth, H. Thierry, & C.J. de Wolff (Eds), *Handbook of work and organizational psychology* (Volume 2, Second edition). Sussex: Psychology Press Ltd.

Cherniss, Cary (1980). *Staff burnout—Job stress in the human services.* Beverly Hills: SAGE.

Cooper, C.L. & Marshall, J. (1978). *Understanding executive stress.* London: Macmillan Press Ltd.

Cordes, C.L. & Dougherty, T.W. (1993). A review and an integration of research on job burnout. *Academy of Management Review, 18*(4), 621–56.

Dijkhuizen, N. van. (1980). *From stressors to strains.* Lisse: Swets and Zeitlinger.

Cropanzano, R., Rupp, D.E., Byrne, Z.S. (2003). The relationship of emotional exhaustion to work attitudes, job performance, and organizational citizenship behaviors. *Journal of Applied Psychology, 88*(1), 160–69.

Edwards, J.R. (1991). Person-job fit: A conceptual integration, literature review, and methodological critique. In C.L. Cooper & I.T. Robertson (Eds), *International review of industrial and organizational psychology, 6,* 283–357. New York: Wiley.

Farahbakhsh, Saed. (2011). The relationship of job burnout and occupational factors in managers of governmental organizations in Lorestan province, Iran. *Journal of Research in Behavioural Sciences, 9*(1).

Golembiewski, R.T. & Munzenrider, R.F. (1988). *Phases of burnout: Development in concepts and applications.* New York: Praeger.

Gold, Y. (1985). Does teacher burnout begin with student teaching? *Education, 105,* 254–57.

Hallsten, L. 1993. Burning out: a framework. In W. B. Schaufeli, C. Maslach & T. Marek (Eds). *Professional burnout: Recent developments in theory and research,* (pp. 95–113). New York: Taylor & Francis.

ILO. (1986). *Manpower planning and development in the petroleum industry.* Report No. III. ILO Petroleum Committee, Tenth Session, Geneva.

Ivancevich, J.M. & Matteson, M.T. (1980). Optimizing human resources: A case for preventative health and stress management. *Organizational Dynamics, 9*(2), 4–25.

Jackson, S.E., Schwab, R.L., & Schuler, R.S. (1986). Toward an understanding of the burnout phenomenon. *Journal of Applied Psychology, 71,* 630–40.

Jackson, S.E., Turner, J.A. & Brief, A.P. (1987). Correlates of burnout among public service lawyers. *Journal of Occupational Behavior, 8,* 339–49.

Janssen, P.P.M., Schaufeli, W.B., & Houkes, I. (1999). Work-related and individual determinants of the three burnout dimensions. *Work & Stress, 13*(1), 74–86.

Kahn, R.L. (1973). Conflict, ambiguity and overload: Three elements in job stress. *Occupational Mental Health, 3*(1).

Kaplan, R.E. & Kaiser, R.B. (2006). *The versatile leader: Make the most of your strengths- without overdoing it.* San Francisco: Pfeiffer.

Keenan, A. & Newton, T.J. (1985). Stressful events, stressors, and psychological strains in young professionals engineers. *Journal of Occupational Behavior, 6:* 151–56.

Kircaldy, B.D., Furnham A.F. & Cooper, C.L. (1999). The relationship between type A, internality-externality, emotional distress and perceived health. *Personality & Individual Differences, 26,* 223–35.

Lee, R.T. & Ashforth, B.E. (1993). A longitudinal study of burnout among supervisors and managers: Comparisons between the Leiter and Maslach (1988) and Golembiewski et al. (1986) models. *Organizational Behavior and Human Decision Processes, 54,* 369–98.

Leiter, M P and Maslach, C. (1988). The impact of interpersonal environment on burnout and organizational commitment. *Journal of Organizational Behavior, 9*(4), 297–308.

Lysonski, S., Singer, A., & Wilemon, D. (1988). Coping with environmental uncertainty and boundary spanning in the product manager's role. *Journal of Services Marketing, 2*(4), 15–26.

Manlove, E.E. (1994). Conflict and ambiguity over work roles: The impact on child care worker burnout. *Early Education and Development,* 5(1), 41–55.

Maslach, C. & Jackson, S.E. (1986). *The Maslach burnout inventory: Manual* (Second edition). Palo Alto, CA: Consulting Psychologists Press.

Maslach, C. & Schaufeli, W.B. (1993). Historical and conceptual development of burnout. In W.B. Schaufeli, C. Maslach, & T. Marek (Eds). *Professional burnout: Recent developments in theory and research* (pp. 1–16). New York: Taylor & Francis.

Maslach, C., Schaufeli, W.B., & Leiter, M.P. (2001). Job burnout. *Annual Review of Psychology, 52,* 397–422.

MBI Maslach, C. & Jackson, S.E. (1981b). *The Maslach burnout inventory: Research Edition.* Palo Alto, CA: Consulting Psychologists Press.

Meier, S.T. (1983). Toward a theory of burnout. *Human Relations, 36*(10), 899–910.

Michie, S. and Williams, S. (2003). Reducing psychological ill health & associated sickness absence: A systematic literature review. *Occupational and Environment Medicine, 50,* 3–9.

Moore, Jo Ellen (2000). Why is this happening? A causal attribution approach to work exhaustion consequences. *Academy of Management Review*, *25*(2), 335–49.

OECD. (1999). *Implementing the OECD job strategy: Assessing performance and policy*. Paris: OECD.

Pareek, U. (1987). *Making organizational roles effective*. New Delhi: Tata McGraw-Hill Publishing Company Ltd.

Peiro, J.M., Gonzalez-Roma, V., Tordera, N., & Manas, M.A. (2001). Does role stress predict burnout over time among health care professionals? *Psychology & Health*, *16*(5), 511–25.

Pfeffer, J. (1998). Seven practices of successful organizations. *California Management Review*, *40*, 96–124.

Phillips, P.S. (2006). What value does coaching add to talent management programs? *Selection and Development Review*, *22*, 5.

Pines, A. & Aronson, E. (1988). *Career burnout*. New York: Macmillan Inc.

Pines, A.M. (1993). Burnout: An existential perspective. In W.B. Schaufeli, C. Maslach, & T. Marek (Eds), *Professional burnout: Recent developments in theory and research*. New York: Taylor & Francis.

Quick, J.C., Cooper, C.L., Quick, J.D., & Gavin, J.H. (2002). *The Financial Times guide to executive health*. London: Prentice Hall.

Rhodewalt, F., Sansone, C., Hill, C.A., & Chemers, M.M. (1991). Stress and distress as a function of Jenkins activity survey-defined Type A behavior and control over the work environment. *Basic and Applied Psychology*, *12*(2), 211–26.

Rosse, J.G., Wayne-Boss, R., & Johnson, A.E. (1991). Conceptualizing the role of self-esteem in the burnout process. *Group & Organization Studies*, *16*(4), 428–51.

Schaufeli, W.B. & Buunk, B.P. (1996). Professional burnout. In M.J. Schabracq, J.A.M. Winnust, & C.L. Cooper (Eds), Handbook of work and health psychology (pp. 311–46). New York: Wiley.

Schaufeli, W.B. & Enzmann, D. (1998). *The burnout companion to study and practice: A critical analysis*. Washington, DC: Taylor & Francis.

Schaufeli, W.B., Leiter, M.P., Maslach, C., & Jackson, S.E. (1996). MBI—General survey. In C. Maslach, S.E. Jackson, & M.P. Leiter (Eds), *Maslach Burnout Inventory: Manual* (Third edition). Palo Alto, CA: Consulting Psychologists Press.

Scott, Elizabeth. (2010). Job burnout: Job factors that contribute to employee burnout. Retrieved from: stress.about.com/od/burnout/a/job_burnout.htm (accessed on Feburary 8, 2012).

Scott, Reinardy (2011). *Newspaper journalism in crisis: Burnout on the rise, eroding young journalists' career commitment* Retrieved from: http://jou.sagepub.com/content/12/1/33.abstract (accessed on Feburary 7, 2012).

Sell, M. Van, Brief, A.P., & Schuler, R.J. (1981). Role conflict and ambiguity: Integration of literature and directions for future research. *Human Relations*, *34*, 43–72.

Sharma, Radha. R. (2002). Executive burnout: Contribution of role related factors. *Indian Journal of Industrial Research*, *38*(1), 81–95.

———— (2005). *Determinants of executive burnout in India*. Unpublished Research Report, WHO & Ministry of Health, Government of India.

———— (2006). Emotional intelligence as a mediator in executive burnout. *Proceedings of Academy of HRD Conference*, Columbus, USA. (Cutting Edge Research Paper Award 2006, Academy of HRD, USA).

———— (2007). Indian model of executive burnout. *Vikalpa*, *32*(2), April–June, 23–38.

Singh, J. & Goolsby, J.R. (1994). Behavioral and psychological consequences of boundary spanning burnout for customer service. *Journal of Marketing Research*, *31*(4), 558–69.

Smith, R.E. (1986). Toward a cognitive-affective model of athletic burnout. *Journal of Sport Psychology, 8*, 36–50.

Stress Directions. (2007). Health and productivity: Presenteeism and productivity analysis. Retrieved from: http://stressdirections.com/content/view/3/23/

Sutherland, V.J. & Cooper, C.L. (2000). *Strategic stress management: An organizational approach.* London: Macmillan Press Ltd.

Terry, D.J., Neilson, M., & Perchard, L. (1993). Effects of work stress on psychological well-being and job satisfaction: The stress-buffering role of social support. *Australian Journal of Psychology, 45*(3), 168–75.

Tubre, T.C. & *Collins*, J.M. (2000). Jackson and Schuler (1985) revisited: A meta-analysis of the relationships between role ambiguity, role conflict, and job performance. *Journal of Management, 26*(1), 155–69.

Veninga, R.L. and Spradley, J.T. (1981). *The work stress connection: How to cope with the burnout?* Boston: Little Brown and Company.

Vingerhoets, A.J.J.M. & Flohr, P.J.M. (1984). Type A behaviour and self-reports of coping preferences. *British Journal of Medical Psychology, 57*, 15–21.

Wanous, J.P. 1973. Effects of a realistic job preview on job acceptance, job attitudes, and job survival. *Journal of Applied Psychology*, 58: 327–332.

———— (1976) Organizational entry: From naive expectations to realistic beliefs. *Journal of Applied Psychology, 61*, 22–29.

Werbel, J.D. & Gilliand, S.W. (1999). Person-environment fit in the selection process. In Ferris, G.R. (Ed.), *Research in personnel and human resource management, 17*, pp. 209–43. Stanford, CT: JAI Press.

Winnubst, J.A.M., Jong, R.D. de, & Schabracq, M.J. (1996). The diagnosis of role strains at work. In M.J. Schabracq, J.A.M. Winnubst, & C.L. Cooper (Eds), *Handbook of work and health psychology* (pp. 106–25). Chichester: John Wiley & Sons.

6

Stress in Extreme Conditions: A Military Perspective

Updesh Kumar, Vijay Parkash, and Manas K. Mandal

Abstract

Stress has become an inevitable part of present-day life. The psychological and environmental conditions of the workplace are considered crucial to stress. From military perspective, extreme conditions in different military settings on land, air, or sea cause distress among soldiers. Deployments in counter-insurgency and low-intensity conflict areas, high altitude, extreme temperatures in glaciers and deserts are the potential stressors for soldiers on land; whereas, extreme temperature and noise in cockpits and high speed are a few major stressors in military aviation; and, repetitive surroundings, social confinement, extreme hydrostatic pressure, and danger from invisible enemy adversely impact the well-being of naval personnel and submariners. Moreover, in future, the soldier will be global soldier serving at global platforms in various peacekeeping missions. The exact nature of the extreme conditions prevailing in different military environments, their psychological impact on soldiers, futuristic vision of soldier's functioning, and measures to manage these stressors are at the centre of this chapter.

Keywords: military settings, soldier, extreme conditions, global soldier

> *Never before has there been so much interest in stress world-wide, among social and biological scientists, and on the part of the general public.... Stress has become a household word, and we are flooded with messages about how it can be prevented, eliminated, managed, or just lived with*
>
> *(Lazarus, 1999: 27).*

The 21st century, which is called as century of technology and globalization, is also called as the age of stress and anxiety. The concept of stress and the stress of daily life have gained increased attention of researchers in the past century. Stress has been primarily conceptualized in three ways: as a stimulus or situation (Holmes & Rahe, 1967); as a response to demands placed on the body (Selye, 1976); and as a person–environment interaction or transaction (Lazarus, DeLongis, Folkman, & Gruen, 1985). Stimulus-oriented approach primarily focuses on external stressors and views humans as reactive to stimulation. The response-oriented approach is guided by the state of stress and treats stress as a response to stressors. Response-oriented theories assert that a specific response pattern is related to the development of distress. The response has two interrelated components: the psychological component (behavior, thought pattern, and emotions) and the physiological component (heightened bodily arousal). *Person–Environment Transaction* approach places emphasis on reciprocal interactions between the person and the environment, with each affecting and being affected by the other (Lazarus and Folkman, 1984; Strealu, 2001; Derogatis and Coon, 1993). It considers that stress is a process in which the person is an active agent who can influence the impact of a stressor. Any stimulus, whether pleasant or unpleasant, can be considered as a source of stress depending on how the stimulus is appraised by the individual (Lazarus, 1966).

Stress is not always bad. Some level of stress helps us to perform at a higher level. However, there are times when stress becomes overwhelming. Having similar thought, Selye (1976) has differentiated between *eustress* and *distress*. Eustress is positive and the pleasant side of stress. On the other hand, distress refers to a destructive type of stress that depletes one's energy reserves and taxes the maintenance and defense of the bodily systems potentially causing harm to both physical and psychological health. Commonsense view of stress is weighted to the negative side. The stressors that people experience can be either *external* or *internal*. External stressors include adverse physical conditions (such as extreme environments, natural calamities, etc.) or stressful psychological environments (e.g., abusive relationships or poor working conditions). *Intensity* and *duration* of the stressors distinguish between acute and chronic stress. *Acute* stress is generally the reaction to an immediate provocative threat and it is commonly observed in the form of fight or flight response. Once the threat has passed, under most circumstances, the response of the individual becomes inactivated and levels of stress hormones return to normal. In contrast to acute stressors, prolonged exposure to *chronic* stressors ultimately exhausts the human potential and hence this chronic stress ultimately becomes a cause of numerous physiological and psychological problems. Anxiety, frustration, hopelessness, and depression are the most prevalent outcomes of chronic stress (e.g., Craig, 2007; Hudd et al., 2000; Lazarus, 1999).

In the earlier sections of this chapter, we will try to enumerate upon the distress in military population and the psychological factors causing and influencing the state of distress. An effort will be made to explain soldier stress by means of a multi-dimensional model including the inherent protective factors, on one hand and the extreme behaviors like suicide, on the other. The chapter will take a shape to deliberate upon various combat stress behaviors and stressors in counter-insurgency and low-intensity conflict environments acting upon the psychological and physiological well-being of the soldiers. Deployments in high altitude and extreme type of temperature conditions are often considered as strenuous and make the deployed personnel vulnerable. The psychological consequences of various stressors related with these extreme deployments will be concisely focused upon. The extreme conditions prevailing for Air Force personnel, Naval Personnel, and Submariners will also find a brief mention. Seeing future soldiers acting upon a global platform will add an extension to the understanding of future stress factors. An attempt will be made to enlist some of the experientially learned and psychologically necessary preventive measures that can minimize soldiers' stress and promote optimum functionality on as well as off the job.

Distress in Military

Although the stress response is an individualized experience, there are, without any doubt, a wide variety of pressures in today's work settings with the potential to generate adverse stress reactions (distress) for many personnel. Excessive demands associated with multiple roles can lead to role strain, characterized by the person feeling stressed or physically and emotionally drained (Barnett and Brennan, 1995). Adverse work experiences, particularly experiences that are uncertain or outside the employee's control result in unpleasant emotional and physiological state (Judge and Colquitt, 2004). The most vulnerable to these adverse experiences are the military personnel, who, most of the times, are deployed in situations that place high demands on them. Though stress during war or counter-insurgency operations is understandable, it is becoming apparent that service life even in the absence of such situations is stressful. Based on the data from US military population, a prominent researcher in this field, Pflanz (2001), asserts that the military personnel are suffering from occupational stress. A majority (60%) reported suffering from significant work stress. Almost half (42.5%) reported that work stress was a significant contributor to the onset of their mental illness (Pflanz, 2001). Though little research exists on the impact of the routine peacetime military work environment on the health of military personnel, it is evident that unexpected mobilizations, all time prevalent combat conditions, deployment to counter-insurgency or war zones, exposure to casualties, and trauma associated with humanitarian missions have serious adverse impact on the emotional functioning of military personnel.

Recent research suggests that work stress may be an important occupational health hazard for military personnel (Pflanz & Sonnek, 2002). In a study conducted on 472 military personnel, Pflanz (2002) found that one-quarter (26%) of respondents were suffering from significant work stress. Nearly one in five reported that work stress was causing them significant emotional distress and almost one in ten (8%) reported suffering from work stress that was severe enough to be damaging their emotional health. The military personnel typically reported job stressors that were common in the civilian arena such as changes in work responsibilities, work hours, or type of work; they did not commonly report military-specific stressors such as deployment overseas, periodic change of station, involuntary assignment, or frequent duty away from home. Only one of the top five and four of the top ten stressors identified by these military personnel were military-specific. Periodic change of station was the only military specific stressor that was endorsed by more than 10% of the respondents (Pflanz, 2001, 2002).

Like the above mentioned, many a research have provided the evidence that professions with little autonomy and long work hours are associated with increased work stress and psychiatric illness. These factors are often attributes of the military work environment and may account for some of the job stress in the military. Work stress in the military cannot be simply dismissed by the fact that the business of war is stressful. As we are moving ahead into the 21st Century, our reliance on the military to protect the nation from terrorism and other threats is increasing. Even when deploying to regions of the world well away from war, there is separation from family, and regular life remains very difficult. Stress has emerged as the invisible enemy and it is definitely making a dent in the spirits of military. Taking an example of Indian military, in places like Jammu and Kashmir where the army has to be constantly vigilant, constantly patrolling, and constantly facing low-intensity conflicts, stress is bound to take its toll. Combined with harsh environmental conditions and very few leave permissions for home, it is very easy to understand why our soldiers could possibly crack under stress. The tensions and worries in pursuit of perfect security coupled with fatigue, loneliness, and depression serve as the immediate enemies for the troops. It may make the toughest of men lose hope.

In context of the military settings, much attention has been primarily devoted to the relationship between combat and the emotional health of soldiers. The aspects of wartime activities have been clearly established as precipitants of psychological stress. Recent research has established that combat, exposure to heavy casualties, deployment of units in a war zone, and unexpected mobilizations of reserve units are all correlated with higher levels of psychological distress (Pflanz and Sonnek, 2002). In recent times, as the role of military personnel in humanitarian and disaster relief missions has increased, so has the focus on the stressful nature of these missions. Researches examining the impact of combat and disasters on the emotional health of military personnel are clearly important. Unfortunately, very little research exists regarding the impact of stress of routine military work on the mental health of military personnel. It is assumed that the stress of military life is primarily attributable to such things as unstable deployments, exposure to combat, and the threat of bodily harm. The periodic change of posting station, stationing of personnel overseas, and lack of control over duty assignments are just a few examples of the more mundane aspects of military life that may affect the mental health of its members (Pflanz & Sonnek, 2002).

Going beyond combat and war-time assignments, researchers have found that work stress is a significant source of distress for military personnel during routine peacetime assignments also. Manning and colleagues (1981) found that military mental health patients identified work-related problems as the primary contributor to their emotional problems and they complained of problems with job satisfaction and relations with supervisors and co-workers. A more recent study examined the prevalence of reported job stress in military mental health patients and concluded that work stress significantly leads to emotional distress and in some cases to mental illnesses (Pflanz, 2001). The most common work stressors reported were change in work responsibilities, change in work hours, and trouble with supervisors. Hence, it may be inferred that job stress in the military may have little to do with the fact that military personnel deal with the difficult business of war and may stem from more subtle aspects of military culture that foster work stress.

Psychological Factors in the Military Stress

The military deployments, in simpler terms, may be called as HARD: Harsh, Ambiguous, Risky, and Distant (Pflanz, 2003). The personnel deployed in the field live in austere conditions. The deployment environments can be uncomfortable, harsh, and severe. The troops have limited basic facilities and recreational options available with them. The temperature and climate can range from the very cold to the very hot. Further to harsh work environments, ambiguity and uncertainty is, to a great deal, a part of military deployments. The troops being deployed are often not aware of when they are deploying, where they are going, or when they are returning. The variability and unpredictability of deployments adds to the experience of their stress. Also, military deployments are risky to a great extent. Especially today, deploying military personnel are heading out to counter-insurgency and low-intensity conflict areas. In these dangerous environments the troops are exposed to the threat of enemy fire and terrorist attacks. These challenging hazardous conditions create stress, irritability, anxiety, and depression among the troops. Lastly, military deployments are distant and military personnel are far away from home. They remain disconnected and separated from family life. When problems occur at home, deployed personnel have little ability to help solve these difficulties.

On the basis of two extensive studies to find out the causal factors for suicides and fratricides in army deployments, we have attempted to comprehensively elaborate upon soldiers' stress from base line to the ultimate consequences through a model of soldier stress. To elaborate the model depicted in Figure 6.1, it may be understood that in military settings, a soldier encounters stresses which may arise due to personal, familial, interpersonal, occupational, and environmental issues. The personal attributes of a troop, relationships at the interpersonal front and the sort of occupational conditions that one is exposed to, serve as a protective layer on the extent of stress experienced by the troops.

The factors which create a protective layer at the personal front are: personal resilience and problem-solving skills, good physical and mental health, a sense of personal control and self-efficacy, a strong sense of meaning and purpose in life, an optimistic outlook, easy temperament, a high level of self-esteem, and social/emotional competence. At the interpersonal front, the support system is provided by the soldier's family and the society one comes from. The level of stress experienced by a soldier is moderated to a great extent if there are strong family bonds, a healthy style of coping is being followed, there is a responsibility of raising children, the partner or spouse is there to provide support, healthy communication patterns exist at home, there is a strong sense of connectedness in the family.

At the occupational front, the level of stress experienced is moderated to a great extent if there is cohesiveness in the unit, the buddy system is well in place, healthy communication patterns exist between the superiors and subordinates,

Figure 6.1 Soldier Stressor Model

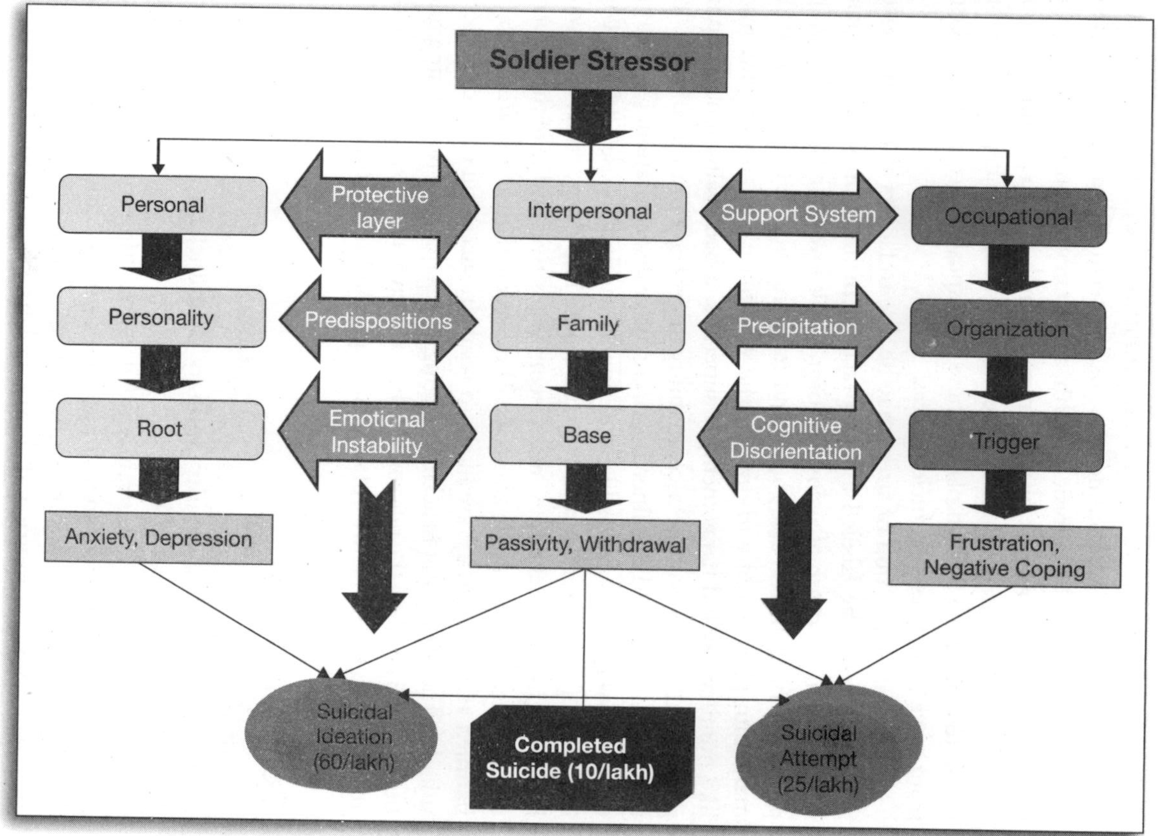

Source. Author.

stress management strategies are being followed and there is an easy access to assistance services in times of need. However, certain predisposing factors at the personal front and precipitants at the interpersonal and occupational front, which if interact, are likely to raise the level of stress experienced by the troops. The predisposing factors at the personal front which can be designated as root factors are: marital isolation, decreased self-esteem, impulsive and aggressive bend of personality, bad physical health, a tendency to abuse alcohol or drugs, or there has been a previous suicidal attempt which make a person emotionally insecure. A soldier may experience feelings of anxiety and depression and may refuse to contribute at workplace. These predisposing factors at the personal front serve as a genesis to suicidal ideas.

The same aggravation of stress may be due to factors at the interpersonal front which can be labeled as basal factors, primary ones being: financial stressors, suicide/death of a close relation, breakdown of a close relation, legal problems, his cultural background and religion, and the like. This is likely to make him passive and withdrawn. The workplace can also provide triggers like humiliation and harassment by superiors, a bad evaluation, disciplinary problem, discharge from service, inability to get leave in times of need. These triggers make the soldier vulnerable to cognitive disorientation. One may start misperceiving orders and is likely to adopt emotion-focused ways of coping in a state of frustration. A soldier may become impulsive, critical, unaware of his strengths and weaknesses, may become sensitive, and take things personally, thus leading to suicide attempts. These suicidal ideas and attempts, if not handled at an early stage are likely to result in successful cases of completed suicides. The key lies not in acknowledging events that may precipitate a suicide, but in understanding the relationship between current stress and the underlying vulnerabilities and resourcefulness that a person brings to a crisis.

Combat Stress

In pursuit of national security, military personnel are always combat-ready and under a great deal of combat stress. *Combat Stress* is the mental, emotional or physical tension, strain, or distress resulting from exposure to combat and combat-related conditions. The primary causal factor underlying combat stress is the exposure to the same conditions during military actions that cause physical injury and disease in battle or its immediate aftermath, and many combat stress reactions occur in persons who are also wounded or ill with disease (US Marine Corps, 2000). It is important to emphasize that combat stress is not restricted only to combat, but may also arise from combat-like conditions present during military operations other than war. In an operational area characterized by continuous action and high danger, our forces may experience high rates of combat stress casualties unless timely interventions are applied to manage this stress. Combat stress reactions have the potential to disable the most courageous soldiers and influence the success or failure of a unit in accomplishing its mission.

REACTIONS TO COMBAT STRESS

The soldiers who are exposed to danger in the combat conditions experience physical and emotional reactions that are generally not present under relatively tranquil circumstances. Some reactions that arise in response to bearable positive stress sharpen abilities to survive and win; other reactions may produce disruptive behaviors and threaten individual and unit safety. In the general sense of understanding, these adverse and disruptive behaviors are collectively termed as *combat stress reactions*. Combat and combat-related military missions can impose combinations of heavy physical work, sleep loss, dehydration, poor nutrition, severe noise, exposure to heat, cold or wetness, poor hygiene facilities, and perhaps exposure to infectious diseases, toxic fumes, or substances. These in combination with other influences—such as concerns about problems back home and lack of social/organizational support at the deployment front—affect the ability to cope with the perception of danger and diminish the skills needed to maintain the optimum morale and motivation to accomplish the operational goals.

The primary causal factor that underlies the combat stress reactions is a perception of imminent external threat to one's life, inability to cope with the threat, and a consequent pervasive feeling of rage and helplessness (Noy, 1991). The fear of death is not unique to the war situations or counter-insurgency operations. This threat is pervasive and difficult in combat. The normal everyday death anxiety which is rationally and irrationally dealt with is especially difficult to restrain in combat circumstances and is felt distinctly by most of the involved troops before and during combat, and most intensely when the odds are poor with intensive and prolonged strains. The risk of developing various combat reactions increases when prolonged intensive threat depletes the resources of the soldiers (Swank and Marchand, 1946) and when at the same time, the social support network collapses. The soldier whose resources have been depleted and who is not protected by unit social support may feel unable to endure the mounting anxiety any longer, and therefore fails to function in combat. This breaking point of losing one's adaptability and control of the situation in the face of an existential threat is traumatic for the soldiers, which creates the feelings of helplessness as well as rage. This is essential to most combat stress reactions and in some cases it is a starting point of post-traumatic stress disorder (Noy, 1991).

In addition to the above mentioned primary level factors, environmental stressors often play an important part in causing the adverse or disruptive combat stress reaction behaviors. A soldier in combat is exposed to extreme hardship and deprivation which wear away the inner resources necessary to cope with the primary cause of combat stress reactions. The secondary level causal factors like extreme hot or cold weather conditions, isolation, physical exertion, sleeplessness, lack of adequate food, lack of communication and support from loved ones, and so on, waste away the soldiers' already depleted resources for coping and enduring. Sleepless long-term sustained operations have been regarded as important causal factors for various combat stress reactions (Haslam and Abraham, 1987). It has been found that deprivation from adequate sleep results in serious psychological, behavioral and somatic disturbances, and many of the sleepless soldiers sometimes develop hallucinations (Belenky, 1987). Most of the troops in combat and in some military operations other than war are affected by ranges of fatigue, fear, stress, anxiety, depression, and in some cases hopelessness.

Stressors in Counterinsurgency and Low Intensity Conflict Environments

The scenario that the military personnel are facing these days is not in the form of conventional warfare; rather it is a unconventional warfare that more prominently involves counter insurgency operations (CI Ops) and the low-intensity conflicts (LIC). Having limited human potential and striving for the security of motherland, the troops deployed in CI Ops and LIC areas become vulnerable to heightened stress experience that have a potential to adversely affect their mental health. Counterinsurgency (CI) aims primarily at preventing, impeding, and defeating anti-government forces or movements in open civil war or similar military conflict and low intensity conflict (LIC) operation is a military term for the use of troops and/or assets in situations other than war. The concept of LIC is a combination of various military and nonmilitary concepts, often not precisely defined. Low-intensity conflicts are territorially limited politico-military struggles to achieve political, social, economic, or psychological objectives. LIC is often characterized by limitations of armaments, tactics, and levels of force. They are often protracted and involve military, diplomatic, economic, and psychological pressure through terrorism and insurgency. Troops trained in conventional warfare experience significant stress in such LIC operations (Goel, 1998; Ray, 1997). In conventional operations of war, limited periods of intense stress followed by adequate recovery phases do not significantly sap the psychological resources of the soldier unless the operations are unduly prolonged. The situation in LIC is diametrically opposite. Prolonged spells of stress punctuated by quantitatively and qualitatively inadequate opportunities for rest and relaxation impose immense and often unbearable demands on even otherwise robust subjects. This may result in psychological distress, combat stress disorder, or post-traumatic stress disorder (Badrinath, 2003; Haas, 2003). Conventional military training makes the soldier think in clear-cut extremes like black and white, friend and foe. This tendency often leads to problems in LIC where the concept of "enemy" is different and cannot be applied in universal sense to one's own people.

The contributory factors, which increase the stress level on soldiers participating in LIC, are the product of a complex interplay of three elements involved—the militant, the local population, and the soldier (Ray, 1997). The development of militancy often has its roots in the regional aspirations and stereotypical affiliations of people. The local population tends to look at the militant as their "own boy" fighting for a just cause, and the security forces as the long and cruel hand of the administration, particularly when there are human rights violations. Propaganda by neighboring countries and international agencies may further alienate the local population. In this background, the soldier is looked upon as an outsider. The security forces thus end up fighting an elusive enemy, in the absence of any reliable intelligence, and lack of cooperation or even active resentment of the local population. Ambiguity of aim, lack of visible success, and high casualty rates tend to erode morale among security forces. Several operational factors such as harsh weather conditions, unavailability of resting times, fatigue, unpredictability of threat, zero error syndromes, extended tenures of stay, absence of recreational avenues, lack of adequate social support in terms of healthy behavior by superiors, domestic worries, problems related to leave may increase the level of frustration (Goel, 1998; Ray, 1997; as cited by Chaudhury, Goel, and Singh, 2006).

The aim in LIC operations is not military conquest, but social control. The typical characteristic of LIC operations is that there is no directly visible enemy in front of the soldiers and the soldiers are under continuous threat of life due to the inability of identification of enemy and also pressures remain on them due to various other issues like human rights and maintenance of peace and stability. Insurgencies have existed for centuries; however, in recent times, the easy availability of high-tech weapons and explosives have made dealing with terrorists and insurgents stressful and painful.

India's experience in Kashmir and Sri Lanka, France's experience in Algeria, Russia's experience in Chechnya, and America's experience in Vietnam, Afghanistan, and Iraq bear testimony to the reality that troops armed with hi-tech weapons and trained for conventional war are at a triple disadvantage when deployed against insurgents and terrorists. First, stress levels in the troops rise abnormally when coping with ingeniously improvised bombs in the hands of insurgents who are supported by the population and not distinguishable from innocent civilians. Second, since freedom struggles go on for decades, there is little respite from repeated tenures of such stressful counterinsurgency deployment. And third, it is unreal to expect troops trained to fight an identifiable enemy in high-intensity battles to be equally proficient in low-intensity conflict involving inadvertent harm to innocent people, and when patriotism and national acclaim are the driving force to sustain morale (Hiranandani, 2007).

Some of the stresses that are peculiar to low-intensity conflict operations are feelings of insecurity with regard to families back home, the lack of societal support, adverse publicity in the media, hostile attitudes of human rights groups, the lack of cooperation on the part of local population, dissatisfaction with regard to financial compensation in risks/hardships involved in counter-insurgency operations, lack of basic amenities like proper food and accommodation, lack of rest, and sense of disgust. Though there remains a paucity of research available on military stress in Indian context, Defence Institute of Psychological Research, in recent years, is engaged in carrying out extensive field studies to find out the causal factors leading to soldier stress in order to take up preventive programs. The stressors, which lead to behavioral changes in the troops working in counterinsurgency operations (CI Ops), are elaborated here.

> *Extended tenures*: The long term postings of troops in the CI environment are subjected to high-risk operations forcing them to remain more vigilant round the clock. Extended and prolonged exposure to such stressful environment adversely affects the physical and mental state of the soldiers.
>
> *Hostile and unfamiliar working conditions*: Since it is quite difficult to identify militants or insurgents in the insurgency areas, the troops therein are always engaged in an invisible threat in a hostile environment that is all around them but unseen. To identify an insurgent or

militant in such an environment is a very tough job and simultaneously, the pressure from the top bears fearful inner state also.

Ambiguity and continuous militant threats: In counter-insurgency low-intensity conflict operations it is quite a tough task to recognize the militants from among the civil population. Even if at certain times they use unconventional methods of devastation, there remains the situation of threat all the time. In such threatening situation, the fear and possibility of getting killed anytime coupled with long duty hours without rest puts tremendous mental pressure on the troops that exceeds their cognitive capacities to resist and which may ultimately lead to maladaptive psychological functions and aberrant behavior.

Prolonged separation from family: Staying away and out of touch from the families due to not getting leave at the time of requirement adds to the stress of the soldiers. Constant worry about the well-being of family and domestic problems, absence of timely and proper communication with family, absence of news from home, and constant deployment in far-flung areas arouses a deep feeling of isolation which might originate depression, hopelessness, and even suicidal ideation in an individual.

Fatigue and unavailability of rest: Besides the strain of operational duties in CI Ops, there is a need for constant vigil and alertness on the part of all ranks. The troops have to carry out additional duty without any time for sleep or rest hours. The sleeplessness and the fatigue due to the long duty hours in absence of the time for rest also cause depressive symptoms.

Poor and inadequate basic facilities: The troops deployed in the border areas and CI Ops zones usually don't get proper basic facilities like proper accommodation, good quality food, transportation facilities, and proper clothing. Such poor living conditions make individuals vulnerable to stress.

Monotonous duties and isolation: The soldiers deployed in CI Ops are always engaged in same kind of duties with any kind of predefined schedule. The boredom associated with this produces the feelings of isolation and detachment. These feelings of isolation coupled with lack of social interaction, sports and other recreational activities, and insecurity of life results in hopelessness and depression which may lead to suicidal thoughts.

Poor interpersonal relations and lack of social support: Social support has always been found having buffering effects in stress experience. In CI Ops areas, everybody is always busy and soldiers' personal problems are not shared and no support is available directly on the part of peer group. There is a wide gap between officers and other ranks and officer–subordinate relationships are poor and strained. Officers do not give ear to the problems of juniors and these unresolved problems cause stress, depression, and hopelessness in troops that take a shape of mental illnesses over a period of time.

Inhospitable terrain and climate: The terrain and the climate in the counterinsurgency environment areas in Jammu & Kashmir and the North East are inhospitable and harsh. Operations have to be conducted under adverse weather conditions without adequate resources. A very high level of endurance is required to sustain over a prolonged period of time since the troops always face different kinds psychological and physical discomforts. In such situations the coping resources of soldiers may fall short of the harsh situational demands which may result into emotional breakdown.

The military deployments are most of the times in inhospitable terrains like high altitudes, glaciers, deserts, and challenging scenarios like counter-insurgency, low-intensity conflict, and peace-keeping missions. It goes without saying that physical environmental conditions always have significant influence on person's ability to adapt, his overall psychological functioning and also general health and well-being. Although their impact may differ based on the variability among the situations, the inhospitable deployment conditions is certainly one of the factors that lead to varied stress experiences of the troops.

Stress in High Altitude and Extreme Temperature Deployments

A significant portion of the world's geography lies above 10,000 feet elevation, an arbitrary designation that separates moderate and high altitude. Although the number of indigenous people living at these elevations is relatively small or negligible, many people travel to high altitude for work. Countries like India, having their borders in these high altitude locations, deploy their military personnel to safeguard the national boundaries. These high altitude deployments expose soldiers to chronic or intermittent hypoxia and the associated risk of acute mountain sickness (AMS) and less frequently, high altitude pulmonary oedema (HAPE) and high altitude cerebral oedema (HACE) (Askew, 2002). The typical symptoms of AMS include headache, nausea, anorexia, fatigue, and lassitude, and these generally occur in those who travel too high and too fast. The development of these symptoms may be linked with the condition of altered blood-brain barrier permeability, possibly related to hypoxia induced free radical formation. The burden of oxidative stress increases during the time spent at altitude and may even persist for some time upon return to the sea level (Askew, 2002). Since the deployments of the military personnel are for long durations, these stressful situations make them vulnerable to many kinds of health related problems.

The physiological consequences of increased oxidative stress may contribute to impaired muscle function and reduced capillary perfusion at altitude or may even play a role in precipitating more serious neurological and pulmonary crisis. Oxidative stress can be observed at altitude without strenuous physical exertion; however, environmental factors other than hypoxia such as exercise, UV light exposure, and cold exposure can also contribute to the burden on the soldiers (Askew, 2002). While a vast knowledge has been acquired about biomedical changes at high altitude and under low oxygen conditions, there is little knowledge available about the psychological changes. Most of the times, soldiers report major psychosomatic complaints and impairments in abilities and work behavior or performance. Concentration problems, fatigue, reduction of their usual activities, shortness of breath on exertion, on average, occur relatively more often (Bocker et al., 2007).

A major driver of the negative effects of high altitude work on employees is the desynchronization of the circadian rhythm (body clock), both in biological and social respects. Due to the lack of adjustment of the body, the person has to work against its demands (Bocker et al., 2007) that engender various kinds of stress reactions, the most common of which include irritability and depression with a probability of hallucinatory experiences and memory function impairment in some cases. The physical and social stress factors at high altitude can promote maladaptive behavior such as alcohol and drugs abuse that can compromise safety.

On similar lines to the stressors prevalent in the high altitude conditions, military personnel do many times remain deployed in extreme temperature conditions that range from the freezing −50°C in snow covered glaciers to the boiling hot 50°C in the deserts. Deserts are extremely dry, cold, or hot environments, exposed to the extremes of UV light radiation and where water is always a very limiting factor for life. Extreme adjustive demands are placed on the soldiers during these desert deployments which are both physiological and psychological in nature. Looking at it from a physiological viewpoint, it is almost beyond human capabilities to survive easily in such harsh conditions for long durations even after sufficient preventive measures.

Skin problems, memory impairments, and hallucinatory experiences are at times common in both extreme cold and hot temperatures. When soldiers face acute physical problems like frostbite in extreme cold snowy deployments, frequent dehydration problems are common in extreme hot conditions. Coupled with the unavoidable physiological adversities, the constant heightened alertness and vigil even in absence of regular enemy encounters, physical, and mental isolation from the external world with continuous worries about the significant others back home, lack of basic requirements to maintain optimum well-being, unavailability of social support are the stressors that deteriorate mental health of military personnel. Though the deployments in such extreme conditions are unavoidable keeping in view the primary objective of military, shortened deployment durations are likely to have lesser negative influences that may be reversible on return to normal conditions.

Stress in Military Aviation

Military aviation is one of the areas that present extreme operational conditions before the personnel involved and the profession of pilots is undoubtedly one of the most demanding, as it is exercised in the circumstances of time pressure, imposed working pace and, above all, continuous psychological, sensory and psychomotor tension. Military aviators work in the physiologically unnatural environment (air), and are exposed to a number of specific loads and extreme stress factors requiring continuous extra efforts from pilots to sustain adjustment (Trutanić, Stražičić, and Koren, 2000).

Stress factors in pilot profession are far more pronounced than others as these are accompanied by a number of pilot-characteristic stress factors. The aviation environment is a high risk environment and rich in potential stressors such as temperature, acceleration, noise and communication, decompression sickness, vibration, hypoxia, exhaust fumes, and motion sickness. Obviously, all these environmental stressors affecting aviation pilots have a negative affect on their mental health. While flying the supersonic aircrafts, pilots move extremely rapidly from one point to another, at a very fast working pace. These highly complex and fine motor movements cause immense psychological strain and emotional tension, especially in critical moments during the flight and failure on the part of a pilot to overcome and resolve these acute stresses for extended times pose a risk of developing chronic stress symptoms resulting in a series of functional disorders (Trutanić, Stražičić, and Koren, 2000).

Among Air Force pilots, acute stress symptoms manifest in the form of initial confusion, tunnel vision, restricted attention, misapprehension of external stimuli, and disorientation. In the conditions of failure to cope with, severe stress may, especially in critical flight stages, lead to loss of concentration, disrupted functioning, and consequently in premature action, slowed functioning, reacting to minor signals, or failure to detect important signals. This may be followed by, exaggerated distress and tension, panic anxiety symptoms (increased heart rate, sweating, etc.) or symptoms of avoidance of stress situations and social isolation. Unresolved acute stress symptoms can accumulate and get replaced by chronic stress symptoms, manifesting in the form of impaired working and social and psychological functioning. Psychological programs focused on stress management, stress coping techniques, ventilation groups, autogenous training as well as demonstration of progressive muscle relaxation, creative visualization, and isometric exercises may prove to have beneficial effect on psychological operative readiness for flight (Trutanić, Stražičić, and Koren, 2000).

Stress among Naval Personnel and Submariners

Like other military personnel operating on ground and in air, the military men working on the surface and in the deep sea also face extreme and adverse work conditions. There are certain unique aspects of the working environment on ships and in submarines. Naval personnel and submariners are exposed to potential stressors such as lack of privacy and cramped living conditions, extended periods of confinement, repetitive conditions and surroundings, and constant presence of physical danger. According to a very recent study by Bridger and associates (2011), the main stressor among Naval personnel associated with strain was an inability to disengage from work and this stressor accounted for a greater proportion of the variance in strain in personnel serving on ships than those serving ashore. Among those serving on ships, the causes associated with heightened distress are lack of autonomy and control and dissatisfaction with living conditions, lack of privacy, and social confinement (Bridger, Brasher, Dew, and Kilminster, 2011).

As compared to the personnel on ships, submariners are more stressed groups as they are exposed to unique and potentially unpleasant environmental conditions like various restrictions, social isolations, poor air quality, deprivation of natural light, and prolonged periods at sea. The stressors specific to personnel working in submarines are unavailability of personnel space, inability to escape from workplace conflicts, total unavailability of sunlight for long periods, disrupted sleep/wake cycles and sleep deprivation, concern for physical danger of excessively elevated hydrostatic pressure of sea, and concern for physical danger from invisible enemy. All these make a physically closed, socially intense, and potentially dangerous environment directly acting upon the psychological functional abilities. Prolonged exposure to these adverse conditions and the probable sea sickness many a times ultimately results into depressive symptoms and even in psychotic problems with inability to adapt with external realities on returning back on ground.

It is obvious that the extreme operative conditions that exist today for the military men in different contexts are not easily bearable even after extensive specified trainings. In the times to come, the intensity and extremity of such conditions is likely to aggravate and the scopes of military personnel are likely to widen forcing him face larger physical and psychological adversities since the role of a soldier is expanding from national to global.

Future Stress Factors: A Global Soldier Perspective

The coming times are expected to face very limited conventional warfare, and the soldiers will be most of the times seen engaged in *unconventional warfare* and various peace time operations and peace-keeping missions. The soldier will not remain restricted to territorial boundaries in the times to come and the whole world will be the platform for his functioning. As this shaping of roles and mixing of boundaries is taking place gradually, the soldiers of different countries are seen engaged out of their homelands in various type of operations like United Nations peace-keeping missions. By global soldier, we refer to the *soldier without territorial restrictions to work, with a global scope of functioning by means of engagement in varied kind of roles even other than war, having varied type of functional platforms including being a part of civilian population, and whose primary objective will be maintenance of peace rather than fighting a war.*

The UN peace-keeping missions that are operative in present-day world project a picture of prevailing stressful situations for the deployed soldiers. The working fields for these peace-keeper soldiers in future are going to be completely unknown, unpredictable, and full of danger wherein they will have to exercise unduly extra cognitive efforts for healthy survival and goal achievements. Following may be the potential stressors inherent in UN peace-keeping deployments (United Nations Department of Peace-keeping Operations, 1995):

The necessities and pressures on the soldier to be ready to shift from one place to another in ultra-short period of time place heightened burden and exhaust the human abilities to a great extent. For the UN peace-keeper soldier, it has very less probability to know the duration of deployment in advance. The longer the separation from family and social support networks, the more is the potential for stressful reactions and developing mental problems. UN missions are likely to be more stressful as there may not be a clearly defined statement of mission and the soldiers will have to adapt to uncomfortable situations and hardships along with lesser psycho-social support in terms of contact with family, friends, etc.

Complex and difficult missions may become even more stressful when media support and national support from one's own land is missing or is somehow misrepresented, which is very likely in during such missions. The peace-keeper soldiers work on foreign land with a little or no acquaintance with the culture of that place. The more involved the peace-keeper is with the population in the local mission area, the greater will be the potential for stress associated with a foreign culture. Some missions, particularly those with overt conflict and involving disaster relief, have a very high potential for exposure to mass death, injury, suffering and bereavement of the survivors. Peace-keeping soldiers may be exposed to extreme atrocities from which they are prohibited to intervene. The exposure to such extreme conditions may be sufficient to cause psychological disorders like PTSD.

Even after being peace-keepers, the soldiers have constant risk of being captured and held hostage. There also prevails a danger of personal injury or being killed by mines or gunfires, etc. Casualties from hostile action increase the potential for battle (conflict) fatigue. If casualties occur under highly frustrating and/or ambiguous conditions, it may also stimulate misconduct stress behavior resulting in lack of contact with realistic appraisal of situation and psychopathological symptoms.

In the times to come, other than the present-day stressors, the number of factors that will separate the global soldier from the conventional soldier in terms of functioning will also add varied types of stressors to be faced. Firstly, when in conventional warfare the soldier is trained for the specific methods of war from the beginning, the future unconventional and technology based warfare will impose a requirement on the soldier to keep himself updated with the rapidly coming change. This will place increased adjustive demands on the soldier and his limited resources will be overburdened, thereby leaving scope for the failure to cope or adjust and resulting in mental health problems. Second, the future soldier will be a part of *coalition forces* engaged in *joint operations* beyond own national territories. This widening of functional role will add to the psychological burden of the soldier by manifolding his cognitive load of processing the information coming from different relatively new and less familiar channels of supervision. Simultaneously, a soldier will be more away from family and in more adverse situation of isolation due to cultural differences, which is quite probable to cause anxiety, depression, and hopelessness.

The future soldier will be having varied type of functional platforms. These futuristic demands will increase the conflicts and role ambiguity and will require more precision on his part. As a result of the role conflicts, ambiguities, and burden of errorless functioning, stress will impinge upon the future soldier and will drain his resources. The continuous deployments in unfamiliar territories will demand excessive psychological and physiological efforts from the soldier for adaptation that is likely to exhaust his resources with a fast pace. Unavailability of favorable social networks and presence of vague environment around will add to the stress level and cognitive abilities are likely to fall short to cope with such a challenging situation. Keeping all the above in mind, the advance preventive measures become the need of the hour for a peaceful world safe in the hand of healthy soldiers.

Managing Soldier Stress: Proactive Measures

Military leadership has a great role to play in managing stress among troops. The leaders must work to keep each soldier's perception of danger balanced by the sense that the unit has the means to prevail over it. The leaders bear entire responsibility to keep themselves and their unit working at the level of stress that sustains optimum performance and confidence. Some of the *proactive measures* to help manage soldier stress are listed in the following:

> *Psychological screening at time of selection:* There are individual differences in people's abilities to deal with varied types of stressors. Person's personality traits and temperamental dispositions are indicative of one's strength and weaknesses and mental stamina to sustain against stress. Screening of the candidates on specific personality attributes at the time of selection for military job may prove crucial to select relatively stronger soldiers.
>
> *Sensitizing the leadership:* Adverse stress reactions are most likely to occur when troops begin to lose confidence in themselves and their leaders. In today's scenario the top management has to give due consideration to the basic privileges, self-esteem, and sentiments of the individual. The leaders, who come in direct contact with the troops most often, need to be sensitive towards the needs of the soldiers as a group and also towards the specific needs of an individual. The leaders need to be approachable for the soldiers at the time of crisis. They need to have

a humane approach towards their problems. Any act or statement on the part of the leader that hurts the ego and lowers the self-esteem of the individual usually becomes the precipitating factor for maladaptive behavior.

Sustenance of morale: A soldier's morale is the best driving force for his overall functioning across various domains of life. Sustained morale at the optimum level keeps the soldier buoyant even under adverse circumstances and brings out willing efforts on his part. These willing efforts in turn develop healthy coping abilities to face stress. Availability of basic amenities, healthy psychological environment prevailing across the units, and the assurance of availability of psychological support from leaders will serve as prime factors to sustain the morale of troops.

Promoting sense of purpose and pride: As asserted by the proponent of the four P's model (Pflanz, 2003), *purpose* involves helping the troops understand and focus on their reasons for choosing to serve in the military. They are serving their country and defending freedom, democracy along with stabilizing peace across the country. The soldiers who are deploying to fight the battle and as well as their family members tending the home fires and providing emotional support, are serving their country and making sacrifices that matter for the nation as a whole. A strong sense of purpose about what they are doing acts as a rational coping mechanism and can comfort them during the difficult times ahead. This sense of purpose can be connected to the sense of *pride*. By developing a *sense of pride* in what they are doing they can feel more devoted to make the duty bound sacrifices and this feeling of devotion again indirectly serves as a defense against negative emotional experiences coming out of the hardships.

Social support: Social support plays a role of protective sheath and acts as a buffer against stress. Isolation, which is viewed as one of the prime causes of stress in extreme environmental conditions, in terms of mental distance from support system is more harmful than the physical one. Promotion of simple means of connectedness with the soldier and the compassionate attitude of leaders towards their followers generate a sense of belongingness and meaning in life which ultimately inculcate inner strengths to bear adversities and adapt to inhospitable environments.

Generating self-awareness and capability building: Most of the times it so happens that soldiers lack awareness of the process of various situation specific and contextual stressors acting upon their mental health. Awareness of such issues makes a person ready to face hazards and the advance mental preparedness acts as adaptive coping strategy. Simultaneously, certain programs focusing on building capabilities to handle inhospitable conditions and to grow personal strengths aimed at optimistic orientation towards future may prove beneficial.

Managing Soldier Stress: Retroactive Measures

First hand redressal of problems: Although soldiers are well trained to handle the minor stressors inherent in the job, it is the herd of numerous minor problems collected over a long period of time that drains the resources of a soldier. A supportive approach on the part of commanders that involves active listening, empathetic understanding of various problems, altruistic dealing with subordinates, and providing possible help provides means of catharsis to vent out the gathered negative loads causing psychological disturbances.

Provision of basic facilities and reduced deployments: The basic facilities for the soldiers need to be improved to make them better equipped to face hardships. Basic facilities like better quality of accommodation, adequate and weather appropriate clothing, good quality of food and ration, communication and transportation facilities are some of the aspects that, if taken care of, add to sustained motivation of soldiers to work with devotion. At the psychological level, proper acclimatization coupled with adequate physical and psychological supports in the form of provision of all basic amenities and the reduced duration of high altitude deployments may help the troops keep themselves physically and mentally healthy.

Rest and recuperation: The soldiers in the CI Ops and LIC areas are working 24 hours under the most stressful conditions and in the most inhospitable climate and terrain. Fatigue and deprivation of sleep prove to be the most potent causes for emotional disturbances, lack of sensory motor coordination, and cognitive malfunction. Regular schedule of work and rest is essential to maintain the physical and mental health of the troops. Provision for mandatory periods of rest, particularly after a soldier is back from a high-stress operation will prove helpful for a soldier's well-being. Along with rest, it is also essential to ensure adequate means of recreation to relax the soldiers, who work under conditions of constant stress.

Identification of early warning signs: In order to intervene promptly for the safety and benefit of the suffering soldier and the unit, it is important for the unit leaders to recognize these adverse behaviors at their onset. Any soldier showing persistent, progressive behavior that deviates from his baseline behavior may be demonstrating the early warning signs and symptoms of a combat stress reaction. At the prevention level, first of all, knowledge about critical behavior and risk factors is essential. *Periodic surveillance of well-being of soldiers or general stress audit* will help in diagnosing a soldier manifesting symptoms of maladaptive behaviors. Early signs and behavioral markers of anxiety, anger, and depression in soldiers can be detected by their immediate supervisors during their routine check-up. Interventions can be tailored to specifically address areas of elevated risk. The services of military psychologists and psychiatrists can be employed to screen soldiers for symptoms associated with depression, substance abuse, etc.

Improved training and spirituality: Though, before deployment in the CI Ops areas, the officers and troops do undergo some training in the specific skills required to operate in these areas, there is a need to enhance the scope of the training to include the aspects of managing the stress, enhancing positive thinking, and surviving with physical, mental wellness even in most adverse circumstances. The training needs to be designed in a manner that it enhances the mental robustness of the soldier. Involvement of the soldiers in the regular spiritual activities also ensures their integration into the group and keeps them engaged in positive behaviors. Certain religious beliefs also act as a deterrent for the faithful to engage in maladaptive behaviors.

Critical incidence stress debriefing: Critical Incidents have the power to overwhelm the normal coping abilities of even the most experienced professional. Typically, these rare but overwhelming events, especially those which may end with a tragic outcome, often have the power to completely immobilize the professional or potentially an entire group of people. Critical Incidence Stress Debriefing needs to be provided to troops of the unit. Debriefing teams can provide assistance to events such as combat deployments, serious accidents, suicides, trauma, and the like.

Destigmatizing and rewarding help-seeking behavior and crisis hotlines: Military personnel are highly reluctant to ask for help because they do not want to be seen as weak. The leader should dispel the stigma from the minds of his men by communicating that recognizing the problems of life is acceptable and a sign of strength. Help seeking behavior needs to be encouraged by the leader and it should be handled in a confidential manner. A leader should encourage soldiers to seek help from mental health professionals if the problem is serious enough. Having crisis hotlines in place for soldiers is expected to help a great deal in initial catharsis of the problem, thus preventing a serious event.

Psychological counseling of troops: Overall, military deployments being HARD, it is quite necessary to help the soldiers manage their stress so that they can perform well under all circumstances. Though use of psychotherapeutic interventions is needed for mental health patients, dealing with deployment stress can be well contributed by the psychological counseling. Personnel manifesting behavioral problems need to be counseled by a trained counselor on a regular basis along with follow-ups.

Conclusion

Conclusively, open communication to and from the deployed setting can be critical as it acts as a stress buffer by taking the form of social support system. Talking about their stress out loud with a friend, family member, or co-worker provides an avenue to vent out the inner stressful resentment and can help blow off steam. Adequate time off for rest and other personal work can be an important part of managing deployment stress (Pflanz, 2003).

The elaborations provided in the preceded text in the chapter make it evident that military personnel, at large, are most of the times at the face of extremely stressful conditions. The soldiers, who are the prime assets of any country and who have the responsibility to keep the nation safe from conflicts, are themselves not safe and they are at constant risk of many physiological, psychological, and behavioral problems in the wake of extreme working environment conditions. Hence, to keep the soldiers' morale high in order to maintain their strengths at the optimum level so that they can adequately discharge the service of the nation, it is necessary to create avenues for their enhanced well-being by means of improving upon the facilities provided, capability building programs, and taking advance adequate preventive measures for tackling the growing stress among soldiers, as only safe soldiers can ensure the safety of all kinds of national assets.

References

Askew, E.W. (2002). Work at high altitude and oxidative stress: Antioxidant nutrients. *Toxicology, 180,* 107–19.

Badrinath, P. (2003). Psychological impact of protracted service in low intensity conflict operations (LICO) on armed forces personnel: Causes and remedies. *Journal of United Service Institution of India, 83,* 38–58.

Barnett, R.C. & Brennan, R.T. (1995). The relationship between job experiences and psychological distress: A structural equation approach. *Journal of Organizational Behavior, 16*(3), 259–76.

Belenky, G.L. (1987). Varieties of reaction and adaptation to combat experience. *Bulletin of the Menninger Clinic, 51,* 64–79.

Bocker, M., Vogt, J., Christ, O., & Muller-Leonhardt, A. (2009). Health, safety and performance in high altitude observatories: A sustainable approach. *The Messenger, 137,* 47–49.

Bridger, R.S., Brasher, K., Dew, A., & Kilmister, S. (2011). Job stressors in naval personnel serving on ships and in personnel serving ashore over a twelve month period. *Applied Ergonomics, 42*(5), 710–18.

Chaudhury, S., Goel, D.S., & Singh, H. (2006). Psychological effects of low intensity conflict (LIC) operations. *Indian Journal of Psychiatry, 48,* 223–31.

Craig, I.W. (2007). The importance of stress and genetic variation in human aggression. *BioEssays, 29*(3), 227–36.

Derogatis, L.R. & Coons, H.L. (1993). Self-report measures of stress. In L. Goldberger & S. Breznitz (Eds), *Handbook of stress: Theoretical and clinical aspects* (Second edition, pp. 200–33). New York: The Free Press.

Goel, D.S. (1998). Psychological aspects of counter-insurgency operations. *Combat, 27,* 43–48.

Haas, K.L. (2003). Stress and mental health support to Australian Defence Health Service personnel on deployment: A pilot study. *Australia Defense Force Health, 4,* 9–22.

Haslam, D.R., & Abraham, P. (1987). Sleep loss and military performance. In G.L. Belenky (Ed.), *Contemporary studies in combat psychiatry.* Westport, CT: Greenwood Press.

Hiranandani, G.M. (2007). Low intensity conflict revisited. *Indian Defence Review, 22*(3), Retrieved from: http://www.indiandefencereview.com/military%20&%20space/Low-Intensity-Conflict-Revisited.html (accessed on December 10, 2010).

Holmes, T.H. & Rahe, R.H. (1967). The social readjustment rating scale. *Journal of Psychosomatic Research, 11,* 213–18.

Hudd, S.S., Dumloa, J., Erdmann-Sager, D., Murray, D., Phan, E., Soukas, N., & Yokozuka, N. (2000). Stress at college: Effects on health habits, health status, and self-esteem. *College Student Journal, 31,* 217–27.

Judge, T.A. & Colquitt, J.A. (2004). Organizational justice and stress: The mediating role of work-family conflict. *Journal of Applied Psychology, 89*(3), 395–404.

Landy, F.J. & Conte, J.M. (2004). *Work in the 21st century: An introduction to industrial and organizational psychology.* Boston: McGraw-Hill.

Lazarus, R.S. (1966). *Psychological stress and the coping process.* New York: McGraw-Hill.

——— (1999). *Stress and emotion: A new synthesis.* New York: Springer.

Lazarus, R.S. & Folkman, S. (1984). *Stress, appraisal, and coping.* New York: Springer-Verlag/Guilford.

Lazarus, R.S., DeLongis, A., Folkman, S., & Gruen, R. (1985). Stress and adaptational outcomes. *American Psychologist, 40,* 770–79.

Manning, F.J., Kukura, F.C., DeRouin, E.M., McCarroll, J.E, Zych, K.A., & Edwards, F. (1981). Outpatient mental health facilities in the U.S. Army, Europe: Patient characteristics, complaints and dispositions at three sites. *Military Medicine, 38,* 7–13.

Noy, S. (1991). Combat stress reactions. In R. Gal & A.D. Mangelsdorff (Eds), *Handbook of Military Psychology* (pp. 507–30). Chichester, West Sussex: John Wiley & Sons Ltd.

Pflanz, S. (2002). Work stress in the military. *Organizational and occupational psychiatry bulletin, 10*(1). Retrieved from: http://www.aoop.org/archive-bulletin/2002fall05.shtml

——— (2003). Military deployments are HARD: The four P's of helping patients cope with deployment stress. *Organizational and Occupational Psychiatry Bulletin, 11*(1). Retrieved from: http://www.aoop.org/archive-bulletin/2003spring01.shtml

Pflanz, S.E. (2001). Occupational stress and psychiatric illness in the military: Investigation of the relationship between occupational stress and mental illness amongst military mental health patients. *Military Medicide, 166,* 457–62.

Pflanz, S. & Sonnek, S. (2002). Work stress in the military: Prevalence, causes, and relationship to emotional health. *Military Medicine, 167,* 877–82.

Ray, A. (1997). *Kashmir diary: Psychology of militancy.* Delhi: Manas Publications.

Selye, H. (1976). *Stress in health and disease. Boston,* MA: Butterworth.

Strelau, J. (2001). The concept and status of trait in research on temperament. *European Journal of Personality, 15,* 311–25.

Swank, R.L. & Marchand, W.E. (1946). Combat neuroses, development of combat exhaustion. *Archives of Neurology and Psychiatry, 55,* 236–47.

Trutanić, V., Stražičić, N., & Koren, B. (2000). Psychological support programmes for pilots of Croatian Air Force. *Proceedings of 36th International Applied Military Psychology Symposium* (pp. 257–60). Split, Croatia.

U.S. Marine Corps (2000). *Combat stress.* Report No. FM 90-44/6-22.5 NTTP 1-15M MCRP 6-11C. Washington, DC: Department of Navy.

United Nations Department of Peace-keeping Operations. (1995). *United Nations stress management booklet.* New York: United Nations.

Section-II

WORK–FAMILY CONFLICT AND STRESS

7

Work–Family Conflict in India: Test of a Causal Model

Ujvala Rajadhyaksha and Kamala Ramadoss

Abstract

The goal of this chapter is to use a derived "etic" approach to arrive at a causal model of work–family conflict for India. We began with an existing theoretical model of work–family conflict—the Frone, Yardley, and Markle (1997) model—developed within the North American context, and used SEM to test its fit within the Indian context. India is well-known for its cultural, economic, linguistic, and religious diversity. It provides an interesting contrast to the environment of the developed English-speaking world which is the background for most studies on work–family conflict. The sample for this study comprised of 405 white-collar men and women employees from health, education, finance, and manufacturing industries. Data tested via SEM provided a very poor fit for the original model (e.g., CFI = 0.497). After several model modifications and changes, fit indices somewhat improved (e.g., CFI = 0.809) though coefficients for some paths were opposite to that hypothesized. Social support was positively rather than negatively related to demands and negative outcomes in both the work and family domains, and work demands was negatively rather than positively related to negative family and work outcomes.

Keywords: work–family conflict, social support, India

Introduction

Changing trends in workforce demographics caused by the entry of women in to paid work has resulted in a redistribution of work and family responsibilities creating new tensions and conflicts for men and women. As employees struggle to balance multiple roles they experience stresses and strains that have negative outcomes not only for themselves but also for the companies that they work for and for the community at large. The work–family interface is characterized by numerous mechanisms linking work and family domains such as spillover, compensation, segmentation, resource drain, congruence, and conflict (e.g., see Edwards and Rothbard, 2000). More recently, other linkages such as facilitation (Grzywacz, J. G. and Marks, N. F. (2000) and work–family enrichment (Greenhaus and Powell, 2006) have also been identified. However, conflict has been and continues to be the dominant paradigm for most work–family research during the past quarter century (Parasuraman and Greenhaus, 2002). This is because work and family tend to work as "greedy" institutions (Pittman, 1994), wherein an individual's fixed or scarce resources of time and energy result in a zero-sum game making conflict inevitable.

While a plethora of research studies have examined specific aspects of WFC such as antecedents, outcomes, mediators, and moderators (e.g., see the review by Eby et al., 2005) few studies have tested complete causal models of WFC. In particular, there is no study that tests a causal model of WFC in India. In this paper we review literature on WFC including a commonly used theoretical model of WFC developed within the North American context. We conduct an exploratory test of this model for fit within the Indian context on a sample of 405 working men and women. Based on previous literature and the rationale of the theoretical model, we begin with the assumption that the fit indices will be adequate for India. We then make modifications in the original model and finally arrive at a derived "etic" model of WFC that has better "fit" for the Indian context. We conclude with some possible explanations for the derived etic model and implications for future research.

Literature Review

WORK–FAMILY CONFLICT

CONCEPT AND MEASUREMENT OF WFC

Work–family conflict (WFC) – The most extensively studied relationship between the work and family domains – is usually defined as a form of role conflict that arises from *"simultaneous pressures from both work and family that are mutually incompatible in some respect"* (Greenhaus and Beutell, 1985, p.77). The conflict approach is based on the "scarcity" hypothesis in that it assumes that time and energy is fixed and in short supply. Participation in one role necessarily reduces resources available for participation in the other role, thus resulting in an experience of conflict and strain. Greenhaus and Beutell (1985) suggested three types of conflict based on the processes by which interference between domains could occur: time-based conflict, strain-based conflict and behavior-based conflict. Later, Frone, Russell & Cooper (1992) and Gutek, Searle, & Klepa (1991) constructed the first widely used measure of conflict that measured separately work-interfering-with-family conflict (WIF) and family-interfering-with-work conflict (FIW). Carlson, Kacmar, & Williams (2000) further refined the measurement of WIF and FIW using Greenhaus & Beutell's (1985) conceptualization, into time-based, strain-based and behavior-based conflict. In this study we use Carlson colleagues' measure of WIF and FIW conflict.

ANTECEDENTS AND OUTCOMES OF WFC

Research on WFC has examined antecedents and outcomes of conflict from both the work and family domains. Antecedents of WFC could include time- and strain-based pressures (Ford, Heinen, & Langkamer, 2007). Work-related antecedents tend to have a stronger influence on WIF than FIW, whereas family-related antecedents tend to have a stronger influence on FIW rather than WIF (Byron, 2005). Work-related antecedents include long work hours (Byron, 2005) and work-schedule related factors such as inflexibility, shift work, and overtime and evening work duties (Parasuraman et al., 1996). Job involvement or the extent to which people identify themselves with their job and center their interests round work, can also cause WIF conflict (Byron, 2005). Both of the above factors create time-based pressure in the work domain making it difficult for the individual to fulfill obligations in the family domain. Time-based pressures could arise in the family realm as well, through housework and childcare related tasks (Byron, 2005).

Strain-based work-related antecedents of work–family conflict include work role stress that can induce strain and tension. Work role stressors such as work role conflict, work role ambiguity and work role overload, can increase WIF and also spillover in to the family domain to influence non-work outcomes (e.g., Kahn & Byosiere, 1992; Parasuraman, Greenhaus, & Granrose, 1992). Family related strain-based antecedents include factors that induce stress within the family such as marital and parental conflict (Byron, 2005).

An increase in the above mentioned work- and family-related, time- and strain-based antecedents, increases work–family conflict. Therefore the two sets of variables are positively related. The greater are work and family demands and stressors, the greater is WFC. Support, on the other hand, acts as a resource for individuals, and tends to serve as a moderator in the stressor–strain relationship (Kahn & Boysiere, 1992). Therefore even though it is treated as an antecedent variable in many models of work–family conflict it works to reduce conflict. Work support has been shown to negatively correlate with several sources of strain in full-time workers (Parasuraman, Greenhaus, & Granrose, 1992). Supervisor support reduced work–family conflict in a study of health care professionals (Thomas & Ganster, 1995). Similarly, family and spousal support has been found to be negatively related to FIW (Adams, King, & King, 1996).

Work–family conflict has been shown to have work-related, family-related, and physical and psychological health related outcomes. The most commonly studied work consequence is job satisfaction, with high conflict resulting in lower job satisfaction (e.g., Bruck, Allen, and Spector, 2002; Ford, Heinen, and Langkamer, 2007) and consequently, lower life satisfaction (Kossek and Ozeki, 1998). Other work-related outcomes of high work–family conflict include greater turnover intentions (Greenhaus, Parasuraman, & Collins, 2002) and less career satisfaction (Martins, Eddleston, and Viega, 2002). The most commonly studied family-domain outcome of work–family conflict is family satisfaction. High levels of conflict have been found to be negatively related to family satisfaction (Ford, Heinen, & Langkamer, 2007). More recently, there has been mention of the role of work–family guilt as an outcome of work–family conflict (McElwain and Korabik, 2005).

High levels of work–family conflict have been found to have negative physical health outcomes for the individual such as greater depression, physical health complaints, hypertension, and greater alcohol consumption (Frone, Russell, & Cooper, 1997). Negative mental health outcomes of work–family conflict include greater psychological distress (Burke & Greenglass, 1999), anxiety disorders, mood disorders and substance abuse disorders (Frone, 2000), greater psychological burnout, psychosomatic symptoms, and negative affective states such as anger, irritation, and depression (Burke, 1988).

WORK–FAMILY CONFLICT AS A MEDIATOR

In an overall sense, work–family conflict has been found to mediate the relationship between work domain and family domain antecedent variables and work domain and family domain outcome variables. For instance, Kopelman, Greenhaus, and Connolly (1983) found that work–family conflict mediated the relationship between work conflict and family conflict with life satisfaction.

The two facets of conflict namely, WIF and FIW conflict have also been found to function as mediator variables between work and family domain variables and outcome variables in the same and opposite domains (crossover effects). WIF has been shown to mediate the relationship between job time demands and psychological strain outcomes such that higher job demands result in higher WIF and greater psychological strain (Major, Klein, and Ehrhart, 2002), whereas FIW has been found to mediate the relationship between off-job (family) demands and psychological strain outcomes in a similar manner (O'Driscoll, Ilgen, and Hildreth, 1992). Some studies have identified crossover mediating effects of WIF and FIW, such that work domain variables may cause WIF which in turn has outcomes in the opposite domain (i.e., family) and family domain variables cause FIW which similarly has outcomes in the opposite domain (i.e., work). This could be in addition to outcomes within the same domain (e.g., Ford, Heinen, and Langkamer, 2007; Luk and Shaffer, 2005).

INTEGRATIVE MODELS OF WORK–FAMILY CONFLICT

Relatively few studies have tested complete causal models of WFC that integrate antecedent, mediating, and outcome effects associated with conflict. One early comprehensive model was developed and tested by Frone, Russell, and Cooper (1992). This model was perhaps the first to clearly distinguish between WIF and FIW. The model tested unique antecedents and outcomes of both forms of WFC including reciprocal relationships between the two. Job demands (such as job involvement) and job stressors were hypothesized to have a direct positive relationship with conflict in the same (work) domain, viz., WIF and outcomes in the same (work) domain (such as job distress), and an indirect positive relationship with conflict in the opposite (family) domain and outcomes in the opposite (family) domain (such as family distress), as well as an indirect positive relationship with individual outcomes (such as depression). Similarly family demands (such as family involvement) and family stressors were hypothesized to have a direct positive relationship with conflict in the same (family) domain, viz., FIW and outcomes in the same (family) domain (such as family distress), and an indirect positive relationship with conflict in the opposite (work) domain and outcomes in the opposite (work) domain (such as job distress), as well as an indirect positive relationship with individual outcomes (such as depression). WIF and FIW therefore acted as mediators between demands and stressors in a specific domain and outcomes in the opposite domain. WIF and FIW were also hypothesized as having a reciprocal positive relationship with each other. The Frone, Russell, and Cooper (1992) model found strong support and it has become the basis for many future integrative tests of WFC. The model was extended and further explicated by Frone, Yardley, and Markel (1997) who included support as an additional antecedent variable. A simplified version of the conceptual model of Frone, Yardley, and Markel (1997) is presented in Figure 7.1.

Figure 7.1   A Simplified Version of the Frone, Yardley, & Markel (1997) Conceptual Model of WFC

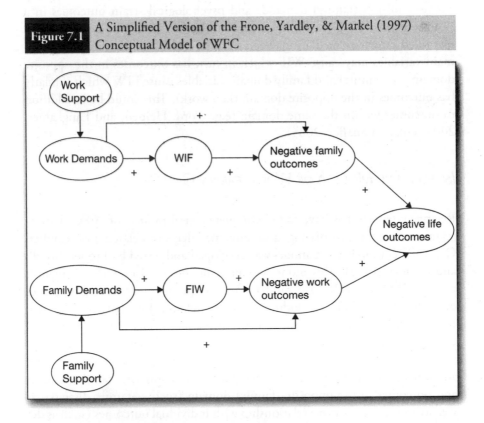

CROSS-CULTURAL TESTS OF WFC MODELS

Much of the research on WFC has been conducted within the context of developed English-speaking countries. While some studies have examined work–family concepts and linkages outside of North America (e.g., Yang et al., 2000), there exist very few tests of *causal models* of WFC outside of North America. One of the earliest examinations of antecedents and outcomes of WFC within the same study was conducted by Aryee (1992) on a sample of married professional women in Singapore. His study indicated that role stressors explained the most variance in job–spouse and job–homemaker conflicts while task characteristics explained the most variance in job–parent conflict. WFC explained only modest amounts of the variance in the well-being and work outcome measures.

Kinnunen & Mauno (1998) studied antecedents and consequences of work–family conflict among employed women and men in Finland. The results showed that work–family conflict was more prevalent than family–work conflict among both sexes, but that there were no gender differences in experience of either work–family or family–work conflict. Family–work conflict was best explained by family domain variables (e.g., number of children living at home) for both sexes, and work–family conflict by work domain variables (e.g., full-time job, poor leadership relations) among the women, and by high education and high number of children living at home among the men. Family–work conflict had negative consequences on family well-being, and work–family conflict, in particular, on occupational well-being.

The generalizability of findings from the US based model of the work–family interface proposed by Frone et al. (1992) was tested by Aryee, Fields, & Luk (1999) on a sample of 320 Hong Kong employees. It was shown that some of the relationships among work and family constructs in the Hong Kong sample were similar to those found by Frone and colleagues in the U.S. sample. For example, consistent with Frone, Russell, & Cooper (1992), Aryee, Fields, and Luk (1999) found a positive relationship between work-to-family conflict and family-to-work conflict. However, life satisfaction of employees in Hong Kong was predominantly influenced by work-to-family conflict, while life satisfaction of the U.S. employees was primarily affected by family-to-work conflict. Aryee, Fields, & Luk (1999) explained these differences with the great importance assigned to family roles in Chinese culture.

A global model of WFC was tested by Hill et al., (2004) in 48 countries covering the east, developing west, west affluent, and west–US. Results supported a transportable rather than culture-specific or gender-specific work–family interface model. Specifically, job flexibility related to reduced work–family conflict, reduced family–work conflict, and enhanced work–family fit. Work–family fit in turn related to increased job satisfaction.

Aryee, Srinivas, & Tan (2005) tested for the cross-cultural generalizability of Frone's (2003) fourfold taxonomy of work–family balance in terms of the direction of influence (work–family vs. family–work) and type of effect (conflict vs. facilitation) on a sample of full-time employed parents in India, and found support for the taxonomy. The focus of their study was to validate the construct of work-life balance outside North America. They also examined antecedents and outcomes of the four components of work life balance using moderated regression analysis, and found that different processes underlay the conflict and facilitation components. Furthermore, gender had only a limited moderating influence on the relationships between the antecedents and the components of work–family balance. Last, work–family facilitation was related to the work outcomes of job satisfaction and organizational commitment.

Aryee, Srinivas, and Tan (2005) have made an important contribution to the work and family literature based on the Indian context. However as with many other studies on WFC, they do not test a *complete causal* model of conflict. To date, there appears to have been no test of a comprehensive WFC model in India or in any of the less-affluent developing countries. Largely, the integrative WFC studies conducted in North America and outside appear to support an overall model of WFC wherein domain specific antecedents cause within-domain and across-domain conflict, and within domain outcomes. In this study we use Frone, Yardley, and Markel's (1997) model as the conceptual base for the examination of WFC in India, as it is to date the most comprehensive *causal model* of WFC available in the literature.

WORK AND FAMILY ISSUES IN INDIA

Research on work and family in India has followed two separate and disconnected paths. One route/path followed sociological and economic perspective with a focus on under-privileged women that looks at structures of patriarchy and their contribution to the subordination of women at work and home. The other path of psychosocial research, conducted largely from a role theory perspective, has examined work family relations within urban settings, (Rajadhyaksha and Smita, 2004) focusing mainly on a conflict perspective, though recently Aryee, Srinivas, and Tan (2005) found support for work–family facilitation in the Indian context.

Studies on work and family roles (conducted mainly in departments of psychology, sociology and more recently in management) have indicated that the division of these roles occurs along traditional lines for working men and women even in dual career and dual earner families (e.g., Sekaran, 1984; Ramu, 1989). Repeatedly studies have indicated that Indian women tend to be more involved with family roles and Indian men with work roles. (Bharat, 2003; Rajadhyaksha and Bhatnagar, 2000). Studies on working women have found that they bear a dual burden across different socio-economic classes which, causes considerable stress and strain (e.g., Khanna 1992), and that they experience psychological spillover of the work domain in to the family domain. Further, gender has been found to moderate the relationship between work variables (such as income, discretionary time, job involvement, career salience, and self esteem from job) and outcomes of life satisfaction and job satisfaction (Sekaran, 1984).

In studies conducted explicitly on work–family conflict, on samples of managerial and professional dual career couples who are presumably matched in terms of their career involvement, no significant differences in the level of overall (global) work–family conflict or organizational stress has been found. However there are differences in the sources of conflict and the kinds of work–family conflict experienced by men and women. Women have reported greater job–homemaker and energy-based conflict, particularly in the middle stage of the family life cycle and career. Men have reported greater job–spouse conflict especially during the early stage of the career and family life cycle (Rajadhyaksha, 2004). Aryee, Srinivas, and Tan (2005) found that work overload significantly increased both work-to-family and family-to-work conflict, and that gender moderated the relationship between parental work overload and work-to-family conflict.

Studies on coping with the stress and strain of balancing work and family role demands (again conducted mainly on samples of urban working women) have indicated that the most common coping strategies tend to be individual-specific and include expanding one's knowledge base by reading and planning and goal setting, actively seeking social support, and investing in developing a social support network. Interestingly, smoking, drinking or relying on medication as a way to relieve stress is not a coping strategy commonly used by Indian working women. This could be attributed to the traditional Indian stereotype of women who smoke or drink as having a "loose" character. Good counseling or psychotherapy appears to be unavailable to most women experiencing stress (Ghadially and Kumar, 1988).

Support for balancing work and family within the Indian context comes primarily from noninstitutional sources that include family members such as spouse, parents and parents-in-law, paid help, friends, and neighbors (Sekaran, 1992). The nature of this support tends to be informal, ad hoc, contingent, and bound in a web of reciprocal relationships of dependence and counter-dependence. For most working Indian women, unless the husband is willing to take on more household responsibilities, her work ambition could be considerably constrained (Ghadially and Kumar, 1988). There is low institutional and organizational support for balancing work and family demands in India. Institutional support takes the form of governmental policies that are progressive on paper (e.g., Factories Act of 1948; Maternity Benefits Act of 1961 and laws to prevent sexual harassment at work) but poorly implemented by organizations that often circumvent the law (Rajadhyaksha & Smita, 2004). Organizational support is generally inadequate – many times companies adopt a fairly rigid, nonflexible and bureaucratic style of functioning that does not give employees control over their schedule or work environment (Poster & Prasad, 2005). However when job control is available to Indian employees, it has been found to predict and reduce general work–family conflict (Pal and Saksvic, 2006). Work support has also been found to be positively related to work–family facilitation (Aryee, Srinivas, & Tan 2005).

Hypotheses

It appears from the above literature review that many relationships between the work and family context in India are fairly similar to the relationships that have been previously established in the literature on WFC. Work demands seem to have negative work, family and life outcomes, and support appears to be an important variable in mitigating the impact of work demands on WFC.

Further given that increasingly many aspects about India seem to mimic the developed world especially in the work domain, we begin by hypothesizing similar within domain and cross domain relationships among the latent constructs in the Frone, Yardley, and Markel model (1997) which is the basis for our current study. More specifically, we hypothesize that:

H1: Work support will have a significant negative relationship with work demands.

H2: Family support will have a significant negative relationship with family demands.

H3: Work demands will have a significant positive relationship with WIF conflict.

H4: Family demands will have a significant positive relationship with FIW conflict.

H5: Work demands will have a significant positive relationship with negative family outcomes.

H6: Family demands will have a significant positive relationship with negative work outcomes.

H7: WIF will have a significant positive relationship with negative family outcomes.

H8: FIW will have a significant positive relationship with negative work outcomes.

H9: Negative work outcomes will be significantly positively related to negative life outcomes.

H10: Negative family outcomes will be significantly positively related to negative life outcomes.

Method

PARTICIPANTS AND DATA COLLECTION

A sample of employees from educational, healthcare, manufacturing, and finance industries was asked to participate in the study and complete a survey on work–family conflict. Data was collected using a purposive sampling approach. The aid of a well known market research agency in India was solicited to identify and survey participants. Data was collected from two cities: Mumbai (N=204) and Bangalore (N=201), comprising a total sample of 405 participants. Trained employees of the agency administered paper/pencil questionnaires to the participants. Participants were married, full time employees working for organizations, and having at least one dependent child still living at home with them. 24% of responses came from the healthcare sector, 23% percent came from the educational sector, 26% from the manufacturing sector, and 25% from the finance sector, and finally 2% from other industries. Females comprised 48% of the sample, and on average participants were 35 years of age. Finally, 64% of the participants were non-managers and 36% were managers. Females comprised 48% of the sample. On average, both male and female participants were 35 years of age and had 17 years of education. Majority (79%) of the sample were Hindu. Finally, 64% of the participants were non-managers and 36% were managers.

MEASUREMENT

The research instrument was a questionnaire that was comprised of 17 parts measuring demands in work and family domains; supports in work and family domains; WIF and FIW; negative outcomes in work and family domains; and negative life outcomes. It was a part of a larger international project exploring the overall construct of the work–family interface. The global study included 10 countries from around the world and aimed to explore and identify cross-cultural differences in the experience of work–family inter-face. (See Korabik, Lero, & Ayman (2003)—Project 3535). Detailed descrip-tion of each of the measures used follows:

WORK DEMANDS AND FAMILY DEMANDS

Work demands and family demands constructs were each measured using three observed variables: job and family control, job and family involvement, and job and family overload, respectively.

1. *Job and family control*: Each measured separately using 5-item scales developed by the Center for Families, Work and Well-being, University of Guelph, Canada. Responses were measured on a 6-point Likert-type format ranging from strongly disagree to strongly agree. Higher scores indicated higher control. A sample item from the job control scale is, "I have influence over the things that happen to me at work," and similarly, a sample item from the family control scale is, "I have influence over the things that happen to me at home." Alpha reliability for job control and family control for the Indian sample was 0.74 and 0.75 respectively.

2. *Job involvement and family involvement*: Each respectively measured using a 4-item scale developed by Frone & Rice (1987). Responses were measured on a 6-point Likert-type format ranging from strongly disagree to strongly agree. Higher scores indicated higher involvement. A sample item from the job involvement scale is, "I am very much involved in my job," and a sample item from the family involvement scale is, "I am very much personally involved with my family." Alpha reliability for job involvement for the Indian sample was 0.60 and for family involvement (after dropping one problematic item) was 0.67.

3. *Work and family overload*: Each measured using a 5-item scale devel-oped by Peterson et al. (1995). Responses were measured on a 6-point Likert-type format ranging from strongly disagree to strongly agree. Higher scores indicated higher overload. A sample item from the work overload scale is, "At work, my workload is too heavy." Similarly, a sample item from the family overload scale is, "At home, my workload is too heavy." Alpha reliability for job overload and family overload for the Indian sample respectively was 0.81 and 0.90.

WORK SUPPORT AND FAMILY SUPPORT

The work and family support constructs were each computed using a measure specially designed for the international work–family project—Project 3535. The measure captured three kinds of support – emotional support, instrumental support and satisfaction with support from work-related and family-related sources for both work and family issues. The work-related sources included the job supervisor and co-workers, and the family-related sources included spouse, children, parents or parents-in-law, paid household helper, neighbors, and friends. Responses were measured using the following scale 1 = never, 2 = not often, 3 = sometimes, 4 = frequently, 5 = not applicable. Mean scores across the work and family sources of support were calculated. The support measures on the work side included work support instrumental for work (wsinsw) (e.g., "Please indicate how often you receive support with respect to your work-related duties from your job supervisor," Indian sample $\alpha = 0.75$); work support instrumental for family (wsinsf) (e.g., "Please indicate how often you receive support with respect to help with household tasks from your job supervisor," Indian sample $\alpha = 0.92$); work support emotional for work (wsemow) (e.g., "Please indicate how often you receive support in the form of listening to and discussing work-related problems from your job supervisor," Indian sample $\alpha = 0.82$); work support emotional for family (wsemof) (e.g., "Please indicate how often you receive support in the form of listening to and discussing family-related problems from your job supervisor," Indian sample $\alpha = 0.87$); and satisfaction with work support (wsgen) (e.g., In general how satisfied are you with the support you receive from your job supervisor, 1 = very dissatisfied to 5 = very satisfied, 6 = not applicable, Indian sample $\alpha = 0.65$).

Similarly on the family side there was family support instrumental for work (fsinsw) (e.g., "Please indicate how often you receive support with respect to your work-related duties from your spouse," Indian sample $\alpha = 0.82$); family support instrumental for family (fsinsf) (e.g., "Please indicate how often you receive support with respect to help with household tasks from your spouse," Indian sample $\alpha = 0.78$); family support emotional for work (fsemow) (e.g., "Please indicate how often you receive support in the form of listening to and discussing work-related problems from your spouse," Indian sample $\alpha = 0.77$); family support emotional for family (fsemof) (e.g., "Please indicate how often you receive support in the form of listening to and discussing family-related problems from your spouse," Indian sample $\alpha = 0.71$); and satisfaction with family support (fsgen) (e.g., in general how satisfied are you with the support you receive from your spouse, 1 = very dissatisfied to 5 = very satisfied, 6 = not applicable, Indian sample α = 0.41).

WORK–FAMILY CONFLICT

Carlson, Kacmar, & Williams (2000) established measure was used to assess the experience of work–family conflict. Their measure allows us to capture both work interfering with family (WIF) and family interfering with work (FIW) conflict. Responses were measured on a 6-point Likert-type format ranging from strongly disagree to strongly agree. Six items were used for WIF. An example item is, "My work keeps me from my family more than I would like," Indian sample α = 0.77. Six items were used for FIW. An example item is, "The time I spend on family responsibilities often interferes with my work," Indian sample α = 0.84.

NEGATIVE WORK OUTCOMES

The construct of negative work outcomes was measured using the following three variables:

1. *Job satisfaction*: Measured using Hackman & Oldham's (1975) 2-item scale. Responses were measured on a 6-point Likert-type format ranging from strongly disagree to strongly agree. Higher scores indicated higher satisfaction. A sample item from the job satisfaction scale is, "I am generally satisfied with the kind of work I do in my present job." Alpha reliability for job satisfaction for the Indian sample was 0.62.
2. *Intention to turnover*: Measured using Camman, Firchman, Jenkins, and Klesh (1979) 3-item scale. Responses were measured on a 6-point Likert-type format ranging from strongly disagree to strongly agree. Higher scores indicated higher intention to turnover. A sample item from the scale is, "I will actively look for a new job in the next year." Alpha reliability for intention to turnover for the Indian sample was 0.88.
3. *Family-interfering-with-work (FIW) guilt*: Measured using a 4-item scale developed by McElwain (2009). Responses were measured on a 6-point Likert-type format ranging from strongly disagree to strongly agree. Higher scores indicated higher WIF guilt. A sample item from the scale is, "I feel guilty for not being able to take care of my children

as well as I would like to." Alpha reliability for WIF guilt for the Indian sample was 0.84.

NEGATIVE FAMILY OUTCOMES

The construct of negative family outcomes was measured using the following three variables:

1. *Family satisfaction*: Adapted from Hackman, and Oldham's (1975) job satisfaction scale. Responses were measured on a 6-point Likert-type format ranging from strongly disagree to strongly agree. Higher scores indicated higher satisfaction. A sample item from the family satisfaction scale is, "I am generally satisfied with the role I play in my family." Alpha reliability for family satisfaction for the Indian sample respectively was 0.72 (after dropping one problematic item).
2. *Work-interfering-with-family (WIF) guilt*: Measured using a 3-item scale developed by McElwain (2009). Responses were measured on a 6-point Likert-type format ranging from strongly disagree to strongly agree. Higher scores indicated higher FIW guilt. A sample item from the scale is, "I regret missing work due to family responsibilities." Alpha reliability for FIW guilt for the Indian sample was 0.85.

NEGATIVE LIFE OUTCOMES

The construct of negative life outcomes was measured using the following two variables:

1. *Life satisfaction*: Measured using Diener, Emmons, Larsen, and Griffin's (1985) 5-item life satisfaction scale. Responses were measured on a 6-point Likert-type format ranging from strongly disagree to strongly agree. Higher scores indicated higher satisfaction. A sample item from the life satisfaction scale is, "I am satisfied with my life." Alpha reliability for life satisfaction for the Indian sample was 0.70.
2. *Psychological well-being*: Measured using Santor and Coyne's (1997) 9-item scale. Responses are measured using the following scale: 0 = less than 1–2 days and 1= 3–7 days. Higher scores indicated lower levels of psychological well-being. A sample item from the psychological well-being scale is, "During the past week, you felt depressed." Alpha reliability for the Indian sample was 0.57.

Analyses and Results

AMOS structural equation modeling program was used to test the full theoretical Frone et al. (1997) model of WFC. SEM also provided a parsimonious way for testing all hypotheses H1 to H10. (See Figure 7.2 for the entire

Figure 7.2   Original Structural Model of Work–Family Conflict Tested

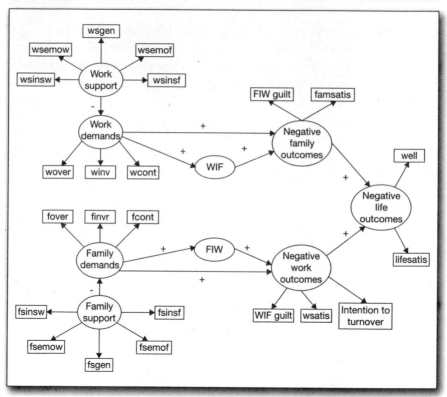

Notes: wover: work overload; fover: family overload; winv: work involvement; finv:
family involvement; wcont: work control; fcont: family control; wsinsf: work support instrumental – family related issues; wsemof: work support emotional – family
related issues; wsemow: work support emotional – work related issues; wsinsw: work
support instrumental – work related issues; fsemof: family support emotional – family related issues; fsinsf: family support instrumental – family related issues; fsemow:
family support emotional – work related issues fsinsw: family support instrumental
– work related issues; wsgen: satisfaction with general work support; fsgen: family
satisfaction with general family support; FIW: family interfering work; WIF: work-
interfering with family; FIW guilt: work-interfering-with-family guilt; famsatis: family satisfaction; lifesatis: life satisfaction; well: psychological wellbeing; WIF guilt:
work-interering-with-family guilt; wsatis: work satisfaction

causal model that was initially tested). As mentioned above, each latent construct was comprised of several observed variables that were measured using standardized scales available in the literature with some items added or modified to accommodate "emic" cultural aspects. In some scales, items were dropped to improve reliability. Data however provided very poor fit to the theoretical model: χ^2/df ratio = 12.862; RMSEA = .171; GFI = .502; IFI = .499; CFI = .497.

To try and improve fit an alternative model was attempted. In this alternative model, many indicators were dropped, and the ones that were retained had the strongest significant correlation values with conflict. (See Figure 7.3 for descriptive statistics of all the variables in the model). Therefore, work and family demands latent variables were measured with only one indicator variable of role overload. Similarly, work and family outcomes were measured with only one indicator variable of family-interfering with work (FIW) guilt and work-interfering with family (FIW) guilt respectively. Since the reliability of work and family general support variables was poor, it was dropped as an indicator of work and family support respectively. Negative life outcomes were measured using one indicator variable of life satisfaction.

Further, based on suggested modification indices provided by the SEM software of AMOS, theoretical rationale and previous research, some additional paths were added in the model and some variables and error terms were allowed to be correlated. Alterations included a path from work support to negative work outcomes, family support to negative family outcomes, work demands to negative work outcomes, family demands to negative family outcomes. (See Figure 7.4 for the alternative model.)

The alternative model provided better fit: χ^2/df ratio = 3.426; RMSEA = .077; GFI = .502; IFI = .81; CFI = .809, TLI = 0.782, RMSEA = 0.077. All paths were significant at $p < 0.001$, however not all paths had standardized coefficients in the hypothesized directions. The support variables were positively rather than negatively related to demands. Work support was positively related to work demands ($\beta = 0.35$, $p < 0.001$) and family support was positively related to family demands ($\beta = 0.76$, $p < 0.001$). Therefore, H1 and H2 were not supported. Even for the additional paths drawn between support and negative work and family outcomes to improve the fit of the alternative model, results indicated that work support was significantly and positively related to WIF guilt ($\beta = 0.16$, $p < 0.001$) and family support was significantly and positively related to FIW guilt ($\beta = 0.33$, $p < 0.001$). In other words, contrary to what may have been expected, the more the support that was received, the more was WIF and FIW guilt.

Work demands (work overload) had a significant positive relationship with WIF conflict ($\beta = 0.51$, $p < 0.001$) and family demands (family overload) had

Figure 7.3 Descriptive Statistics Matrix of Variables Included in the Study

Variables	1	2	3	4	5	6	7	8	9	10	11	12	13	14	15	16	17	18	19	20	21	22	23	24	25
wcont	1																								
winv	.62[b]	1																							
wover	.37[b]	.38[b]	1																						
fcont	.69[b]	.71[b]	.36[b]	1																					
finv	.59[b]	.65[b]	.28[b]	.62[b]	1																				
fover	.37[b]	.27[b]	.64[b]	.33[b]	.33[b]	1																			
wsgen	.28[b]	.31[b]	.17[b]	.30[b]	.28[b]	.12[a]	1																		
wsemof	.14[b]	.04	.22[b]	.12[a]	.08	.38[b]	.37[b]	1																	
wsemow	.13[b]	.18[b]	.21[b]	.17[b]	.19[b]	.22[b]	.48[b]	.56[b]	1																
wsinsf	.17[b]	.08	.23[b]	.15[b]	.07	.36[b]	.30[b]	.79[b]	.47[b]	1															
wsinsw	.11[a]	.12[a]	.24[b]	.17[b]	.12[a]	.27[b]	.37[b]	.53[b]	.67[b]	.53[b]	1														
fsgen	.29[b]	.37[b]	.16[b]	.30[b]	.30[b]	.06	.44[b]	.15[b]	.31[b]	.10[a]	.28[b]	1													
fsemof	.25[b]	.23[b]	.31[b]	.25[b]	.20[b]	.33[b]	.35[b]	.58[b]	.46[b]	.54[b]	.39[b]	.50[b]	1												
fsemow	.26[b]	.20[b]	.36[b]	.20[b]	.16[b]	.39[b]	.33[b]	.66[b]	.45[b]	.66[b]	.36[b]	.41[b]	.81[b]	1											
fsinsf	.26[b]	.30[b]	.34[b]	.26[b]	.20[b]	.33[b]	.28[b]	.53[b]	.39[b]	.61[b]	.43[b]	.49[b]	.82[b]	.76[b]	1										
fsinsw	.26[b]	.23[b]	.34[b]	.21[b]	.18[b]	.41[b]	.26[b]	.62[b]	.38[b]	.70[b]	.40[b]	.38[b]	.77[b]	.85[b]	.78[b]	1									
WIF	.30[b]	.21[b]	.50[b]	.27[b]	.14[b]	.58[b]	.13[b]	.43[b]	.17[b]	.49[b]	.20[b]	.12[a]	.37[b]	.45[b]	.40[b]	.49[b]	1								
FIW	.19[b]	.14[b]	.43[b]	.22[b]	.15[b]	.57[b]	.14[b]	.46[b]	.17[b]	.49[b]	.17[b]	.10[a]	.39[b]	.45[b]	.37[b]	.50[b]	.79[b]	1							
wksatis	.39[b]	.42[b]	.15[b]	.42[b]	.37[b]	.01	.15[b]	-.14[b]	-.01	-.15[b]	-.05	.27[b]	.08	-.02	.07	-.05	-.06	-.17[b]	1						
intturn	-.01	-.04	.24[b]	-.06	-.03	.39[b]	.15[b]	.55[b]	.24[b]	.58[b]	.28[b]	.03	.37[b]	.43[b]	.37[b]	.49[b]	.46[b]	.49[b]	-.25[b]	1					

FIW guilt	.17[b]	.10[a]	.29[b]	.13[b]	.16[b]	.58[b]	.14[b]	.44[b]	.19[b]	.43[b]	.18[b]	.07	.37[b]	.42[b]	.33[b]	.41[b]	.52[b]	.63[b]	-.19[b]	.47[b]	1				
famsatis	.39[b]	.45[b]	.09	.45[b]	.41[b]	-.01	.12[a]	-.16[b]	.01	-.21[b]	-.10	.31[b]	.03	-.05	.08	-.06	-.05	-.10[a]	.56[b]	-.25[b]	-.21[b]	1			
WIF guilt	.07	.11[a]	.27[b]	.04	.06	.42[b]	.10[a]	.42[b]	.23[b]	.43[b]	.21[b]	.12[a]	.35[b]	.42[b]	.37[b]	.46[b]	.47[b]	.53[b]	-.15[b]	.55[b]	.67[b]	-.12[a]	1		
lifesatis	.33[b]	.35[b]	.20[b]	.30[b]	.05	.23[b]	-.02	.08	-.11[a]	.06	.36[b]	.14[b]	.15[b]	.09	.04	.01	.01	.45[b]	-.07	-.04	-.49[b]	-.08		1	
well	-.08	-.13[b]	.23[b]	-.15[b]	-.14[b]	.29[b]	.04	.33[b]	.19[b]	.35[b]	.17[b]	.05	.32[b]	.34[b]	.27[b]	.37[b]	.29[b]	.40[b]	-.23[b]	.46[b]	.40[b]	-.30[b]	.40[b]	-.06	1
M	4.4	4.5	4.1	4.4	3.9	4.2	2.9	3.3	3.3	2.8	3.3	3.4	3.3	3.2	3.1	3.9	3.7	4.7	3.1	3.6	4.7	3.6	4.5	1.4	
SD	.66	.69	.97	.72	1.1	.84	1	.77	.70	1.1	.55	.57	.53	.68	.76	.86	1	.82	1.4	1.16	.76	1	.65	.21	

Notes: wover: work overload; fover: family overload; winv: work involvement; finv: family involvement; wcont: work control; fcont: family control; wsinsf: work support instrumental – family related issues; wsemof: work support emotional – family related issues; wsemow: work support emotional – work related issues; wsinsw: work support instrumental – work related issues; fsemof: family support emotional – family related issues; fsinsf: family support instrumental – family related issues; fsemow: family support emotional – work related issues fsinsw: family support instrumental – work related issues; wsgen: satisfaction with general work support; fgen: family satisfaction with general family support; FIW: family interfering work; WIF: work-interfering with family; FIW guilt: work-interfering-with-family guilt; famsatis: family satisfaction; lifesatis: life satisfaction; well: psychological wellbeing; WIF guilt: work-interering-with-family guilt; wsatis: work satisfaction.

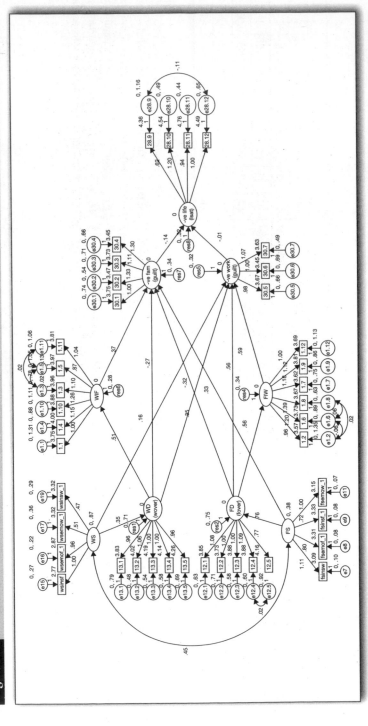

Notes: WD: Work demands; FD: Family demands; WS: Work support; FS: Family support; wover: family over-load; wsinsf: work support instrumental – family related issues; wsemof: work support emotional – family related issues; wsemow: work support emotional – work related issues; fsemof: family support emotional – family related issues; wsinsw: work support instrumental – work related issues; fsinf: family support instrumental – family related issues; fsemow: family support emotional – work related issues; fsinsw: family support instrumental – work related issues; fiw: family interfering work; wif: work–interfering with family; lifesatis: life satisfaction; -ve fam out: Negative family outcomes (WIF guilt); -ve w out: Negative work outcomes (FIW guilt).

a significant positive relationship with FIW conflict (β = 0.56, p < 0.001). Therefore, H3 and H4 were supported. However H5 was not supported because work demands (work overload) was negatively rather than positively related to negative family outcomes, i.e., WIF guilt (β = –0.27, p < 0.001). The additional path from work demands to negative work outcomes (FIW guilt) drawn to improve the fit of the alternative model also had a significant negative coefficient (β = –0.32, p < 0.001). Family demands however had a significant positive relationship with negative work outcomes (FIW guilt) as hypothesized (β = 0.56, p < 0.001). Therefore H6 was supported. The additional path from family demands to negative family outcomes (WIF guilt) was also significantly positive (β = 0.35, p < 0.001).

With regard to the relationship between conflict and outcomes, as hypothesized, WIF was significantly and positively related to negative family outcomes (WIF guilt) (β = 0.37, p < 0.001), and similarly, FIW was significantly and positively related to negative work outcomes (FIW guilt) (β = 0.59, p < 0.001). Therefore H7 and H8 were supported.

H9 and H10 hypothesized that there would be a significant positive relationship between negative work and family outcomes and negative life outcomes. In the alternative model work and family outcomes were measured with only one observed variable, viz., FIW guilt and WIF guilt respectively. Similarly just one observed variable, viz., life satisfaction measured the construct of negative life outcomes. As both of these variables were measured in such a manner that high scores indicated high values on both variables, the correct relationship between these two variables would actually be negative rather than positive. A negative relationship would appropriately indicate that as guilt increased, life satisfaction decreased. Results of analyses showed that there was indeed a significant negative relationship between WIF guilt and life satisfaction (β = –0.14, p < 0.001), and also between FIW guilt and life satisfaction (β = –0.01, p < 0.001). Therefore one could consider that H9 and H10 also found support.

Discussion

In this chapter we conducted an exploratory test within the Indian context of a commonly used theoretical model of WFC in North American, viz., the Frone, Yardley, and Markel (1997) model. We relied on a sample of 405 working men and women from two cities in India. Based on previous literature and the rationale of the theoretical model we began with the assumption that the fit indices would be adequate for India. However the original model had poor fit indices. We then made modifications in the original model and arrived at a derived "etic" model of WFC that had better "fit" for the Indian context. Although all the paths in the alternative model were significant, some of the standardized path coefficients were not in the hypothesized direction.

Indian data moderately supports within and cross domain relationships hypothesized by Frone et al. (1997). However the nature of the relationship between constructs begs further examination. Results indicated most obviously, that the relationship between support and demands and support and outcomes works differently in the Indian context. This could be because the study measured received rather than perceived support. As mentioned earlier, support for work–family conflict within the Indian context comes primarily from non-institutional sources that include family members such as spouse, parents, and parents-in-law, paid help, friends, and neighbors. The nature of this support tends to be informal, ad hoc, contingent, and bound in a web of reciprocal relationships of dependence and counter-dependence. There is always some give-and-take between the support provider and receiver, and therefore even if easily available, support is not guaranteed to alleviate conflict and stress. For instance, studies in the Indian context have indicated that support from the spouse is critical for the working woman's career, but is usually inadequate and generally non-negotiable – the woman takes what she gets and is expected to be thankful that it is no less (e.g., Ghadially and Kumar, 1988; Sekaran, 1985). Support from paid help though cheap and commonly available for purposes of household care, child care, and elder care is unorganized and not very reliable. It is fairly common among urban middle class homes to employ more than one "maid" as a back-up for the days when the primary maid absents herself from work. Even unpaid support provided by family members such as parents and parent-in-law comes with its share of duties and responsibilities that can consume a person's time and energy resources, especially as family member's age and develop health issues that need taking care of. For example, a working woman's mother-in-law may take care of her children while she is away at work, relieving the woman's worries regarding her children's well-being. However if her mother-in-law suffers from diabetes, then the responsibility of accommodating the demands placed by her health condition, for example, cooking special meals that are suitable for diabetics, falls on the working woman who may thus end up trading in one source of stress for another. Likewise, the demands to financially provide for health care expenses of the ailing mother tend to fall on the working man (son).

Similar to the relationship between family support and family demands, results indicated that work support had a positive rather than the expected negative relationship with work demands. Previous studies in the Indian context have found that paternalistic values and a nurturant-task leadership style are fairly common (e.g., Aycan et al., 2000; Sinha, 1984). The influence of the traditional family structure where members are expected to comply with the decisions of the father tends to get replicated in the workplace. Consequently, leaders are expected to maintain strong authority while subordinates are expected to accept the leader's values and to learn and imitate these values as if they were their own (Sinha, 1990). In such a work context, it is possible that supportive bosses and colleagues could inadvertently encourage employees to put in more time and effort in to work thereby increasing work demands.

Another contrary result in the Indian model was that work demands rather than increasing negative work and family outcomes (such as FIW and WIF guilt) actually reduced it. This could be because work is seen as a means to an end (good family life) and higher work demands may be tolerated as a "necessary evil," especially if it is your boss' encouragement on the job that causes you to lengthen your work day. It has been suggested that value congruence across work and family roles may be more prevalent in collectivistic cultures (Yang, 2005). This factor coupled with high power distance at work in India (Chhokar, Brodbeck, and House, 2007) and traditional division of work and family responsibilities may actually work in a curious way to buffer Indian employees to some extent from experiencing negative outcomes of high work demands. Larson, Verma, and Dworkin (2001) have reported in their study that Indian working men tend not to bring their work frustrations home because they view it their duty to provide for the family and therefore face up to the unpleasantness of work with fewer complaints.

Conclusions

To conclude the results of the study—the Indian context does provide moderate support for within and cross domain relationships between work and family domain demands and stressors and work and family outcomes as given in the Frone et al. (1997) model. However two significant differences emerge in the Indian context, viz., that support does not work as an unambiguous resource as suggested in the WFC literature, and work demands do not necessarily cause negative outcomes.

Clearly social support, whether from family or work is not a one-way street in India's relationship oriented culture. It is possible that the expectations of reciprocity could actually create more rather than less strain for working Indians. This may also explain the significant positive relationship between family and work support on the one hand and FIW and WIF guilt in the Indian model—the greater is the social support received and utilized, the more are the feelings of guilt, as future expectations of having to reciprocate the favors build up in the mind of the Indian employee.

Implications of the Study

The results suggest that appropriate work–family interventions for the Indian context could include any form of help that is reliable and comes with "no strings attached," especially in the family domain. One can clearly see a future market for childcare, household chores maintenance and eldercare facilities, that includes bonded and secure services as are offered in many developed countries. For the work front, perhaps what may be required is a culture change, where bosses begin to take more cognizance of the impact of the nature of their boss–subordinate relationships on work–family conflict. Perhaps a less benevolent leadership style could place subordinates in a position to disassociate work more easily from the rest of their lives, giving Indian employees a better chance at managing work–family balance.

Limitations of the Study

In future research on WFC in India, it may be more appropriate to treat social support as a moderator variable between demands and conflict, and between demands and outcomes, rather than as an antecedent variable as has been done in the Frone, Yardley, and Markel (1997) model. It may also be useful to examine more closely the impact of social support from different work and family sources on conflict. Finally, other than conflict, work–family balance and work–family facilitation and their relationship with demands and support could also be studied.

References

Adams, G.A., King, L.A., & King, D.W. (1996). Relationships of job and family involvement, family social support, and work-family conflict with job and life satisfaction. *Journal of Applied Psychology, 81*, 411–20.

Aryee, S. (1992). Antecedents and outcomes of work-family conflict among married professional women: Evidence from Singapore. *Human Relations, 45*, 813–37.

Aryee, S., Fields, D., & Luk, V. (1999). A cross-cultural test of a model of the work-family interface. *Journal of Management, 25*(4), 491–511.

Aryee, S., Srinivas, E.S., & Tan, H.H. (2005). Rhythms of life: Antecedents and outcomes of work-family balance in employed parents. *Journal of Applied Psychology, 90*, 32–146.

Aycan, Z., Kanungo, R.N., Mendonca, M., Yu, K., Deller, J., Stahl, G., & Kurshid, A. (2000). Impact of culture on human resource management practices: A 10-country comparison. *Applied Psychology: An International Review, 49*, 192–221.

Bharat, S. (2003), Women, work, and family in urban India: Towards new families? In J.W. Berry, R.C. Mishra, & R.C. Tripathi (Eds), *Psychology in human and social development: Lessons from diverse cultures* (pp. 155–69). New Delhi, India: SAGE Publications.

Burke, R.J. (1988). Some antecedents and consequences of work-family conflict. *Journal of Social Behavior and Personality, 3*(4), 287–302.

Burke, R.J. & Greenglass, E.R. (1999). Work-family conflict, spouse support, and nursing staff well being during organizational restructuring. *Journal of Occupational Health Psychology, 4*, 327–36.

Bruck, C.S., Allen, T.D., & Spector, P.E. (2002). The relation between work–family conflict and job satisfaction: A finer-grained analysis. *Journal of Vocational Behavior, 60*, 336–53.

Byron, K. (2005). A meta-analytic review of work-family and its antecedents. *Journal of Vocational Behavior, 67*, 169–98.

Cammann, C., Fichman, M., Jenkins, D., & Klesh, J. (1979). *The Michigan organisational assessment questionnaire*. Unpublished manuscript, University of Michigan, Ann Arbor, Michigan, USA.

Carlson, D.S., Kacmar K.M., & Williams, L.J. (2000). Construction and initial validation of a multidimensional measure of work–family conflict. *Journal of Vocational Behavior, 56*, 249–76.

Chhokar, J., Brodbeck, F., & House, R. (2007). *Culture and leadership across the world: The GLOBE book of in-depth studies of 25 societies*. Global Leadership and Organizational Behavior Effectiveness Research Program, Routledge.

Diener, E., Emmons, R.A., Larsen, R.J., & Griffin, S. (1985). The satisfaction with life Scale. *Journal of Personality Assessment, 49*, 71–75.

Eby, Lillian T., Casper, Wendy J., Lockwood, Angie, Bordeaux, Chris, & Brinley, Andi. (1980–2002). Work and family research in IO/OB: Content analysis and review of the literature. *Journal of Vocational Behavior, 66*, 124–97.

Edwards, J.R. & Rothbard, N.P. (2000). Mechanisms linking work and family: Clarifying the relationship between work and family constructs. *Academy of Management Review, 25*, 178–99.

Ford, Micheal T., Heinen, Beth A., & Langkamer, Krista L. (2007). Work and family satisfaction and conflict: A meta-analysis of cross domain relations. *Journal of Applied Psychology, 92*, 57–80.

Frone, M.R. (2000). Work-family conflict and employee psychiatric disorders: The National Comorbidity Study. *Journal of Applied Psychology, 85*, 888–95.

Frone, M.R. & Rice, R.W. (1987). Work-family conflict: The effect of job and family involvement. *Journal of Occupational Behaviour, 8*, 45–53.

Frone, M.R., Russell, M., & Cooper, M.L. (1992). Antecedents and outcomes of work family conflict: Testing a model of the work-family interface. *Journal of Applied Psychology, 77*, 65–78.

——— (1997). Relation of work-family conflict to health outcomes: A four-year longitudinal study of employed parents. *Journal of Occupational and Organizational Psychology, 70*, 325–35.

Frone, M.R., Yardley, J.K., & Markel, K.S. (1997). Developing and testing an integrative model of the work–family interface. *Journal of Vocational Behavior, 50,* 145–67.

Frone, M.R. (2003). Work–family balance. In J.C. Quick & L.E. Tetrick (Eds), *Handbook of occupational health psychology* (pp. 143–62). Washington, DC: American Psychological Association.

Ghadially, R. & Kumar, P. (1988). Bride-burning: The psycho-social dynamics of dowry deaths. In R. Ghadially (Ed.), *Women in Indian society: A reader.* New Delhi: India, SAGE.

Greenhaus, J. & Beutell, N. (1985). Sources of conflict between work and family roles. *Academy of Management Review, 10,* 76–88.

Greenhaus, J.H., Parasuuraman, S., & Collins, K.M. (2001). Career involvement and family involvement as moderators of relationships between work-family conflict and withdrawal from a profession. *Journal of Occupational Health Psychology, 6,* 91–100.

Greenhaus, J. & Powell, G. (2006). When work and family are allies: A theory of work-family enrichment. *Academy of Management Review, 31,* 72–92.

Grzywacz, J.G. & Marks, N.F. (2000). Reconceptualizing the work-family interface: An ecological perspective on the correlates of positive and negative spillover between work and family. *Journal of Occupational Health Psychology, 5,* 111–26.

Gutek, B.A., Searle, S., & Klepa, L. (1991). Rational versus gender-role explanations for work family conflict. *Journal of Applied Psychology, 76,* 560–68.

Hackman, J.R., & Oldham, G.R. (1975). Development of the job diagnostic survey. *Journal of Applied Psychology, 60,* 159–70.

Hill, E.J., Yang, C., Hawkins, A.J., & Ferris, M. (2004). A cross-cultural test of the work-family interface in 48 countries. *Journal of Marriage and the Family, 66,* 1300–16.

Kahn, R.L. & Byosiere, P. (1992). Stress in organizations. In M.D. Dunnette & L.M. Hough (Eds), *Handbook of industrial and organizational psychology* (Volume 3, Second edition, pp. 571–650). Palo Alto, CA: Consulting Psychologists Press.

Khanna, S. (1992). Life stress among working and non-working women in relation to anxiety and depression. *Psychologia, 35,* 111–16.

Kinnunen, U. & Mauno, S. (1998). Antecedents and outcomes of work-family conflict among employed women and men in Finland. *Human Relations, 51,* 157–77.

Kopelman, R.E., Greenhaus, J.H., & Connolly, T.F. (1983). A model of work, family, and interrole conflict: A construct validation study. *Organizational Behavior and Human Performance, 32,* 198–215.

Korabik, K., Lero, D., & Ayman, R. (2003). A multi-level approach to cross-cultural work-family research: A micro- and macro-level perspective. *International Journal of Cross-Cultural Management, 3*(3), 289–303.

Kossek, E.E. & Ozeki, C. (1998). Work-family conflict, policies, and the job-life satisfaction relationship: A review and directions for organizational behavior-human resources research. *Journal of Applied Psychology, 83,* 139–49.

Larson, R., Verma, S., & Dworkin, J. (2001). Men's work and family lives in India: The daily organization of time and emotion. *Journal of Family Psychology, 15*(2), 206–24.

Luk, D. & Shaffer, M. (2005). Work and family domain stressors and support: Within- and cross-domain influences on work-family conflict. *Journal of Occupational and Organizational Psychology, 78,* 489–508.

Major, V.S., Klein, K.J., & Ehrhart, M.G. (2002). Work time, work interference with family, and psychological distress. *Journal of Applied Psychology, 87,* 427–36.

Martins, L.L., Eddleston, K.A., & Veiga, J.F. (2002). Moderators of the relationship between work-family conflict and career satisfaction. *Academy of Management Journal, 45,* 399–409.

McElwain, A. & Korabik, K. (2005). Work-family guilt. In Pitt-Catsouphes, M. & Kossek, E.E. (Eds), *The work-family Encyclopedia*. Retrieved from: http://www.bc.edu/bc_org/avp/wfnetwork/rft/wfpedia

McElwain, A.K. (2009). *An examination of the reliability and validity of the work-family guilt scale*. Ph.D. dissertation, No. AAT NR47606, University of Guelph, Canada.

O'Driscoll, M.P., Ilgen, D.R., & Hildreth, K. (1992). Time devoted to job and off-job activities, interrole conflict, and affective experiences. *Journal of Applied Psychology, 77*, 272–79.

Pal, S., & Saksvik, P.O. (2006). A comparative study of work and family conflict in Norwegian and Indian hospitals. *Nordic Psychology, 58*, 298–314.

Parasuraman, S., Greenhaus, J.H., & Granrose, C.S. (1992). Role stressors, social support and well-being among two-career couples. *Journal of Organizational Behavior, 13*, 339–56.

Parasuraman, S., Purohit, Y.S., Godshalk, V.M., & Beutell, N.J. (1996). Work and family variables, entrepreneurial career success, and psychological well-being. *Journal of Vocational Behavior, 48*, 275–300.

Parasuraman, S. & Greenhaus, J.H. (2002). Toward reducing some critical gaps in work family Research. *Human Resource Management Review, 12*, 299–312.

Peterson, M.F., Smith, P.B. et al. (1995). Role conflict, ambiguity and overload: A 21 nation study. *Academy of Management, 38*(2), 429–52.

Pittman, J.F. (1994). Work/family fit as a mediator of work factor on marital tension: Evidence from the interface of greedy institutions. *Human Relations, 47*, 183–209.

Poster, W.R. & Prasad, S. (2005). Work-family relations in transnational perspective: A view from high-tech firms in India and the United States. *Social Problems, 52*, 122–46.

Rajadhyaksha, U. & Bhatnagar, D. (2000). Life role salience: A study of dual-career couples in the Indian context. *Human Relations, 53*, 489–511.

Rajadhyaksha, U. (2004). Work-family balance and dual career couples: What do organizations of the future need to know? In R. Padaki, N.M. Agarwal, C. Balaji, & G. Mahapatra (Eds), *Emerging Asia: An HR agenda*. New Delhi: Tata-McGraw Hill.

Rajadhyaksha, U. & Smita, S. (2004). Tracing a timeline for work and family research in India. *Economic and Political Weekly of India*, Review of women's studies, April 24, pp. 1674–80.

Ramu, G.N. (1989). *Women, work and marriage in urban India: A study of dual and single-earner couples*. New Delhi: SAGE Publications.

Santor, D.A. & Coyne, J.C. (1997). Shortening the CES-D to improve its ability to detect cases of depression. *Psychological Assessment, 9*, 233–43.

——— (1984). Job and life satisfaction experienced by dual-career family members. *Journal of Psychological Research, 28*, 139–44.

Sekaran, U. (1992). Middle-class dual-earner families and their support systems in urban India. In S. Lewis, D.N. Izraeli, & H. Hootsmans (Eds), *Dual-earner families: International perspectives* (pp. 46–61). Newbury Park, CA: SAGE Publications.

Sinha, J.B.P. (1980). *The nurturant task leader*. New Delhi: Concept Publishing House.

——— (1990). *Work culture in Indian context*. New Delhi: SAGE Publications.

Thomas, L.T. & Ganster, D.C. (1995). Impact of family-supportive work variables on work-family conflict and strain: A control perspective. *Journal of Applied Psychology, 80*, 6–15.

Yang, N., Chen, C.C., Choi, J., & Zou, Y. (2000). Sources of work-family conflict: A Sino-US comparison of the effects of work and family demands. *Academy of Management Journal, 43*, 113–23.

8

Work Stress, Work–Family Conflict, and Health: A Multilevel Perspective

Kamala Ramadoss

Abstract

Advances in information technologies have led to an increase in outsourcing jobs in the knowledge-based service industry from the West to the East and India has emerged as a forerunner in this sector. The goal of this study was to examine the relationship between work environment (job demands, job control, and support in the workplace), work–family conflict, and health among employees working in the Information Technology enabled Services (ITeS) in India from a multilevel perspective. Seven hundred and seventy-four employees working in 54 organizations participated in this survey. Karasek's Demand-Control-Support model and Role theory were used as the theoretical perspectives to guide this research. Multilevel modeling was used to differentiate between individual and organizational effects. Job demand and work–family conflict at the individual level were significantly related to health and the direction of the relationship was negative. There were significant differences between organizations in how supportive they were of their employees' work–family issues, and when employees reported their organizations to be more supportive then they reported better health. This study extends Karasek's Demand-Control-Support model by including work-to-family conflict in the model and also by looking at the model from a multilevel perspective, thereby delineating individual and organizational effects.

Keywords: demand-control-support model, work–family conflict, health, multilevel modeling

Introduction

The new economy is characterized by a dramatic shift from manufacturing to knowledge based service industry (Budhwar, Varma, Singh, and Dhar, 2006).

Advances in information technologies coupled with cost consciousness have led to an increase in outsourcing jobs in the knowledge-based service industry from the West to the East (Batt et al., 2005). India has emerged as a forerunner in this market by providing an attractive amalgamation of cost, quality, and scalability (PricewaterhouseCoopers, 2005). The National Association of Software and Services Companies, NASSCOM, (an apex body responsible for the Business Process Outsourcing—Information Technology Enabled Services sector in India) estimates that export revenue will reach $50.1 billion for 2010. Currently the Indian Business Process Outsourcing—Information Technology Enabled Services (ITeS) sector employs about 2 million people (National Association of Software and Services Companies, 2010).

The ITeS market in India is quite heterogeneous; the West is the principal consumer of the ITeS market. The US with a market share of 66% is the main consumer of India's ITeS, followed by Western Europe including the UK (20% of the market share). With respect to service offerings, customer care and customer services accounted for about 34% of the revenues followed by financial services (22%), administrative services (13%) and content development services which accounted for 19% of the revenues generated by the Indian ITeS market (PricewaterhouseCoopers, 2005). In terms of vertical markets, global financing (including banking, financial services, and insurance) remained the largest user of Indian ITeS followed by telecom, healthcare, airline, retail, and utilities segments (National Association of Software and Services Companies, 2010; PricewaterhouseCoopers, 2005).

What are the reasons for India's dominance in the global offshore ITeS market? The first wave of reforms in 1991 led to the liberalization of the Indian economy followed later by the second wave of reforms particularly in the highly regulated telecom industry. These economic reforms heralded the emergence of India as a preferred destination for ITeS market (Budhwar, 2001). A country-level analysis comparing India's competitive edge with respect to other countries such as China, Israel, Africa, Ireland, Czech Republic, Poland, Hungary, and Russia rated India as "Excellent" with respect to government support, labor pool, and cost, "Very good" for education system and overall climate to do business, "Good" for data/IP security and "Fair" for infrastructure, political stability, and cultural compatibility (Gartner Research, 2004). Government support include the setting up of Information Technology Parks or Special Economic Zones that provide location specific incentives like tax holiday, preferential treatment in the allocation of physical infrastructure such as power, water, telecom, etc. The labor pool includes an English speaking labor force and the availability of skilled labor to the tune of over a million graduates which includes 350,000 engineers. This particular aspect puts India ahead of other low-cost countries such as Brazil, Hungary, Philippines, and

China. Other factors including a favorable exchange rate with the dollar and the time difference between India and principal consumers in the west such as the US and UK have contributed significantly to the growth of the ITeS industry in India (PricewaterhouseCoopers, 2005; Budhwar et al., 2006).

The ITeS sector in India is not without its challenges. A major issue is high employee turnover which is estimated to be about 15–25 percent. Anecdotal and exploratory research reports the reasons for the high attrition rate to be-assuming pseudo-identities, learning a foreign accent, high burnout due to the long work hours, shift work, a mismatch between work and social life, and lack of work–family balance for employees (Singh, 2005; Sushmul, 2005 as cited in Budhwar et al, 2006). Employees in the ITeS sector report health issues such as gastric ulcer, hypertension, diabetes, clinical depression, spondylitis, etc. (Jayaswal, 2005; Wadhwa, 2004). Human Resources personnel and managers in ITeS centers reported stressful work conditions and its effect on health as one of the major challenges faced by employees working in these centers leading to high attrition (Budhwar et al., 2006; Mehta, Armenakis, Mehta, and Irani, 2006). This chapter extends previous research by examining the effects of the stressors in the work environment (particularly job demands and work–family conflict) and resources available to employees in the workplace (such as organizational support and job control) on employees' self-reported health from a multilevel (specifically, individual, and organizational effects) perspective.

Work Environment

Among the various aspects in the work environment that affects employees in the workplace, in this study, the focus is on job demands, job control, and support in the workplace. Jobs in the ITeS sector are very demanding with daily and monthly targets that need to be met. Moreover, pay and benefits are linked to performance—employees' own performance and that of their teams. One such incentive is performance based incentive scheme. The parameters for calculation of performance-based monetary benefit are process performance, that is, speed, accuracy, and productivity of each process (PricewaterhouseCoopers, 2005; Suri and Rizvi, 2008). Closely allied to the concept of job demands are job control and support in the workplace. For instance, the concept of job control (such as autonomy, workgroup control, task, and routine control) relates to how workers can reduce or cope with exposure to occupational stressors. Tausing and Fenwick (2001) observed that alternate work schedule (such as shift work) does not necessarily lead to work–family conflict. Perceived control of work schedules increases work–family balance, net of work, and family characteristics.

Furthermore, the subjective experience of stress may be further exacerbated (or decreased) depending on the social support available in the workplace (Cohen and Syme, 1985; Smith and Gardner, 2007). Organizational support includes both formal family-supportive policies and benefits, such as those administered through Human Resources departments, and informal family-supportive work cultures. For instance, analyses of data from the 2002 National Study of the Changing Workforce revealed that a more family-supportive work culture was related to increased job satisfaction, increased organizational commitment, increased life satisfaction, decreased work-life interference, and decreased mental health problems (Bond et al., 2002). Further analyses of the data from the National Study of the Changing Workforce revealed that job autonomy and informal organizational support were associated with job satisfaction, family satisfaction, life satisfaction, stress and well-being, turnover intentions, positive spillover, and family–work conflict (Thompson and Prottas, 2006).

In studying employees' health, the demands-control-support model is often used to explain how the work environment affects an employee's health situation. Karasek (1979) hypothesized that jobs characterized by high-demand and low control (Demand-Control or DC model) will create arousal which will be directed internally with severe consequences including fatigue and exhaustion. As this model was not comprehensive to explain stress, Johnson and Hall (1988) included support into the model and stated that workers in jobs with high demands, low control, and low support on the job would report poor health. As a refinement of the earlier model, Karasek and Theorell (1990), added support as a third dimension (Demand-Control/Support or DC/S model) to their original job demands-control model.

A large body of research has tested Karasek's model and the results did not always support the hypothesis (for reviews, see de Jonge and Kompier, 1997; de Lange et al., 2004; Kristensen, 1996; Theorell and Karasek, 1996; van der Doef and Maes, 1999). There is modest support in the literature for the strain and iso-strain hypotheses; support for the moderating effects of job control and support is less consistent (van der Doef and Maes, 1999). With the exception of a few studies (e.g., Van Yperen and Snijders, 2000), failure to differentiate between individual and contextual effects has led to inconsistent findings being reported (Allen et al., 2000; Van der Doef and Maes, 1999). Moreover, Karasek's model was proposed at a time when employees' work and family life was on the same time. This is not always the case for the workforce in today's global economy. The type of work done in ITeS is characterized by long work hours, a mismatch between work and family/social life. When people in India work with clients in the UK and US, it results in working in evening and/or graveyard shifts, because of the time difference between the two countries. As a consequence employees working in the ITeS in India report a lack of work–family balance (Singh, 2005; Sushmul, 2005; as cited in Budhwar et al, 2006).

In order to help employees balance their work and non-work lives, organizations in the ITes sector in India offer various work-life benefits such as job sharing, schedule flexibility, services such as gymnasiums, day-care facilities, cafeteria, laundry facilities, and rest area with futons to sleep on during breaks (Uma Devi, 2002). According to Organizational Support Theory, employees have a tendency to attribute humanlike characteristics to the organization, which results in perceived organizational support (Eisenberger et al., 1986; Rhoades and Eisenberger, 2002; Shore and Shore, 1995). This personification is brought about by:

1. The fact that organizations assume legal, moral, and financial responsibility for the actions of its agents (supervisors, managers).
2. The organizational policies, norms, and culture that prescribe role behaviors and provide continuity.
3. The power that agents of the organizations (managers, supervisors) have over their subordinates.

Based on this personification of the organization, employees tend to view the treatment received from the organization (both favorable and unfavorable) as an indication of how much the organization cares about the employees' well-being as also the extent to which the employee's contributions are valued by the organization.

In summary, Organizational Support Theory postulates that employees develop perceived organizational support to determine the organization's readiness to reward increased efforts made on its behalf (indicating the organization's proclivity to provide help when needed to carry out one's job effectively), and also to meet their own socio-emotional needs (Eisenberger, Huntington, Hutchinson, and Sowa, 1986; Shore and Shore, 1995). Employees, therefore, trade effort and dedication to their organization for incentives such as pay, fringe benefits, esteem, approval, and caring (Eisenberger et al., 1986). However, organizations differ in how supportive they are of their employees and it is important to study the same.

WORK–FAMILY CONFLICT

Work and family issues have been extensively studied for the past four decades (for recent reviews, see Allen et al., 2000; Frone, Russell, and Cooper, 1992). A major theme in this literature is that both work and family responsibilities demand time and energy. When employees are unable to cope with the conflicting demands of work and family, they may experience work–family conflict. Increased work–family conflict has been found to be associated with (*a*) poor health outcomes such as increased depressive symptoms (Frone, 2000; Hammer et al., 2005) and decreased physical health (Allen and Armstrong, 2006; Frone, Russell, and Cooper, 1997); (*b*) reduced levels of reported life satisfaction (Allen, 2001; Kossek and Ozeki, 1998) and marital satisfaction (Neal and Hammer, 2007); and (*c*) compromised work-related outcomes such as lower job satisfaction (Kossek and Ozeki, 1998; Allen et al., 2000) and less commitment to the employer (Lyness and Thompson, 1997). Excessive work–family conflict, therefore, presents challenges for employees, their families, employers, and for society as a whole (MacDermid, 2005; Parasuraman and Greenhaus, 2000).

For the most part, the basis for theory and research related to conflict between family and work roles comes from Role theory (MacDermid, 2005). According to Role Theory, conflict occurs when the demands of one domain (work) are incompatible with demands of the other (family). Role conflict is defined as the "simultaneous occurrence of two (or more) sets of pressures such that compliance with one would make more difficult compliance with the other" (Kahn et al., 1964: 19). Extending Kahn and colleagues' hypothesis, Greenhaus and Beutell (1985) defined work–family conflict as "a form of inter-role conflict in which the role pressures from the work and family domains are mutually incompatible in some respect" (Greenhaus and Beutell, 1985: 19). They also defined three specific forms of conflict, namely, (*a*) time-based conflict (when involvement in one role is weighed down by time pressures in the other); (*b*) strain-based conflict (when performance in one role is affected by tension in the other); and (*c*) behavior-based conflict (when fulfilling the requirements of one role is made more difficulty by the behavior required in the other). Role conflict is thought to be greater when these roles are central to the individual's sense of self and when there is pressure to conform to expectations in a role (Greenhaus and Beutell, 1985; Kahn et al., 1964).

Although there was initial support for Kahn (1964) and Greenhaus and Beutell's (1985) hypotheses (MacDermid, 2005), subsequent research indicated that occupying multiple roles did not necessarily result in conflict (by using up resources and energy) but that occupying multiple roles may in fact be beneficial in some instances. For example, positive experiences in one role were found to offset the effects of negative experiences in another role (Baruch and Barnett, 1986; Marks, 1977; Ruderman et al., 2002; Sieber, 1974). Participation in multiple roles was also associated with increased levels of well-being (Kandel, Davies, and Ravies, 1985; Thoits, 1983; Verbrugge, 1983). Factors associated with the quality of the role experience include personal, dispositional factors, situational factors, and social support. Contemporary thinking focuses on the premise that conflict between work and family can originate from either domain and that different antecedents produce the conflict arising from each domain. Two distinct constructs have been proposed, namely work-to-family conflict and family-to-work conflict, and research suggests that family "boundaries" are more permeable than job "boundaries," resulting in a higher prevalence of work-to-family conflict (Carlson and Frone, 2003; Frone, Yardley, and Markel, 1997).

Work–family conflict has been associated with situational factors such as job demands and control (Karasek, 1979) and with contextual factors such as family-friendly policies, a family supportive work culture or supervisor support (Allen, 2001; Thompson, Beauvais, and Lyness, 1999; O' Driscoll et al., 2003; Thomas and Ganster, 1995). There is some research evidence in Western literature that high work–family conflict is associated poor health outcomes, both physical health (Frone, Russell, and Cooper, 1997; Thomas and Ganster, 1995) and psychological health (Frone, Russell, and Cooper, 1992; O' Driscoll et al. 2003) as reported by employees. A similar trend is seen in exploratory research done on employees engaged in ITeS in India; there is some research evidence that work environment is associated poor health outcomes for employees working in the ITeS (Subramanian and Vinothkumar, 2009; Suri and Rizvi, 2008) which then leads to high attrition rates (Budhwar et al., 2009; Mehta et al., 2006). Consequently, it is important to examine the relationship between work variables (such as job demands, job control, and support) and work–family conflict on health from a multilevel perspective (Refer Figure 8.1 for a conceptual model).

The major focuses of this investigation are guided by the following hypotheses:

- Hypothesis-1: At the individual level, job demand will be significantly related to health and the direction of the relationship will be negative, such that higher job demands will be related to poorer health.
- Hypothesis-2: At the individual level, job control will be significantly related to health and the direction of the relationship will be positive, such that higher job control will be related to better health.

Figure 8.1   Conceptual Model

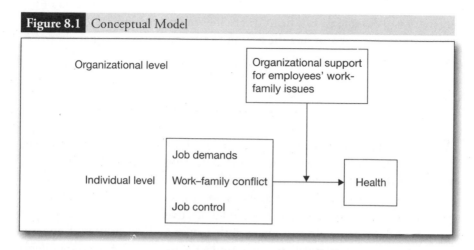

- Hypothesis-3: At the individual level, work–family conflict will be significantly related to health and the direction of the relationship will be negative, such that higher work–family conflict will be related to poorer health.
- Hypothesis-4: Organizations will differ in how supportive they are of their employees and higher levels of organizational support will be significantly related to better health as reported by employees.

Method

PROCEDURES

Human resources managers of various ITeS centers in south and western India were contacted and permission to recruit participants was obtained. Due to heightened security in ITeS centers, the investigator was allowed access to the reception area and cafeteria. Research participants were recruited from the cafeteria when they were there for their break periods. Snowball technique was also used to recruit participants for the study. A total of 804 respondents participated in the study but only 774 returned usable surveys (30 people completed only a page of the survey and could not be used in the study; as the information available was very limited it was not possible to evaluate if the people who did not complete the full survey were significantly different from those who did). The final sample comprised of 774 respondents who participated in the study and the research participants were from 54 organizations from three cities in western India and one city in south India. Participants had the option to use the survey in either electronic format or paper–pencil format.

SAMPLE

A majority of the sample of employees surveyed in the ITeS centers were male (79%); 76% of the respondents reported as being single, 23% reported as being married and 1% included divorced, separated, and widowed. Nineteen percent of the sample reported as living in extended family and 76% of the respondents reported as living in nuclear family, that is, living with parents and siblings if one was single and living with spouse and/or children if one was married. This was a relatively young sample; the mean age of the respondents was 25.46 years. These findings are similar to those reported in the literature (Budhwar et al., 2009; Mehta, Armenakis, Mehta, and Irani, 2006; Poster and Prasad, 2005) wherein employees in the ITeS sector in India tend to be relatively young in age. Total work experience reported was 3 years on average and tenure on the current job was 1.9 years on average. Employees were engaged in various types of services such as customer care and customer services, financial services, administrative services, health services such as medical transcription, and content development services and worked in organizations that were both captive units and third-party service providers.

MEASURES

Health: The scale developed and standardized by Derogatis, Rikels, and Rock (1976) was used to measure employees' self-reported health. This scale was then given to two Human Resources managers and five employees working in Business Process Outsourcing centers in India for their feedback. The final scale included eight items related to physical health such as "In the past two weeks how often did you have trouble sleeping, have back pain, have severe headaches, have stomach pains due to hyperacidity or ulcer, etc." Response categories included Never (coded 1) to all the time (coded 5). The items were reverse coded so that a higher score indicated better self-reported physical health. The mean was 3.67, standard deviation was 0.78, and scale reliability was 0.79.

Job demands: This scale includes items related to job complexity and the items were drawn from Fenwick and Olsen's (1986) scale and Karasek's skill discretion scale. These items related to the degree to which a worker has to work hard, challenges in job about learning new skills, etc. A higher score indicated greater job demands. The mean was 3.63, standard deviation was 0.83 and Cronbach's alpha was 0.65. Factor analysis was done and a single factor was extracted using the criteria of eigenvalue greater than 1.00. Bartlett's test of sphericity was significant ($p < 0.01$) and all factor loadings were above 0.30.

Job control: This scale combined items from Fenwisk and Olsen's (1986) scale related to decision latitude and items from Schat and Kelloway's (2000) scale related to predictability in the job and work environment, because they represent three aspects of the job control concept. The response categories ranged from 1 (strongly disagree) to 5 (strongly agree) and higher scores indicated greater job control. The mean was 3.42, standard deviation was 0.63 and Cronbach's alpha was 0.63. As the reliability computed for job control was less than the recommended 0.70, factor analysis was done and a single factor was extracted using the criteria of eigenvalue greater than 1.00. Bartlett's test of sphericity was significant ($p < 0.01$) and all factor loadings were above 0.30.

Work–family conflict: This scale included items from MacDermid et al. (1999) regarding the impact of work/life tension on personal life. Responses ranged from rarely (coded 1) to almost always (coded 5) to the following statements that were prefixed by the question: "How often in the past three months have you experienced the following?—"I came home from work too tired to do some of the things I wanted to do"; "My job made it difficult to maintain the kind of relationships with my family that I would like"; "My work schedule or shift made it difficult for me to fulfill personal responsibilities"; "Because of my job, I didn't have enough time to participate in the leisure and recreational activities I find relaxing and enjoyable"; "My job caused me to behave in ways that are unacceptable at home." A higher score indicated more work–family conflict. The mean for work–family conflict scale was 3.08, the standard deviation was 0.68 and scale reliability was 0.73.

Organizational support: A report of organizational support for employees' work–family issues was obtained and included items from the National Study of the Changing Workforce (2002) on organizational support for work–family issues. Response categories range from strongly disagree (coded 1) to strongly agree (coded 5) to the following statements—"There is an unwritten rule at my company that you cannot take care of family needs on company time"; "My company does not look favorably on employees who put their family or personal needs ahead of their jobs"; "If employees have a problem managing their work and family responsibilities, the company believes that: 'they made their bed, now they must lie in it.'" Reverse coding was done for all three items so that higher score indicated greater organizational support for employees' work–family issues. Other items included statements such as: "My company really cares about me" and "My company is willing to help me when I need a special favor." A higher score indicated greater organizational support. The mean for organizational support was 3.38, the standard deviation was 0.88 and scale reliability was 0.76. Using the aggregate function in SPSS, a level 2 dataset was created for the variable organizational support. For each of the 54 organizations, the average score of all the employees' report of organizational support for that particular organization was computed into one aggregate score of organizational support for that particular organization and so on till all 54 aggregate scores of organizational support were computed.

Data Analysis

Data management was done using SPSS as HLM software is not a standalone software. The data was analyzed using HLM 6.02 software to conduct multilevel modeling analyses. This technique takes into consideration the nested data structure of organizational data. Data collected in the workplace from employees is hierarchical in nature because 774 employees were nested within 54 different organizations. Conventional analyses such as OLS regression and ANOVA assume that observations are independent of one another. Data collected from research participants from the same organization violates the assumption that observations are independent of one another as every organization has a unique culture. When autocorrelation (or more formally intra-class correlation or ICC) is present, information coming from the same unit (as in employees in the same organization) tends to be more alike than information from independent units (such as data from a set of unrelated workers). Due to this autocorrelation, some of the information in a nested dataset is redundant. When we use conventional regression models, it fails to adjust for the intra-class correlation and so tends to give a smaller standard error for the coefficient of interest than it should be, thereby making a finding spuriously significant (Raudenbush and Bryk, 2002).

Multilevel modeling is a more appropriate technique for analyzing nested data because multilevel modeling corrects for autocorrelation and gives more robust standard errors. Second, multilevel modeling allows researchers to differentiate between individual and organizational effects. Third, multilevel modeling allows researchers to ask more interesting research questions. We can test how individual characteristics interact with organizational characteristics and therefore test the joint level (or cross-level interactions) effects on the outcome (Hofman, 1997; Raudenbush and Bryk, 2002).

For the purpose of these analyses, job demands, job control, and work–family conflict were entered into the model at the individual level and organizational support was entered into the model at the organizational level as organizations tend to differ in how supportive they are of their employees. At the organizational level, grand mean centering of the variable, organizational support, was done. In the grand mean centered model, the explanatory variable is centered on the overall mean. This is the standard procedure of choice of location for X_{ij} in the classical ANCOVA model and the procedure includes subtracting the mean for the entire sample from each observation in the sample. When grand mean centering is used, the expected outcome (β_{0j}) is the expected outcome for a case whose value on predictor 'X' is equal to the grand mean. Grand mean centering also yields an intercept that can be interpreted as an adjusted mean for group 'j'. Similarly, τ_{00} or the variance of β_{0j} is the variance among the level-2 units in the adjusted means (Raudenbush and Bryk, 2002: 33).

Results

Prior to conducting multilevel modeling analyses, one needs to first ascertain if it is desirable to conduct multilevel modeling analyses by computing intraclass correlation. Intra-class correlation is the coefficient of between organizational variance (τ_{00}) and the sum of between-organization variance (τ_{00}) and within-organization variance (σ^2). Intra-class correlation indicates the proportion of variance between groups, that is, how much of the variance in the outcome is due to organizational effects. A high intra-class correlation indicates that much of the variation in the outcome variable is due to organizational effects and signifies the need to do multilevel analyses (Raudenbush and Bryk, 2002).

Intra-class correlation was computed for the outcome variables of interest, health. Intra-class correlation was computed by performing an unconditional ANOVA with random effects (Raudenbush and Bryk, 2002: 36) with outcome variable, health, and no predictors in the model.

Individual level: (health)ij = $\beta_{0j} + r_{ij}$
Organizational level: $\beta_{0j} = \gamma_{00} + u_{0j}$

Where "i" denotes individual, "j" denotes organization, "r" is error variance at the individual level and "u" is error variance at the organizational level. From the output, the between-organization variance (τ_{00}) was 0.09 and the within organization variance (σ^2) was 0.54 and intra-class correlation computed was

0.14. This means that 86% of the variance in health for this sample can be attributed to individual level factor(s) and 14 percent of the variability in health can be attributed to organizational level factor(s), thereby suggesting the need to conduct multilevel modeling analyses.

The results of a sequence of multilevel models associated with health as the outcome variable of interest are presented in Table 8.1. Model 1 includes the effect an unconditional ANOVA with random effects (colloquially known as an empty model because there are no predictors in the model), on employees' health. Model 2 addresses individual level effects whereas Model 3 addresses organizational level effects. Specifically, Model 2 presents the results for hypotheses 1, 2, and 3 which predicted that high job demands, low job control, and high work–family conflict will be significantly related to poorer health at the individual level. Model 3 presents the results for hypotheses 4 which predicted that there will be significant differences between organizations in how supportive organizations are and organizational support will moderate the relationship between high job demands, low job control, and high work–family conflict on health. In other words,

At the individual level (or level 1):

$$(\text{health})_{ij} = \beta_{0j} + \beta_{1j} \text{ (job demands)} + \beta_{2j} \text{ (job control)} + \beta_{3j} \text{ (work–family conflict)} + r_{ij}$$

At the organizational level (or level 2):

$$\beta_{0j} = \gamma_{00} + \gamma_{01} \text{ (organizational support)}_{0j} + U_{0j}$$
$$\beta_{1j} = \gamma_{10} + U_{1j}$$
$$\beta_{2j} = \gamma_{20} + U_{2j}$$
$$\beta_{3j} = \gamma_{30} + U_{3j}$$

The intercept of Model 1 shows that employees employed in ITeS centers in India reported above average health situation (Estimate = 3.76, $p < .01$). Model 2 presents the results of hypotheses 1, 2, and 3; at the individual level, job demands (Estimate $= -0.15$, $p < .01$) and work–family conflict (Estimate $= -0.15$, $p < .01$) were significantly related to health and the direction of these relationships were negative, that is, when employees reported higher job demands and higher work–family conflict then they reported poorer health. However, job control was not significantly related to health (Estimate $= 0.05$) and the direction of the relationship was in the hypothesized direction, that is individuals reporting greater job control reported better health but this relationship was not statistically significant. From these results it is seen that

Table 8.1 Multilevel Model Results Predicting Health from Organizational and Individual Level Variables Using Full Maximum Likelihood Estimation (N = 774 Individuals from 54 Organizations)

	Health					
	Model 1		Model 2		Model 3	
Predictors	Unstandardized Coefficient	SE	Unstandardized Coefficient	SE	Unstandardized Coefficient	SE
Organizational-level						
Organizational support (γ_{01})					.56**	.19
Individual-level						
Intercept (γ_{00})	3.76**	.06	4.87**	.21	4.61**	.21
Job demands (β_{1j})			-.15**	.05	-.15**	.05
Job control (β_{2j})			.05	.05	.05	.05
Work-family conflict (β_{3j})			-.15**	.06	-.16**	.06
Estimated parameters	3		6		7	
Deviance	1769.90		1737.29**		1728.85**	

Note: Convergence criterion = .001.
*$p < .05$. **$p < .01$.

there is support for hypothesis-1 and hypothesis-3 but hypothesis-2 is not supported. From the results of the deviance statistics (1737.29, $p < .01$), it is seen that Model 2 is significantly different from Model 1, that is, variables entered in Model 2 (job demands, job control, and work–family conflict) explain unique variance in health at the individual level.

Model 3 presents the results of hypotheses 4. There were significant differences between organizations in how supportive they are of their employees work and family issues (Estimate = 0.56, $p < .01$) and support at the organizational level moderated the effects of high job demands and high work–family conflict on health. The direction of the relationship was in the hypothesized direction, that is, when employees perceived their organizations to be supportive of their work and family issues, then they reported better health. There is support for hypothesis 4 and Model 3 was found to be significantly different that Model 2. From the results of the deviance statistics (1728.85, $p < .01$) it is seen that Model 3 is significantly different from Model 2, that is, organizational support explained unique variance in health at the organizational level over and above the variance explained by variables in Model 2 which were at the individual level. Taken together, high job demands and high work–family conflict were significantly related to poor health at the individual level. But when employees perceived their organizations to be supportive of their work and family issues then support at the organizational level moderated the effect of high job demands and high work–family conflict at the individual level among employees in ITeS in India. Moreover, organizations are different significantly from each other in how supportive they were of their employees' work and family issues.

Discussion

The phenomenal growth of the ITeS sector put India on the global map and India is seen as one of the emerging economies. In a knowledge-based sector such as ITeS sector, employees are a valuable resource. As employees in the ITeS sector work mostly with clients in the West, they tend to work long hours and/or engaged in shift work. In an exploratory study of employees in the ITeS sector, 79% reported that the call center job is a physically draining one and 76% reported that call center job affected their health in some way or other (Budhwar et al., 2009). This paper extends previous research by examining the effects of the stressors in the work environment, particularly high job demands and work–family conflict and resources available to employees in the workplace such as organizational support and job control to alleviate the effect of these stressors on employees' self-reported health from a multilevel perspective.

Multilevel modeling analyses revealed that high job demands were significantly associated with poor health. Jobs in the ITeS sector are very demanding with daily and monthly targets that need to be met. Moreover, pay and benefits are linked to performance—employees' own performance and that of their team's. One such incentive is performance-based incentive scheme. The parameters for calculation of performance-based monetary benefit are process performance, that is, speed, accuracy and productivity of each process (PricewaterhouseCoopers, 2005). High job demands were, therefore, associated with poor self-reported health. These findings are supported by previous research (Budhwar et al., 2009; Subramanian and Vinothkumar, 2009; Suri and Rizvi, 2008). Furthermore, participants in this study were a relatively young sample; the mean age of the respondents was 25.46 years. Total work experience reported was 3 years on average and experience on the current job was 1.9 years on average. During data collection one constant theme that the researcher heard from the respondents with respect to their jobs is "one should make hay while the sun shines," meaning that if one works hard and is very productive then one's take-home pay is substantially higher as monetary incentives are tied to productivity. This may come at a price though as in the long-term it may lead to poorer health. Further research is needed to investigate the long-term effects of working in a stressful work environment.

High work–family conflict was found to be significantly related to poor health. Similar findings were reported both in Western literature and research done on employees in ITeS centers in India. In the Western literature, increased work–family conflict has been found to be associated with poor health outcomes such as increased depressive symptoms (Frone, 2000; Hammer et al., 2005) and decreased physical health (Allen and Armstrong, 2006; Frone, Russell, and Cooper, 1997). There is some evidence that stressful work conditions and its effect on health is a major challenge faced by employees working in ITeS centers (Budhwar et al., 2006; Mehta et al., 2006). Employees working in ITeS have to deal with issues such as assuming pseudo-identities, learning a foreign accent, high burnout due to the long work hours, shift work, a mismatch between work and social life, and lack of work–family balance for employees (Singh, 2005; Sushmul, 2005, as cited in Budhwar et al., 2006).

The moderating effects of job control at the individual level and support for work–family issues at the organizational level to alleviate work stress and work–family conflict on health were tested. Job control was not significantly related to health. Unlike ITeS centers in the West (Hutchinson, Purcell, and Kinnie, 2000), those in India are characterized by a highly controlled environment with employees having very little autonomy on the job. Budhwar et al. (2009) reported low job control as one of the reasons for the high attrition in ITeS centers in India. With respect to support for employees' work and family issues, in the ITeS sector, organizations provide a wide range of work-life policies and benefits but organizations differ in the type and number of supportive work-life policies and benefits they provide to their employees (Uma Devi, 2002). According to neo-institutional theory (DiMaggio and Powell, 1991), adopting family-friendly policies has an economic value (recruiting and retaining talented labor), and is also a means to maintain legitimacy in a climate where incorporating family-friendly policies is normative. There is some concern among experts, however, that organizational support for employees' work–family issues has not been very successful in helping employees in the Business Process Outsourcing sector in India balance their work-life demands (Rajadhyaksha, 2009).

In order to test this concern among experts, multilevel modeling analyses were done and there is support for the hypothesis that organizations significantly differ in how supportive they are for their employees' work–family issues and the more supportive they were their employees reported better health. In the ITeS sector, "poaching of employees" by competitive firms is an important challenge (Budhwar et al., 2009) and the significance of organizational support is very important in this context. Results from this analysis are supported by research done in the US Analyses of data from the 2002 National Study of the Changing Workforce revealed that a more family-supportive work culture was related to increased job satisfaction, increased organizational commitment, increased life satisfaction, decreased work-life interference, and decreased mental health problems (Bond et al., 2002). Further analyses of the data from the National Study of the Changing Workforce revealed that job autonomy and informal organizational support were associated with job satisfaction, family satisfaction, life satisfaction, stress and well-being, turnover intentions, positive spillover, and family–work conflict (Thompson and Prottas, 2006). In conclusion, from the overall model, it is seen that low job demands, low work–family conflict at the individual level and support at the organizational level were significantly associated with better health. This model explained 12% of the variance in health among employees working in the ITeS sector. A unique contribution of this study is that it extends Karasek's Demand-Control-Support model by including work-to-family conflict in the model and also by looking at the model from a multilevel perspective, thereby delineating individual and organizational effects.

IMPLICATIONS FOR FUTURE RESEARCH

The reliabilities for job demand variable and job control variable was below the acceptable norm of 0.70 although a single factor was extracted for each of these two scales. Future research needs to focus on developing a better measure of job demands and job control for employees working in the ITeS sector as they face a unique set of circumstances. To measure job demands one needs to include items such as those related to daily, weekly and/or monthly targets, the mismatch, if any, between training and job requirements as an employee who feels less prepared for a task will find the task more challenging, and whether or not one is engaged in shift work. Similarly, there is the need to explore the job control variable in ITeS sector. Budhwar et al. (2009) reported that jobs in ITeS are characterized by a lack of control as these jobs include a very high level of scrutiny. This aspect needs to be further investigated in future studies.

This survey used a cross-sectional research design; consequently causal statements cannot be made. Data was collected from single informants, namely, employees working in the ITeS sector. Data from multiple informants such as colleagues and supervisors will enrich the data quality in future studies. Also, surveys need to be complemented with other methods such as daily dairy method. Majority of the respondents in this study were male and single. Future studies need to include more women and married people, particularly parents in the study. The type and nature of the job should be taken into consideration in future studies as job demands may vary depending on the type of work done. For example, a customer service representative needs to be constantly available and work with customers whereas someone working in process development may have relatively more control over their work day. Also, in this study the focus was on employees nested in organizations and therefore a 2-level model was used. In reality, employees are nested in workgroups which are further nested in organizations. Future studies need to include workgroup level effects on health and a 3-level model needs to be used, thereby delineating individual, workgroup level, and organizational level effects. Moreover, an important challenge for organizations is the high attrition rate. Therefore, future studies need to look at the impact of the stressors (such as high job demands and work–family conflict) and the moderating effect of resources available in the workplace for managing work–family issues on absenteeism, organizational commitment, and employees' turnover intentions.

IMPLICATIONS FOR POLICY AND PRACTICE

An aspect leading to high job demands over which neither employees nor organizations have any control is the lack of continuous power supply. Data collection was done in India during the summer when unscheduled power outages for a few minutes or hours are common. This creates a problem for time sensitive service providers, for example, employees working in organizations providing customer service to a 24-hour online bidding for a product. To cope with this issue, organizations typically spread themselves to multiple sites in the same city or nearby cities (some organizations have started operations in nearby East Asian countries like Philippines to combat the issue of power outages due to inclement weather particularly during monsoon period in India). When there is an unscheduled power outage in one site, the nearby sites that have electric power supply pick up the workload. All trained personnel regardless of rank attend to the job and anyone who is on break is pulled back onto the job till the crisis is over. This increases the job demands and stress experienced by employees. Government needs to ensure better infrastructure facilities for ITeS centers not only in the Special Economic Zones but at all sites.

Organizations need to adopt cultural sensitive practices that can help alleviate stress and burnout. There is some evidence that mindfulness programs such as yoga and meditation which have been practiced in the Indian subcontinent for hundreds of years help alleviate stress and these needs to be incorporated in the workplace. Furthermore, it does not suffice to offer one-time events such as a seminar or workshop conducted by Brahmakumaris or Art of living institutes on mindfulness meditation. These need to be incorporated on a more regular basis. Currently the ITeS sector in India is in its nascent phase and organizations are more occupied with growth, development, and consolidation of businesses. But programs aimed at investing in employees' health would be a sound long-term investment.

Conclusion

India has emerged as the preferred destination for the knowledge-based service sector. A major challenge faced by the ITeS sector in India is high attrition;

anecdotal and exploratory research suggests that long work hours, lack of balance between work and family life leading to poor health as some of the important reasons for this high attrition rate. Findings from this investigation show that high job demands and high work–family conflict were significantly related to poor health at the individual level. At the organizational level, organizations significantly differed from each other in how supportive they were of their employees' work and family issues. Furthermore, when employees perceived their organization to be supportive of their work and family issues then support at the organizational level moderated the effect of high job demands and high work–family conflict on employees' health. Thus it is seen that workplaces in today's global economy are stress inducing and this has a negative effect on employees' physical and psychological health. This is an important area that needs to be researched further as understanding the antecedents and consequences of workplace stress can help design interventions and workplace policies that will mitigate this stress leading to better quality of life for all employees.

References

Allen, T.D. (2001). Family supportive work environments: The role of organizational perceptions. *Journal of Vocational Behavior, 58*, 414–35.

Allen, T.D. & Armstrong, J. (2006). Further examination of the link between work-family conflict and physical health: The role of health-related behaviors. *American Behavioral Scientist, 49*, 1204–21.

Allen, T.D., Herst, D.E.L., Bruck, C.S., & Sutton, M. (2000). Consequences associated with work-family conflict: A review and agenda for future research. *Journal of Occupational Health Psychology, 5*, 278–308.

Baruch, G.K., & Barnett, R.C. (1986). Role quality, multiple role involvement, and psychological well-being in midlife women. *Journal of Personality and Social Psychology, 51*, 578–85.

Batt, R., Doellgast, V., Kwon, H., Nopany, M., Nopany, P., & da Costa, A. (2005). The Indian call centre industry: National benchmarking report strategy, HR practices, & performance. CAHRS Working Paper, No. 05–07, Cornell University, School of Industrial and Labor Relations, Center for Advanced Human Resource Studies, Ithaca, NY.

Bond, J. T., Thompson, C., Galinsky, E., & Prottas, D. (2002). *Highlights of the national study of the changing workforce.* New York: Families and Work Institute.

Budhwar, P.S. (2001). Doing business in India. *Thunderbird International Business Review, 43*(4), 549–68.

Budhwar, P.S., Varma, A., Malhotra, N., & Mukherjee, A. (2009). Insights into the Indian call center industry: Can internal marketing help tackle high employee turnover? *Journal of Services Marketing, 23*(5), 351–62.

Budhwar, P.S., Varma, A., Singh, V., & Dhar, R. (2006). HRM systems of Indian call centers: An exploratory study. *International Journal of Human Resources Management, 17*(5), 881–97.

Carlson, D.S. & Frone, M.R. (2003). Relation of behavioral and psychological involvement to a new four-factor conceptualization of work-family interference. *Journal of Business and Psychology, 17*, 515–35.

Cohen, S. & Syme, S.L. (1985). *Social support and health.* San Diego, CA: Academic Press.

de Jonge, J. & Kompier, M.A.J. (1997). A critical examination of the Demand-Control-Support Model from a work psychological perspective. *International Journal of Stress Management, 4*, 235–58.

de Lange, A.H., Taris, T.W., Kompier, M.A.J., Houtman, I.L.D., & Bongers, P.M. (2004). The relationship between work characteristics and mental health: Examining normal, reversed and reciprocal relationships in a 4-wave study. *Work and Stress, 18*, 149–66.

Derogatis, L.R., Rikels, K., & Rock, A.F. (1976). The SCL–90 and MMPI: A step in the validation of a new self report scale. *British Journal of Psychiatry, 128*, 280–89.

DiMaggio, P.J. & Powell, W.P. (1991). The iron cage revisited: Institutional isomorphism and collective rationality in organizational fields. *American Sociological Review, 48*, 147–60.

Ducharme, L.J. & Martin, J.K. (2000). Unrewarding work, co-worker support and job satisfaction: A test of the buffering hypothesis. *Work and Occupations, 27*, 223–43.

Edwards, J.R. & Rothbard, N.P. (2000). Mechanisms linking work and family: Clarifying the relationship between work and family constructs. *Academy of Management Review, 25*, 178–99.

Eisenberger, R., Huntington, R., Hutchison, S., & Sowa, D. (1986). Perceived organizational support. *Journal of Applied Psychology, 71*, 500–07.

Family and Work Institute. (2002). *National study of the changing workforce.*

Fenwick, R. & Olson, J. (1986). Support for worker participation: Attitudes among union and non-union workers. *American Sociological Review, 51*, 505–22.

Frone, M.R. (2000). Work-family conflict and employee psychiatric disorders: The national comorbidity survey. *Journal of Applied Psychology, 85*, 888–95.

Frone, M.R., Russell, M., & Cooper, M.L. (1992). Antecedents and outcomes of work-family conflict: Testing a model of work-family interface. *Journal of Applied Psychology, 1*, 65–78.

Frone, M.R., Yardley, J.K., & Markel, K.S. (1997). Developing and testing an integrative model of the work-family interface. *Journal of Vocational Behavior, 50*, 145–67.

Gartner Research. (2004). Retrieved from: www.gartner.com.

Gillen, M., Baltz, D., Gassel, M., Kirsch, L., & Vaccaro, D. (2002). Perceived safety climate, job demands and co-worker support among union and nonunion injured construction workers. *Journal of Safety Research, 33*, 33–51.

Greenhaus, J.H., & Beutell, N.J. (1985). Sources of conflict between work and family roles. *Academy of Management Review, 10*, 76–88.

Hammer, L.B., Cullen, J.C., Neal, M.B., Shafiro, M.M., & Sinclair, R.R. (2005). The effects of work-family fit on depression: A longitudinal study. *Journal of Occupational Health Psychology, 10*, 138–54.

Hammer, T.H., Saksvik, P.O., Nytrø, K., Torvatn, H., Bayazit, M. (2004). Expanding the psychosocial work environment: Workplace norms and work–family conflict as correlates of stress and health. *Journal of Occupational Health Psychology, 9*, 83–97.

Hofman, D.A. (1997). An overview of the logic and rationale of hierarchical linear models. *Journal of Management, 23*, 723–44.

Hopkins, K.M. (2005). Supervisor support and work-life integration: A social identity perspective. In E.E. Kossek & S.J. Lambert (Eds), *Work and Life Integration: Organizational,*

Cultural and Individual Perspectives (pp. 445–67). Mahwah, NJ: Lawrence Erlbaum Associates.

Hutchinson, S., Purcell, J., & Kinnie, N. (2000). Evolving high commitment management and experience of RAC call center. *Human Resource Management Journal, 10*(1), 63–79.

Jayaswal, R. (2005). Generation Y logs out of BPO honeymoon. *The Economic Times,* February 14.

Johnson, J.V. & Hall, E.M. (1988). Job strain, work place social support and cardiovascular disease: A cross-sectional study of a random sample of the Swedish working population. *American Journal of Public Health, 78,* 1336–42.

Jones, B., Flynn, D.M., & Kelloway, E.K. (1995). Perceptions of support from the organization in relation to work stress, satisfaction, and commitment. In S.L. Sauter & L.R. Murphy (Eds), *Organizational risk factors and job stress.* Washington, DC: American Psychological Association.

Kahn, R.L., Wolfe, D.M., Quinn, R.P., Snoek, J.D., & Rosenthal, R.A. (1964). *Organizational stress: Studies in role conflict and ambiguity.* New York: Wiley.

Kandel, D.B., Davies, M., Raveis, V.H. (1985). The stressfulness of daily social roles for women: Marital, occupational and household roles. *Journal of Health & Social Behavior, 26*(1), 64–78.

Karasek, R.A. Jr. (1979). Job demands, job decision latitude, and mental strain: Implication for job redesign. *Administrative Science Quarterly, 24,* 285–311.

Karasek, R.A. & Theorell, T. (1990). *Healthy work.* New York: Basic Books.

Kossek, E. (2005). Workplace policies and practices to support work and families. In S. Bianchi, L. Casper & R. King (Eds), *Work, family, health & well-being* (pp. 97–116). Mahwah, NJ: Lawrence Erlbaum Associates.

Kristensen, T.S. (1996). Job stress and cardiovascular disease: A theoretical critical review. *Journal of Occupational Health Psychology, 3,* 246–60.

Liukkonen, V., Virtanen, P., Kivimaki, M., Pentti, J., & Vahtera, J. (2004). Social capital in working life and health of employees. *Social Science and Medicine, 59,* 2447–58.

Lyness, K.S. & Thompson, D.E. (1997). Above the glass ceiling? A comparison of matched samples of female and male executives. *Journal of Applied Psychology, 82,* 359–75.

MacDermid, S.M. (2005). (Re)Considering conflict between work and family. In E.E. Kossek & S.J. Lambert (Eds), *Work and life integration: Organizational, cultural and individual perspectives* (pp. 19–40). Mahwah, NJ: Lawrence Erlbaum Associates.

MacDermid, S.M. with Barnett, R., Crosby, F., Greenhaus, J., Koblenz, M., Marks, S., Perry-Jenkins, M., Voydanoff, P., Wethington, E., & Sabbatini-Bunch, L. (1999). *The measurement of work/life tension: Recommendations of a virtual think tank.* Inaugural white paper of the Sloan Work-Family Researchers' electronic network.

Marks, S.R. (1977). Multiple roles and role strain: Some notes on human energy, time, and commitment. *American Sociological Review, 42,* 921–36.

Mehta, A., Armenakis, A., Mehta, N., & Irani, F. (2006). Challenges and opportunities of business process outsourcing in India. *Journal of Labor Research, 27*(3), 323–38.

Nakata, A., Haratani, T., Takahashi, M., Kawakami, N., Arito, H., Kobayashi, F., & Araki, S. (2004). Job stress, social support and prevalence of insomnia in a population of Japanese daytime workers. *Social Science and Medicine, 59,* 1719–30.

National Association of Software and Services Companies. (2010). *IT-BPO sector in India: Strategic review.* Retrieved from: http://www.nasscom.in/upload/SR10/ExecutiveSummary. pdf 20100226 (accessed on February 26, 2010).

O' Driscoll, M.P., Poelmans, S., Spector, P.E., Kalliath, T., Allen, T.D., Cooper, C.L., Sanchez, J.I. (2003). Family-responsive interventions, perceived organizational support and supervisor support, work-family conflict, and psychological strain. *International Journal of Stress Management, 10*, 326–44.

Parasuraman, S. & Greenhaus, J.H. (2000). Toward reducing some critical gaps in work-family research. *Human Resource Management Review, 12*, 299–313.

Poster, W.R. & Prasad, S. (2005). Work-family relations in transnational perspective: A view from high-tech firms in India and the United States. *Social Problems, 52*, 122–46.

PricewaterhouseCoopers. (2005). The evolution of BPO in India. Retrieved from: http://www.pwc.com/en_IN/in/assets/pdfs/evolution-of-bpo-in-india.pdf (accessed on October 14, 2010).

Rajadhyaksha, U. (2009). Work-life in India. *Executive Briefing Series*. Boston College: Center for work and family.

Raudenbush, S.W. & Bryk, A.S. (2001). *Hierarchical linear models: Application and data analysis method* (Second edition). London: SAGE Publications.

Rhoades, L. & Eisenberger, R. (2002). Perceived organizational support: A review of literature. *Journal of Applied Psychology, 87*, 698–714.

Ruderman, M., Ohlott, P.J., Panzer, K., & King, S.N. (2002). Benefits of multiple roles for managerial women. *Academy of Management Journal, 45*, 369–86.

Schat, A.C. & Kelloway, E.K. (2000). Effects of perceived control on the outcomes of workplace aggression and violence. *Journal of Occupational Health Psychology, 5*, 386–402.

Shanock, L.R. & Eisenberger, R. (2006). When supervisors feel supported: Relationships with subordinates' perceived supervisor support, perceived organizational support, and performance. *Journal of Applied Psychology, 91*, 689–95.

Shore, L.M. & Shore, T.H. (1995). Perceived organizational support and organizational justice. In R. Cropanzano & M. Kacmar (Eds), *Organizational politics, justice and support: Managing the social climate in the work place* (pp. 149–64). Westport, CT: Quorum.

Sieber, S.D. (1974). Toward a theory of role accumulation. *American Sociological Review, 39*, 467–78.

Singh, H. (2005). Is the BPO iceberg melting under attrition heat? *The Economic Times*, February 10.

Smith, J. & Gardner, D. (2007). Factors affecting employee use of work-life balance initiatives. *New Zealand Journal of Psychology, 36*(1), 3–12.

Subramanian, S. & Vinothkumar, M. (2009). Hardiness personality, self-esteem and occupational stress among IT professionals. *Journal of the Indian Academy of Applied Psychology, 35*, 48–56.

Suri, S. & Rizvi, S. (2008). Mental health and stress among call center employees. *Journal of the Indian Academy of Applied Psychology, 34*, 215–20.

Tausig, M. & Fenwick, R. (2001). Unbinding time: Alternate work schedules and work-life balance. *Journal of Family and Economic Issues, 22*, 101–19.

Theorell, T. & Karasek, R.A. (1996). Current issues relating to psychosocial job strain and cardio-vascular disease research. *Journal of Occupational Health Psychology, 1*, 9–26.

Thoits, P.A. (1983). Dimensions of life events that influence psychological distress: An evaluation and synthesis of the literature. In H.B. Kaplan (Ed.), *Psychosocial stress: Trends in theory and research* (pp. 33–103). New York: Academic Press.

Thompson, C.A., Beauvais, L.L., & Lyness, K.S. (1999). When work-family benefits are not enough: The influence of work-family culture on benefit utilization, organizational attachment and work-family conflict. *Journal of Vocational Behavior, 54*, 392–415.

Thompson, C.A. & Prottas, D.J. (2006). Relationships among organizational family support, job autonomy, perceived control, and employee well-being. *Journal of Occupational Health Psychology, 10,* 100–18.

Uma Devi, S. (2002, October 26). Globalisation, information technology and Asian Indian women in US. *Economic and Political Weekly.* Retrieved from: http://www.epw.org.in. (accessed on November 4, 2006).

Van der Doef, M. & Maes, S. (1999). The job demand-control (-support) model and psychological well-being: A review of 20 years of empirical research. *Work and Stress, 13,* 87–114.

Verbrugge, L.M. (1983). Multiple roles and physical health of women and men. *Journal of Health & Social Behavior, 24*(1), 16–30.

Wadhwa, R. (2004). Oh honey! I need a good night's sleep. *The Economic Times,* August 4.

9

Gender Issues in Work and Stress

Shubhra P. Gaur and Shikha S. Jain

Abstract

During the last decade of the twentieth century the number of women participating in paid work has increased across the globe including India. In addition, the projections in WHO report of 2003 indicate that stress related illnesses will be the second most important cause of disease within the next two decades. Against this backdrop it becomes mandatory for stress management researchers and talent management specialists to understand the stress-related issues concerning women in particular. This chapter attempts to delineate myriad aspects related to stress and gender in workplace. It begins with a discourse on the reasons of considering gender as a variable and covers the broad spectrum of gender differences and similarities on work-related stressors and coping. Further, it discusses the importance of having two separate models for males and females and is followed by a discussion on dual career families and specific issues concerning them. The chapter concludes with implications for organizations for achieving the agenda of bringing gender inclusivity in stress management interventions and directions for future research in the field.

Keywords: gender, work-related stressors, coping, dual career families, gender inclusivity

Introduction

Total working population of India was 384 million, i.e., 32.5% of the overall population, by 2010. Out of this, approximately 100 million were women and the rest were men. The sex ratio of working population reveals that there are 259 employed females for every 1,000 employed males. Although the number of working women has been remarkably low in India, it has increased continually. In 1981, work participation rate for women in India was 19.7%, which increased to 25.7% in 2001. Women's participation in organized sector has also increased from 49.5 lacs in 2001 to 51.2 lacs in 2006.

During the last decade of the twentieth century, the number of women participating in paid work has increased across the globe including India. As compared with the participation rates for females in Europe and America, India's figures are dismal. In 1981, work participation rate for women in India was 19.7%, which increased to 25.7% in 2001. Approximately, around similar period in European Union, e.g., the labor force participation for females was 47% in 1977, which increased to 61% in 2000 and in the United States, it was 55% in 1977 and 72% in 2000. The global trend clearly indicates an optimistic picture which is also supported by current figures in India.

INEVITABILITY OF STRESS

In most workplace settings, stress is a daily occurrence. Studies spanning a myriad of occupations and organizations have identified both the sources of job-related stress as well as the often negative behavioral outcomes associated with high levels of stress (Grossi, Keil, and Vito, 1996; Lambert, 2004; Lambert, Edwards, Camp, and Saylor, 2005; Moon and Maxwell, 2004; Robinson, Porporino, and Simourd, 1997; Slate, Vogel, and Johnson, 2001; Van Voorhis, Cullen, Link, and Wolfe, 1991; Walters, 1996). With increasing number of women in work places, it becomes important to specifically understand the issues concerning women in particular. This chapter attempts to delineate the aspects related to stress and gender in workplace. Stress at workplace has been variously referred to as work-related stress, occupational stress and organizational stress (Gaur, 1996; Gaur, 2000). In this chapter the term work-related stressor is used to indicate stressors arising because of paid work engagement.

Why is Gender an Important Variable?

GENDER AND SEX DIFFERENTIATED

Gender and sex are sometimes used interchangeably but the two concepts have very distinct meanings (Reeder, 1996). Basically sex is a term based on biology, whereas gender is socially and psychologically constructed by the process of interactions in the family, social and educational settings. As research on biological sexuality is relatively new, there are many questions for which we lack conclusive answers, e.g., whether hormones or socialization influences sexual orientation, cognitive abilities, or levels of aggression. However, there is a general consensus among researchers that environment is at least as great an influence as biology on our thoughts, feelings, and behavior and that culture is all pervasive important environmental variable. The culture shapes the understanding of the gender by perpetuating gender stereotypes.

There are two types of stereotypes—namely, descriptive and prescriptive. *Descriptive stereotypes* are those which a person provides as a description of the personality characteristics he/she believes that men and women possess. *Prescriptive stereotypes* are those which a person provides as a description of the personality characteristics she/he believes that men and women should have. Gender stereotypes have important implications for gender roles, gender-role identity and gender typing. They eventually guide individuals' behavior and affect their well-being. These four terms have been defined in literature clearly. Gender stereotypes have been defined as a set of widely held beliefs about characteristics deemed appropriate for males and females in a particular culture. They include information about physical appearance, attitudes and interests, psychological traits, social relations, and occupations (Ashmore, DelBoca, and Wohlers, 1986; Deause and Lewis, 1984; Huston, 1983, 1985). Gender roles are a reflection of these stereotypes in everyday behavior (Ruble and Ruble, 1982). *Gender role identity* refers to the perception of the self as relatively masculine or feminine in characteristics, abilities, and behaviors, whereas *gender typing* refers to the process of developing gender-linked beliefs, gender roles, and a gender-role identity (Huston, 1983).

One explanation for gender differences comes from the gender role theory. It illustrates that the differential self expectations, others' expectations and gender role identity influence behavior of people in both social and organizational contexts. Thus individual's behavior is mediated by gender role stereotypes prevalent in a culture.

Gender differences can also be explained through Social Learning Theory. It posits that we learn a great deal through modeling and observation, i.e., emphasis on vicarious learning. Humans acquire behaviors by observing others belonging to the same gender. For example, if a mother screams at sight of a cockroach, her daughter would also show a similar response; and if a boy observes that his dad shouts when he is angry and stressed out for his office work, he thinks it is the response he also has to display to be accepted in the family and society.

This constant conditioning, expectations, and individuals' experiences gradually develop role identity in them. This self identity begins with one's perception towards one's body and its association with gender role. Stress is experienced when a person is not able to fulfil the predefined gender appropriate roles. These predefined gender appropriate roles continue through adolescence and adulthood. A study on school going adolescents clearly shows that boys get more affected than girls by agentic stressors. The term "agentic" stressor refers to impediments to personal achievements, physical victimization, and concern over life chances. On the other hand, girls get more affected by ambient stressors. Here, *ambient stressors* refer to environmental threats from school and neighborhoods that cause stress (Kort-Butler, 2009). Thus, the stressors by which men and women get stressed are different or the same type of stressor influences them differently.

As accepted by and large in most societies, man is the breadwinner of the family and woman is the care provider. Most of the activities and emotional expressions revolve around these basic role expectations. Men have been found to get stressed out more at functional level; and for women major source of stress is associated with maintenance of relationship. Similarly, sources of stress for men and women are different at workplace too. Men are more sensitive to work-related problems; women are more sensitive to problems of getting along with others, with their colleagues. Both genders are equally susceptible to encounter stress. But as indicated by many studies, there is no clear-cut reason why women suffer from depression more than men do.

According to a neurological study (Nauert, 2007), it has been observed that when men and women are faced with performance-related stress, different parts of the brain activate in differential levels. This further leads to assumption that stress responses may be consequently different in each gender. Developmentally, men may have had to deal with a stressor either by overcoming or evading it, whereas women may have reacted with more socially or emotionally influenced response. These are called "fight-or-flight" and "tend-and-befriend" responses, respectively. They help in times of adversity, resulting in survival of species. At workplace, too, these strategies, which are mainly gender specific, are employed in order to relieve stress.

The hormone connection of stress varies between the two genders and thus provides evidence for justifying gender differences on biological ground. Research studies point out towards "oxytocin" as the hormone that leads to maternal behavior, affiliation, and induces relaxation. Apparently, this is a critical factor which leads to gender differences to reactions of stress. It has been found that individuals with higher levels of oxytocin have a calmer disposition, are less anxious and more social. Typically in the vent of stress experience, body secretes cortisol and adrenaline. These hormones prepare the body for fight or flight and lead to rise in blood pressure and suppression of the immune system. Although both men and women are equally prone to the effects of cortisol and adrenaline, the women's pituitary glands secrete oxytocin that counters the production of cortisol and adrenaline thus reducing their harmful effects and promoting nurturing and relaxing emotions. Men also produce oxytocin during exposure to stressful experiences; however, first it is in smaller quantity and second its effects are also inhibited by male hormones like testosterone (Sujatha, 2007).

Recently studies have begun to investigate stress responses, and differences between men and women, in functional and structural neuroimaging studies (Dedovic, Wadiwalla, Engert, & Pruessner, 2009). Evidence from endocrine and neuroimaging studies have been found to explain these differences using either sex (i.e., biological differences between male and female) or gender (i.e., socialization differences between men and women) as the mediating factor and the summary of these evidences have been provided by Dedovic et al. (2009). Some of the aspects of differential stress responses have been shown to be sex related, like phase of the menstrual cycle and levels of estrogen. But studies manipulating the stressor context, or using stressors emphasizing achievement versus social integration, provide strong support for the notion that gender may play an important role in explaining male–female variation in stress responses as well.

In conclusion, one can say that research points towards major differences between the two genders in all the three domains—stressors, strains, and coping. Further, these differences can be explained on the basis of biological as well as socialization related differences between the two genders. Thus there is a clear case for considering gender as a variable in stress and work.

Gender and Work-related Stressors

There are many studies which indicate that stressors are a function of the occupation and that within an occupational group the stressors for men and women would be more or less similar. However, there have been many more studies which support the hypothesis that the men and women experience different stressors even within the same occupational group.

Some have suggested that men and women experience different stressors (e.g., Misra, McKean, West, & Russo, 2000). Research has shown that men's stressors relate to finances (McDonough & Walters, 2001), work-related power (Spielberger & Vagg, 1999; Vagg, Spielberger, & Wasala, 2002), and job responsibility (Sharada & Raju, 2001). On the other hand, women's stressors relate to social life (McDonough & Walters, 2001), interpersonal issues (Thompson, Kirk, & Brown, 2006), work–family conflicts (Vagg et al., 2002), role conflict, and role ambiguity (Sharada and Raju, 2001). Spielberger and Vagg (1999) found that lack of participation and conflict with other departments was more stressful for men, whereas inadequate salary, insufficient personal time, and competition for advancement were more stressful for women. Interestingly, Wu and Shih (2010) found the effect of Gender role on perception of stress. In a study on bank clerks they found that high level of feminine traits were related to higher perception of job-related stress in case of women and the opposite was found for men. A high level of masculine traits was found to be related to lower perception of job-related stress among men.

Stress is also a common and usual phenomenon when one works in the opposite gender dominant work areas. According to Savicki et al. (2003: 603), "although women tend to perform as well in correctional employment setting as do men, women's sources of stress in the workplace are quite different than men's sources of stress." Prison setting is highly masculinized work environment. In such a setting, female correctional officers experience more than usual stressors as they require to adapt to traditionally male-dominant environment (Jurik, 1985). Studies have shown that in addition to the normal pressures associated with working as a correctional officer, female officers also had to navigate a complex work environment made more difficult because of negative expectations, informal stereotypes, denial of informal training and socialization, and resistance from inmates and fellow officers (Britton, 2003; Jurik, 1985; Hemmens et al., 2002; Huckabee, 1992; Pogrebin and Poole, 1998; Savicki et al., 2003; Wright and Saylor, 1991; Zimmer, 1986). The present chapter examines multiple sources and levels of job stress on male and female employees.

Building on research that links gender to differences in well-being and differences in stress exposure and vulnerability, the study examined how coping styles are gendered in ways that may contribute to sex differences in depressive symptoms and delinquent behavior. The study disaggregates stress measures to reflect gender differences in the experience of stress, examining whether avoidant, approach, and action coping condition the relationship between stress and well-being. Regression analyses were conducted using data from the National Longitudinal Study of Adolescent Health. Results revealed both, sex differences and similarities. The interaction of avoidant coping and stress helped explain why girls had more depressive symptoms than boys, action coping increased delinquent behavior for girls, while approach coping decreased delinquent behavior for boys and girls. Assisting adolescents in developing coping styles that discourage avoiding problems

Table 9.1 Review of Stressors Which Are Different in the Two Genders in Different Studies

	Profession	Female	Male	Methodology	Author(s)
1	University Faculty and staff (N=336)	Interpersonal conflicts: Conflicts with one's coworker, supervisor, student, or the administration Lack of job autonomy: Lack of autonomy on work-related issues, such as making work schedule, making decisions, etc.	Workload: Heavy workload, deadlines, or time constraints Work mistakes: Dereliction of duty or unsuccessfulness at work	Qualitative Approach: The Stress Incident Record (SIR); Content analysis of responses. Quantitative Scales: Interpersonal Conflict at Work Scale (ICAWS); Frustration scale (Peter and O'Connor); Patient Health Questionnaire (Spitzer et al.); Job-Related Affective Well-Being Scale (JAWS)	Liu, Spector and Shi, 2008
2	IT (N=399)	interpersonal conflict	Job requirements, work-load and responsibility	Quantitative Measures: General Job Stress Questionnaire (Japanese edition); Center for Epidemiological Studies Depression Scale (CES-D, Japanese version) Qualitative Measure: Content analysis of Interviews (N=8)	Ogiwara et al, 2008
3	Not mentioned (N=900)	Workplace relationship difficulties, Bullying/ Harassment	**Change in job situation:** Organizational change, shift in role responsibility, workload expectation; **workload;** Organizational/ employment issues	Clinical Outcomes for Routine Evaluation (CORE)	Rowlands, 2008

4	Police officers (N=1100)	None	Negative exposure: Tragic accident, making violent arrest, police funeral, shooting someone	Quantitative Measures—Work-related stress instrument developed by Davis (1988); Likert-type scale for negative exposure and unfairness	McCarty, Zhao, and Garland, 2007
5	Not mentioned (N=203)	Loss of control stress: Things that were unpredictable, uncontrollable and overloaded	Financial stress: Managing and maintaining financial commitments, supporting family and saving money	Index of Financial stress developed on the basis of Turner et al.'s (1991) measure Perceived Stress Scale (PSS)	Gaunt and Benjamin, 2007
6	Correctional officers (N=2576)	Safety, organizational support for employee	Organizational support for equal treatment policies, work–family conflict	Quantitative Measure: Quality of Work Life survey; Six scales for employee perception: Quality of supervision, and Organizational support (used by Armstrong and Griffin); Coworker support (used by Haines, Hurlbert, & Zimmer); Workplace safety (used by Griffin); Organizational support for equal treatment policies (Likert-type used by Griffin, Armstrong & Hepburn); Work–family Conflict (Likert-type)	Griffin, 2006

(Table 9.1 Continued)

(*Table 9.1 Continued*)

	Profession	Female	Male	Methodology	Author(s)
7	Not mentioned	Workload, discrimination, maternal wall, isolation, sexual harassment, stereotyping, home-work conflict	Long working hours, corporate politics, little time for children	Based on a chapter comprising review of many studies	Nelson and Burke, 2002
8	Professor (N=124)	Interpersonal conflict, lack of reward/recognition	Time/effort wasted, Lack of control	Modified version on Stress Incident Record (SIR) used by Newton and Keenan, responses content analyzed	Narayanan, Menon and Spector, 1999
	Salesperson (N=130)	Interpersonal conflict, time/effort wasted	Lack of reward/recognition		
9	Athlete (N=332)	Coach related (argument, unfairness,	None	Sources of Acute Stress Scale (SASS)	Anshel, Sutarto, and Jubenville, 2009
10	Information system Professionals (N=240)	Role ambiguity	None	Items from Measurement of role stress by developed by Rizzo (1970)	Gaan, 2008
11	Mixed (N=2498)	Relationships with other people, Organizational structure and climate, home-work interface	None	The sources-of-pressure scale	Fotinatos and Cooper, 2005

12	Communications Workers (N=190)	Office politics (role conflict and role ambiguity), time pressure, workload, long hours	None	Questionnaire developed by the authors based on focus group discussions and extensive literature review	Fielden, Tench, and Fawkes, 2003
13	Teachers (N=30) Doctors (N=30) Bank-officers (N=30) Bureaucrats (N=30)	Career development Organizational interface with oneself and family Stressors specific to working women Quantitative workload		Work-related Stress Scale (WRS) developed by Gaur and Dhawan (1996)	Gaur and Dhawan, 2000

Table 9.2 Review of Stressors Which Are Similar in the Two Genders in Different Studies

	Profession	Stressors	Author(s)
1	Athletes	Performance related: Unfairness from referee, injury and pain caused, negative comments from others, cheating from opponent	Anshel, Sutarto, and Jubenville, 2009
2	University Faculty and staff	Organizational constraints: A variety of issues including equipments, budget cuts, or inadequate training	Liu, Spector, and Shi, 2008
3	Not mentioned	Low social support, i.e., support of supervisors, co-workers and spouses	Ogiwara et al., 2008
4	Information System Professionals	Role conflict, Work overload	Gaan, 2008
5	Not mentioned	Career issues, Violence, Work conditions (low stress)	Rowlands, 2008
6	Not mentioned	Stress spillover into marriage and parenthood.	Gaunt and Benjamin, 2007
7	Police officer	Unfairness	McCarty, Zhao, and Garland, 2007
8	Correctional officers	Work–family conflict: Lack of balance between work and personal obligation	Griffin, 2006
9	Not mentioned	Role ambiguity, Job insecurity, Downsizing, and Time pressures	Nelson and Burke, 2002
10	Professors and salespersons	Role ambiguity, Role conflict (low stress)	Narayanan, Menon, and Spector, 1999

or taking quick action, but that encourage problem-solving, can improve well-being, regardless of sex.

GENDER DIFFERENCES IN COPING

Stress researches conducted in various professions offer distinct results as the diverse work environment presents employees with different challenges. Anshel and Kaissidis (1997) found that male and female highly skilled athletes used more approach-oriented coping strategies than did their lower skilled counterparts. However, among the less skilled male and female athletes, women applied avoidance coping more often than did men. Also, Anshel, and Delany (2001) found gender differences for 11- and 12-year-old male and female field hockey players. For example, girls used considerably more confidence-building self-talk than did boys, whereas boys more often used resignation (e.g., "I reminded myself that things could be much worse") than did girls. Anshel, Jamieson, and Raviv (2001) found gender differences in the use of coping strategies among Israeli athletes, whereas Lane, Jones, and Stevens (2002) found no gender differences in coping with failure and changes in self-efficacy among male and female tennis players as a function of self-esteem. In addition, maladaptive coping (e.g., self-blame, behavioral disengagement) was associated with low self-esteem for both genders.

ROLE OF PERCEPTION IN COPING

Femininity is noted for traits that reflect an emotional, interpersonal orientation toward others, such as being sensitive to needs of others, and understanding. This emotional orientation is associated with the ability to characterize others' emotions in a detailed, complex manner (Conway, 2000). Masculinity pertains to a more instrumental and assertive orientation, with measure items that include independence, aggressiveness, and competitiveness. This orientation discourages any detailed consideration of people's emotional reactions (Conway, 2000). Stereotypes and role perceptions play an important role in the understanding of gender-specific behavior. Harriman (1985) defined roles as the expected and actual behaviors or characteristics that attach to a particular social status, and stereotypes as the set of attributes that are attributed to all individuals who occupy a particular role. Since gender stereotypes dictated the approved masculine or feminine image, they are powerful in terms of their ability to influence how people act and what they believe in (Kohlberg, 1966). In addition, the distinctions between male-valued and female-valued components of the sex-role stereotypes have principal implications for the self-concept of men and women (Kohlberg, 1966). Bem (1975) indicated that psychologically androgynous individuals might be more likely than either feminine or masculine individuals to show gender role adaptability across situations, and engage in effectual behavior without regard for stereotypes that suggest this type of behavior is more appropriate for one gender or the other.

As seen in the previous section on stressors, there are some common stressors observed in both the genders apart from exclusive ones pertinent to a specific gender. They are extrinsic and have the potential to act on an individual. On the contrary, coping responses are intrinsic and hence gendered. Very few similarities have been found in the way both the genders respond to a stressor. This is because of the fundamental differences between them which we have discussed earlier. However, there is some similarity also observed in the coping responses. "Approach Coping" strategy was found to be used by both the genders almost equally (Narayanan, Menon, and Spector, 1999). Approach coping strategy uses positive reappraisal of the stressful situation, wherein the individual tries to think though in terms of what can and cannot be done to overcome it (Kort-Butler, 2009). Narayanan et al. (1999) have observed that most of the employees had "talked to their boss" whenever confronted with a stressful situation. However, the stressors may or may not be the same for both males and females.

Need for two Separate Models for Males and Females

In many meta-analytic studies researchers have found absence of or negligible gender differences in occupational stress (Gyllensten and Palmer, 2005), but at the same time there is a plethora of research that shows that the same model of stress does not work equally for males and females and that different models may be needed in order to understand how males and females respond to and cope with organizational change (Barnett et al.,1995; Hendrix et al., 1994; Tamres, Janicki, and Helgeson, 2002). Researchers have, for example, shown that males and females have unique sources of stress (Almeida, Wethington, and Kessler, 2002; Korabik, McDonald, and Rosin, 1993; Nelson and Quick, 1985; Trocki and Orioli, 1994) and that the same stressors have a different impact on males and females (Hendrix et al., 1994; Zappert and Weinstein, 1985). In addition, researchers have studied the effects of personal and work

Table 9.3 Review of Coping Responses Reported by the Two Genders in Different Studies

	Profession	Women	Men	Methodology	Study
1	Athletes	Approach Behavioral (Social support, help seeking, social interaction, efforts towards "emotion-coping" functions) Avoidance Cognitive	**Active coping-** Behavioral and cognitive attempts to confront, Venting emotions	Coping Style in Sport Scale (CSSS)	Anshel, Sutarto, and Jubenville, 2009
2	Not mentioned	Indirect aggression (gossip, rumour)	Verbal/physical aggression	Not mentioned	Rowlands, 2008
3	Police officers	Constructive coping (exercise regularly, make a plan)	Destructive coping (drinking, smoking, gambling)	Likert-type scale for Constructive and Destructive coping	McCarty, Zhao, and Garland, 2007
4	Not mentioned	Social support, task strategies, home–work relationships, effective use of time, involvement	Use logic	Likert-type rating scale	Fotinatos and Cooper, 2005
5	Not mentioned	Emotion-focused strategies (expression of emotion, seeking social support) (self-blame, denial, avoidance)	Problem-focused strategies (planned/rational actions, humor, fantasy	Based on a chapter comprising review of many studies	Nelson and Burke, 2002

(Table 9.3 Continued)

(*Table 9.3 Continued*)

Profession	Women	Men	Methodology	Study
6 Professors Salesperson	Talk to co-worker/family Talk to co-worker/family	Took direct action Took direct action	Questions designed and incorporated in SIR, responses content analyzed	Narayanan, Menon, and Spector, 1999
7 Communication Workers	Social support (emotion-focused coping strategy)	None	Based on focus group discussions	Fielden, Tench, and Fawkes, 2003
8 Teachers DoctorsBank officers Bureaucrats	Active coping stance, planfulness, forbearance	None	Behavioral Attribute of Psychosocial competence (BAPC), Rotter Internal External Scale (RIE), Rotter Trust Scale (RT)	Gaur and Dhawan, 2000

stressors on males and females and found that women have a higher sensitivity to stressors and experience higher levels of strain than males. Females have reported higher levels of mental, physical, and emotional exhaustion (Geller and Hobfoll, 1994; Hendrix et al., 1994), depression (Hendrix et al., 1994; Zappert andWeinstein, 1985), psychosomatic symptoms (Frankenhaeuser, Lundberg, Fredrikson, Melin, Tuomisto, Myrsten, Hedman, Bergman-Losman, andWallin, 1989; Hendrix et al., 1994), and perceived stress (Hendrix et al., 1994: Ptacek et al., 1992). In a research study by Trocki and Orioli (1994), it was found that females perceived more personal and work changes, greater personal and work pressures, and higher levels of physical, behavioral, and emotional symptoms than males. While work changes were predictive of physical symptoms for males, they were directly predictive of physical, behavioral, and emotional symptoms for females. Even when variance due to work change, pressures, and satisfaction was controlled, females still showed greater physical and emotional symptoms. Tamres et al. (2002) found that females used more coping strategies than males regardless of the type of strategy and that stressor type or stressor appraisal may account for coping differences. Similarities and differences between males and females regarding the relationships between amount of change and appraisal have been found. A major difference between the model applicable for males and for females was that the male model, in contrast to the female model, included a path from uncertainty to challenge. For males, higher levels of uncertainty also predicted higher levels of challenge. Perceived stress was directly predicted by amount of change in work relationships and appraisal of uncertainty in the male and female models. However, in case of model for females challenge appraisal and amount of change in facility significantly predicted perceived stress as well. The pattern of relationships for control and avoidance coping were similar for males and females.

Perception and appraisal of stressor account for the level of stress, wherein gender/sex operates as a moderator. Some studies have shown that different models are needed to understand how both the genders appraise, respond to and cope with organizational stressors (Kohler, Munz, and Grawitch, 2006). This is supported by another study concluding that women rated stressors as more severe and used more coping strategies than men (Tamres et al., 2002). According to Kohler et al. (2006), organizational change is one of the major sources of stress among employees. They found indicative evidence that men and women appraise challenge and uncertainty, respectively, more negatively than their opposite gender co-workers. They have recommended that the model applicable for females was a poor fit for the male sample, hence suggesting for the development of unique models for males and females.

Dual Career Families: Stressors and Coping

DUAL CAREER FAMILY DEFINED

Dual career families are those families wherein both the husband and the wife are committed to their own careers. In addition to the time they need to progress speedily in their respective careers, they need time to contribute to the future careers of their children. Such families are under tremendous stress and consequently they are prone to negative outcomes of stress. A separate section is required to deal with this subject because the context of dual career families is very different and also because "family is one unit" in dual career contexts and not the individual. The context of a dual career family is different in many ways from a single career family. First of all, the traditional gender roles come in the way of well-being of the family and need to be revised. Second, the time pressures plaguing a dual career family are far more intense and demanding. Third, a dual career family has almost double work load in comparison to single career family. The term "family is one unit" means that actions and decisions of individuals in a dual career family are so interlinked that individuals cease to function individually and their response as a family becomes a major determiner of their consequences and that common context is intervened by the coping pattern of the family as a unit to determine the consequences for the family.

DUAL CAREER FAMILY: STRESSORS

Domains of stressors specific to a dual career family are as follows:

1. *Job location*: Deciding to stay in two separate places or compromise on career growth by one of the spouses. Long distance relationships have their own uncharted pathways and challenges.
2. Decision regarding whether to have children and if yes when and how many. The whole notion of marriage and ideal family are undergoing change.
3. Role conflict or incompatibility can happen in three broad ways:

    (i)   Cumulative role overload: time spent in one role may leave little time for other roles.
    (ii) Inter-role strain spill-over: Strain within one role may spill over to other roles.

(iii) Inter-role functionality mismatch: behavior functional in one role(s) may be dysfunctional to other role(s)

4. *Child rearing and elderly care*: They are two major areas of attention for dual career families which opt for children and value elderly care.
5. *Quality time to self and spouse*: There is a great deal of effort spent in building dual careers and balance other traditionally expected responsibilities like elderly and child care. Consequently, despite financial affluence, two oft neglected people are self and spouse and the time they spend with each other. Notably, even the quantity of time they spend with each other is insufficient.

Researches show that although pursuing a career is very demanding for women, the sense of fulfillment and well being tilts the balance in favor of the career as compared to lack of it.

Dual Career Family: Coping with Stressors

Studies have indicated that dual career families range from the "perfect models" with everything running smoothly on one end and "chaotic households" with disharmony and bitterness on the other end. One aspect that emerged salient in this relationship is the type of husband and wife relationship and its impact on outcomes for the family. Handy (1978) proposed a four-fold model in which different marriage patterns were derived by combining the husband's orientations with that of the wife.

Pattern-1: The most common pattern that emerged was on the lines of *traditional sex role stereotypes*. This involves a thrusting husband and caring wife. These marriages show little stress because life is structured and predictable.

Pattern-2: The *chaotic household* is the one in which both the husband and wife are thrusting and have a high need for achievement. Their energies, time and effort is directed toward their work and career aspirations and the problems increase manifold if the child arrives. At this juncture the husband tries to convince wife to adopt traditional role.

Pattern-3: The *ideal pair* is the one with two involved persons who are high achievers, enjoy their careers but at the same time understand each other. Although the stress levels in such marriages are fairly high but it is tempered by their caring attitude and resolve problems by compromise and discussion. Such marriages are resilient and flexible where partners take turns to compromise and ensuring that the other partner gets what he/she wants.

Table 9.4   Tabular Presentation of the Model Proposed by Handy (1978)

	Caring Wife	Involved Wife (high achiever, enjoys career but understands spouse)	Thrusting Wife (high achiever-energy and effort focused on career aspirations)
Thrusting Husband (high achiever, energy and effort focused on career aspirations)	Traditional Stereotyped roles		Chaotic Household
Involved Husband (high achiever, enjoys career but understands spouse)	Intense emotional Relationship	Ideal Pair	

Pattern-4: Intense emotional relationship in which the husband is involved and the wife is caring. Here the husband focuses on his career without hurting others' interests. He feels guilty because she devotes her life to him. Due to their emotional intensity such relationships have potential for problems.

A similar categorization has also been reported by Francine and Tim Hall (1980). The four patterns were labeled as *accommodators, adversaries, acrobats,* and *allies* corresponding to the four patterns of Handy. The slight addition is in the last categorization of allies. Halls reported two orientations within allies: (*a*) where both identify with the home and (*b*) where both identify with work and have no interest in home and relationship.

Lewis & Cooper (1989) have summarized three approaches to coping with stress by dual career couples:

1. *Coping by Structure role redefinition*: In this strategy, the attempt is to alter the role expectation of the spouse or significant others in a particular role by either refusing to take extra load or delegating some of the duties expected by others.
2. *Coping by personal role redefinition*: In this strategy, the attempt is to alter his/her own self expectations from different roles by either eliminating certain self expectations within one or many roles, reducing time allocated for some activities or prioritizing.

3. *Coping by reactive role behavior or role expansion*: In this strategy, instead of changing self or other's expectations, the attempt is to meet the demands of all roles equally.

The relative efficacy of each of these strategies depends on the self role perception of the woman (Agrawal, 2001). In a separate work, four-step recommendation has been made by Campbell-Moore (1988)—(*a*) find time to talk in a relaxed way to resolve tricky issues, (*b*) learn techniques of effective communication, (*c*) listen to what other person has to say, and (*d*) do not try to solve all the problems at once.

Bringing Gender Inclusivity in Stress Management Interventions: Implications for Organizations

GENDER INCLUSIVITY DEFINED

Gender inclusivity can be understood as inclusion of both the genders at workplace not only in terms of increasing number but also including them in making decisions, sharing responsibilities, taking leadership roles, formulating regulations for an organization, having equal opportunities, etc. Organizations should be flexible in their policies to accommodate the special needs of both the genders. It also means creating an environment in which none of the genders feels that they are trapped in the "opposite" gender dominant environment. However, this term in contemporary literature has been used for women employees. Considering the social context, even organizations where women are in majority, the chances of males considering the environment dominated by women are not very high since the top positions are in most cases with majority of men.

Padma R. Ravichandar, Country Head, Mercer Consulting said:

> *Gender inclusivity is not about a set of simple initiatives that corporations need to undertake to increase the female population within their organization or policies to ensure that women have a harassment-free and secure work environment. It is a far more complex multi-dimensional, transformation journey, with multiple stakeholders that must work together in order to help create a holistic and empowered society where men and women have different but equal roles to play.*
>
> *(Singh, 2011)*

NASSCOM efforts proved effective. In mid 1980s, only 5–8% of students in engineering colleges and approximately 25–30% of the population entering the IT industry were women. By 2005, 40.4% of the entrants into institutions of higher education were women. Women in IT workforce grew from 421,460 in 2005 to 670,984 in 2008.

A major section of female employees found in organized sector in various arenas include 27% in HR, 21% in marketing, 12% in finance and 33% in technical field. However, out of these working women only 7% are found at top level, 7% at directorial level, 14% at managerial level and the rest 72% at entry level (graduates with no supervisory role). A very striking reason behind women not reaching top level is the "leaking pipeline," which means majority of women tend to leave the workforce in their 30s due to the inability to achieve balance in their work-life at critical times when they could have otherwise progressed through leadership roles.

A study was conducted by Accenture in 2008 on 4,000 male and female business professionals in 17 countries. It has revealed some interesting findings:

- 43% of women felt well-equipped to compete in the global business economy
- Women in many emerging markets such as India, China, and Brazil seem to be better equipped than those in developed countries
- 83% of women showed willingness to learn new technologies for future success
- 23%, 22%, and 18% of women attributed "gender," "the need to devote energy to family" and "an unwillingness to relocate," respectively, as three factors limiting their career, which were considered to be the top reasons for voluntary attrition of working women.

NASSCOM in collaboration with Mercer has taken a functioning initiative to promote gender inclusivity in India. They have proposed a holistic multidimensional framework incorporating an ecosystem that comprises individuals, organization, social environment, and government. The purpose of this model is to identify forces that were overlooked until recently and then provide solution for the newly defined problems.

The framework is divided into the following three parts:

1. *Stakeholders and influencers*: There are two types of influencers, i.e., extrinsic and intrinsic. Extrinsic influencers include law, policies, and other mandatory requirements, whereas intrinsic influencers are the

ones at the subconscious level such as unstated beliefs and rules. All stakeholders have been functioning on the external front of gender inclusivity and diversity. Deeper levels need to be tapped in order to bring about a radical change. For example, government glorifying success stories of female role models like Kalpana Chawla and implicitly encouraging women to strive for such accomplishments.

2. *The journey from identification to empowerment*:

- Phase 1: Recognizing the need for inclusivity. Steps in the first phase include communicating intent, formulating a team, designing, and implementing the policies, supporting women in the course of essential transitions such as marriage, childbirth, etc.
- Phase 2: Standardizing processes, policies, and metrics so that the smallest change could be noticed.
- Phase 3: Striving to achieve a level where chief positions include 50% women and they do not opt for care-taking and home management as key challenges while considering career growth. Focus is shifted more towards culture, and softer and intangible issues.
- Phase 4: Reaching the optimum level where both men and women perform diverse roles and are found at all career levels. They work together to eradicate the practices that reduce equity. Equal participation is expected in all activities, especially decision-making processes.

3. *Metrics*: Measuring on a regular basis is required to check where an organization has reached in terms of gender inclusivity. For example, if we are in Phase 1, gender inclusivity is measured through number of recruitment, percentage of women participation in workforce, etc. Similarly, for each phase there are some measures which tell us whether the optimal state has been achieved.

Few important practices that companies can adopt to enhance gender inclusivity:

1. Acknowledge gender inclusivity as a decisive factor in overall growth and progress of the company by making "culture of inclusion" an essential component of organizational policy.
2. Appreciate the unique and different competencies of women and foster the working environment in such a way that encourages them to assume/adopt leadership roles.

3. Increase the opportunities to involve women in decision-making processes at higher level by setting up a new relevant department or introducing a new program.
4. Follow strict and stringent rules to ensure women employees' dignity and security.
5. Demonstrate appropriate and effective "role models" to encourage younger women to feel confident and take up leadership positions, hence enhancing gender inclusivity.
6. Plan organizational support, especially when a couple has young children including that of flexi time, crèche facility, and work from home options for both men and women.

Directions for Future Research and Training Interventions

There are four distinct areas where the review of literature suggests directions for researchers on a priority basis. The first area that needs attention is the statistics related to (*a*) women's participation in part-time, full-time and self-employment, (*b*) sector-wise male–female comparisons, (*c*) hierarchy-wise male–female comparisons. The second area that will add to existing body of knowledge is in the domain of identifying magnitude and type of stressors in different professional groups. The third area that draws attention is the gender comparisons in coping mechanisms. The fourth agenda should be in the domain of developing two separate models to understand the dynamic nature of stress-coping-strain relationship for the two genders and related questions of similarities and differences across the two genders.

Research also points out that stress management programs in organizations need to be focusing on couples since individual coping is inadequate for the desired outcomes of well-being and realization of one's potential in personal and professional spheres. It is important that in a dual career family coping strategies are formulated jointly by the couples. Based on their findings that some dual career couples never learn to manage their problems as a result of which there were more divorces in dual career couples than single career couples (McCook, Folzer, Charlesworth, and Scholl, 1991). They have reported workshops for dual career couples at Du Pont. Believing that stable couples make better employees, Du Pont instituted a series of workshops for its employees in its Field Engineering Program with their spouse or partners and the feedback from workshop participants was clearly in favor of conducting such programs and the major recommendation to the management was that spouses should be present even if they are working from home. The participants benefitted at three levels: personal, marital, and work.

Conclusion

The *sex ratio* of working population reveals that there are 259 employed females for every 1,000 employed males. Although the number of working women has been remarkably low in India, it has increased continually. In 1981, work participation rate for women in India was 19.7%, which increased to 25.7% in 2001. Women's participation in organized sector has also increased from 49.5 lacs in 2001 to 51.2 lacs in 2006. Considering the projections in WHO report of 2003 indicating that stress related illnesses will be the second most important cause of disease within the next two decades and inevitability of stress at workplaces, it becomes important for stress management researchers and talent management specialists to understand the stress related issues concerning women in particular.

Evidence from endocrine and neuroimaging studies have been found to explain these differences using *either sex* (i.e., biological differences between male and female) *or gender* (i.e., socialization differences between men and women) as the mediating factor and the summary of these evidences have been provided by Dedovic et al. (2009). Some of the aspects of differential stress responses have been shown to be sex related, like phase of the menstrual cycle and levels of estrogen. But studies manipulating the stressor context, or using stressors emphasizing achievement versus social integration, provide strong support for the notion that gender may play an important role in explaining male–female variation in stress responses as well.

The two sections on *work-related stressors* and *coping* pointed toward some common stressors observed in both the genders apart from exclusive ones pertinent to a specific gender. They are extrinsic and have the potential to act on an individual. On the contrary, coping responses are intrinsic and hence gendered. Very few similarities have been found in the way both the genders respond to a stressor. This is because of the fundamental differences between them which have been discussed earlier in the context of biological and sociological reasons. However, there is some similarity also observed in the coping responses. "Approach Coping" strategy was found to be used by both the genders almost equally (Narayanan, Menon, & Spector, 1999). Approach coping strategy uses positive reappraisal of the stressful situation, wherein the individual tries to think though in terms of what can and cannot be done to overcome it (Kort-Butler, 2009). Narayanan et al. (1999) have observed that most of the employees had "talked to their boss" whenever confronted with a stressful situation. However, the stressors may or may not be the same for both males and females.

The individual-level understanding of stress-coping strain is the *primary level intervention* in stress management literature and herein the importance of *two separate models for the males and females* was identified. It was found that perception and appraisal of stressor account for the level of stress, wherein gender/sex operates as a moderator. Some studies have shown that different models are needed to understand how both the genders appraise, respond to and cope with organizational stressors (Kohler, Munz, and Grawitch, 2006). This is supported by another study concluding that women rated stressors as more severe and used more coping strategies than men (Tamres et al., 2002). According to Kohler et al. (2006), organizational change is one of the major sources of stress among employees. They found indicative evidence that men and women appraise challenge and uncertainty, respectively, more negatively than their opposite gender co-workers. They have recommended that the model applicable for females was a poor fit for the male sample, hence suggesting for the development of unique models for males and females.

It was considered important to have a separate section on *Dual Career families*. This can be understood as *secondary level intervention*. Dual career families are those families wherein both the husband and the wife are committed to their own careers. In addition to the time they need to progress speedily in their respective careers, they need time to contribute to the future careers of their children. Such families are under tremendous stress and consequently they are prone to negative outcomes of stress. Specific stressors and coping patters have been identified in this section. The section highlights the importance of coping style used as a couple rather than simply as individuals and the outcomes for the family and dual career couple.

As a *tertiary level intervention* the section on *gender inclusivity* in stress management interventions has been discussed. It begins with defining gender inclusivity as inclusion of both the genders at workplace not only in terms of increasing number but also including them in making decisions, sharing responsibilities, taking leadership roles, formulating regulations for an organization, having equal opportunities, etc. A framework consisting of three parts with the objective of identifying forces that were overlooked until recently and providing solutions for the newly defined problems has been discussed. A few important practices that companies can adopt to enhance gender inclusivity have also been highlighted.

The chapter ends with directions for future research and training interventions. Four distinct areas identified were:

1. Collecting statistics related to

    (i) women's participation in part time, full time, and self employment;
    (ii) sector-wise male–female comparisons;
    (iii) hierarchy-wise male–female comparisons.

2. Identifying magnitude and type of stressors in different professional groups.
3. Examining gender comparisons in coping mechanisms.
4. Developing two separate models to understand the dynamic nature of stress-coping-strain relationship for the two sexes/genders and related questions of similarities and differences across the two sexes/genders.

References

Agrawal, R. (2001). *Stress in life and at work*. California: SAGE.

Almeida, D.M., Wethington, E., & Kessler, R.C. (2002). The daily inventory of stressful events: An interview-based approach for measuring daily stressors. *Assessment, 9*(1), 41–55.

Anshel, M.H., Sutarto, T., & Jubenville, C. (2009). Racial and gender differences on sources of acute stress and coping style among competitive athletes. *The Journal of Social Psychology, 149*(2), 159–77.

Anshel, M.H. & Delany, J. (2001). Sources of acute stress, cognitive appraisals, and coping strategies of male and female child athletes. *Journal of Sport Behaviour, 24,* 329–53.

Anshel, M.H., Jamieson, J., & Raviv, S. (2001). Cognitive appraisals and coping strategies following acute stress among skilled competitive male and female athletes. *Journal of Sport Behaviour, 24,* 75–94.

Anshel, M.H. & Kaissidis, A.N. (1997). Coping style and situational appraisals as predictors of coping strategies following stressful events in sport as a function of gender and skill level. *British Journal of Psychology, 88,* 263–76.

Barnett, R.C., Raudenbush, S.W., Brennan, R.T., Pleck, J.H., & Marshall, N.L. (1995). Change in job and marital experiences and change in psychological distress: A longitudinal study of dual-earner couples. *Journal of Personality and Social Psychology, 69*(5), 839–50.

Bem, S.L. (1975). Sex role adaptability: One consequence of psychological androgyny. *Journal of Personality and Social Psychology, 31,* 634–43.

Britton, D.M. (2003). *At work in the iron cage: The prison as gendered organization*. New York: New York University Press.

Conway, M. (2000). On sex roles and representations of emotional experience—Masculinity, femininity, and emotional awareness. *Sex Roles, 43,* 687–98.

Dedovic, K., Wadiwalla, M., Engert, V., & Pruessner, J.C. (2009). The role of sex and gender socialization in stress reactivity. *Developmental Psychology, 45*(1), 45–55. (doi: 10.1037/a0014433).

Fielden, S.L., Tench, R., & Fawkes, J. (2003). Freelance communications workers in the UK: The impact of gender on well-being. *Corporate Communications, 8*(3), 187–96. Retrieved from: ABI/Inform Complete (accessed on January 20, 2011).

Fotinatos, R. & Cooper, C. (2005). The role of gender and social class in work stress. *Journal of Managerial Psychology, 20*(1/2), 14–23. Retrieved from: ABI/Inform Global (accessed on May 15, 2011).

Frankenhaeuser, M., et al. (1989). Stress on and off the job as related to sex and occupational status in white-collar workers. *Journal of Organizational Behavior, 10*, 321–46.

Gaan, N. (2008). Stress, social support, job attitudes and job outcome across gender. *The Icfai University Journal of Organizational Behaviour, 7*(4), 34–44.

Gaunt, R. & Benjamin, O. (2007). Job insecurity, stress and gender: The moderating effect of gender ideology. *Community, Work and Family, 10*(3), 341–55. (doi: 10.1080/13668800701456336).

Gaur, S.P. (1996). Employment status, occupational stress and adaptation patterns among women. Unpublished doctoral dissertation in psychology, University of Allahabad, Allahabad.

Gaur, S.P. & Dhawan, N. (2000). Work related stress and adaptation pattern among women professionals. *Psychological Studies, 45*(1 & 2), 58–64.

Gaur, S.P. (2006). Achieving inter-gender communication effectiveness in organizations. *VISION—The Journal of Business Perspective, 10*(2), 11–19.

Geller, P.A. & Hobfoll, S.E. (1994). Gender differences in job stress, tedium and social support in the workplace. *Journal of Social and Personal Relationships, 11*, 555–72.

Genre, V., Salvador, R.G., & Lamo, A. (2005, March). European women: Why do(n't) they work? Working paper series. Retrieved from: http://www.ecb.int/pub/pdf/scpwps/ecbwp454.pdf (accessed on February 5, 2012).

Griffin, M.L. (2006). Gender and stress: A comparative assessment of sources of stress among correctional officers. *Journal of Contemporary Criminal Justice, 22*(1), 4–25. (doi: 10.1177/1043986205285054).

Gyllensten, K. & Palmer, S. (2005). The role of gender in workplace stress: A critical literature review. *Health Education Journal, 64*(3), 271–88 (doi: 10.1177/001789690506400307).

Harriman, A. (1985). *Women/men/management.* New York: Praeger.

Hemmens, C., Stohr, M., Schoeler, M., & Miller, B. (2002). One step up, two steps back: The progression of perceptions of women's work in prisons and jails. *Journal of Criminal Justice, 30*, 473–89.

Hendrix, W.H., Spencer, B.A., & Gibson, G.S. (1994). Organizational and extra-organizational factors affecting stress, employee well-being, and absenteeism for males and females. *Journal of Business and Psychology, 9*(2), 103–28.

Huckabee, R.D. (1992). Stress in corrections: An overview of the issues. *Journal of Criminal Justice, 20*, 479–86.

Jurik, N. (1985). An officer and a lady: Organizational barriers to women working as correctional officers in men's prisons. *Social Problems, 32*, 375–88.

Kohlberg, L. (1966). A cognitive-developmental analysis of children's sex-role concepts and attitudes. In Maccoby, E. (Ed.), *The development of sex differences* (p. 82–173). Stanford, CA: Stanford University Press.

Kohler, J.M., Munz, D.C., & Grawitch, M.J. (2006). Test of a dynamic stress model for organizational change: Do males and females require different models? *Applied Psychology: An International Review, 55*(2), 168–91.

Korabik, K., McDonald, L.M., & Rosin, H.M. (1993). Stress, coping, and social support among women managers. In B.C. Long & S.E. Kahn (Eds), *Women, work, and coping: A multidisciplinary approach to workplace stress* (pp. 133–53). Montreal: McGill-Queen's University Press.

Kort-Butler, L.A. (2009). Coping styles and sex differences in depressive symptoms and delinquent behaviour. *Journal of Youth and Adolescence, 38,* 122–36. (doi: 10.1007/s10964-008-9291-x).

Lane, A.W., Jones, L., & Stevens, M.J. (2002). Coping with failure: The effects of self-esteem and coping on changes in self-efficacy. *Journal of Sport Behaviour, 25,* 331–45.

Liu, C., Spector, P. E., & Shi, L. (2008). Use of both qualitative and quantitative approaches to study job stress in different gender and occupational groups. *Journal of Occupational Health Psychology, 13*(4), 357–70. (doi: 10.1037/1076-8998.13.4.357).

McCarty, W.P., Zhao, J.S., & Garland, B.E. (2007). Occupational stress and burnout between male and female police officers: Are there any gender differences? *International Journal of Police Strategies & Management, 30*(4), 672–91. (doi: 10.1108/13639510710833938).

McDonough, P. & Walters, V. (2001). Gender and health: Reassessing patterns and explanations. *Social Science and Medicine, 52,* 547–59.

Misra, R., McKean, M., West, S., & Russo, T. (2000). Academic stress of college students: Comparison of student and faculty perceptions. *College Student Journal, 34,* 236–45.

Narayanan, L., Menon, S., & Spector, P.E. (1999). Stress in the workplace: A comparison of gender and occupations. *Journal of Organizational Behaviour, 20*(1), 63–73. Retrieved from ABI/Inform Complete (accessed on February 2, 2011).

Nauert PhD, R. (2007). Response to stress is gender specific. *Psych Central.* Retrieved from: http://psychcentral.com/news/2007/11/20/response-to-stress-is-gender-specific/1559.html (accessed on September 12, 2011).

Nelson, D.L. & Burke, R.J. (Eds) (2002). *Gender, work stress, and health.* Washington, DC: American Psychological Association.

Nelson, D.L. & Quick, J.C. (1985). Professional women: Are distress and disease inevitable? *Academy of Management Review, 10*(2), 206–18.

Ogiwara, C., Tsuda, H., Akiyama, T., & Sakai, Y. (2008). Gender-related stress among Japanese working women. *Transcultural Psychiatry, 45*(3), 470–88. (doi: 10.1177/1363461508094677).

Pogrebin, M.R. & Poole, E.D. (1998). Women deputies and jail work. *Journal of Contemporary Criminal Justice, 14,* 117–34.

Ptacek, J.T., Smith, R.E., & Zanas, J. (1992). Gender, appraisal, and coping: A longitudinal analysis. *Journal of Personality, 60,* 747–70.

Ministry of Labour and Employment, Govt. of India. (2010, October). *Report on employment and unemployment survey 2009–10.* Retrieved from: http://labourbureau.nic.in/Final_Report_Emp_Unemp_2009_10.pdf (accessed on January 31, 2012).

Rowlands, R. (2008, June). Stress agender. *Occupational Health, 60*(6). Retrieved from: ABI/Inform Global (accessed on May 10, 2011).

Savicki, V., Cooley, E., & Gjvesvold, J. (2003). Harassment as a predictor of job burnout in correctional officers. *Criminal Justice and Behaviour, 30,* 602–19.

Sharada, N. & Raju, M.V.R. (2001). Gender and role stress in organizations. *Journal of Indian Psychology, 19,* 50–55.

Singh, S. (n.d.). Gender equity: Not an even match. *Softdisk India.* Retrieved from: http://softdiskindia.com/articles.php?show=24 (accessed on January 20, 2012).

Spielberger, C.D. & Vagg, P.R. (1999). *The job stress survey: JSS professional manual.* Odessa, FL: Psychological Assessment Resources.

National Institute of Public Cooperation and Child Development (2010). Statistics on Women in India. Retrieved from: http://nipccd.nic.in/reports/ehndbk10.pdf (accessed on February 1, 2012).

Sujatha, B. (2007). Managing the stress: The gender divide. In Sen, P. (Ed.), *Gender equity in management: An introduction* (pp. 136–41). Hyderabad: The Icfai University Press.

Tamres, L.K., Janicki, D., & Helgeson, V.S. (2002). Sex differences in coping behavior: A meta-analytic review and an examination of relative coping. *Personality and Social Psychology Review, 6*(1), 2–30.

Trocki, K.F., & Orioli, E.M. (1994). Gender differences in stress symptoms, stress producing contexts, and coping strategies. In G.P. Keita & J.J. Hurrell Jr. (Eds), *Job stress in a changing workforce: Investigating gender, diversity, and family issues* (pp. 7–22). Washington, DC: American Psychological Association.

Vagg, P.R., Spielberger, C.D., & Wasala, C.F. (2002). Effects of organizational level and gender on stress in the workplace. *International Journal of Stress Management, 9,* 243–61.

World Health Organization. (2003). *Gender, health and aging.* Geneva, Switzerland: Department of Gender and Women's Health, World Health Organization.

Wright, K. & Saylor, W. (1991). Male and female employees' perceptions of prison work: Is there a difference. *Justice Quarterly, 8,* 505–24.

Wu, Y.C. & Shih, K.Y. (2010). The effects of gender role on perceived job stress. *The Journal of Human Resource and Adult Learning, 6*(2), 74–79.

Zappert, L.T. & Weinstein, H.M. (1985). Sex differences in the impact of work on physical and psychological health. *American Journal of Psychiatry, 142,* 1174–78.

Zimmer, L.E. (1986). *Women guarding men.* Chicago: University of Chicago Press.

Section-III

POSITIVE STRESS MANAGEMENT

10

Coping with Stress

Paulomi Sudhir and Arathi Taksal

Abstract

Stress is a ubiquitous phenomenon and references to it can be found as early as the 14th century. The understanding of the concept of stress has likewise undergone several changes over the years. One model integral to our understanding of stress is the transactional model proposed by Folkman and Lazarus (1984). This model stresses on the process of appraisal and effort at coping with stress based on the appraisal. Coping refers cognitive and behavioral efforts at mitigating stress and there is a vast amount of literature on coping styles, effectiveness, and its outcomes. Researchers delineate between problem and emotion-focused coping and argue that flexibility in adopting coping strategies is essential for coping efforts to be effective. Social support is another important contribution to the understanding of coping with stress and is a buffer for stress. Social support is also dynamic and reliant on various individual factors. Recent work on this topic has added newer perspectives on this process. This includes dual process models of coping, proactive, religious, social, and communal coping. Another recent development is the association between emotion regulation and coping and positive affect. These new directions in the field of coping with stress will contribute extensively to our understanding of coping and have important theoretical and clinical implications.

This chapter is an attempt to provide the reader with an overview of the field of coping with stress, and some the recent advances in this area.

Keywords: stress, coping, coping effectiveness, coping styles, emotions and coping, social support

Introduction

Reference to the term stress can be found as early as the early 14th century. However, the usage of the term "stress" has undergone considerable changes over time; from early reference to a physical load to more recently, an emotional breakdown in response to traumas of war (Lazarus, 1993). The term stress refers to both the demands placed on the person to adjust and the person's biological and psychological response to these demands. The word "stressor" refers to the events, and situations which make these demands.

Stress has been defined relationally (Holroyd and Lazarus, 1982), with reference to the person who experiences stress and the environment in which it occurs. Both positive and negative events can make demands on the individual. Positive stress is also called eustress (e.g., being promoted, getting married) and negative stress is called distress (e.g., losing a job or getting divorced).

Stress and coping are interrelated. Research on coping has increased tremendously over the years. A Google search keying the words "coping and stress" yielded 3,560,000 results, while a search on PubMed Central yielded 9857 results.

Stress can be experienced in several ways such as having to encounter frustrating situations, when personal goals are thwarted or due to pressures arising from internal or external sources, e.g., when personal expectations of topping an exam are high or experiencing conflicts between goals or shifting to a new city for better job prospects while having to stay away from family or choosing between two equally good colleges. Three main models of stress have been discussed. These include the *biological model* amongst which the "General Adaptation Syndrome" (GAS; Selye, 1956), describing the process of biological decompensation under continuous stress, is best known; the *field Model* of stress, based on Lewin's Field Theory which suggests that the psychological experience of a person is a function of the interaction between environment and the self; and the *transactional model* that emphasizes the appraisal and perception of the situation as critical (Lazarus & Folkman, 1984). Transactional model has generated immense research and continues to be a relevant approach to understanding stress and coping (Rao, 2009) and will be referred to in detail in the following section.

The Transactional Model of Stress and Coping

Lazarus & Folkman (1984: 19) define stress as a particular relationship between the person and the environment that is appraised by the person as taxing or exceeding his or her resources and endangering his or her well-being. The key points in the definition are *appraisal* and the *transaction*.

They propose that people use three types of appraisals when encountering a situation—primary, secondary, and reappraisal. *Primary appraisal* has been viewed as having motivational significance and involves evaluating the importance of the encounter for the self. If the individual perceives that the encounter is harmful or threatening, then it gives rise to negative emotions such as anxiety, sadness, or anger and the individual will engage in secondary appraisal to change the conditions that are stressful. *Secondary appraisal* consists of reviewing available options for altering or managing the perceived stress. Attribution is an important part in the appraisal process. According to Lazarus (1991), three secondary appraisal decisions are likely, assigning the blame or credit to either oneself or onto another, assessing one's coping potential and considering future expectations. Coping efforts have been strongly related to an individual's cognitive appraisal of the situation. The choice of coping efforts is made based on the stakes at hand and options available. The choice of a coping mechanism is also influenced by perceptions of personal control. Personal control refers to an individual's belief about one's ability to bring about change in the desired direction on the environment (Greenberger and Strasser, 1986: 165). Secondary appraisals are considered to be evaluative processes. Here the individual considers coping options that are available, and expectancies regarding outcome, self efficacy with regard to performing the response and the consequences of using that response (Lazarus and Folkman, 1984). The third cognitive appraisal, that of *re appraisal* is a feedback process in which reaction and counter reactions are appraised by the individual and leads to reappraisal of the person–environment relationship (Perrewe and Zellara, 1999).

The appraisal a person makes is influenced by individual factors such as values, goals, motivation, and general expectancies. Further, the more predictable, controllable the situation is, the less stressful it is perceived to be. If the potentially stressful event is highly likely to occur, the stress is greater. The transactional model is closely linked to the construct of coping and the person's repertoire of coping is a significant component in this model.

Coping refers to the constantly changing cognitive and behavioral efforts to manage specific external and/or internal demands that are appraised as exceeding the resources of the person (Lazarus and Folkman, 1984, p.141). Coping is a contextual and effortful process, which changes based on an evaluation of how successful the current coping is. The emphasis is on the ability to manage the situation rather than gaining mastery over it. Coping choice is affected by both primary and secondary appraisals (Folkman, Lazarus, Dunkel-Schetter, DeLongis, and Gruen, 1986).

Theoretical Issues and Framework in Coping with Stress

Diverse theoretical perspectives have contributed to our current understanding of coping and the measures of coping. Four major lines of theoretical perspectives have shaped our conceptualizations. These perspectives include ego/psychodynamic perspectives, developmental perspectives, lifecycle, and evolutionary perspectives. That ego processes serve to resolve intra-psychic conflicts were described first by Freud. Their aim is to reduce tension caused by the conflicts and the mechanisms adopted are largely cognitive in nature. The *developmental perspective* focuses on the growth or accumulation of personal coping resources over one's lifespan (Erikson, 1963). They develop during adolescence and are later consolidated and integrated into the self-concept. *The life cycle perspective* influenced the understanding of several coping resources such as self-esteem, competence motivations, stimulus seeking behavior and selection of coping responses, as well as appraisal of potentially threatening situations.

The influences of Darwin's *evolutionary perspective* can be seen on descriptions of behavioral problem-solving activities that contribute to the individual's survival. More recent aspects of this perspective are the functional aspects of problem-solving behavior and cognitive-oriented intervention components. Bandura's (1986) concept of self-efficacy as a coping resource is a related construct. The concept of environmental coping and environmental coping resources, such as culturally relevant coping resolutions, are important contributions of this perspective. These four perspectives have been integrated into a model that conceptualizes a link between life stress and functioning with coping resources and appraisal as mediating factors (Moos and Billings, 1982).

Theories of coping are classified into *trait and state oriented* and *macro and micro oriented* theories (Krohne, 1996). *Trait-oriented* theories are based on the strategy of early identification of people whose coping resources are insufficient to meet stressful encounters. *State-oriented* theories deal with actual coping and enhancing coping efficacy. Trait oriented theories identify both vigilance and moving towards the stressful situation and cognitive avoidance, or a move away from the stressful encounter. *Repression-sensitization* (Byrne, 1964) and *monitoring-blunting* (Miller, 1987) are two important theories described under this approach. The repressor typically denies or minimizes the negative consequences resulting from the stressful encounter or may fail to verbalize or avoids thinking about them. At the other end of this dimension are sensitizers, who react to the stressful situation by seeking out information, worry about it excessively. *Monitoring and Blunting* are conceptualized as cognitive information styles. According to this theory, people vary their arousal responses to stress depending on the amount of attention that is directed to the stressor. When a person employs cognitive avoidant strategies (denial, distraction), arousal can be lowered as the impact of the stressful situation also reduces. This is called *blunting* while the former strategy is referred to as *monitoring*. Blunting can be adaptive, when events are uncontrollable (an impending surgery). When events are controllable, monitoring (looking for information) may be more adaptive. Situational and personality factors influence the use of either of these strategies.

Defense mechanisms, problem-focused and emotion-focused coping strategies are examples of the macroanalytical approach. Defense mechanisms are also examples of state-oriented approaches.

A more recent approach has been that of the models of coping model (MCM; Krohne, 1993). The MCM states that stress situations have qualities of aversive stimulation and ambiguity. While the former leads to emotional arousal, the latter lead to the experience of uncertainty. In turn, these two reactions are linked to vigilance and cognitive avoidance, two independent personality dimensions (Krohne, 2002).

DIMENSIONS OF COPING

Researchers have examined two basic dimensions of coping—a vigilant, confrontative, *active* coping and another *avoidant*, emotional or palliative coping. Lazarus (1991) separates *problem-focused coping* from *emotion-focused coping*. Another distinction is that of *assimilative* (modifying the environment) and *accommodative* (modifying oneself) (Brandtstädter, 1992). This has also been referred to as mastery versus meaning (Taylor, 1983) or primary versus secondary control (Rothbaum et al., 1982). Individuals often change their coping strategies over time.

Problem-focused coping refers to efforts that are directed at solving the problem at hand and includes several strategies such as seeking information talking to friend, spouse, acquiring necessary skills (Lazarus and Folkman, 2004), making alternate plans or specific action taken and negotiation (Moos and Billings, 1982).

Problem-focused coping can be meaningful as well. This is because the person using problem-focused approach engages his or her attention on a certain goal. In turn, the achievement of these goals increases the individual's sense of mastery and control over the situation, both of which are essential for positive well being (Carver and Scheirer, 1998). Problem-focused coping occurs when the individual perceives the stressful situation as controllable and has been related to better adjusted outcomes (Billings and Moos, 1981; Endler and Parker, 1990b; Mitchell, Cronkite, and Moos, 1983).

Emotion-focused coping refers to attempts directed at emotions that accompany the stress. Emotion-focused coping is exhibited in behaviors such as avoidance, minimization, distancing, and selective attention, all of which work to cognitively reduce emotional distress (Lazarus and Folkman, 1984). It has been empirically related to maladapted outcomes (Endler and Parker, 1990a, 1990b). Some of the strategies under this dimension include *affective regulation* which involves direct efforts at controlling emotions associated with a stressful encounter through strategies of postponing, paying attention to an urge, working through one's problems; *resigned acceptance* (waiting for time to remedy the problem or accepting things as they are). Emotional discharge refers to verbal expression (crying, smoking or acting out) (Moos and Billings 1982). *Appraisal-focused coping* includes *logical analysis* or trying to identify the cause of the problem, paying attention to one aspect of the situation at a time, drawing on relevant past experiences, and mentally rehearsing possible actions and their consequences. *Cognitive redefinition* involves the individual accepting the reality of the situation, but restructuring it in a favorable manner. These cognitive strategies include thinking how it might have been worse, focusing on something good that has happened. *Cognitive avoidance* is another appraisal-focused coping and includes denying fear or anxiety, trying to forget the situation, engaging in wishful fantasies.

Problem-focused coping behaviors are more observable while emotion-focused coping involves covert cognitive processes (Compas et al., 1993). A third coping function labeled avoidance-oriented coping has also been empirically distinguished (Billings and Moos, 1981; Endler and Parker, 1990b). This coping has received less attention in research. *Avoidance-oriented coping* involves both task-oriented and emotion-oriented behaviors that help the individual forestall dealing with the stressor and includes behaviors such as seeking support from other people or purposely engaging in another activity. Although some researchers have found avoidance oriented coping beneficial in adolescents in high stress (Gonzales et al., 2001), others suggest that it is related to maladapted outcomes (Billings and Moos, 1981; Ebata and Moos, 1994; Endler and Parker, 1990a, 1990b).

Table 10.1 Dimensions of Coping

Type	Definition
Problem-focused	Dealing with the cause of the distress; looking at the ways of solving the problem.
Emotion-focused	Regulating the emotions associated with the problem or the distress.
Acceptance	Accepting that one is facing a problem that one cannot solve.
Instrumental social support	Seeking practical help or support from one's social circle, which can help solving the problem.
Emotional social support	Seeking emotional support form one's group, which provides space for ventilation and deburdening.
Attention diversion	Engaging in tasks, which will make one's mind and attention to divert away from the cause of distress.
Fostering meaning related activities	Engaging in tasks or activities, which foster a sense of meaning or purpose in life.
Religious coping	Relying on faith that (*a*) there is a *reason* why one has to face this problem, (*b*) that experiencing the problem may be a result of one's past *karma* so one has to deal with it, or (*c*) that God or some higher power will help in dealing with the situation.
Communication skills	Enhancing one's communication skills in order to solve the problem, to reach out to people who can provide emotional or instrumental social support.
Relaxation training	Learning how to relax using methods such as deep breathing, pranayama, meditation, or muscle relaxation.
Self statements	Giving oneself positive statements about being able to deal with the stress.
Emotion regulation	Using behavioral and cognitive strategies to calm oneself down.
Cognitive reappraisal	Since coping is a matter of belief or perception, restructuring one's beliefs about not being able to cope or that the situation is threatening.
Positive reappraisal	Seeing positives in the problem or challenging situation, aiming to reduce its threat component.

(Table 10.1 Continued)

(Table 10.1 Continued)

Type	Definition
Maladative coping strategies	
Substance use	Using addictive or psychoactive substances such as alcohol, nicotine to regulate the negative emotional state associated with the problem situation.
Denial	A defense mechanism where one denies having the problem at all.
Avoidance	Accepting that one has a problem and actively staying away from it.
Fantasy	Actively imagining or fantasizing, which creates positive affect, reducing the negative feelings associated with the problem.
Blaming	Blaming others for the problem situation or the difficulty, thereby absolving oneself of the responsibility; and thus reducing the distress.

PROBLEM-SOLVING ABILITIES

Effective problem-solving behaviors are crucial for successful adaptation. Social problem-solving refers to cognitive and behavioral skills that help the individual deal effectively with stressful situations and encounters that arise in everyday life (D'Zurilla et al., 2006). Problem-solving includes problem recognition and definition, generating possible solutions and selecting the best solution after evaluating the consequences of all alternatives (Spivack, Platt, and Shure, 1976). D'Zurilla et al. (2002) also include problem orientation, a general motivational and appraisal component, problem-solving style, which constitutes the cognitive and behavioral skills to cope with problems.

SOCIAL SUPPORT

Social support is closely linked to stress and coping. It includes social networks and social integration. Three categories of social support distinguished are social networks, social relationships, and social support (Cohen and Williams, 1985; House and Kahn, 1985). *Social networks* form the objective basis for both social support and social integration. *Social integration* refers to factors such as density, size of relationships *social support* refers to, the function and quality of these relationships, the perceived availability as well as the actual help or support received. In a comprehensive review of the construct of social support, Cohen and Williams (1985), describe the buffering role of social support. It can buffer stress by influencing the appraisal of the stress response. That is, the individual views the situation as less stressful due to having social support and considers it as something that can be coped with. It can also buffer stress through the actual presence of support, leading to reduction in physiological responses and even a practical solution for the stress.

Social networks are an important source of positive experiences and social rewards. Through them, social support can have a broader beneficial effect and in turn can improve affect and increase well-being as well as reduce negative experiences (Thoits, 1995). A social network provides a person with "psychosocial supplies" for the maintenance of mental and emotional health. Social support has two basic elements: (*a*) the perception that there are a sufficient number of available people on whom one can rely on, and (*b*) satisfaction with the available support. Personality impacts the seeking and use of social support (Sarason et al., 1983).

The important types of social support are *instrumental* (e.g., assisting with a specific problem), *tangible* (providing clothes), *informational* (giving advice), and *emotional* such as providing reassurance. Social support arises in a socially meaningful context and is reciprocal. An individual receiving support may feel obligated to return it and thus set up a harmonious network of both support and obligation. Two broad distinctions are made with reference to social support—actual social support received and perceived available social support. Perceived social support is more prospective and while actual support is retrospective.

Studies on social support show that it is linked to mortality and physical health (Schwarzer and Leppin, 1991; Schwazer, Knoll, and Rieckmann, 2003) through psychological pathways to recovery and diverse physical outcomes ranging from common cold to HIV infection (Glynn, Christenfeld, and Gerin, 1999; Hemingway, Nicholson, and Marmot, 1999). Several factors determine differences in who receives social support and these arise due to variations in need for social support, mobilization of relationships, and perception of social support. Gender differences in social support have been noted and women are reported to have greater number of close friendships than men, beginning from childhood, and are much more likely to develop close intimate relationships, although men may have larger numbers of friends. Women have also been found to provide greater emotional support to both men and women and also receive greater support than men (Klauer and Winkeler, 2002).

COPING EFFECTIVENESS

The belief that coping can either be more or less effective has been discussed by researchers. Coping outcomes can vary based on the context. What is effective in one situation may be ineffective at a later point. Characteristics of the stressful situation such as controllability also influence coping effectiveness. Several points need to be considered while evaluating the effectiveness or ineffectiveness of coping. Outcomes of coping are goals that are determined either by the individual (personal goals) or *a priori* goals set by the researcher, based on research objectives. These goals have varied from specific to generic goals, e.g., feeling better, solving a problem effectively (Cummings et al., 1994, McCrae and Costa 1986) to better management of emotions, improved social interactions, and increased self-esteem (Laux and Weber, 1991). Limiting oneself to specific goals narrows down the understanding of coping and its complexities. Goals of coping can be *proximal* (an immediate psycho-physiological change) or *distal,* which occurs over a course of time being influenced by other factors (improving social interactions).

In addition to the contextual nature of coping, the fit between the coping response and the stressful encounter is also important. Folkman and Moskovitz (2004) raise several other issues in their discussion of coping effectiveness. These include evaluation of the goal and its personal significance. Focusing exclusively on mastery and resolution would limit the understanding of effective coping to those situations in which the stress is time-limited and not applicable to chronic strains that do not completely resolve and the individual has to learn to continuously adapt to the stress. The ability to change one's responses in response to changing situational demands in referred to as *coping flexibility* and is said to be a good fit between characteristics of coping strategies and the nature of stressful events (Aldwin, 1994; Cheng, 2003).

In general, adaptive strategies of problem-focused coping and reappraisal are found to help in better adaptation, and in effectively reducing the experience of stress. Predominant use of emotion-focused coping such as denial, distraction has been associated with higher negative psychological outcomes and poorer overall adjustment and maintenance of the stress and distress (Folkman, Lazarus, Gruen, and DeLongis, 1986; Moffat, McConnachie, Ross, and Morrison, 2004).

COPING RESOURCES AND COPING STRATEGIES

Coping resources are social and personal characteristics which people may draw from while dealing with stressors (Pearlin and Schooler, 1978). According to Schwazer and Taubert (2002), personal resources are internal coping options available to an individual in a particular stressful situation. A person with resources such as perceived competence, being affluent, healthy, optimistic, or capable is less vulnerable toward stress. Social competence, empathy, and assertiveness are needed to deal with specific interpersonal demands. Adaptive strategies develop when people estimate their potential for action accurately and are labeled "perceived self-efficacy" or "optimistic self-beliefs" by Bandura (1977). These two are prerequisites for coping with several kinds of stress. A sense of control and mastery over life are believed to influence the choice and the efficacy of coping strategies.

Issues of Measurement

Measurement of coping is a challenging issue. The interest in theoretical models of stress and coping led to the development of various measures, checklists, and questionnaires to assess the process and methods of coping. Early attempts at measuring coping included asking respondents to list thoughts and behaviors in response to stressful events. Most of these measures capture retrospective reports of how people cope with a specific event using case vignettes.

Skinner (2006) identifies "families of coping" that include an organization of different ways of coping into one higher order family. This family includes a variety of coping that serve the same functions when dealing with stress (e.g., planning, decision-making, and action under problem-solving). Difficulties in conceptually separating coping from coping resources (hardiness, self-efficacy, optimism) and cognitive coping from cognitive appraisal have complicated measurement of coping. The other issue has been of *stability* or patterns in the use of stable coping strategies at different time points in individuals and *generality* which refers to the consistency in coping across different situations and assumes that people generalize strategies to some degree across situations. The third issue is that *coping behaviors* or strategies can be grouped on the basis of their function or value which makes assessment more parsimonious (Schwarzer and Schwarzer, 1996).

Over the years, a large number of scales to assess coping have been developed. Skinner et al. (2003) identified nearly 100 assessments that covered about 400 ways of coping. The complexity of coping phenomenon itself poses an important problem in the assessment of coping and accurately capturing this construct has been difficult.

The difficulty in drawing distinctions between cognitive coping and appraisal is a major issue in coping research. Lazarus tries to answer this difficulty in his statement "… *coping* refers to what a person thinks or does to try to manage an emotional encounter; and *appraisal* is an evaluation of what might be thought or done in that encounter" (Skinner et al., 2003: 113). The gap between theory and research in coping is an ever widening one. Theorists develop explanations to understand adaptation to stress and different methods of coping. However, researchers have predominantly used cross-sectional models and multi-wave approaches to study stress and coping. While single subject designs are best suited to understand an individual's coping processes, this method has been used infrequently. Prospective measurements such as daily or within-day are used to measure coping and adaptation in process-oriented research.

Time intensive, idiographic approaches or research designs allow researchers to study proximal stressors, coping efforts, and adaptational outcomes in settings in which they actually occur and allow one to track changes due to mood or coping, close their context of occurrence (Somerfield & McCrae, 2000) and minimize recall errors. It overcomes problems due to retrospective accounts of stress and coping.

Most of the coping measures have been developed and validated using one of two general approaches (Edwards & Baglioni, 1999). The first involves assembling items from various sources (e.g., open-ended descriptions of coping episodes, existing coping measures) to represent a range of coping strategies and empirically determining the structure underlying the items, based on exploratory factor analyses Examples include the *ways of coping questionnaire* (Folkman and Lazarus, 1980; Folkman and Lazarus, 1988), *coping strategy indicator* (Amirkhan, 1990). A second approach uses an *a priori* method of defining a set of coping dimensions, generating or adapting items to represent each dimension, and then determining empirically the extent to which each item is associated with its intended dimension. Existing theory is used to both generate and define coping dimensions as well as to assign them to dimensions. Exploratory factor analysis is used to determine and evaluate the degree to which items represent their intended dimensions. The Coping Orientation to Problems Experienced (COPE; Carver et al. 1989) and the Coping Inventory for Stressful Situations (CISS; Endler & Parker, 1990a) are examples of this second approach.

MEASURES OF COPING

The following section enumerates some coping measures available in literature. There are a large number of measures available in literature and a complete review would be beyond the scope of this chapter (see Schwarzer and Schwarzer, 1996 for review). Table 10.2 summarizes some of the important measures and their properties.

The CCL has generated considerable research covering several populations. Among executives, a personality constellation characterized by a high control, commitment, and challenge were associated with greater problem-focused coping and higher well-being, while avoidance coping and distraction were correlated with greater psychological distress and lower well-being (Ahuja, Rao, and Subbakrishna, 1999). A study on married working women indicated that coping behaviors are stable over stressful episodes and type of stressor as well as the domain in which it occurred and the perceived control over it influenced the coping behavior used (Murthy, 2007). Studies on coping behaviors in clinical samples indicate the use of denial and escape more frequently in patients with depression. Normals also report greater use of problem-focused coping than clinical samples (Sharma, 2007). Rammhohan, Rao, and Subbakrishna, (2002) report that caregivers of patients with schizophrenia used religious coping in the initial stages, and denial and the strength of religious beliefs contributed to psychological well-being.

Interventions to Enhance Coping

Integral to coping with stress are interventions developed to enhance coping. These have aimed at increasing coping repertoire, coping strategies associated with better outcomes. Cognitive behavioral programs that include strategies such as reappraisal of the stressful situations, problem-solving skills, skills to enhance coping effectiveness and self-efficacy, and emotion regulation skills and anxiety management have greatest efficacy. The stress inoculation (SIT) model (Meichenbaum, 2007) postulates that stressful situations can be anticipated and individuals can acquire skills to inoculate themselves against it. Stress inoculation programs focus on reconceptualization of the stress, acquisition of skills to deal with the stress, rehearsal and application in real life. SIT has been used widely in populations such as paramilitary forces, patients who are posted for surgeries, and exam-related fears. Recent studies indicate the need for adaptive emotion regulation strategies using therapeutic strategies such as Mindfulness Based Stress Reduction, Acceptance and

Table 10.2 An Overview of Psychometric Instruments Used for Measuring Coping Strategies/Styles

Instrument	Authors	Psychometric Properties	Model	Items	Scoring	Dimensions
Ways of Coping Question- naire	Folkman and Lazarus (1980)	Reliability estimates average— 0.77 and range from .56 to .91.	Transactional model	68	4 point Likert type 0–4	Cognitive and behavioral strategies used in stressful situations
Coping Orientation to Problems Experienced (COPE)	Carver et al. (1989)	Construct validity and test–retest reliability; Internal reliabilities for 10 of the 13 three-item scales have alphas ranging from 0.65 to 0.90	Behavioral self-regulation and cognitive relational	60	4 point Likert type 1–4	15 subscales (Acceptance, Alcohol–Drug Disengage- ment, Behavioral Disengage- ment, Denial, Focus on and Venting of Emotion, Humor, Mental Disengagement, Positive Reinterpretation and Growth, Seeking Social Sup- port for Emotional Reasons, Turning to Religion.)
The Coping Responses Inventory (CRI)	Moos (1993)	Internal consistency ranges from 0.51 to 0.74	Approach- avoidance orientation cognitive and behavioral coping	48	4 point likert type 1–4	Approach and avoidance (Logical Analysis, Positive reappraisal, Seeking Guid- ance and Support, Problem- solving, Cognitive Avoidance, Acceptance or Resignation, Seeking Alternative Rewards, and Emotional Discharge)

Measure	Author	Reliability		Scoring	Construct
Coping Strategy Indicator (CSI)	Amirkhan, (1990)	Internal consistency for each of the subscales ranges from 0.86 to 0.98 for Problem-solving, 0.89 to 0.98 for Seeking Social Support and from 0.77 to 0.96 for Avoidance	78		problem-solving, seeking social support, avoidance
Coping Inventory for Stressful Situations	Endler and Parker (1990)	internal consistency was tested using coefficient alpha reliabilities which ranged from 0.87 to 0.92 for the task oriented scale, 0.82 to 0.90 for the emotion-oriented scale, and 0.69 to 0.85 for the avoidance oriented scale	48	5 point frequency scales	task-oriented, emotion-oriented and avoidance-oriented coping strategies
Miller Behavioral Style Scale	Miller (1987)	The internal consistency of the monitoring and blunting sub-scales of the MBSS was alpha = 0.65 and 0.41 respectively. Test-retest analyses show the MBSS subscales to be highly stable over a 4-month period: for the monitoring subscale = .72; for the blunting subscale = .75	Attentional styles 32	Items scored as loading on Monitoring (M) or Blunting (B).	Monitoring and blunting information processing styles

(Table 10.2 Continued)

(Table 10.2 Continued)

Instrument	Authors	Psychometric Properties	Model	Items	Scoring	Dimensions
Health and Daily Living Coping Response Index	Moos, Cronkite, Billings, and Finney (1986)	Coefficient alphas for the coping response indexes were low to moderate: 0.69, 0.66, and 0.48 for Active Behavioral, Active Cognitive, and Avoidance Coping, respectively		32	3 point rating	Active Behavioral Coping, Active Cognitive Coping, Avoidance coping
Life Events and Coping Inventory	Dise-Lewis, (1988)	0.74			9-point Likert-type scale (1–9)	
Cybernetic Coping Scale	Edwards, (1988, 1992)	Reliability estimates 0.79 to 0.94.	Cybernetic theory			Accommodation, devaluation, avoidance, symptom reduction, changing the situation
Life Situations Inventory	Feifel and Strack (1989)	Pooled within-situations correlations between the scales r = 0.01 for problem-solving with avoidance, r = 0.22 for problem-solving with resignation, and r = 0.51 for avoidance with resignation.	Principal coping inventories	28 items	4 point rating scale	5 Conflict areas Problem-solving, avoidance, and resignation
Coping Checklist (CCL)	Rao, Subbakrishna and Prabhu (1989)	Retest reliability 0.74		70		Problem-solving and five emotion focused coping (denial, distraction positive, distraction negative, religion/faith and acceptance) and social support

Commitment Therapy (ACT). These approaches recommend reappraising emotional experiences and viewing them non-judgmentally (Barlow et al., 2004, Hayes et al., 1999, Linehan, 1993, Majgi Sharma, and Sudhir 2006; Mennin et al., 2002, Segal et al., 2002).

Worksite stress management interventions have been researched extensively and involve principles similar to individual stress management. Organizational factors are also taken into account to reduce factors that contribute to the experience of stress. Semmer (2003) classifies work site stress prevention programs as being person-focused interventions, organization-focused interventions, or both. Person focused interventions include stress management approaches based on cognitive behavioral principles. Organization-based programs focus on: (*a*) the nature of tasks, (*b*) the work environment, and (*c*) social relationships at work. Research indicates that SMT programs with relaxation component are most effective. A major lacuna in this area is lack of follow up and emphasis on process issues (Bamberg & Busch, 2006; Lamontagne et al., 2007; van der Klink et al. 2001). Several interventions have been reported with students, workforce women executives, paramilitary forces, and IT (Information Technology) professionals (Barmi, 2007, Majgi, Sharma, & Sudhir 2006; Majgi, 2008; Manpreet, 2010; Verma, 2007). Training medical students in stress management has shown to produce positive benefits such as better immunological functions, increased empathy, and positive coping skills (Shapiro et al., 2000).

Future Directions

The field of coping with stress is ever growing; and in this process, we are faced with newer issues and challenges in understanding nature of coping and stress. In this section, we highlight the emerging research issues on different themes of coping.

PROACTIVE COPING

People often cope in *anticipation* of stressful events and act before the occurrence of stressful events or take steps to avoid or minimize them. *Proactive coping* consists of efforts that the individual undertakes in advance of a potentially demanding event and aim is to prevent or modify it before it actually occurs (Aspinwall and Taylor, 1997). Proactive coping is temporally *prior* to coping and anticipatory coping. It is a *general preparation* for coping with stressful situations such as accumulation of knowledge resources and acquisition skills. These are not designed to address any specific or particular stressor but help prepare the individual with the understanding that stressors do occur in life, and that one needs to be prepared. Recently, there have been mixed findings about the use of proactive coping. Choudior, Norton et al. (2011) reported that persons with HIV/AIDS did not use proactive coping to deal with the stress of the illness; instead spiritual peace moderated the effect of HIV stigma on depression when the stigma was high. A metaanalysis of 63 studies, however, indicated that it was associated with greater physical and psychological well-being in persons living with HIV/AIDS (Moskowitz, Hult, Bussolari, & Acree, 2009).

DUAL PROCESS MODEL OF COPING

Though it is understood that coping is contextual, Cheng (2003) raises the question how do people actually generate alternate coping mechanisms and what helps them in being flexible in the use of coping strategies? Two constructs were proposed to explain this are that of *discriminative facility*, defined as the person's active appraisal of situational characteristics, and their choice among alternative behaviors in response to changing contingencies and *need for closure*, defined as difficulty in tolerating ambiguity or uncertainty (Chiu, Hong, Mischel, & Shoda, 1995; Shoda, 1996). It was proposed that when people with a high need for closure face stress, they are highly motivated to quickly use a coping strategy which will "close" the situation, which brings about pleasant emotions or relief. Cognitive closure, however, does not allow for sufficient information processing. The person also quickly stops or "closes" the cognitive process of searching for an appropriate coping strategy, ending in a premature judgment and ineffective handling of stress. However, in the effort to reduce ambiguity, the person is likely to have used an inappropriate strategy to cope. This model has been researched in various contexts such as coping with loss and bereavement (Stroebe & Schut, 2001), positive emotions, and coping.

SOCIAL ASPECTS OF COPING

More recently the social aspects of coping such as communal coping and prosocial coping have been considered (Folkman & Moskowitz, 2004; Wells et al, 1997). *Communal coping* refers to the pooling of resources and efforts of several people (families, friends) in order to deal with a difficult situation (Lyons, Mickelson, Sullivan, and Coyne, 1998). Evidence of this type of coping can be seen in communities that get together to cope with natural disasters.

RELIGIOUS COPING

The interest in religious coping has increased with the knowledge that religion and spirituality impact aspects of physical and mental health. The RCOPE, measures religious coping and consists of five religious coping functions in response to stressors (Pargament et al., 2000) such as achieving a sense of mastery, finding comfort, fostering social solidarity, and aspects related to meaning making. In an Indian study of caregivers of patients with schizophrenia (Rammhohan, Rao, and Subbakrishna, 2002), the strength of religious belief was found to play an important role in helping family members to cope with the stress of caring for a mentally ill relative. Recently, in a study on coping with stressful interpersonal events, positive religious coping and reaching out were found to be related to post-traumatic growth; negative religious coping was correlated with depression; and isolation was related to both depression and angry feelings (Hashim, Pargament, and Mahoney, 2011). Though studies have shown that religious/spiritual coping helps in dealing with stress, the challenge lies in incorporating components of these in counseling or therapy or stress management programs. Secular aspects of religious coping, spirituality, and need to be addressed in future research.

EMOTION REGULATION

Our understanding of the activation of stress has also accommodated the view that the experience of stress can lead to a variety of emotions. Appraisal theorists contend that emotions are elicited in response to the person's evaluation of an event or encounter as being central to their well-being (Roseman, 1984; Scherer, 1984; Schmidt, Tinti, Levine, and Testa, 2010). Various emotion regulation strategies have been identified (Gross 1998; Thayer et al. 1994; Walden and Smith, 1997). Gross (1998) describes five sets of strategies that include: (*a*) situation selection, which consists of approaching or avoiding people, places, or objects in order to regulate emotions; (*b*) situation modification, aimed at changing the situation to alter its emotional impact; (*c*) attentional deployment, includes strategies like distraction and rumination; (*d*) cognitive change, entailing reappraisal which transforms the initial appraisal of the event; and (*e*) Response-focused strategies that influence physiological, experiential, or behavioral aspects of the emotional response. Empirical evidence shows that reappraisal and distraction are more effective than expressive suppression in down-regulating emotions (Gross 2001; Richards and Gross 2000). Effective regulation of emotions is crucial to successful outcomes of coping. Some strategies such as rumination, suppression, and avoidance increase the emotional distress in the long run and maintain negative affective states and are related to onset of depression (Ciesla and Roberts 2007; Nolan, Roberts, and Gotlieb, 1998). However, adaptive suppression can lead to better adjustment. Evidence for this comes from studies on bereavement (Bonanno, Keltner, Holen, and Horowitz, 1995), sexual abuse (Bonanno, Noll, Putnam, O'Neill, and Trickett, 2003), and other traumatic events (Gross and John 2003).

COPING AND POSITIVE AFFECT

There is increasing evidence that positive affect has significant adaptive functions in the coping process (Folkman and Moskowitz, 2000). Researchers have tried to understand how positive affect is generated and what sustains it in the face of stress over long periods of time. Positive affect acts as a buffer against stress and the negative physiological consequences of stressful encounters. Positive reappraisal, goal-directed problem-focused coping and the infusion of ordinary events with positive meaning (Folkman and Moskowitz, 2000) are related to the occurrence and maintenance of positive affect (Folkman, Moskowitz, Ozer, and Park, 1997). *Positive reappraisal* refers to cognitive strategies for framing a situation in a positive light. It helps particularly in chronic stressful situations, such as care giving in chronic illness. People who use positive reappraisal focus on not only their efforts but on the value of these efforts.

Theories on stress-related growth also suggest that personal growth occurs as a result of an individual's crisis experience and struggle. Positive growth related aspects of stress and coping have been documented by various researchers working with grief (Strobe and Schut, 1999), caregivers of patients with HIV/AIDS (Folkman et al., 1997).

A closely associated construct to the positive aspects of coping is that of meaning making (Park, 2010; Schwarzer and Knoll, 2003). This includes both situational meaning as well as global meaning (Park and Folkman, 1997). *Situational meaning* refers to a personal significance of a stressful situation or event in relation to the goals and beliefs of the individual and *global meaning* refers to an individual's beliefs, values, and purpose/goal (Folkman and Moskowitz, 2000). There is a need to broaden existing models of stress and coping and to examine positive affect generated by stressful events as well as to go beyond negative affect.

COPING PROCESSES AND ADAPTATION

There has been considerable work in the area of coping and adaptational outcomes. The work on coping and adaptation primarily began with work in the field of health and health-related outcomes. Effective coping has been associated with lower mortality and better health outcomes, although this needs to be viewed keeping in mind the complexity of interrelationships between stress and health and health and coping. Coping is also a major factor in relation to stress and psychological outcomes such as depression and somatic illness (Schwazer and Leppin, 2008). Coping and adaptation is closely associated with the range, quality, and availability of social relations.

Conclusion

Coping is a dynamic process that includes multidimensional, interrelated constructs of appraisal, coping strategies, and styles. Research on coping has spanned several decades, but the gaps between theoretical research and clinical applications continue. The broad dimensions of coping are of problem-focused and emotion-focused coping and they remain prominent in coping research. There is growing emphasis on other dimensions of coping such as avoidant or assimilitative. Coping measurement is a challenging area and due to its complex nature, a complete effort to capture coping is difficult.

Several Indian studies have been carried out on stress, coping, and stress management interventions. However, there are several methodological difficulties with these studies. Major conclusions that can be drawn from the stress management interventions are that interventions are *based on building cognitive behavioral skills*. Programs with a relaxation component have yielded the best results. Worksite stress management programs are carried out both at individual and organizational levels. Researchers in the area of coping and stress emphasize the need to modify research deigns in order to capture the complexity of coping process. These may include longitudinal studies, intensive sampling methods on a relatively continuous basis, and experience sampling.

Further research on understanding newer dimensions of coping such as proactive coping, religious and communal coping are required. Emotion regulation and coping as well as positive emotions and coping are promising areas that will take the field forward and extend to people who are coping effectively.

References

Hashim, A., Pargament, K., & Mahoney, A. (2011). Examining coping methods with stressful interpersonal events experienced by Muslims living in the United States following the 9/11 attacks. *Psychology of Religion and Spirituality, 3*(1), 1–14.

Ahuja, J., Rao, K., & Subbakrishna, D.K. (1999). Psychological health in executives–The role of hardiness and coping behaviours. *Behaviour Medicine Journal, 2,* 30–38.

Aldwin, C.M. (1994). *Stress, coping, and development: An integrative perspective.* New York: Guilford.

Amirkhan, J.H. (1990). A factor analytically derived measure of coping: The coping strategy indicator. *Journal of Personality and Social Psychology, 59,* 1066–74.

——— (1994). Criterion validity of a coping measure. *Journal of Personality Assessment, 62,* 242–61.

Aspinwall, L.G. & Taylor, S.E. (1997). A stitch in time: Self regulation and proactive coping. *Psychological Bulletin, 121*(3), 417–36.

Bandura, A. (1977). *Social learning theory.* Englewood Cliffs, NJ: Prentice-Hall.

——— (1986). *Social foundations of thought and action: A social cognitive theory.* Englewood Cliffs, NJ: Prentice-Hall.

Bamberg, E. & Busch, C. (2006). Stressbezogene interventionen in der arbeitswelt [Stress-related interventions at the workplace]. *Zeitschrift für Arbeits- und Organisationspsychologie, 50,* 215–26.

Barlow, D.H., Allen, L.B., & Choate, M.L. (2004). Toward a unified treatment for emotional disorders. *Behavior Therapy, 35,* 205–30.

Barmi, B. (2007). Stress management in executives. M.Phil thesis. In A. Shah & K. Rao (Eds), *Psychological research in mental health & neurosciences, 1957–2007* (p. 371). Bangalore: NIMHANS (Deemed University).

Billings, A.G. & Moos, R.H. (1981). The role of coping responses and social resources in attenuating the stress of life events. *Journal of Behavioral Medicine, 4,* 139–57.

Brandtstädter, J. (1992). Personal control over development: Implications of self-efficacy. In R. Schwarzer (Ed.), *Self-efficacy: Thought control of action* (pp. 127–45). Washington, DC: Hemisphere.

Bonanno, G.A., Keltner, D., Holen, A., & Horowitz, M.J. (1995). When avoiding unpleasant emotions might not be such a bad thing: Verbal-automatic response dissociation and midlife conjugal bereavement. *Journal of Personality and Social Psychology, 69,* 975–89.

Bonanno, G.A., Noll, J.G., Putnam, F.W., O'Neill, M., & Trickett, P. (2003). Predicting the willingness to disclose childhood sexual abuse from measures of repressive coping and dissociative experiences. *Child Maltreatment, 8,* 1–17.

Byrne, D. (1964). Repression–sensitization as a dimension of personality. In B.A. Maher (Ed.), *Progress in experimental personality research* (Volume 1, pp. 169–220). New York: Academic Press.

Carver, C.S. & Scheier, M.F. (1998). *On the self-regulation of behavior*. New York: Cambridge University Press.

Carver, C.S., Scheier, M.F. & Weintraub, J.K. (1989). Assessing coping strategies: A theoretically based approach. *Journal of Personality and Social Psychology, 56*, 267–83.

Cheng, C. (2003). Cognitive and motivational processes underlying coping flexibility: A dual process model. *Journal of Personality and Social Psychology, 84*(2), 425–38.

Chiu, C., Hong, Y., Mischel, W., & Shoda, Y. (1995). Discriminative facility in social competence: Conditional versus dispositional encoding and monitoring-blunting of information. *Social Cognition, 13,* 49–70.

Ciesla, J.A. & Roberts, J.E. (2007). Rumination, negative cognition, and their interactive effects on depressed mood. *Emotion, 7*(3), 555–65.

Cohen, S. & Williams, T.A. (1985). Stress, social support and the buffering hypothesis. *Psychological Bulletin, 98*(2), 310–57.

Compas, B.E., Orosan, P.G., & Grant, K.E. (1993). Adolescent stress and coping: Implications for psychopathology during adolescence. *Journal of Adolescence, 16*, 331–49.

Coyne, J.C., & Fiske, V. (1992). Couples with Chronic illness. In T.J. Akamatse, J.C., Crowther, S.C. Hobfoll, & M.A.P. Stevens (Eds), *Family health psychology*. Washington DC: Hemisphere.

Cummings, E.M., Davies, P.T., & Simpson, K.S. (1994). Marital conflict gender and children's appraisals and coping efficacy as mediators of child adjustment. *Journal of Family Psychology, 8*(2), 141–49.

Dise-Lewis, J.E. (1988). The life events and coping inventory: An assessment of stress in children. *Psychosomatic Medicine, 50*, 484–99.

D'Zurilla, T.J., Nezu, A.M., & Maydeu-Olivares, A. (2002). *Social problem solving inventory— revised: Technical manual*. New York: Multi-Health Systems Inc.

D'Zurilla, T.J., Nezu, A.M., & Nezu, C.M. (2006). *Problem-solving therapy: A positive approach to clinical intervention* (Third edition). New York: Springer Publishing Company.

Ebata, A.T. & Moos, R.H. (1994). Personal, situational, and contextual correlates of coping in adolescence. *Journal of Research on Adolescence. 4*(1), 99–125.

Edwards, J.R. (1992). A cybernetic theory of stress, coping, and well-being in organizations. *Academy of Management Review, 17*, 238–74.

———— (1988). The determinants and consequences of coping with stress. In C.L. Cooper & R. Payne (Eds), *Causes, coping, and consequences of stress at work* (pp. 233–63). New York: Wiley.

Edwards, J.R. & Baglioni, A.J. (1999). Empirical versus theoretical approaches to the measurement of coping: A comparison using the ways of coping questionnaire and the cybernetic coping scale. In P. Dewe, T. Cox, & M. Leiter (Eds), *Coping and health in organizations* (pp. 21–50). London: Taylor & Francis.

Endler, N.S. & Parker, J.D.A. (1990a). *Coping inventory for stressful situations (CISS):* Manual. Toronto: Multi Health Systems.

Endler, N.S. & Parker, J.D.A. (1990b). Multidimensional assessment of coping: A critical evaluation. *Journal of Personality & Social Psychology, 58*, 844–54.

Erikson, E.H. (1963). *Childhood and society* (Second edition). New York: Norton.

Feifel, H. & Strack, S. (1989). Coping with conflict situations: Middle-aged and elderly men. *Psychology and Aging, 4*(1), 26–33.

Folkman, S. & Lazarus, R.S. (1980). An analysis of coping in a middle-aged community sample. *Journal of Health and Social Behavior, 21*, 219–39.

Folkman, S. & Lazarus, R.S. (1988). *Manual for the ways of coping questionnaire.* Palo Alto, CA: Consulting Psychologists Press.

Folkman, S., Lazarus, R.S., Dunkel-Schetter, C., DeLongis, A., & Gruen, R.J. (1986). Dynamics of a stressful encounter: Cognitive appraisal, coping, and encounter outcomes. *Journal of Personality and Social Psychology, 50,* 992–1003.

Folkman, S., Lazarus, R.S., Gruen, R., & DeLongis, A. (1986). Appraisal, coping, health status, and psychological symptoms. *Journal of Personality and Social Psychology, 50,* 572–79.

Folkman, S. & Moskowitz, J.T. (2000). Positive affect and the other side of coping. *American Psychologist, 55(6),* 647–54.

——— (2004). Coping: Pitfalls and promise. *Annual Review of Psychology, 55,* 745–74.

Folkman, S., Moskowitz, J.T., Ozer, E.M., & Park, C.L. (1997). Positive meaningful events and coping in the context of HIV/AIDS. In B.H. Gottlieb (Ed.), *Coping with chronic stress.* New York: Plenum Press.

Glynn, L., Christenfeld, N., & Gerin, W. (1999). Gender, social support, and cardiovascular responses to stress. *Psychosomatic Medicine, 61(2),* 234–42.

Gonzales, N.A., Tein, J., Sandler, I.N., & Friedman, R.J. (2001). On the limits of coping: Interactions between stress and coping for inner-city adolescents. *Journal of Adolescent Research, 16,* 372–95.

Greenberger, D.B. & Strasser, S. (1986). Developing and application of a model of personal control in organizations. *Academy of Management Review, 11,* 164–77.

Gross, J.J. (1998). Antecedent and response focused emotion regulation: Divergent consequences for experience, expression and physiology. *Journal of Personality and Social Psychology, 74(1),* 224–37.

——— (2001). Emotional regulation in adulthood: Timing is everything. *Current Direction in Psychology Science, 10,* 214–19.

Gross, J.J. & John, O.P. (2003). Individual differences in two emotion regulation processes: Implications for affect, relationships, and well-being. *Journal of Personality and Social Psychology, 85,* 348–62.

Hayes, S.C., Strosahl, K.D., & Wilson, K.G. (1999). *Acceptance and commitment therapy.* New York: The Guilford Press.

Hemingway, H., Nicholson, A., & Marmot, M. (1997). The impact of socioeconomic status on health functioning as assessed by the sf-36 questionnaire: The whitehall II study. *American Journal of Public Health, 87(9),* 1484–90.

Holroyd, K.A. & Lazarus, R.S. (1982). Stress, coping and somatic adaptation. In L. Goldberger & S. Breznitz (Eds), *Handbook of stress: Theoretical and clinical aspects.* New York: Free press.

House, J.S. & Kabarl, R.L. (1985). Measures and concepts of social support. In Sheldon Cohen and S. Leonard Syme (Eds), *Social support and health* (pp. 83–108). New York: Academic Press.

Klauer, T. & Winkeler, M. (2002). Gender, mental health status, and social support during a stressful event. In G. Weidner, M. Kopp, & M. Kristenson (Eds), *Heart disease: Environment, stress, and gender* (*NATO Science Series*, Series I: *Life and behavioural Sciences*, Volume 327, pp. 223–36). Amsterdam: IOS Press.

Krohne, H.W. (1996). Individual differences in coping. In M. Zeidner & N.S. Endler (Eds), *Handbook of coping: Theory, research, and applications.* New York: Wiley.

Krohne, H.W. (2002). Stress and coping theories. Retrieved from: http://userpage.fuberlin. de/~schuez/folien/Krohne_Stress.pdf

Lamontagne, A.D., Keegel, T., Louie, A.M., Ostry, A., & Landsbergis, P.A. (2007). A systematic review of the job-stress intervention evaluation literature, 1990–2005. *International Journal of Occupational and Environmental Health, 13*, 268–80.

Laux, L. & Weber, H. (1991). Presentation of self in coping with anger and anxiety: An intentional approach. *Anxiety Research, 3*(4), 233–55.

Lazarus, R.S. (1991). *Emotion and adaptation.* New York: Oxford University Press.

——— (1993). From psychological stress to the emotions: A history of changing outlooks. *Annual Review of Psychology, 44*, 1–22.

——— (1993). Coping theory and research: Past, present, and future. *Psychosomatic Medicine, 55*, 234–47.

Lazarus, R.S. & Folkman, S. (1984). *Stress, coping, and adaptation.* New York: Springer.

Linehan, M.M. (1993). *Cognitive behavioral treatment of borderline personality disorder. New York: Guilford Press.*

Lyons, R.F., Mickelson, K.D., Sullivan, M.J.L., & Coyne, J.C. (1998). Coping as a communal process. *Journal of Personal and Social Relations, 15*(5), 579–605.

Manpreet, K. (2010). Mindfulness based stress reduction in IT professionals. Unpublished MPhil thesis, NIMHANS (Deemed University), Bangalore.

Majgi, P., Sharma, M.P., & Sudhir P. (2006). Mindfulness based stress reduction program for paramilitary personnel. In U. Kumar (Eds), *Recent developments in Psychology* (pp. 115–125). Defence Institute of Psychological Research.

Majgi, P. (2008). Mindfulness based stress reduction program for paramilitary personnel. Unpublished PhD Thesis, NIMHANS (Deemed University), Bangalore.

McCrae, R.R. & Costa, P.T. (1986). Personality, coping, and coping effectiveness in an adult sample. *Journal of Personality, 54*, 385–405.

Meichenbaum, D. (2007). Stress inoculation training: A preventative and treatment approach. In P.M. Lehrer, R.L. Woolfolk, & W.E. Sime (Eds), *Principles and Practice of Stress Management* (Third edition, pp. 497–516). London: Guilford Press.

Mennin, D.S., Heimberg, R.G., Turk, C.L., & Fresco, D.M. (2002). Applying an emotion regulation framework to integrative approaches to generalized anxiety disorder. *Clinical Psychology: Science and Practice, 9*, 85–90.

Miller, S.M. (1980). When is little information a dangerous thing? Coping with stressful events by monitoring versus blunting. In S. Levine and H. Ursin (Eds), *Health and coping* (pp. 145–169). New York: Plenum.

——— (1987). Monitoring and blunting: Validation of a questionnaire to assess styles of information seeking under threat. *Journal of Personality and Social Psychology, 52*, 345–353.

Mischel, W. & Shoda, Y. (1995). A cognitive-affective system theory of personality: Reconceptualising situations, dispositions, dynamics, and invariance in personality structure. *Psychological Review, 102*, 246–68.

Mitchell, R.E., Cronkite, R.C. & Moos, R.H. (1983). Stress, coping, and depression among married couples. *Journal of Abnormal Psychology, 92*, 433–48.

Moffat, K.J., McConnachie, A., Ross, S. & Morrison, J.M. (2004). First year medical student stress and coping in a problem-based learning medical curriculum. *Medical Education, 38*(5), 482–91.

Moos, R.H. (1993). *Coping responses inventory.* Odessa, FL: Psychol. Assess. Resource.

Moos, R.H. & Billings, A.G. (1982). Conceptualizing and measuring coping resources and coping processes. In L. Goldberger & S. Breznitz (Eds), *Handbook of stress: Theoretical and clinical aspects* (pp. 212–30). New York: Free Press.

Moos, R.H., Cronkite, R.C., Billings, A.G., & Finney, J.W. (1986). *Health and Daily Living Form Manual* (Revised edition). Palo Alto, CA: Social Ecology Laboratory, Stanford University.

Moskowitz, J. T., Folkman, S., & Acree, M. (2003). Do positive psychological states shed light on recovery from bereavement? Findings from a 3-year longitudinal study. *Death Studies*, *27*, 471–500.

Moskowitz, J.T., Folkman, S., Collette, L., & Vittinghoff, E. (1996). Coping and mood during AIDS-related care giving and bereavement. *Annals of Behavioral Medicine*, *18*(1), 49–57.

Moskowitz, J.T., Hult, J.R., Bussolari, C., & Acree, M. (2009). What works in coping with HIV? A meta-analysis with implications for coping with serious illness. *Psychological Bulletin*, *135*(1), 121–41.

Murthy, V. (2007). *Coping patterns of working women across stressful episodes*. M.Phil thesis. In A. Shah & K. Rao (Eds), *Psychological research in mental health & neurosciences, 1957–2007* (p. 371). Bangalore: NIMHANS (Deemed University).

Nolan, S.A., Roberts, J.E., & Gotlib, I.H. (1998). Neuroticism and ruminative response style as predictors of change in depressive symptoms. *Cognitive Therapy and Research*, *22*, 445–55.

Pargament, K.I. (1997). *The psychology of religion and coping*. New York: Guilford.

Pargament, K.I, Koenig, H.G., & Perez, L.M. (2000). The many methods of religious coping: Development and initial validation of the RCOPE. *Journal of Clinical Psychology*, *56*(4), 519–43.

Park, C.L. (2010). Making sense of the meaning literature: An integrative review of meaning making and its effects on adjustment to stressful life events. *Psychological Bulletin*, 136(2), 257–301.

Park, C.L. & Folkman, S. (1997). Meaning in the context of stress and coping. *Review of General Psychology*, 1 (2), 115–14.

Pearlin, L.I. & Schooler, C. (1978). The structure of coping. *Journal of Health and Social Behaviour*, 19, 2–21.

Perrewe, P.L. & Zellara, K.L. (1999). An examination of attributions and emotions in the transactional approach to the organisational stress process. *Journal of Organisational Behavior*, *20*, 739–52.

Pillay, U. & Rao, K. (2002). The structure and function of social support in relation to help-seeking behavior. *Family Therapy*, *29*(3), 153–67.

Rammohan, A., Rao, K., & Subbakrishna, D.K. (2002). Religious coping and psychological wellbeing in carers of relatives with schizophrenia. *Acta Psychiatrica Scandinavia*, 105(5), 356–62.

Rao, K. (2009). Recent research in stress, coping and women's health. *Current Opinion in Psychiatry*, *22*(2),188–93.

Rao, K., Apte, M., & Subbakrishna, D.K. (2003). Coping and subjective well-being in women with multiple roles. *International Journal of Social Psychiatry*, 49(3), 175–84.

Rao, K., Subbakrishna, D.K., & Prabhu, G.G. (1989). Development of a coping checklist. *Indian Journal of Psychiatry*, *31*, 128–33.

Richards, J.M., & Gross, J.J. (2000). Emotion regulation and memory: The cognitive costs of keeping one's cool. *Journal of Personality and Social Psychology, 79*, 410–24.

Roseman, I.J. (1984). Cognitive determinants of emotions: A structural theory. In P. Shaver (Ed.), *Review of personality and social psychology* (Volume 5, pp. 11–36). Beverly Hills, CA: SAGE Publications.

Rothbaum, F., Weisz, J. R., & Snyder, S. (1982). Changing the world and changing the self: A two-process model of perceived control. *Journal of Personality and Social Psychology, 42*, 5–37.

Sarason, I.G., Levine, H.M., Basham, R.B.B., & Sarason, B.R. (1983). Assessing social support: The social support questionnaire. *Journal of Personality and Social Psychology, 44*(1), 127–39.

Scherer, K.R. (1984). On the nature and function of emotion: A component process approach. In K.R. Scherer & P.E. Ekman (Eds), *Approaches to emotion* (pp. 293–317). Hillsdale, NJ: Erlbaum.

Schmidt, S., Tinti, C., Levine, L.J., & Testa, S. (2010). Appraisals, emotions and emotion regulation: An integrative approach. *Motivation and Emotion, 34*, 63–72.

Schwarzer, R. & Knoll, N. (2003). Positive coping: Mastering demands and searching for meaning. S.J. Lopez & C.R. Snyder (Eds), *Handbook of positive psychological assessment*. Washington, DC: American Psychological Association.

Schwarzer, R. & Schwarzer, C. (1996). A critical survey of coping instruments. In M. Zeidner & N.S. Endler (Eds) (1996). *Handbook of coping: Theory, research, applications* (pp. 107–32). New York: Wiley.

Schwarzer, R. & Leppin, A. (1991). Social support and health: A theoretical and empirical overview. *Journal of Social and Personal Relationships, 8*, 99–127.

Segal, Z., Williams, J.M.G. & Teasdale, J. (2002). *Mindfulness-based cognitive therapy for depression: A new approach to preventing relapse.* New York: Guilford Press.

Selye, H. (1956). *The stress of life.* New York: McGraw-Hill.

Semmer, N.K. (2003). Job stress interventions and organization of work. In L.E. Tetrick & J.C. Quick (Eds), *Handbook of occupational health psychology* (pp. 325–353). Washington DC: American Psychological Association.

Shapiro, J., Morrison, E.H., & Boker, J.R. (2000). Stress management in medical education. *Academic Medicine, 75*, 748–59.

Sharma, P. (2007). Vulnerability to depression: A study of personality and cognitive process and coping behaviour. PhD Thesis. In A. Shah & K. Rao (Eds), *Psychological research in mental health & neurosciences, 1957–2007* (p. 371). Bangalore: NIMHANS (Deemed University).

Shoda, Y. (1996). Discriminative facility as a determinant of coping. Paper presented at the 8th Annual Convention of the American Psychological Society, San Francisco.

Skinner, E. A., Edge, K., Altman, J., & Sherwood, H. (2003). Searching for the structure of coping: A review and critique of category systems for classifying ways of coping. *Psychological Bulletin, 129*, 216–69.

Skinner, E.A. & Zimmer-Gembeck, M.J. (2007). The development of coping. *The Annual Review of Psychology, 58*, 119–44.

Somerfield, M.R. & McCrae, R.R. (2000). Stress and coping research: Methodological challenges, theoretical advances, and clinical applications. *American Psychologist, 55*(6), 620–25.

Spivack, G., Platt, J.J., & Shure, M.B. (1976). *The problem-solving approach to adjustment.* San Francisco: Jossey-Bass.

Stroebe, M.S. & Schut, H. (2001). Meaning making in the dual process model of coping with bereavement. In R.A. Neimeyer (Ed.), *Meaning reconstruction, the experience of loss* (pp. 55–73). Washington, DC: American Psychological Association.

Taylor, S.E. (1983). Adjustment to threatening events: A theory of cognitive adaptation. *American Psychologist, 38,* 1163–71.

Thayer, R.E., Newman, J.R., & McClain, T.M. (1994). Self regulation of mood: Strategies for changing a bad mood, raising energy, and reducing tension. *Journal of Personality and Social Psychology, 67,* 910–25.

Thoits, P.A. (1995). Stress, coping, social support processes: Where are we? What next? *Journal of Health and Social Behaviour,* (Extra issue), 53–79.

Walden, T.A. & Smith, M.C. (1997). Emotion regulation. *Motivation and Emotion, 21,* 7–25.

Wells, J.D., Hobfoll, S.E., & Lavin, J. (1997). Resource loss, resource gain, and communal coping during pregnancy among women with multiple roles. *Psychology of Women's Quarterly, 21*(4), 645–62.

11

Flourishing at Work

Seema Mehrotra and Ravikesh Tripathi

Abstract

Flourishing is a state of positive mental health that comprehensively captures the "feeling good" as well as the positive psychosocial functioning aspects. However, the term "flourishing" is rarely used at the level of a psychological construct in the organizational science/business literature. The chapter brings together the relevant literature on the constituents of flourishing, viz., emotional, psychological, and social well-being and examines their relevance in work settings. Although some attempts have been made to develop models of psychological well-being specific to work; the positive indicators of well-being that are most often measured in the organizational literature are those that tap emotional well-being. A case is made for the potential utility of a context-specific meta-level construct of "flourishing at work" and various steps for theory building and research are outlined. The chapter highlights the implications of further research on this construct for development and testing of workplace-interventions that go beyond stress management and are aimed at enhancement of well-being and functioning.

Keywords: flourishing, psychological well-being, well-being at work, social well-being, occupational well-being

Acknowledgment

The feedback and suggestions provided by Professor Shivaprakash, A.R. on the draft version of this chapter are gratefully acknowledged.

Introduction

Conceptualizations of Well-being: Current Trends

The utility of embracing a construct of health that goes beyond absence of illness has received widespread attention amongst researchers, practitioners, and policy makers in the last one decade or so. With respect to mental health in particular, emotional well-being has been the most frequently examined variable in the burgeoning literature in positive psychology (Vazquez, Hervas, Rahona, and Gomez, 2009; Mehrotra, and Tripathi, 2011). Emotional well-being is defined as a cluster of symptoms reflecting the presence/absence of positive feelings about life (Keyes, 2002). This term is used more or less synonymously with subjective well-being and is conceptualized in terms of an affective component (presence of positive affect and low negative affect) and a cognitive–evaluative component namely, sense of satisfaction in life (Diener, 1984). In the emerging literature, the frequent experience of positive emotions is being seen not only as a positive outcome in itself but also as a predictor of other positive outcomes such as building of physical, psychological, and social resources in the longer run along with beneficial consequences in turn, on health, resilience to stress and functioning (Lyubomirsky, King, and Diener, 2005; Fredrickson and Kurtz, 2011). However, the notion of positive mental health does not merely comprise of emotional well-being or the "feeling good" (hedonic) aspect. There is a growing consensus about the need to investigate constructs that may be indicative of high positive psychological functioning or what may be loosely termed as the "doing well" (eudaimonic) aspect (Ryan and Huta, 2009; Keyes and Annas, 2009). The latter is often operationalized in terms of psychological well-being. The most popular conceptualization of psychological well-being incorporates six dimensions, namely, self acceptance, positive relations with others, personal growth, purpose in life, environmental mastery, and autonomy (Ryff, 1989). In addition, it has been argued that positive mental health needs to extend beyond the personal sphere to incorporate high functioning with respect to social criteria, too. Individuals high in social well-being are likely to see society as meaningful and possessing a growth potential, feel belonged to and accepted in their communities, and see themselves as contributing to society in some way or another (Keyes, 1998).

Keyes (2002) proposed that the conceptualization and measurement of mental health should include not merely absence of mental illness but also the presence of positive features of mental health which in turn should include emotional, psychological, and social well-being, with the former representing the hedonic dimension of well-being and the latter two representing eudaimonic well-being. Further, he operationalized the construct of flourishing as indicative of a state of mental health reflected through high levels of emotional as well as psychological and social well-being. On the other hand, languishing refers to a state wherein individuals are low on these dimensions of well-being (Keyes, 2002). Keyes's landmark analysis of data from the "Midlife in the United States Study" of 3032 adults indicated that 17.2% of the adults in the sample met the criteria for flourishing whereas 12.1% met the criteria for languishing. On the other hand, 56.6% were moderately healthy (neither flourishing nor languishing) while 14.1% fit the criteria for diagnosis of major depressive episode during the previous 12-month period (Keyes, 2002). "Completely mentally healthy" adults (defined as free of a mental disorder during a 12-month period and fulfilling the criteria for flourishing) reported the fewest missed days of work, the fewest half-day work cutbacks, healthiest psycho-social functioning (low helplessness, clear life, goals, high resilience, and high intimacy) lowest cardiovascular risk, lowest number of chronic physical diseases with age, fewest health limitations in activities of daily living and lower health care utilization (Keyes, 2007; Keyes and Grzywacz, 2005). These results highlight the implications of flourishing as a construct for the stress and coping literature.

The numerous potential benefits that seem to correlate with flourishing states as well as the observations that a bulk of the general population of adults are likely to be functioning only at moderate levels of mental health rather than flourishing, suggest the immense potential of the construct of flourishing and the role of promotive programs in the field of mental health.

WORK IN THE CANVAS OF LIFE

Workplaces not just occupy a highly significant proportion of adult lives but are also often considered one of the central domains in life wherein individuals seek/find means for fulfillment of their various psychological needs (Harter, Schmidt, and Keyes, 2003; Baumeister, 1991). Work also provides opportunities to use one's potentials and hone not just task-related skills but also emotion management, self regulation, and interpersonal skills by offering numerous opportunities for varied experiences. Although, the centrality/ salience of work varies from person to person, it often constitutes one of the top domains of significance in life (e.g., Harpaz, Honig, and Coetsier, 2002). Thus the context of work may be assumed to be an important arena, the experiences within which are likely to shape the overall/global levels of well-being.

SCOPE OF THE CHAPTER

In the above context, this chapter attempts to provide a background and a framework for conceptualizing flourishing in the context of workplace. Strands of relevant research in the field of organizational science and positive psychology are reviewed with this overall aim in view. The chapter is not meant to provide a comprehensive coverage of all the constructs and studies that fall under the rubric of positive organizational scholarship or positive organizational behavior. Its focus is on the construct of flourishing that subsumes effective management of stress but goes beyond it to include high psychological functioning. Its scope is thus limited to synthesizing and connecting research carried out from multiple perspectives, in order to build a case for exploring a meta-level construct called "flourishing at work."

Research on Positive Constructs at Work: An Overview

Several researchers have highlighted the extent of under-representation of studies on positive processes in business and health literature (e.g., Walsh, Weber, and Margolis, 2003; Vazquez, Hervas, Rahona, and Gomez, 2009). However, the numerous studies since the year 2000 onwards that focus on positive processes, determinants, and outcomes in the field of psychology in general as well as organizational science in particular, including those on Positive Organizational Scholarship and Positive Organizational Behavior (Bakker and Schaufeli, 2008; Bakker and Derks, 2010; Fredrickson and Dutton, 2008), seem to be redressing this imbalance in perspectives to some extent. There is ample evidence now to suggest that antecedents and consequences of both positive and negative states at work should be examined separately and one cannot substitute the other (e.g., Hart and Cooper, 2001).

Rodríguez-Carvajal et al. (2010) used manual based and electronic searches for articles during the years 2005 to 2010 and observed that although multiple positive concepts and constructs have been raised, there exist significant limitations in terms of lack of consensus on meaning and insufficient theory building. In this review, the use of the keyword "flourishing" yielded only five articles. Donaldson and Ko (2010) reviewed peer-reviewed journal publications between 2001 and 2009 on positive constructs in organizational contexts through the use of five electronic databases. This review too does not mention any studies with an explicit focus on flourishing at work.

FLOURISHING AS A PSYCHOLOGICAL CONSTRUCT AT WORK

Unfortunately, flourishing is a term that has been used in multiple ways and its meaning as a psychological construct needs to be clearly and consistently spelt out across studies. Behavioral sciences literature suggests that this term is not as much in vogue as other terms such as satisfaction/well-being. When it does occur, especially in the organizational literature, it is often as a broad term referring to positive outcomes in general at the individual/ organizational level. These outcomes are not clearly specified but refer to any positive consequence such as productivity, innovation, creativity, growth, etc. (e.g., Fredrickson and Dutton, 2008; Bakker and Schaufeli, 2008). At times, conglomerations of such ill defined positive outcomes actually refer to external tangible outcomes. Thus most often, the term "flourishing" even when used, is not at the level of a scientific construct. On the other hand, in terms of a rigorous scientific conceptualization, flourishing as a psychological construct is best viewed as an "internal psychological state, having distinct characteristics that serve as indicators of emotional well-being as well as positive functioning at the psychosocial level" (Keyes, 2002). Some theorists have questioned the need for making distinctions between emotional (roughly equated with hedonic or "feeling good") and eudaimonic well-being (positive psychological functioning or "doing well"). Addressing this debate, Keyes and Annas (2009) conducted a reanalysis of Keyes's data on mental health which revealed that almost half (48.5%) of the adult participants had high emotional well-being but 30% of them had only moderate levels of eudaimonic well-being and only 18.5% met the criteria for flourishing (high emotional as well as psychological and social well-being). This data support the distinction between the two forms of well-being and the need for their separate examination.

Horn, Taris, Schaufeli, and Schreurs (2004) noted that operationalizing well-being in a context-specific way can be useful in understanding work-related factors and their interplay with other factors as well as in designing programs for enhancing occupational well-being. One example of such a framework applies the construct of flourishing in the context of workplace-coaching (Grant, 2007a). This model for coaching is based on Keyes's (2002) conceptualization of flourishing and languishing but reportedly extends beyond it. Grant (2007a) argued that the languishing-flourishing continuum does not explicitly incorporate intentional goal striving, a paramount theme in coaching endeavors. He proposed the incorporation of two dimensions: (*a*) mental health-illness and (*b*) high-low goal striving for a comprehensive model of coaching. His model is based on the premise that the individuals may be high on mental health and yet low on intentional goal striving. A quadrant called acquiescence was proposed that refers to individuals "experiencing high subjective and psychological well-being" but not being actively engaged in intentional goal striving. The languishing quadrant involves low well-being with varying levels of intentional strivings. Flourishing in Grant's coaching model is thus redefined to include high level of mental health as well as high intentional goal striving. The last quadrant involves individuals with major psychopathology/clinical syndromes along with low level of intentional striving. This model thus collapses the two bipolar dimensions of mental health and illness proposed by Keyes (2005) into a single dimension. This strategy is a significant departure from the original conceptualization of flourishing and its validation needs rigorous examination. In addition, the assumption that individuals high on mental health may have low intentional striving towards personally meaningful and self-concordant goals also warrants conceptual debate and empirical examination. As discussed earlier, Keyes' (2005) original model of complete mental health includes not just absence of illness and presence of emotional well-being but also high psychological and social well-being (positive psychological functioning). On the other hand, the "happy disengaged" quadrant (acquiescence) in Grant's model is described as "experiencing high subjective and psychological well-being" but not being actively engaged in intentional goal striving. Grant's proposition is tantamount to the reasoning that individuals high on positive psychosocial functioning as identified through Keyes' criteria may not be high on intentional goal striving. The assumption that high positive functioning does not subsume high intentional goal striving is open to debate. High positive functioning involves dimensions such as autonomy, sense of purpose, mastery, and personal growth, etc., which are likely to facilitate intentional goal striving. Grant's model (2007a) hence requires further conceptual and empirical examination.

Andrews (2010) used a qualitative approach to explore the experience of flourishing in the lives of professional women. This study used a subset of data from a study called "The changing landscape of American women: understanding work, family and personal issues." The transcripts of focus group discussions held with professional women were coded using *a priori* criteria for flourishing, in addition to the use of narrative analysis techniques. This is one of the rare attempts to qualitatively explore the experience of flourishing in the process of navigating the challenges across life domains, through utilizing predetermined indicators of flourishing as given by Keyes (2002).

Examining Constituents of Flourishing at Work

Examination of "flourishing at work" as a state of mental health would require conceptualizing and operationalizing individuals' experience of emotional, psychological, and social well-being within the context of work. As there is a significant dearth of studies on flourishing per se, the following subsections discuss the different constituents of flourishing, viz., emotional, psychological, and social well-being at workplace.

A. EMOTIONAL WELL-BEING AT WORK

The construct of subjective/emotional well-being has generated a lot of research and discussion in the broad field of organizational psychology. Emotional well-being as mentioned earlier refers to frequent experience of positive affect and life satisfaction. Warr (1990) used the term affective well-being to refer to feelings about either life in general ("context-free"), or affect in relation to a specific domain (i.e., "job-related" and "facet-specific"). Wright and Cropanzano (2000) noted that affective well-being is very often treated as synonymous with happiness in organizational research; moreover, it has been usually measured through indices of job satisfaction which tap a cognitive evaluation component, more than the affective aspect of work-experience. However, the last one decade has witnessed a shift in this trend towards examining indices of well-being beyond life satisfaction.

Various models of affective well-being at work have been described involving dimensions such as anxiety–discomfort, tiredness–vigor, etc. (e.g., Warr, 1990; Daniels 2000). While the earlier studies mainly focused on determinants of stress, emotional well-being and particularly job satisfaction at work (e.g., Sinha and Singh, 1995; Rodríguez-Carvajal et al., 2010; Mehrotra and Tripathi, 2011), recent studies indicate a broadening of the focus by including happiness/or well-being not just as an outcome but also examining its role as a potential determinant of other desirable outcomes such as productivity (e.g., Harter, Schmidt, and Keyes, 2003). One of the examples of this trend is reflected in the studies on "happy worker–productive worker" hypothesis (Zelenski, Murphy, and Jenkins, 2008; Taris and Schreurs, 2009). There is also a small yet growing body of literature on the optimum balance between positivity and negativity that may predict high functioning and well-being in various contexts (e.g., Losada, 1999; Fredrickson and Losada, 2005).

Fisher (2010) conducted an extensive review of studies on happiness at work including an examination of the ways in which it has been defined in the context of work and noted that many work-related happiness constructs focus mostly on hedonic aspects of well-being whereas some others focus on eudaimonic aspects such a learning, growth, autonomy, etc. They highlighted the need for a higher order construct in the field of happiness—studies at work.

B. PSYCHOLOGICAL AND SOCIAL WELL-BEING IN CONTEXT OF WORK

As mentioned earlier, emotional/affective well-being comprises only one of the facets of positive mental health, the other two being psychological and social well-being. Compared to individual outcomes such as emotional well-being or job satisfaction, there is a relative dearth of studies on psychological and social well-being in the work context.

The term social well-being has been often used to refer to social indicators which are operationalized in terms of economic measures/indices (e.g., poverty). However, as a psychological construct, social well-being has been defined in terms of the five dimensions, namely, social integration, social contribution, social coherence, social acceptance, and social actualization (Keyes, 1998; Keyes and Shapiro, 2004). Examining social well-being from the lens of workplace psychology would entail seeing the organization as the society or the community. Thus high social well-being at workplace would be a reflection of the extent to which individuals perceive their work-organizations as meaningful/understandable systems that possess a growth potential, feel a sense of belongingness to the organization, are generally accepting of the organizations and see themselves as making a contribution to it in some way or another. Boros (2008) discussed in detail the myriad conceptualizations of organizational identification as well as affective organizational commitment, the variables that have high relevance for social well-being. Affective commitment is viewed in the organizational literature as the emotional attachment that individuals have towards their organizations but this does not cover all the dimensions of social well-being.

Scholars have speculated about the overlap of social well-being with one of the Ryff's dimensions of psychological well-being, namely, "positive relations with others." The construct of social well-being is however considered multi-dimensional and broader than that of positive relations with others. Beyond the personal level of analysis, social well-being could also be conceptualized in terms of an organization's connections to and perceptions of the larger society within which it operates as a system. Pro-social organizational behaviors, entrepreneurship, and organizational citizenship behaviors (e.g., Srivastava, 2010; Organ, 1988) are some of variables that may arguably be seen as some of the consequences/manifestations of high social well-being. Jobs have been viewed as having pro-social characteristics that enable employees to contribute to and benefit others, in line with their other-oriented values and motives. Recent studies suggest that when jobs are designed to provide opportunities for impact on and contact with beneficiaries/customers, employees display higher levels of affective commitment to the beneficiaries, greater motivation, and performance (Grant, 2007b; Grant 2008). In one of the very few studies on social well-being at work, de Jager, Coetzee, and Visser (2008) examined dimensions of social well-being in employees of a motor manufacturing organization in South Africa and found that Keyes' five factor model could not replicated.

On the whole, there is a fair case for the relevance of social well-being as a psychological construct at work place and several lines of research in the organizational context incorporate variables that are conceptually linked to the various dimensions of social well-being and/or its potential antecedents or consequences.

The term psychological well-being has also been often used rather loosely/broadly and sometimes synonymous with emotional well-being or has been conceptualized very differently across different studies. It has been observed that the wide array of conceptualization of psychological well-being are inferable many a times only through the nature of the measure that is used in a given study and the theoretical bases are not made explicit or verified (Diener, 1994, Danna and Griffin, 1999). In a thought-provoking review that clearly brought to focus the conceptual confusions in this area, Dagenais-Desmarais, and Savoie, (2011) surveyed the existing literature and identified 23 operationalizations of psychological well-being (PWB) comprising of 42 distinct dimensions under the "aegis of five slightly different terminologies."

Using the terms "psychological well-being" and "India"/"Indian" in a popular electronic database (EBSCO) along with other combinations of key words such as "work," "occupation," "organization" threw up only a handful of studies. Further, we observe that psychological well-being has been investigated by Indian researchers in various contexts ranging from clinical to normal community dwelling people, in as well as outside the domain of work. At workplace, its assessment has involved the use of a variety of conceptually distinct measures such as Ryff's psychological well-being scale, Warr's affective well-being scale, Bradburn's affect balance scale, and an indigenous measure

(*Psychological well-being questionnaire*, Bhogle and Jaiprakash, 1995). Factor structure of Ryff's measure of psychological well-being in Indian samples is yet to be well determined and the other commonly used measures tend to tap features of emotional well-being rather than psychological well-being/positive functioning. Bhogle and Jaiprakash (1995) operationalized psychological well-being in terms of the degree of happiness, satisfaction, or gratification that is subjectively experienced by an individual. The authors mention more than ten factors, ranging from meaninglessness, somatic symptoms, positive affect, personal control to suicidal thoughts, etc. This measure appears to utilize a rather broad-based conceptualization of well-being that includes aspects pertaining to both emotional and psychological well-being (hedonic and eudaimonic aspects). The PGI well-being scale developed by Verma, Dubey, and Gupta (1983) consists of 20 items of low difficulty level. The utility of PGI well-being scale in the context of work was examined by Singh and Singh (2003). They reported that factor analysis revealed five factors: social support, emotionality, psychosomatic, personal adjustment, and global attitude toward life. It was concluded that this measure would benefit from revisions.

A scan of the literature suggests that work-related/individual level variables are most commonly examined as predictors of context free psychological well-being. It might also be important to see the relationships between predictors and outcomes at the same level by using the construct of "psychological well-being at work," rather than overall level of psychological well-being in global/general sense. This may provide a clearer picture of work-related variables that could have a stronger bearing on workplace well-being. The effects of workplace—psychological well-being on psychological well-being-in-general—could also be then examined analogous to the examination of the relationship between job satisfaction and life satisfaction. The most researched measures of psychological well-being are based on the Ryff's model (Ryff, 1989) and an attempt to capture the experience of the six dimensions of well-being in one's life in general. In view of this, it would be pertinent to explore the potential applicability of Ryff's model at work.

Ryff's Psychological Well-Being Dimensions: Relevance and Potential Applicability at Work

Keyes, Shmotkin, & Ryff (2002) stated that each of the six dimensions of psychological well-being "articulates different challenges individuals encounter as they strive to function positively." Reframing of the general psychological well-being measures in a way that requires the respondents to answer keeping in view the work life as a context for rating, might be one small step in the direction. But before this, each of the dimensions needs to be scrutinized as well as field- tested to ensure that these lend themselves to rating when workplace-experiences are taken as the context. There are strands of research that directly/indirectly highlight the applicability and relevance of variables at workplace which are similar to the dimensions of psychological well-being as proposed by Ryff. The key observations across such studies on these variables are summarized here, along with their implications on the use of Ryff's model of PWB at work.

Autonomy at Work

Ryff & Keyes (1995) describe individuals high on a sense of autonomy to be self-determining and independent, who are able to resist social pressures to think and act in certain ways, regulate behavior from within, and evaluate themselves by their personal standards.

Autonomy has been a highly researched topic in the context of work. Several researches have focused on the various outcomes of autonomy, including job satisfaction, well-being, and productivity (e.g., Denton & Kleiman, 2001; De-Jonge & Schaufeli, 1998). It has been measured in various ways but most of the organizational literature has focused on autonomy as a job/task characteristic, i.e., the degree to which the task provides a scope for latitude and discretion in scheduling, procedures used, and evaluation standards (e.g., Van den Broeck et al., 2010). The dominant conceptualization of autonomy as a task/job characteristic variable in the organizational context is different from its conventional usage in the mainstream psychology literature, including the self determination theory. It would be worthwhile to consistently distinguish between autonomy as a task characteristic and the perception of a global sense of autonomy at work.

Sense of Purpose and Meaning at Work

Ryff & Keyes (1995) defined purpose in life as having meaningful goals and a sense of directedness. Experienced meaningfulness of work was considered as one of the critical psychological states proposed to mediate the relationship between core job characteristics and outcomes in the job characteristic model proposed by Hackman & Oldham (1980). As per this model, the variety of skills required, task-identity (the degree to which the job involved completing a whole, identifiable unit of work), and task significance (the extent to which the job has an impact on others within and outside the organization) were considered as the three core job characteristics that would predict the sense of meaningfulness of work. The growing literature on spirituality at work also emphasizes the sense of purpose and meaning at work and how that relates to well-being and performance. Ulrich & Ulrich (2010) proposed the model of an abundant organization that relies on the experience of meaning at work as a key component. Studies suggest that several individuals seek and derive meaning in life and sense of personal development from a sense of purpose and meaning at work and see work as a "calling"—fulfilling and socially useful (Avolio & Sosik, 1999). Individuals who perceive their work to be meaningful also experience it as stimulating and satisfying and tend to report higher levels of well-being (Brown and Leigh, 1996; Begat, Ellefsen, and Severinsson, 2005).

Environmental Mastery at Work

Ryff & Keyes (1995) defined environmental mastery in terms of the extent to which a person feels competent in managing his/her immediate and distal environment. Need for competence (the desire to feel effective in meeting the environmental demands) is considered one of the basic psychological needs in the self-determination theory (Deci and Ryan, 2000). While the sense of mastery refers to the general affective experience of mastery, self efficacy refers to the cognitions regarding one's capacity to successfully accomplish specific future tasks (Van den Broeck et al. 2010). In general, sense of mastery has been defined as an outlook in which one believes that he/she is efficacious across a broad range of life domains and that he/she can or does master one's life (Geis and Ross, 1998). Sense of mastery has been associated with a wide range of behaviors, health, well-being, as well as work-related outcomes (e.g., Chou and Chi, 2001). It is likely to be influenced by several variables such as knowledge and skills, skill utilization, and nature of the challenge involved in the tasks as well as macro-level variables. Greenberg and Gruenberg (2003) explored how workplace changes can impact on employees' sense of mastery. Leppanen (2001) attempted to demonstrate how development programs can influence conceptual mastery of work processes which in turn can enhance well-being.

POSITIVE RELATIONS AT WORK

"Positive relations" is conceptualized as yet another dimension of psychological well-being by Ryff and there is an abundance of research indicating its relevance in the workplace. This aspect also finds a place in the self determination theory as one of the three basic psychological needs, i.e., the need to feel connected. The various aspects related to this dimension that have been examined at workplace include perceived organizational support, supervisory and co-worker support, and their role in prediction of well-being, health, commitment, performance and work-family conflict, engagement and thriving, etc. (e.g., Rhoades and Eisenberger, 2002; Halbesleben, 2006; Pati and Kumar, 2010). It is important to remember that positive relations at work is a broader construct than perceived support as it refers to a sense of high quality interpersonal connections in general.

PERSONAL GROWTH AT WORK

Experience of personal growth at work may contribute to satisfaction, high functioning, and provide a buffer against burnout. The role of organizations as facilitators/inhibitors of adult learning and personal development are being increasingly researched. Petterson and Arnetz (1997) examined individuals' personal development in work context by operationalizing it as employees' efforts toward developing their work competencies, ability to learn new work-related skills, and the degree to which their job stimulated additional personal development. Personal development thus defined was observed to be correlated with indices of well-being and health. Although there is emergent literature on how individuals see themselves as changing for better through their work experiences, this area requires the benefit of systematic and rigorous scientific inquiry.

There has been a significant amount of theory building and research on the construct of thriving at work and this is a construct that overlaps highly with the construct of personal growth. Thriving at work has been defined as the psychological state in which individuals experience both a sense of vitality and a sense of learning at work (Spreitzer, Sutcliffe, Dutton, Sonenshein, and Grant, 2005). Vitality refers to the positive feeling of having energy available reflected in a sense of aliveness (Nix, Ryan, Manly, and Deci, 1999). Learning refers to the sense that one is acquiring and can apply knowledge and skills (Elliott and Dweck 1988). Thriving as a construct focuses on the joint operation of these two components. A relationship of thriving at work with various outcomes such as career development initiative, burnout, health, and individual job performance was documented by Porath, Spreitzer, Gibson, and Garnett (2011). The various dimensions in Ryff's construct of psychological well-being (other than personal growth) are seen as enablers of thriving in the process—model of thriving proposed by Spreitzer and colleagues. Flourishing in their model is differentiated from thriving in as much as the former refers to a much broader positive state involving multiple dimensions including personal growth. Moreover, these researchers highlight that it is possible to score high on flourishing as defined by Keyes without necessarily scoring high on the personal growth dimension. On the whole, personal growth seems to be a more narrowly defined construct that does not capture fully the construct of thriving as operationalized in the context of work.

Self Acceptance at Work

Ryff & Keyes (1995) defined self-acceptance as the degree to which people acknowledge and accept all aspects of themselves, both good and bad. According to the notion of multiplicity of selves, as well as the Multiple Self-aspect Framework (MSF), (McConnell, 2011), self concept may be viewed as collection of multiple context-dependent selves. This line of thinking in turn indicates that it might be possible and pertinent to examine the level of self acceptance as experienced in the work environment. The available literature does suggest the possibility that individuals can experience shifts in their sense of self-acceptance with change in their contexts (family vs. work) and consequent change in the roles they undertake in such contexts. It would be pertinent to briefly examine the relevance of the construct of "Reflected Best Self" (RBS) as researched in the work-context. RBS has been defined as changing self-knowledge structure/cognitive representation about who one is at one's best (Roberts, Dutton, Spreitzer, Heaphy, and Quinn, 2005). RBS is seen as a relational representation as it emerges through an interaction between one's self-schema and other's schema of the self and is thus likely to be influenced by social experiences at work. There is also a scope to examine related constructs such as organizational-based self-esteem. In what ways and under what conditions individuals experience a shift in their sense of self acceptance at work as well as how there might be interplay between experiences in various domains of life needs further empirical attention.

There have been a few other conceptualizations of psychological well-being (other than Ryff's) in the context of work and these are discussed in the following section.

Other Conceptualizations of Psychological Well-being at Work

Warr (1990, 1994) synthesized the available literature to propose a vitamin model which states that health is affected by environmental psychological features, such as job characteristics, in analogy with the non-linear effects of vitamins on physical health. For example, job autonomy is hypothesized to have a curvilinear effect on mental health at work. As far as mental health at work is concerned, Warr (1994) distinguished between four primary dimensions (affective well-being, aspiration, autonomy, and competence) and a secondary fifth dimension ("integrated functioning"). The dimensions of autonomy and competence overlap with the corresponding dimensions of Ryff's model. The hypothesis generated based on the Vitamin model that job autonomy is non-linearly associated with work outcomes (e.g., emotional exhaustion) has been examined in some studies (e.g., De-Jonge and Schaufeli, 1998).

Using a sample of Dutch teachers, Horn, Taris, Schaufeli, and Schreurs (2004) proposed a multidimensional model of occupational well-being that combined Ryff's and Warr's models and expanded the same. Three dimensions of their model were similar to Ryff and Warr's models and were labeled as affective, social, and professional well-being. In addition, cognitive functioning and psychosomatic well-being were two new two dimensions added to reflect the common manifestations of stress/low well-being. However, this was an *a priori* model designed to examine occupational well-being as a composite of five-dimensions and the authors caution that their findings may not cover all key aspects of occupational well-being. Cognitive and psychosomatic correlates/manifestations of stress and distress are well recognized; but whether these should be included as separate dimensions of well-being is debatable. Albano (2010) attempted to develop a measure of well-being specific to the context of work, namely Workplace Happiness Index (WHI), using a theory driven approach and relying on the eudaimonic notion of happiness.

Another conceptualization of psychological well-being at work was proposed by Dagenais-Desmarais, and Savoie, (2011). They brought to light the problematic methodological issues in researches that measure context-free general PWB and its components for predicting organizational level outcomes. This view is in consonance with observations that PWB contains components that can fluctuate across life domains (Diener, 1984, 1994). This line of reasoning led them to explore the construct of PWB within a "work frame of reference." For generation of items to measure PWB at work, they adopted an exploratory, inductive bottom-up approach to operationalize psychological well-being that utilizes experiences of individuals, rather than any theory driven, top-down operationalization (Dagenais-Desmarais and Savoie, 2011). A pool of items was generated, based on interviews with twenty workers from various industry sectors. The items were subsequently examined for theoretical pertinence, frequency of occurrence in the interviews, etc. These were then utilized in the quantitative arm of the study that led to identification of six factors; namely, interpersonal fit at work, thriving at work, feeling of competence at work, desire for involvement at work, and perceived recognition at work. The first factor seems to closely resemble the Ryff's factor of positive relations as experienced in the work context. The third factor (competence at work) bears a resemblance to Ryff factor called environmental mastery, again contextualized to tap sense of mastery perceived at work. Thriving at work dimension was defined as "perception of accomplishing a significant and interesting job that allows one to realize oneself as an individual." Its similarity to the sense of purpose and personal growth, the two dimensions of Ryff's model, is worth exploring. Perceived recognition at work as a factor was defined as being appreciated within the organization for one's work and personhood. It needs a closer look to understand whether perception of being appreciated and recognized should be viewed as an antecedent/predictor of well-being or it rightfully deserves a place as an internal psychological indicator of psychological well-being, itself, at work. Its conceptual overlap with the factor labeled "interpersonal fit" needs clarification. Reciprocal perceptions of being valued/cared for and recognized may be inherent to the sense of interpersonal fit/positive relations. The factor labeled "desire for involvement at work" was defined as the will to involve oneself and to contribute to success. This has a strong resemblance to the heavily researched construct of engagement at work. The sense of engagement does not form part of the Ryff's dimension though it has been research in general as a sense of vital engagement. There have been different approaches to conceptualizing engagement at work and its antecedents and outcomes have been examined across multiple studies in the recent few years (e.g., Harter, Schmidt, and Keyes, 2003; Bhatnagar and Biswas, 2010). Schaufeli, Salanova, Gonzalez-Roma, and Bakker (2002) defined engagement independently from job resources and positive organizational outcomes as a positive fulfilling affective motivational state of work-related well-being. Based on this conceptualization, it was operationalized by three interrelated dimensions (vigor, dedication, and absorption) and considered to be a relatively stable indicator of occupational well-being. Whether engagement as an internal psychological state should be included as a marker of PWB in general at work or whether it should be examined as a consequence of high PWB at work is again an interesting point of scientific debate. The framework of PWBW by Dagenais-Desmarais and

Savoie (2011) does not include factors that explicitly pertain to perception of autonomy, sense of meaningfulness, and self-acceptance, although there is clear support for the pertinence of at least the first two of these dimensions at workplace. It remains a possibility that their initial item pool may not have clearly captured all the relevant dimensions, having been based on a sample of only twenty interviews in a given culture.

In a recent study, an attempt was made to examine Ryff's model of psychological well-being at work by utilizing items from Ryff's measure and rephrasing them to reflect work life/professional-self as the frame of reference for responding (Schultz, 2008). Six dimensions were thus created; namely, positive organizational relationships, professional self-acceptance, job autonomy, job purpose, environmental mastery, and job growth. Substantial correlations between various dimensions were observed; for example, "job growth" and "job purpose" were strongly correlated. A possibility that "self-acceptance" and "environmental mastery" at work might be a shared factor was also raised. It was surmised that future research should consider a more thorough approach to theory development including interviews with individuals about well-being experiences at work, thematic analysis, and reviewing of features of existing theories to develop a robust model specific to occupational well-being.

Flourishing at Work: Future Directions in Theory-building and Research

To recapitulate, flourishing is a state of positive mental health that comprehensively captures the "feeling good" and the positive psychosocial functioning aspects (emotional, psychological and social well-being). However, the term "flourishing" is rarely used at the level of a psychological construct in the organizational science/business literature. The instances when the term does appear in the organizational literature, it is most commonly used in a broad and generic sense to refer to ill-defined positive outcomes pertaining to employee behaviors and performance, general well-being, as well as tangible business outcomes such as profits etc. On the other hand, the emergent literature in psychology points towards the potential benefits of examining a comprehensive index of positive mental health and highlights the scope for promotive mental health interventions for a substantial proportion of individuals in a given community who are likely to experience moderate mental health rather than flourishing.

Although there is a plethora of positive constructs being examined in the field of organizational science, many of these constructs pertain to positive work- characteristics (e.g., task-autonomy, decision latitude), group/organizational level features (e.g., authetizotic psychological climate) or positive attitudinal and behavioral characteristics (e.g., organizational citizenship behaviors). There is less attention to positive internal psychological states which are potential mediators of the relationships between positive individual or work characteristics/organizational level variables on one hand and positive outcomes, on the other hand. A few examples of exceptions to this trend include the research on constructs such as psychological capital and thriving at work. However, these constructs do not reflect a comprehensive set of indicators of positive mental health as such.

Most often, the positive indicators of well-being measured in the organizational literature are those that tap emotional well-being (e.g., job satisfaction, affective well-being at work). A meta-level construct such as flourishing at work would comprehensively capture all the three aspects of positive mental health, viz., emotional, psychological, and social well-being as manifest in the context of work. This would broaden as well as enrich the focus on well-being at work which is currently often examined in a global and yet non-comprehensive fashion. In the longer run, this can facilitate the development of more nuanced understanding of (a) the role of various kinds of antecedents in differentially influencing the various dimensions of flourishing as well as (b) the multiple outcomes of flourishing states that may ensue at individual and organizational levels.

As highlighted earlier, well-being is very often examined as an outcome variable in itself and there is an under-representation of studies exploring outcomes of positive mental health/well-being. Having a context-specific model and measure of flourishing at work could be useful. This is because context-specific, comprehensive indices may be more powerful predictors of various outcomes at work and would also provide opportunities to examine the complex interplay between experiences of well-being across life domains.

In view of a dearth of studies on flourishing per se, the chapter has attempted to bring together the relevant literature on the constituents of flourishing, viz., emotional, psychological, and social well-being. Significant progress has been made in understanding emotional/affective well-being at work. The construct of social well-being at work seems highly relevant but is researched the least. The relevance and robustness of various dimensions of social well-being in the context of work as well as their relationships and conceptual overlaps with other organizational science constructs need to be thoroughly explored. This exercise was not undertaken extensively, keeping in view the broader scope of the chapter. Compared to social well-being, psychological well-being at work has received more scientific attention, although its myriad operationalizations do not help in creation of a coherent picture. The few available models of psychological well-being have taken either theory-driven, top-down or a bottom-up, data-driven approach to conceptualizing psychological well-being. Both these approaches have thrown up a few dimensions of psychological well-being at work that are similar to the psychological well-being dimensions as proposed in the Ryff's model.

In the backdrop of a high volume of empirical literature on the Ryff's model of psychological well-being in general, the chapter explored the relevance and applicability of its various dimensions in the context of work through reviewing the available literature on related constructs. It is observed that four of the six dimensions of psychological well-being (as per the Ryff's model) are likely to be relevant in the context of work. Perception of meaningfulness and a sense of purpose in one's work, sense of autonomy, as well as sense of mastery have been frequently investigated in work-contexts. Similarly, perceived sense of positive relations with others has also been independently investigated in myriad forms. Such studies lend support to the view that these dimensions can be conceptualized/recast as dimensions of psychological well-being as experienced at work. On the other hand, empirical literature on the other two dimensions of psychological well-being, viz., personal growth and especially self-acceptance as experienced at work is relatively sparse. The extent to which the experiences of self acceptance and that of growing "as a person" might be meaningfully assessed in the context of work is a topic for further inquiry.

On the whole, an observation of the available literature suggests that it would be useful to adopt a combination of inductive and deductive approaches for theory building in this area, perhaps by beginning with Ryff's already available theoretical framework of context-free psychological well-being and attempting to develop a richer qualitative understating of the manifestations of its dimensions at work, as experienced by individuals as well as exploring the interrelationships among these dimensions. This step is best attained through the use of qualitative methods such as focus group discussions, interviews, as well as experience sampling of daily work-lives. Qualitative approaches provide scope for in-depth understanding of the linkages between various facets of experiences, both positive and negative, that form the complex, paradoxical, and yet coherent realties of living. It would however be critical to keep lines of general inquiry open so as to allow emergence of newer themes or the possibility of inclusion of dimensions that have not been examined in a given theoretical model. For example, one contender could be the construct of "thriving at work." Thriving at work has been examined independently of the studies on psychological well-being, but it has also emerged as relevant in some of the available models of psychological well-being at work. Its relationship with personal growth and sense of purpose dimensions of psychological well-being (as experienced at work) requires empirical testing. However, vitality which is seen as an essential component of thriving at work is not represented in the Ryff's model.

It would be important to start with certain basic criteria for inclusion of newer dimensions. Some of these could be as follows: Whether the construct refers to an internal "psychological experience"? [For example a construct like emotional intelligence would not meet this criterion.] Whether it is variable that is not a trait or trait-like variable (e.g., extraversion)? The focus needs to be on the "state of mental health/well-being" within a given time frame which is expected to vary somewhat over time/malleable. Lastly, any new dimension being considered must be closely examined to decide whether it is best viewed as a psychological antecedent/outcome of flourishing or whether it is justified to conceptualize it as an indicator of flourishing/psychological well-being as such, in the context of work.

An in-depth understanding of the interrelationships between the dimensions of psychological well-being, especially in the context of work, is sorely needed. Also, the consideration of any new dimension must be weighed against the criteria of conceptual overlap/redundancy with the existing model. The possibility that certain dimensions (e.g., personal growth and sense of purpose) could be collapsed to form newer ones (e.g., thriving) to capture the manifestations of psychological well-being at work also requires further conceptual debate and testing.

With sufficient theory building, data generation, and refinement of psychological and social well-being dimensions in the context of work, it would be possible to examine the emergence of a higher order construct of flourishing at work that integrates all the three dimensions. An examination of flourishing at work as a higher order construct is likely to be useful for drawing and building upon the available literature on cultivation/promotion of various dimensions of well-being. A standardized assessment of flourishing at work that provides a holistic index of positive mental health can pave way for theory building through systematic accumulation and synthesis of research studies that consistently utilize a clearly operationlized construct of flourishing at work. Moreover, it would also be a useful tool for tracking well-being experiences at work as well as for development and testing of individual and organizational level workplace—interventions that are not merely restricted to identifying sources of stress and effective stress management but are promotive in nature.

Both within-individual factors such as personality or background history, beliefs, attitudes, values as well as current life events and a host of work-related factors and macro-contexts could be examined as antecedents of flourishing states at work which in turn could be examined as mediators of multiple outcomes at both individual, team/unit, and organizational levels. The criteria of flourishing as proposed by Keyes do not necessitate that individuals high on flourishing are high on all the dimensions of emotional, psychological, and social well-being. This leaves scope for individuals to be identified as flourishing despite variations in terms of the combinations of psychological and social well-being dimensions on which they may score high. Whether individuals flourishing at work may exhibit different meaningful configurations of well-being dimensions is an issue worthy of examination. However, this exercise is best taken up at a later stage of research, following a systematic and cumulative building up of the basic theoretical and empirical knowledge on flourishing at work.

Conclusion

Flourishing at work, as a meta-level psychological construct, deserves attention from theoreticians, researchers, and practitioners in the field of psychology and organizational science. The existing lines of theorizing and evidence provide sufficient leads for its relevance and space in the nomological networks of well-being constructs being examined at work. Most importantly, this line of inquiry holds numerous implications for theory building, hypothesis generation, and testing as well as for development of mental health promotive interventions at workplace.

References

Albano, J.F. (2010). Developing a measure and an understanding of the individual experience of happiness at work. *Dissertation Abstracts International—Section B: The Sciences and Engineering*, 70 (9-B), 5877.

Andrews, M. (2010). That rich, rich, quality of existence: Mothers with professional careers talk about their experiences of flourishing. Doctoral dissertation, University of Minnesota. Retrieved from: http://purl.umn.edu/91785

Avolio, B.J. & Sosik, J.J. (1999). A life span framework for assessing the impact of work on white-collar workers. In S.L Willi & J.D. Reid (Eds), *Life in the middle: Psychogical and social development in middle age* (pp. 251–74). San Diego, CA: Academic Press.

Bakker, A.B. & Derks, D. (2010). Positive occupational health psychology. In S. Leka & J. Houdmont (Eds), *Occupational health psychology: A key text* (pp. 194–224). Oxford: Wiley-Blackwell.

Bakker, A.B. & Schaufeli, W.B. (2008). Positive organizational behavior: Engaged employees in flourishing organizations. *Journal of Organizational Behavior*, 29, 147–54.

Baumeister, R.F. (1991). *Meanings of life*. New York: The Guilford Press.

Begat, I., Ellefsen, B., & Severinsson, E. (2005). Nurses' satisfaction with their work environment and the outcomes of clinical nursing supervision on nurses' experiences of well-being—a Norwegian study. *Journal of Nursing Management, 13*, 221–30.

Bhatnagar, J., & Biswas, S. (2010). Predictors & outcomes of employee engagement: Implications for the resource-based view perspective. *The Indian Journal of Industrial Relations 46*(2), 273–85.

Bhogle, S. & Prakash, I.J. (1995). Development of the Psychological Well-Being (PWB) questionnaire. *Journal of Personality and Clinical Studies, 11*(1–2), 5–9.

Boros, S. (2008). Organizational Identification: Theoretical and empirical analyses of competing conceptualizations. *Romanian Association for Cognitive Science, 12*(1), 1–27.

Brown, S.P. & Leigh, T.W. (1996). A new look at psychological climate and its relationship to job involvement, effort, and performance. *Journal of Applied Psychology, 81*, 458–368.

Chou K.L., & Chi I. (2001). Stressful life events and depressive symptoms: Social support and sense of mastery as mediators or moderators? *International Journal of Aging and Human Development, 52*, 155–71.

Dagenais-Desmarais, V. & Savoie, A. (2011). What is psychological well-being, really? A grassroots approach from the organizational sciences. *Journal of Happiness Studies*. Springer (doi: 10.1007/s10902-011-9285-3).

Daniels, K. (2000). Measures of five aspects of affective well-being at work. *Human Relations, 53*, 275–94.

Danna, K. & Griffin, R.W. (1999). Health and well-being in the workplace: A review and synthesis of the literature. *Journal of Management, 25*(3), 357–84.

de Jager, M., Coetzee S, & Visser, D. (2008). Dimensions of social well-being in a motor manufacturing organization in South Africa. *Journal of Psychology in Africa, 18*(1), 57–64.

De Jonge, J. & Schaufeli, W. (1998). Job characteristics and employee well-being: A test of Warr' s Vitamin Model in health care workers using structural equation modeling. *Journal of Organizational Behavior, 19*(4), 387–407.

Deci, E.L. & Ryan, R.M. (2000). The 'what' and 'why' of goal pursuits: Human needs and the self-determination of behaviour. *Psychological Inquiry, 11*(4), 227–68.

Denton, D.W. & Kleiman, L.S. (2001). Job tenure as a moderator of the relationship between autonomy and satisfaction. *Applied H.R.M. Research, 6*(2), 105–14.

Diener, E. (1984). Subjective well-being. *Psychological Bulletin, 95*(3), 542–75.

——— (1994). Assessing subjective well-being: Progress and opportunities. *Social Indicators Research, 31*, 103–57.

Donaldson, S.I. & Ko, I. (2010). Positive organizational psychology, behavior, and scholarship: A review of the emerging literature and evidence base. *Journal of Positive Psychology, 5*(3), 177–91.

Elliott, E.S. & Dweck, C.S. (1988). Goals: An approach to motivation and achievement. *Journal of Personality and Social Psychology, 54*, 5–12.

Fisher, C.D: (2010). Happiness at Work. *International Journal of Management Review, 12*, 384–412.

Fredrickson, B.L. & Dutton, J.E. (2008). Unpacking positive organizing: Organizations as sites of individual and group flourishing. *The Journal of Positive Psychology, 3*(1), 1–3.

Fredrickson, B.L. & Losada, M.F. (2005). Positive affect and the complex dynamics of human flourishing. *American Psychologist, 60*, 678–86.

Fredrickson, B.L. & Kurtz, L.E. (2011). Cultivating positive emotions to enhance human flourishing. In S.I. Donaldson, M. Csikszentmihalyi, & J. Nakamura (Eds), *Applied positive psychology: Improving everyday life, health, schools, work, and society* (pp. 35–48). New York: Routledge Academic.

Geis, K.J. & Ross, C.E. (1998). A new look at urban alienation: The effect of neighborhood disorder on perceived powerlessness. *Social Psychology Quarterly, 61*(3), 232–46.

Grant, A.M. (2007a). A model of goal striving and mental health for coaching populations. *International Coaching Psychology Review, 2*(3), 248–62.

——— (2007b). Relational job design and the motivation to make a pro-social difference. *Academy of Management Review, 32*, 393–417.

——— (2008). Designing jobs to do good: Dimensions and psychological consequences of prosocial job characteristics. *Journal of Positive Psychology, 3*(1), 19–39.

Greenberg, E.S. & Grunberg L. (2003). The changing American workplace and the sense of mastery: Assessing the impacts of downsizing, job redesign and teaming. Institute of Behavioral Science. Working Paper PEC 2003–2006. Retrieved from: www.colorado.edu/ibs/PEC/workplacechange/papers/WP – 006.PDF.

Hackman, J.R. & Oldham, G.R. (1980). *Work redesign*. MA: Addison-Wesly.

Halbesleben, J.R.B. (2006). Sources of social support and burnout: A meta-analytic test of the Conservation of Resources Model. *Journal of Applied Psychology, 91*(5), 1134–45.

Harpaz, I., Honig B., & Coetsier, P. (2002). A cross cultural longitudinal analysis of the meaning of work and socialization process of career starters. *Journal of World Business, 37*, 230–44.

Hart, P.M. & Cooper, C.L. (2001). Occupational stress: Towards a more integrated framework. In N. Anderson, D.S. Ones, H.K. Sinangil, & C. Viswesvaran (Eds), *Handbook of industrial, work and organizational psychology* (Volume 2: *Personnel Psychology*, pp. 93–114). London: SAGE.

Harter, J.K., Schmidt, F.L., & Keyes, C.L.M. (2003). Well-being in the workplace and its relationship to business outcomes: A review of the Gallup studies. In C.L.M. Keyes and J. Haidt (Eds), *Flourishing: Positive psychology and the life well-lived* (pp. 205–24). Washington DC: APA.

Horn, J.E. van., Taris, T.W., Schaufeli, W.B., & Schreurs, P.J.G. (2004). The structure of occupational well-being: A study among Dutch teachers. *Journal of Occupational and Organizational Psychology, 77*, 365–75.

Keyes, C.L. (1998). Social well-being. *Social Psychology Quarterly, 61*, 121–40.

Keyes, C.L.M. (2002). The mental health continuum: From languishing to flourishing in life. *Journal of Health and Social Research, 43*, 207–22.

——— (2005). Mental illness and/or mental health? Investigating axioms of the complete state model of health. *Journal of Consulting and Clinical Psychology, 73*(3), 539–48.

——— (2007). Promoting and protecting mental health as flourishing: A complementary strategy for improving national mental health. *American Psychologist, 62*(2), 95–108.

Keyes, C.L.M. & Annas, J. (2009). Feeling good and functioning well: Distinctive concepts in ancient philosophy and contemporary science. *The Journal of Positive Psychology, 4*(3), 197–201.

Keyes, C.L.M. & Grzywacz, J.G. (2005). Health as a complete state: The added value in work performance and healthcare costs. *Journal of Occupational & Environmental Medicine, 47*(5), 523–32.

Keyes, C.L.M. & Shapiro, A. (2004). Social well-being in the United States: A descriptive epidemiology. In O.G. Brim, C.D. Ryff, & R.C. Kessler (Eds), *How healthy are we?: A national study of well-being at midlife* (pp. 350–72). Chicago: University of Chicago Press.

Keyes, C.L.M., Shmotkin, D., & Ryff, C.D. (2002). Optimizing well-being: The empirical encounter of two traditions. *Journal of Personality and Social Psychology, 82*(6), 1007–22.

Leppanen, A. (2001). Improving the mastery of work and the development of the work process in paper production. *Industrial Relations, 56*(3), 579–609.

Losada, M. (1999). The complex dynamics of high performance teams. *Mathematical and Computer Modelling, 30*(9–10), 179–92.

Lyubomirsky, S., King, L., & Diener, E. (2005). The benefit of frequent positive affect: Does happiness lead to success? *Psychological Bulletin, 131*(6), 803–55.

McConnell, A.R. (2011). The multiple self-aspects framework: Self-concept representation and its implications. *Personality and Social Psychology Review, 15*(1), 3–27.

Mehrotra, S. & Tripathi, R. (2011). Positive psychology research in India: A review and critique. *The Journal of the Indian Academy of Applied Psychology, 37*(1), 9–26.

Nix, G., Ryan, R.M., Manly, J.B., & Deci, E.L. (1999). Revitalization through self regulation: The effects of autonomous and controlled motivation on happiness and vitality. *Journal of Experimental Social Psychology, 25*, 266–84.

Organ, D.W. (1988). *Organizational citizenship behavior: The good soldier syndrome.* Lexington, MA: Lexington Books.

Pati, S.P. & Kumar, P. (2010). Employee engagement: Role of self-efficacy, organizational support & supervisor support. *The Indian Journal of Industrial Relations, 46*(1), 126–37.

Petterson, I.L. & Arnetz, B.B. (1997). Measuring psychosocial work quality and health: Development of health care measures of measurement. *Journal of Occupational Psychology, 2*, 229–41.

Porath, C., Spreitzer, G., Gibson, C., & Garnett, F.G. (2011). Thriving at work: Toward its measurement, construct validation, and theoretical refinement. *Journal of Organizational Behavior* (doi: 10.1002/job.756).

Rhoades, L. & Eisenberger, R. (2002). Perceived organizational support: A review of the literature. *Journal of Applied Psychology, 87*(4), 698–14.

Roberts, L.M., Dutton, J.E., Spreitzer, G.M., Heaphy, E.D., & Quinn, R.E. (2005). Composing the reflected best-self portrait: Building pathways for becoming extraordinary in work organizations. *Academy of Management Review, 30*(4), 712–36.

Rodríguez-Carvajal, R., Moreno-Jiménez, B., de Rivas-Hermosilla, S., Álvarez-Bejarano, A. Y., & Sanz-Vergel, A.I. (2010). Positive psychology at work: Mutual gains for individuals and organizations. *Revista de Psicología del Trabajo y de las Organizaciones (Journal of Work and Organizational Psychology), 26*(3), 235–53.

Ryan, R.M. & Huta, V. (2009). Wellness as healthy functioning or wellness as happiness: The importance of eudaimonic thinking (response to the Kashdan et al. and Waterman discussion). *The Journal of Positive Psychology, 4*(3), 202–04.

Ryff, C.D. (1989). Happiness is everything, or is it? Explorations on the meaning of psychological well-being. *Journal of Personality and Social Psychology, 57*(6), 1069–81.

Ryff, C. D. & Keyes, C.L. (1995). The structure of psychological well-being revisited. *Journal of Personality and Social Psychology, 69*(4), 719–27.

Schaufeli, W.B., Salanova, M., Gonzalez-Roma, V., & Bakker, A.B. (2002). The measurement of engagement and burnout: A two sample confirmatory factor analysis approach. *Journal of Happiness Studies, 3*, 71–92.

Schultz, M.L. (2008). Occupational well-being: The development of a theory and a measure. Doctoral dissertation, Kansas State University. Retrieved from: http://hdl.handle.net/2097/746.

Singh, S. & Singh, R. (2003). Construct validation of P.G.I. well-being scale in work set up. *Journal of the Indian Academy of Applied Psychology, 29*(1–2), 53–60.

Sinha, J.B.P. & Singh, S. (1995). Employees satisfaction and its organizational predictors. *Indian Journal of Industrial Relations, 31*(2), 135–152.

Spreitzer, G., Sutcliffe, K., Dutton, J., Sonenshein, S., & Grant, A.M. (2005). A socially embedded model of thriving at work. *Organization Science, 16*(5), 537–49.

Srivastava, S. (2010). Culture-intrapreneurship relationship: Reward as a moderator. *Management and Labour Studies, 35*(2), 249–63.

Taris, T.W. & Schreurs, P.J.G. (2009). Well-being and organizational performance: An organizational-level test of the happy-productive worker hypothesis. *Work & Stress, 23*(2), 120–36.

Ulrich, D. & Ulrich, W. (2010). *How great leaders build abundant organizations that win: The why of work.* New York: McGraw Hill.

Van den Broeck, A., Vansteenkiste, M., De Witte, H., Soenens, B., & Lens, W. (2010). Capturing autonomy, competence, and relatedness at work: Construction and initial validation of the Work-related basic need satisfaction scale. *Journal of Occupational and Organizational Psychology, 83*(4), 981–1002.

Vazquez, C., Hervas, G., Rahona, J.J., & Gomez, D. (2009). Psychological well-being and health: Contributions of positive psychology. *Annuary of Clinical and Health Psychology, 5*, 15–27.

Verma, S.K., Dubey, B.L., & Gupta, D. (1983). PGI general well-being scale. *Indian Journal of Clinical Psychology, 10*, 299–304.

Walsh, J.P., Weber, K., & Margolis, J.D. (2003). Social issues in management: Our lost case found. *Journal of Management, 29*, 859–81.

Warr, P. (1990). The measurement of well-being and other aspects of mental health. *Journal of Occupational Psychology, 63*, 193–210.

——— (1994). A conceptual framework for the study of work and mental health. *Work and Stress, 8*(2), 84–97.

Wright, T.A. & Cropanzano, R. (2000). Psychological well-being and job satisfaction as predictors of job performance. *Journal of Occupational Health Psychology, 5*, 84–94.

Zelenski, J.M., Murphy, S.A., & Jenkins, D.A. (2008). The happy-productive worker thesis revisited. *Journal of Happiness Studies, 9*(4), 521–37.

Section-IV

STRESS AND SPIRITUALITY

12

Existential Rhythm, Spiritual Synergy, and Spiritual Immunity: Spiritual Approaches to Stress Management

Akbar Husain

Abstract

The distinctive feature of theoretical and philosophical psychology of Indian thinking is its spiritual approach, by which I mean to integrate new experience and understanding into an evolving scheme of ideas, all leading and pointing to spiritual approach to stress management. In this article, certain key concepts such as existential rhythm, spiritual synergy, and spiritual immunity are introduced to manage stress. These concepts can help us in the process of spiritual growth. The author advocates that these concepts are closely linked to the Indian culture and spirituality. The article is concluded with a discussion of how spiritual practices may provide strength in individuals in coping with stress.

Keywords: stress management, spirituality, and stress management

Unnatural work produces too much stress.

—*Bhagwad Gita 3.35*

It's not stress that kills us; it is our reaction to it.

—*Hans Selye*

Introduction

Industrial Revolution caused an increase in social problems. In the present era, which is called the era of computerization, millions of people worldwide are affected by mental, behavioral, neurological, and social disorders. Stress not only affects our body and corrupts its natural functioning, but also affects our mind and spirit. Everyday, each of us experience stress mild or severe. We adopt different ways to cope with stress. Behavioral scientists have suggested a number of effective methods for managing stress. Even then the stress remains the major affliction of modern life.

Most of us use physical, social, behavioral, emotional, cognitive, and religious approaches to cope with stress, but we remain ignorant of spiritual approaches. Recently, there has been a growing interest to the development of a new interdisciplinary field, psychoneuroimmunology, which studies stress, psychological responses, and the immune system simultaneously. Psychologists and professionals have neglected the place of spiritual dimensions in the field of stress management. Stress is a cardinal state of existence. The present chapter introduces three basic elements of spiritualism, i.e., "Existential Rhythm," "Spiritual Synergy," and "Spiritual Immunity" and points out their relevance to stress management and psychoneuroimmunology.

What is Spirituality?

Spirituality is the state of ultimate well-being, which is qualitatively different from what is ordinarily experienced. It is regarded as a state of inner peace, and tranquility. Spirit is hidden in all beings. Some are spiritual aspirants. They believe that the mind flows for the sole purpose of attaining the Infinite, and hence they focus their energies on the contemplation of the transcendental entity. They are more attracted to God and reach the stage which marks the end of mental existence and the beginning of spirituality. At the spiritual state, one is no longer a human being, one is a spiritual being. Spiritual state directs us how we live consciously, aware of every movement and awake to every existential rhythm of life.

According to Husain (2011), human spirituality can be viewed conceptually as having two principal components—knowledge and practice (see Figure 12.1). Krishna says in Bhagavad Gita spirituality is sovereign knowledge, the secret of all things, meant to be experienced and practiced, "There is nothing pure as the knowledge" (chapter 4, verse 38). Knowledge deals with both

Figure 12.1 An Analytical Model of Spirituality

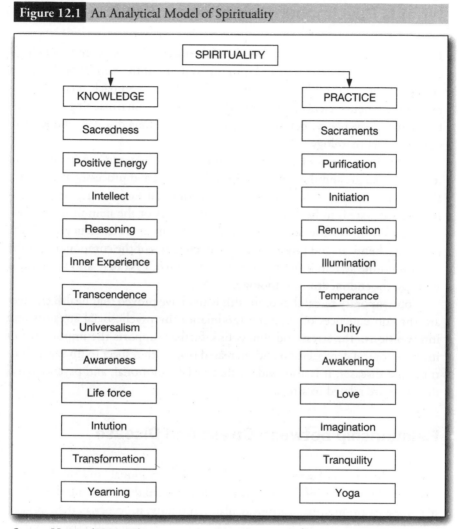

Source: Husain (2011: 27).

spiritual as well as material science. Spirituality helps the practical application of new modes and concepts for the benefit of humanity.

The word *spirituality* has twelve letters; each letter connotes two concepts related to knowledge and practice. The concepts related to knowledge and practice is so powerful and elevating that it deals with every domain of human experience. They are stationed in the higher realms of human consciousness.

What is Psychoneuroimmunology (PNI)?

Psychoneuroimmunology is the study of the interaction between psychological processes and the nervous and immune systems of the human body (Irwin and Vedhara, 2005). PNI takes an interdisciplinary approach incorporating psychology, neuroscience, immunology, physiology, pharmacology, molecular biology, psychiatry, behavioral medicine, infectious diseases, endocrinology, and rheumatology.

The main interests of PNI are the interactions between the nervous and immune systems and the relationships between mental processes and health. PNI studies, among other things, the physiological functioning of the neuroimmune system in health and disease; disorders of the neuroimmune system (autoimmune diseases, hypersensitivities, immune deficiency); and the physical, chemical, and physiological characteristics of the components of the neuroimmune system in vitro, in situ, and in vivo. PNI may also be referred to as psychoendoneuroimmunology (PENI).

Contemporary researches on health issues have proved that health changes are the consequences of immune modulation by psychosocial stressors and interventions. The stress and illness link further supports the importance of immunological deregulation and increased risks with respect to diverse conditions and diseases. It is also evident that social, emotional, and psychological disorders are related to stress.

Relationship between Stress and Disease

Most of the causes of stress are related to social, emotional, and psychological disorders. Husain (1999) has categorized stress related disorders into the following types: gastrointestinal, cardiovascular, respiratory, urogenetial, dermatological, musculo-skeletal, endocrine, exocrine, neurological, and affective disorders.

Stressors can produce profound health problems. In one epidemiological study, for example, all-cause mortality increased in the month following a severe stressor—the death of a spouse (Kaprio, Koskenvuo, and Rita, 1987). Researchers have propagated that cognitive and affective responses are precipitated and aggravated by stressful events which ultimately affect the sympathetic nervous system and hormonal changes leading to the permanent impairment of immune system (Chrousos and Gold, 1992; Glaser and Kiecolt-Glaser, 1994). Potential health consequences are broad, but include rates of infection (Cohen, Tyrrell, and Smith, 1991; Cohen and Williamson, 1991), HIV progression (Leserman et al., 1999, 2000) and cancer incidence and progression (Andersen, Kiecolt-Glaser, and Glaser, 1994; Kaprio, Koskenvuo, and Rita, 1987; Kiecolt-Glaser and Glaser, 1999).

Many emotional and behavioral responses such as anxiety, fear, tension, anger, and sadness lead to psychophysiological changes like pulse rate, heart rate and blood pressure, etc. All these factors affect the immune system. Researchers have shown that the physiological changes that are of short duration (Chrousos and Gold, 1992) may be beneficial to the system and chronic stress disturbs the homeostasis.

Immune changes in response to very brief stressors have been a central theme in the last decade of PNI research, but older literature also provides early illustrations. In a study published in 1960, subjects were led to believe that they had accidentally caused serious injury to a companion through misuse of explosives (McDonald and Yagi, 1960).

Diseases of the Immune System

Diseases of the Immune System Disorders range from mild allergies to serious transplant rejections. Auto immune diseases and disorders may result in allergies and rejection of a foreign body in the organism. Antigens that provoke an allergic response are known as allergens. The immune system recognizes and attacks anything that is different from the substances that are normally present in an individual, even those that are only slightly different like transplanted tissues and organs. When an organ is donated to an individual, the immune system recognizes it as a foreign body and might attack it. Most transplant recipients are given drugs to suppress their immune response and prevent rejection of the transplant.

Autoimmunity is the response of the immune system against the cells and tissues of the body. It may involve cell-mediated responses, humoral responses, or both. The mechanism of autoimmune responses is not clearly understood and much research needs to be done before it could result in cures. Autoimmune responses could result in allergies, arthritis, multiple sclerosis, and other stress-related disorders.

Existential Rhythm

O'Dea (1966) quantified three fundamental characteristics of human existence—*uncertainty*, *powerlessness*, and *scarcity*. These, he perceived as challenges to the order upon which social life is based. He came to the conclusion that such experiences as these create questions in the mind which cannot be satisfied within the realm of normal human existence; therefore, he stated that the explanations of rationalization for such experiences must arise from outside the enclosures of the individual's world—from the "beyond"—so to speak. This would suggest that marginal experiences compel humans to search the transcendent for meaningful answer.

The concept of existential rhythm leads to the creation of a new field, i.e., Psycho-neuro-immunology. As we know the relationship of necessity exists between body and mind, internal environment and external environment, life, mind, and the metacognitions (i.e., the higher possibilities of consciousness) that are not exhausted by mind. The consciousness arises out of the very requirements of mind. According to Sartre (1956) consciousness is freedom. The ability of men to see himself as a self, to have consciousness, to question his own existence is powers and possibilities of humans alone. Man must be understood as an "existence." Life is the rhythm of God. Therefore, an individual is seen as "a being-in-the-world" or "rhythmist." Compare Tillich's statement: "Man is essentially 'finite freedom'; freedom not in the sense of indeterminancy but in the sense of being able to determine himself through decisions in the center of his Being" (Tillich, 1956: 52) with that of Freud (1956: 214): "What we call our ego is essentially passive ... we are 'lived' by unknown and uncontrollable forces." The rhythm of existence implies two things: (a) preparation and the rise of necessary and sufficient conditions of organization constituting the dynamism within one plane of existence, (b) rise and emergence of the higher visible principle creating meaning and purpose in the dynamism and its operations.

If we analyze the behavior of "matter," we find attractions, repulsions, motion, vibrations, and so on. They give rise to tendencies where contractions, expansions, and all the forces operating in matter that have brought into existence the necessary and sufficient conditions for the emergence of the visible principle of life. And all this has happened of necessity.

At every plane of existence the entire sequence of the creation of a higher principle of existence is repeated till we arrive at the plane of mind which constitutes the basis of the integral principle of the existentialism synthesizing spiritual principle with materialism to the greatest advantage of science that is likely to evolve in the next century.

Mind can be viewed in two ways: (a) a self exhausting force acting under those absorptions that are its characteristics, e.g., cognitive process and functions; (b) a creative power capable of transcending its own functions. As we know that consciousness is not determinate, and mind as a visible principle does not exhaust all possibilities of awareness. Man has a hidden aspiration to transcend from one realm of possibilities into another. This aspiration is not restricted to the material realm. Man has the urge to transcend and to spiritualize himself, to create meaning of his physical being, his material existence, and his mental phenomena of a non-material plane. The prolonged suppression on this urge—consciously or otherwise—has given rise to boredom, meaninglessness, loneliness, suicidal inclinations, and sufferings like anxiety that have no immediate cause. They must, therefore, be located in the arrested growth of human potential because this materialistic civilization has served the relationship of our being with the transcendent reality. The rhythm of existence has been disturbed. This rhythm cannot be restored unless the suppressed urge to transcend is released.

The secret of psycho-neuro-immunology lies in releasing this urge: in its fulfillment and in accepting the fact that be possibilities of our consciousness are not exhausted by mental functions. In order to reach into the holistic paradigm of existentialism, we have to note that supermind starts from the whole and seen in its parts and properties it does not build up the knowledge of the whole by an increasing knowledge of the parts and properties; and even the whole is to it only a unity of sum, only a partial and inferior term of the higher unity of infinite essence.

Spiritual Synergy

What I visualize is that the cause of mental suffering and ailments is the absence of spiritual synergy and the disturbance in the existential rhythm which impeded the growth of the self. Since the growth of our self is a necessity embedded in our very existence, the conditions of life that allow the said growth, implying transcendence, are the natural conditions—which has been brought about by the materialistic civilization—giving rise to most agonizing conflicts because mind and the life force sinks under their own absorptions which also begin to decompose because they are only the preconditions for reaching into the higher possibilities of our being. This state of sinking and deterioration, which is an inevitable consequence of it, has thrown us into an existential crisis where the higher possibilities of our being and existence are all blocked up.

In the language of psycho-neuro-immunology the theory of stress would tell us that our real problem lies in minimizing the susceptibility to stressful conditions of life. Hence, in order to create a state of immunity from stress-inducing and tension-inducing conditions of life, the disturbed rhythm of one existence must be set right by understanding the fact that the meaning and coherence, stability, balance, and the natural movement of life gets seriously disturbed if our affinity with any of the primary relational patterns is broken down. The immense power of self creates the state of spiritual synergy necessary for onward movement of life force.

The creative power of *Mantra* has effects within the vast subliminal consciousness and helps the individual. Since there is a shared consciousness in all living beings also within ourself, i.e., between mind and every living cell of the body, the *Mantra*s can induce a power and accentuate its effects. The expositions of the *Mantra*s tend to transform into forces with the rhythm of vibrations created by recitals and interiorized through the *prana* in a state of high energy concentration at the psychic level, while some hidden channels begin to *trans*, the pooled energy with immediate or delayed somatic effects. *Mantra*s also help us in our experience of superman whose essential being is beyond all analysis.

Those who have spent their life learning to live in the spiritual stream through meditation have nothing to fear from stress. They face their stresses with serenity. They have learned the art of rising above body-consciousness. They know how to transcend beyond their physical energies. Those who learn spiritual exercises early in life are fortunate. They can devote sometime daily to their spiritual practices so that they can master the art of rising above body-consciousness in their life. Meditation requires practice. Daily meditation will build up our spiritual abilities so that we can experience the spiritual rhythm within.

Silence is one the methods for coping with stressful situations. "Right speech comes out of silence, and right silence comes out of speech," says Dietrich Bonnhoeffer. In silence our speech patterns are refined because silence develops a self-awareness that enables us to choose better the words that we say. When you are under stress, remain silent, do spiritual practices, and have trust in the spirit of God. In other words, keep silence and consciously focus on God rather than anything else.

Practising rhythms of silence and stillness helps us learn to cope with stress. It is not something easy for those of us who are busy trying to make things happen. It takes energy to be restrained and to wait for the miracle of God in our lives and in the world around us. What we are learning these days is to use words. The more distressing things are, the more active process that is required of us, the more silence we need.

Every individual must realize the importance of spiritual synergy in every activity. One may attain spiritual synergy more quickly if he seeks to attune himself with it in his daily activities. From a spiritual perspective, spiritual synergy maximizes our abilities in every sphere of life. Spiritual synergy rooted in faith can develop confidence and solutions to every problem.

Spiritual Immunity

We are blessed with an immune system that protects us from all sorts of stresses and diseases. We maintain reasonably good health despite exposure to stress-related diseases. We have an in-built immune system that we maintain with healthy lifestyles. Just as we develop immunity in the body, we need to develop immunity of the spirit to protect the purity of our heart, mind, and soul and stay free from stresses.

Most of us are exposed and liable to a number of life stresses originating from the external world, and from within. We need to transform ourselves from within to overcome distresses and influences. Stresses block the very light of the soul. Mind is a gift from God and we should not allow it to get polluted. In order to increase spiritual immunity, let us learn to overcome stresses and unnecessary worldly desires.

Another highly common tendency is that we keep remembering and reliving the past, both achievements and traumas. We blame others for our misfortunes and take credit for our successes. But often we are responsible for our misfortunes, and we come to fear the future. Stop thinking of past achievements and failures and learn to live in the present. Then only we can come back to the original state of purity and build the immunity of spirit.

When the stresses trouble us, we need to be patient and not get upset. At the same time, we must acknowledge that stress is a part of life. Thus, when we calmly react to any stressful situation, we become immune to our system. Then our coping mechanism will be able to shore up good karma.

Older people are able to absorb divine vibrations easily because they tend to be cool-headed and patient. This develops the purity of their mind and heart. When stress develops, grace stops flowing and you begin to have bad karma! The present generation needs to come out of their comfort zone to deal with stress. We must be willing to identify and firmly develop positive traits right from young age itself so that the process of cultivating immunity begins.

Spiritual immunity protects us from distresses and negative vibrations operating in the present lives. It draws the best things to us. It makes us strong with emotional and mental stability and builds up self-confidence. It makes us have self-control. Owing to spiritual immunity our innate powers are awakened and activated. We not only realize but also actualize that we are born as a light to spread light.

On a practical level, if you wish to develop your immune function, you need to be conscious of and improve the quality of your air, water, and especially nutrition—the food you eat (i.e., *sattavic*). Regular periods of rest have also been found to be important for good immune function. These periods of health-inducing rest are characterized by increases in alpha and theta brain wave activity. Certain types of meditation are ideal for generating these kinds of stress reducing brain states. Research has shown that those who meditate twenty minutes, once or twice a day tend to have better immune function and wellness than those who do not (Kenyon, 2006).

Conclusion and Suggestions for Future Research

Beyond the use of bodily strengths, we can utilize the mental and spiritual strengths. As we are of a finite nature, our mental and spiritual capacities are also finite. Stress is generally perceived by the presence of negative thoughts. It may be questioned along with physical and psychological symptoms of stress there is also the existence of spiritual symptoms. In fact, if there is the existence of bodily, mental, emotional, and spiritual symptoms or even beyond that, the spiritual practices may provide strength in individuals in coping with stress.

Although the physical body is always impure, the mind and heart should be kept clean. This will help us refine our spiritual powers so that we are able to decide what to do and how to do to cope with stress. Only when we are willing to learn do we begin to recognize, adopt, and cultivate the spirituality in us.

Future researches should explore the spiritual symptoms and sources of stress with reference to age, gender, religious beliefs differentials, etc.

Spiritual immunity may be linked to psycho-immunology or psychoneuroimmunology. This field of research needs new looks at how our thoughts and especially emotions affect our immune systems. And while such ephemeral things as thought and feeling are only one small part of the immune puzzle, they are an intriguing and important aspect.

Fields of medicine and psychology should support the concept of spiritual synergy. Spiritual synergy is forever our reality. It is a true state of being. Practicing rhythms of silence may help to cope with distressing things. More silence is needed to enjoy real peace of mind.

References

Andersen, B.L., Kiecolt-Glaser, J.K., & Glaser, R. (1994). A biobehavioral model of cancer stress and disease course. *American Psychologist 49*(5), 389–404.

Chrousos, G.P. & Gold, P.W. (1992). The concepts of stress and stress system disorders: Overview of physical and behavioral homeostasis. *JAMA 267(Mar 4),* 1244–52.

Cohen, S., Tyrrell, D.A., & Smith, A.P. (1991). Psychological stress and susceptibility to the common cold. *The New England Journal of Medicine, 325*(9), 606–12.

Cohen, S. & Williamson, G.M. (1991). Stress and infectious disease in humans. *Psychological Bulletin, 109*(1), 5–24.

Freud, S. (1956). *Erinnerungen an Sigmund Freud* (Memories of Sigmund Freud). Berne.

Glaser, R. & Kiecolt-Glaser, J.K. (1994). *Handbook of human stress and immunity.* San Diego: Academic Press.

Husain, A. (1999). Management of stress disorders through individual control techniques. In D.M. Pestonjee, U. Pareek, & R. Agrawal (Eds), *Studies in stress and its management* (pp. 235–48). New Delhi: Oxford & IBH Publishing Co. Pvt. Ltd.

———— (2011). *Spirituality and holistic health: A psychological perspective.* New Delhi: Prasad Psycho Corporation.

Irwin, M. & Vedhara, K. (2005). *Human psychoneuroimmunology.* Oxford University Press.

Kaprio, J., Koskenvuo, M., & Rita, H. (1987). Mortality after bereavement: A prospective study of 95,647 widowed persons. *American Journal of Public Health, 77*(3), 283–87.

Kenyon, T. (2006). Explorations in self-haling and transformation. Soundings.

Kiecolt-Glaser, J. K., & Glaser, R. (1999). Psychoneuroimmunology and cancer: Fact or fiction? *European Journal of Cancer, 35,* 1603-07.

Leserman, J., Jackson, E.D., Petitto, J.M., Golden, R.N., Silva, S.G., Perkins, D.O., Cai, J., Folds, J.D., & Evans, D.L. (1999). Progression to AIDS: The effects of stress, depressive symptoms, and social support. *Psychosomatic Medicine, 61*(3), 397–406.

Leserman, J., Petitto, J.M., Golden, R.N., Gaynes, B.N., Gu, H., Perkins, D.O., Silva, S.G., Folds, J.D., & Evans, D.L. (2000). Impact of stressful life events, depression, social support, coping, and cortisol on progression to AIDS. *The American Journal of Psychiatry, 157*(8), 1221–28.

McDonald, R.D. & Yagi, K. (1960). A note on eosinopenia as an index of psychological stress. *Psychosomatic Medicine, 2*(22), 149–50.

O'Dea, T. (1966). *The sociology of religion.* Englewood Cliffs, NJ: Prentice Hall.

Sartre, J.P. (1956). *Being and nothingness* (trans. by H. Barnes). New York: Philosophical Library.

Tillich, P. (1952). *The courage to be.* Nishet and Co. Ltd.

13

Managing Constructive and Destructive Emotions: Indian Psycho-spiritual Perspective

Mala Sinha

Abstract

The paper presents The Rasa-Guna (R-G) theory of emotions based on the Rasa theory from *Natyasastra* and Guna theory from Bhagavad Gita. The theory outlines the sequential arousal of emotions and their impact on human consciousness positing that negative emotions with dominance of *Rajasic* and *Tamasic guna* like fear, anger or grief have a destructive impact on self and impairs cognitive capabilities. Positive emotions like love, heroism, and serenity, on the other hand, have a preponderance of *Satwic guna*, the impact of which on the consciousness is constructive. Negative emotions are associated with narrow ego centered ethics while positive emotions, contribute to social and cosmic order that is beyond the self. The RG model has many parallels within contemporary discourse on emotions particularly psycho-neurobiological researches of emotions. The paper concludes by suggesting a strategy to manage constructive and destructive emotions based on the principles of reducing the habit tendencies (*vasanas*) of destructive emotions through certain yoga practices.

Keywords: destructive emotions, rasa, guna, satwic, rajasic, tamasic, yoga, ethics

Introduction

The Indian *Rasa* theory as described in *Natyasastra* by Bharata Muni (Sanskrit text developed around 200–500 BC), complemented by Bhagavad Gita's Guna theory, offers an etiologically advanced meta theory of emotions. The

Rasa theory in particular describes the sequential arousal of different types of emotions, and their link with three *gunas* (*Satwic, Rajasic,* and *Tamasic*) explains effects of emotions on consciousness. *Rasa* or aesthetic relish is an emotion experienced by audience while viewing any form of art; for example, the dramatist through the use of props, plot, situations, dialogue, and expressions of actors along with accompaniments of music and dance simulates the determinant and excitatory causes of a specific emotion it wishes to arouse in viewers. It is hypothesised that if emotions can be aroused vicariously in drama, in real life too there will exist several causes, because of which individuals will go through both positive and negative emotions that impact consciousness and subsequently the behavior in various ways. The *Rasa* theory lends itself extremely well to an understanding of human emotions in real life and ancient scholars like Bhatta Lollata, Sankuka, and Abhinavagupta (ninth to eleventh century) have elaborated on the seminal work of Bharata (J. Sinha, 1958); and many modern scholars have critiqued and examined the theory in contemporary idioms from social sciences (Jain, 2002; Menon and Schweder, 1994; Paranjpe, 1998, 2009; Paranjpe and Bhatt, 1997; Shweder and Haidt, 2000).

The theory of *Guna* (described in Chapter 18 of Bhagavad Gita) describes three characteristic ways energy (*prakriti*) organizes to give rise to different forms we see in creation. Drawing from Indian Sankhya philosophy, creation is envisaged as play of expressive creative energy called *prakriti*—a manifestation of unmanifest *purusa* or the cosmic unified intelligence (Pande, 1990). Within this framework emotions are constituted of three *gunas* and expression and consequences thereof will reflect the properties of particular *guna* which dominates. This paper presents Bharata's *Rasa* theory in conjunction with Bhagavad Gita's *Guna* theory: alignment of the two perspectives allowing a more comprehensive understanding of why certain emotions will be constructive, while others are destructive to human consciousness and endeavors. The case of Arjuna, one of the key protagonists in the great Indian epic Mahabharata is illustrative. The surge of grief and fear in valiant Arjuna that made him put down his weapons and desire to flee from battleground when he first witnessed the vast Kaurava army arrayed opposite him, comprising of venerable teachers, elders, and brothers, demonstrates the destructive power of negative emotions on consciousness: we find Arjuna of *kshatriya–svabhava* (warrior nature) whose duty is to fight for justice is now unwilling to fight a war he has been waiting for many long years. The *Rasa* theory elaborates on how emotions are aroused and develop due the dynamic interplay of external stimulus causes, physiological changes and cognitive appraisals which cumulatively impact the consciousness of the individual experiencing the emotion. The theory presents a number of intersection points during ongoing emotion episode that provides space for modifications in the trajectory of an emotion and perhaps changes its course, and this has implications for management of emotions. In the first part of paper, researches on emotions both within Indian knowledge tradition and contemporary context will be developed, followed by description of *Rasa-Guna* (R-G) theory of emotions; and in the last section ways to manage constructive and destructive emotions will be discussed.

Theoretical Framework

CONTEMPORARY DISCOURSE ON EMOTIONS

Historically, the discourse on emotions can be traced to Lange and James (1922) who saw emotions as mere bodily sensations. That is, when we observe ourselves displaying certain patterns of physiological arousal, we tend to put the label of a particular emotion on it: hence we do not smile because we are happy, but because we smile we are happy. Later researchers found it was difficult to differentiate physiological states among emotions, a fact underscored in *Rasa* theory, which says that the *sattvika*s (the physiological and organic expression of emotions) remain largely undifferentiated in different emotional experiences. Walter Cannon (1927) questioned: if bodily sensation is undifferentiated information about what we are feeling, then this awareness must come from somewhere else and Singer and Schacter (1962) attributed this to cognitive appraisal that accompany bodily changes. Therefore when we appraise a situation as threatening we experience fear, subsequently primary and secondary ways of interpreting relations between events, goals, motives, and concerns further lead to development of emotions—a line of thinking supported by several other scholars (Frijda, 1986; Lazarus, 1984,1991; Roseman, Spindal, and Jose, 1990; Scherer, 1997, 2005). In 1980 Zajonc's work reinstated the viewpoint that it is not necessary that emotions must flow from appraisal since they often arise even when the person is unconscious of the stimuli. According to Scherer (2005), the appraisal first view point is apparently opposite the bodily reactions first viewpoint and arises when we do not take a dynamic systems approach, treating emotions as standalone experiences that reoccur in specific stimulus situation in isolated time zones.

Inspired by social constructionist's paradigms (Gergen, 1985; Harre and Gillet, 1994) emotions have also been viewed as socially constructed rather than being an inner individualized experience. Protagonists posit that the way a community uses language and meaning derived from social relations that are locally created interpretative systems is that which give rise to emotional experiences (Armon-Jones 1986; Levenson et al., 1992). For example Finlay Jones and Harre (1986) note that *accidie* is a medieval and now obsolete emotion that refers to sense of boredom and dejection in fulfilling religious duties (rather than with joy as was expected by social-cultural interpretative system of that time). There is also evidence that emotions are rooted in preconscious intuitions only slightly modified by cultural influences that are pan cultural. Caroll Izard (1971) proposed ten discrete emotions each with a distinct neuro-physiological state, which like colors on the palate, mix and match to give rise to a host of other emotions that organize cognition and motivate action. Similarly Paul Ekman (1982) has proposed seventeen basic emotions of which seven are positive and the remaining negative or neutral. Research has also shown that emotions emerge according to genetic time table which show stability across ontogenesis and cultures (Ackerman, Abe, and Izard, 1998). In line with these researches *Rasa* theory also proposes existence of nine permanent predispositions of emotions (*sthayi–bhava*) which when aroused due to causative conditions (*vibhava*) give rise to an emotional experience with characteristic impact on consciousness.

A number of psychologists are beginning to take a non linear, dynamic system and context sensitive view of emotions giving importance to feedback components to understand the relationship between emotions, moods, and personality changes (Parkinson, 2004; Teasdale and Barnard, 1993). In 1993, Fogel proposed that emotions are self organizing products of psychological and bodily processes that arise and develop continuously as we transact interpersonally. Camras (1992) examined developing emotions as dynamic assemblies of hedonic, motor, appraisal and expressive constituents. Several researches within the dynamic systems approach have related emotions to personality formations, (Lewis 1995; Cloniger, Svaric, and Svrakie, 1997); adult personality change (Magai and Nusbaum, 1996); identity development (Haviland and Kalbaugh, 1993); development of self (Schore, 1997); and consolidation of temperament (Derryberry and Rothbart, 1997).

Although there is still lack of clarity regarding definition of emotions (Rozen and Cohen, 2003) there is consensus on the view that emotions are multifaceted, context dependent; and monitoring, regulation, and expression of emotions are socially constructed (Armon, 1986; Frijda & Mesquito, 1998). Scherer (2000) distinguishes two major pairs of competing approaches in studies on emotions: (*a*) psycho-biological versus socio-psychological and (*b*) structural–modular versus component–dynamic approaches. Psycho-biological theories underline pre formation of discrete emotional tendencies that are limited in number and have a neural base meant for biological adaptation where culture only plays the role of modulating or controlling the underlying psychobiological mechanisms (Ekman, 1992, 1993; Panksepp, 1998; Tomkins, 1984). The socio-psychological theories, on the other hand, believe that culture and language play a central role in constitution, elicitation, and expression of emotions (Averill, 1980; Harre and Jones, 1986). The structural–modular approaches of Zajonc (1980) espouse that cognitions, emotions, and motivations are strictly independent systems while the component–dynamic approach envisage emotions to be continuously changing configurations consisting of cognitive component and motivational processes (Ellsworth and Scherer 2003; Frijda, 1986; Lazarus, 1991). Scherer (2005) proposes the component process model to cope with these dichotomies and conceptualizes emotions as a sequence of state changes in five organismic systems—cognitive system (appraisal), autonomic nervous system (arousal), motor systems (expression), motivational system (action tendencies), and monitor system (feeling). That these processes are not sequential but work on each other through feedback loops leading to emergent co-processes is supported by neurobiological researches (Damasio, 1994; Freeman, 1995).

POSITIVE AND NEGATIVE EMOTIONS

The key objective of the paper is to examine the impact of emotions on consciousness and this creates the necessity to classify emotions as positive or negative with respect to impact on self. Researchers have shown positive and negative emotions are not continuous but separate—like apples and oranges—and different parts of the brain are associated with them. Le Doux found (1996) when a particular word was presented to left hemisphere of brain injured patients the left brain could read, report, and evaluate the word but when the same word was presented to right hemisphere, patients were unable to evaluate the word as being good or bad, showing that roots of transferring of emotional meaning and verbal meaning are different. The Osgood Suci and Tannenbaum study in 1957 through analysis of ratings of affect laden words found evaluation, activity, and potency to be the three primary dimensions through which we differentiate words with respect emotional arousal. Russel and Carroll (1999) and Watson et al. (1999) have mapped affect words as falling along two axes based on high and low activation versus positive and negative, strengthening the two dimension view of emotions. Norma Bradburn (1969), in a survey of thousands of people, found that number of positive emotions a person experiences is independent of number of negative emotions, in the sense that one cannot predict how happy a person is from how unhappy he or she was. The classic two factor study of job satisfaction, by Herzberg Mausner and Synder (1959) found that factors that contribute to satisfaction are different from those that contribute to dissatisfaction. For example, presence of money may not lead to satisfaction, but its absence will lead to dissatisfaction. Similarly sense of achievement and growth promotes satisfaction, but may not be linked with dissatisfaction.

The neurology of positive and negative emotions has different neurobiological functions and perhaps distinct anatomical structures also. Considerable work has been done, for example, on the association between depletion of serotonin in brain and presence of negative emotions (Malenka, Hamblin, and Barcha, 1989; Panksepp, 1998). Biological psychiatry uses drugs based on this principle to treat depression and other affective disorders. Similarly neurochemical dopamine has been linked with positive states (Wise and Hoffman, 1992) and another neurotransmitter called Corticotropin releasing hormones (CRH) increases significantly when in stress and mobilizes neuro-mechanism associated with fear and anxiety. Positive and negative emotions also activate different areas of brain as shown by brain imaging techniques like Positron Emission Tomography (PET), Magnetic Resonance Imaging (MRI), and Electro Encephalography (EEG). Detractors, however, believe that processes related to emotions draw from the whole brain rather than certain anatomical parts of it (Davidson, 2000), but there is sufficient evidence to state that positive and negative emotions are not two ends of the same continuum both can be independent of each other.

CONSTRUCTIVE AND DESTRUCTIVE EMOTIONS

It is important to understand how positive and negative emotions impact the way people feel, think, and behave and Jeffrey Gray (1982) uses two behavioral criteria to assess the inner workings underlying human action and reaction during an emotional experience—behavioral activation and behavioral inhibition. The former suggests that approach motivation is strengthened by positive affective information and avoidance is strengthened with negative effect. The work of Lang, Bradley, and Cuthbert (1998) use the terms defensive and appetitive action orientations and suggest when one system is in engagement the other is suspended while experiencing a particular emotion. Generally negative affect dynamics involve motives of reduction of aversive state through avoidance behavior that is accompanied by fear and anxiety, cognitions of pessimism with hopes to end the fear and becoming secure and safe. On the other hand, the dynamics of positive affect states involves motives of promotion of positive affect by approach and goal pursuit behaviors, accompanied by emotions of interest and excitement and optimism of fulfillment and happiness (Zautra, 2003). Positive and negative emotions set forth two parallel trajectories and Clynes (1978) uses the metaphor of reins of a horse drawn carriage to explain the relationship between the two systems. When you pull the reins to activate positive emotions you cannot push the same reins to get the opposite (that is negative emotion), for which you need to pull the reins, on the other hand.

Stress is difficult to differentiate from negative emotions, but it is well-established that in stress the cognitive capacity to process affective information is constrained when compared to when we are calm and serene. It has been found that stress narrows field of vision, makes judgments bipolar and leads to less receptivity (Zautra, Berkhof, and Nicholson, 2002). The researchers also found in stressful situations the two dimensional nature of emotions get diffused, thus greater the negative feelings, lesser the positive feelings, making it reasonably clear that stress, emotions, and cognitive capacities are interrelated. Damasio (1999) has shown through brain imaging that decision-making is often prompted by states of physiological arousal triggered by lower brain like amygdale, driving decisions even before one is consciously aware of it. Gray (1982) also found that in a happy mood learner will recall more items than is possible in a sad mood indicating that conscious reasoning strategies are biased by non-conscious affective processes.

Viewpoint from Indian Knowledge Traditions

Ancient text *Natyasastra* by Bharata Muni provides the most detailed account of *rasa* (emotions) in Indian knowledge tradition. *Rasa* exemplifies a particular aesthetic experience and a mental state aroused specifically in the audience, with certain practical means that create a distinct mood through artistic expression. For example, everything in drama is subordinate to aim of producing *rasa,* which includes plot, accessories, props, dialogue, and expressions of actors. Bharata states that *rasa* is aesthetic relish experienced by suitably cultivated individuals, and only the more cultured theatergoers will have this optimum experience (Higgens, 2007). Through an artistic performance the latent predispositions of different emotions are aroused, and in discerning audiences over a period of time there is development of emotional maturity and honing of artistic sensibilities due to recurrence of stimulus conditions and reinforcement of attendant causes witnessed (Jain,

2002). *Natyasastra* makes a subtle distinction between *bhava* and *rasa*; the former is existence of latent psychological–mental state (*sthayi bhava*) and latter is its affective transformation leading to an emotional experience. It is underscored that *rasa* is an aesthetically transformed emotional state "quintessence of something" (Chakrabarti, 2002) and is experienced with elevated consciousness by audience, while experience of *bhava* is rooted largely in mind and body. Bharata mentions nine *sthayi bhava* that can be transformed into *rasa* (*nava rasa*) to which two more were added later making a total of eleven *rasa*s; examples of which are *Rati* (erotic love), *Bhaya* (fear) or *Hasya* (humor), and *Vatsalya* (parental love). It is noteworthy that unlike in Indian tradition, Western classification of emotions (Izard 1971 and Ekman, 1992) does not include erotic emotion and parental love and have listed more negative than positive emotions. Through the combination of determinant causes (*vibhava*), consequents (*anubhava*), and transient complementary psychological states (*vyabhicari-bhava*), a particular *sthayi bhava* is aroused and transformed into *rasa* experience. For example, in the Indian epic Mahabharata, the latent emotion of grief (*sthayi bhava)* in fearless and valiant Arjuna is aroused when he surveys venerable elders, kith and kin arrayed opposite him on battle ground, who he would definitely have to kill if he fought the war. There is physiological expression of nervousness, a sinking feeling and weakness (*anubhava*) accompanied by involuntary organic and physiological changes (*sattvikas*) like sweating and trembling in Arjuna, which accentuate and deepen feelings of grief and give rise to secondary and transitory emotions like fear, detachment, and alienation (*vyabhichari bhava*). The cumulative impact of the emotion episode impacts Arjuna's consciousness in such a way that he almost chooses to withdraw from the impending war, one that was a logical and inevitable outcome of series of tragic events that had developed over decades.

The Vedanta philosophy offers some insights regarding the nature of human emotions. To begin with emotions are physiological interface between body and mind in which the ego plays a critical role. Unlike *rasa* which is enjoyment of emotions chiefly due to noninvolvement of the audience's ego, in real life the person experiencing emotions is also the character in the situation (plot) and thus pain is suffered and pleasure enjoyed. The Gita says that the degree of involvement of individual in the emotion arousing situations depends on dominance of *Rajasic* and *Tamasic guna* which degenerate a constructive impact on consciousness to becoming progressively destructive. In fact, intelligence (*buddhi*) benefits the individual as long as it is not distorted by ego (*ahamkara*), as a sense of agency embodied by ego predisposes individuals to pay attention to aspects that are in favor of ego, thereby distorting perceptions, reason, and judgment (Radhakrishnan and Moore, 1957). The sense of ego signifies greater *Rajasic guna*, a component of negative emotions (Baral and Das, 2004; Das, 1994). Emotions are believed to have their roots in organic body, but do not stay there and are stored in the mind (*manas*) as memory, and can play out their character as feelings even when the determinant causes of emotions (*vibhavas*) are absent. Feelings are natural to humans but are meant to pass, as clouds do over the sun. However, most of us allow feelings to coalesce and get anchored in mind as emotions when we ruminate obsessively and ascribe judgmental labels to them, thereby cultivating conditioning and predisposing the mind to experience specific emotions more frequently than others (Iyengar, 2005).

The Bhagavad Gita traces all emotions to interweaving and interpenetration of three-fold nature of energy (*triguna*). *Satwic guna* is luminosity, essence, clarity, equilibrium, interconnectedness, perceives failures, and success as processes in dynamic whole and therefore its energy is constant and non-diminishing. *Rajas* is dynamism, passion, goal-focused, pleasure- and dominance-seeking with strong sense of ownership (ego) and failures and success affect the motivation and energy levels. *Tamasic guna* is fixed on patterns, is habit-driven, with propensity for routine, slowness, inertia, rigidity, and stagnation. Its actions are guided by immediacy and ignorance and energy is sporadic (Sinha, 2005; Bhal and Debnath, 2006). *Satwa* produces constructive emotions characterized by joy, cheerfulness, and equanimity; *Rajas* and *Tamas* are modes for destructive emotions like lust, anger, greed, pride, vanity, and hatred and it is the proportion of *guna* in emotions that modifies the consciousness. The emotion of love and humor leads to blooming (*vikasa*) of consciousness, while heroic and wonder emotion expands (*vistara*) the consciousness. Conversely, fear and disgust agitates (*kshobha*), while anger and fear obstructs (*viksepa*) consciousness. *Vikasa and vistara* or blooming and expansion of consciousness are because of *Satwa* and *kshobha* and *viksepa* is due to *Rajas–Tamas* (Sinha, 1958; Das, 2008). The Buddhists specifically refer to five common negative emotions that distract one from taking good decisions, namely: (*a*) passion, including desire, greed, and lust; (*b*) aggression including anger, hatred, and resentment; (*c*) ignorance, which includes bewilderment, confusion and apathy; (*d*) pride, especially wounded pride, low self-esteem; and (*e*) jealousy, which includes envy, and paranoia (Goleman, 1988; Guenther, 1974).

Lewis (2000) presents a multiscale theory that views emotions as self organizing systems in micro, meso, and macro timescales which is based on psycho-neurobiological researches. For example, an angry appraisal minimizes attention to threat and maximizes attention to goal blockage while an angry feeling and sense of power consolidates. This is similar to *viksepa* of consciousness. At the meso level, recurrence of the emotional interpretations (EI) over time leads to entrainment of emotions triggering an angry mood that can last minutes, hours, and even days. Finally, with recurrent experiences there is consolidation leading to personality change (macro-development) and the resultant emotional entrainment that stabilizes helps sense making on subsequent occasions strengthening interpretive habits. Lewis's conceptualization of "interpretive habits" is similar to *vasana or sanskars that* human beings acquire through life experiences that predispose individuals to respond in different situations with characteristic value orientations, attitudes, and emotional states (Iyengar, 2005). In spite of similarities, the *Rasa-Guna* theory of emotions is a departure in several ways from the way modern scholars have looked at emotions. First, it is noteworthy that the deepest etiological theoretical account of emotions has existed in Indian knowledge traditions, in the treatise on drama and aesthetics *Natyasastra*, as also within the scriptural text of Bhagavad Gita (*Guna* theory). Second, both *Rasa* and *Guna* theory are not reductionist and rest on underling principles of Indian nondualistic Vedanta philosophy which considers physical, mental, social, and environmental aspects of existence to be part of the same unified reality. Finally, the most significant feature is conceptualizing the functional aspects of emotions as not just adaptability of individual with his or her micro and local realities, but also a way to achieve harmony and equilibrium at macro—physical, social and even cosmic—levels adding the hitherto less discussed ethical dimension to emotions in contemporary researches.

Rasa-Guna (R-G) Model of Emotions

The etiology of an emotional experience is a non linear process with a number of stages. Arousal of emotions is dependent on perception of causes called *vibhava* which lead to intermediary expressions called *anubhava*, accompanied by transient psychological feelings (*vyabhiachara bhava*) and physiological expression (*sattvic bhava*); and these antecede a full blown emotional experience. According to Bharata Muni every individual has nine latent predispositions of emotions (*sthayi bhava*), namely : (1) *Rati*—Erotic pleasure (*sringara*) and platonic love; (2) *Hasya* or laughter, merriment, humor, and ridicule; (3) *Shoka* is grief, pity, and compassion (*karuna*); (4) *Krodha* is anger, wrath, and terrible (*raudra*); (5) *Bhaya* is fear, alarm, fearful (*bhaynaka*); (6) *Utsaha* is effort, determination, perseverance, courage, and heroism (*vira*); (7) *Jugupsa* is equivalent to dislike, censure, and disgust (*Vibhatsa*); (8) *Vismaya* is wonder, surprise, awe, and marvelous (*Adhabhuta*); (9) *Shanta* is tranquility, rest, and restraint of senses. Later scholar like Abhinavagupta added two more *rasa* (10) *Vatsalya* or affection for offspring and children and (11) *Bhakti* or worship and devotion. *Sringara* is subdivided as *Sambhoga Sringara* (union of lovers) and *Vipralambha Sringara* (separation). *Utsaha also* has four categories: (*a*) *Danavira*—enthusiastic generosity; (*b*) *Dharmavira*—extraordinary piety and righteousness; (*c*) *Dayavira*—chivalrous liberality; and (*d*) *Yuddhavira*—heroism in battle (Mishra, 1964).

The latent predispositions (*sthayi bhava*) are first aroused due to presence of potential determinant cause (*Alambana vibhava*) followed by secondary excitatory causes (*uddipana vibhava*). *Anubhāvas* are outward expressions that develop in accordance to relevant emotion that has been initiated by *vibhava* and *vyabhicāri bhāvas* are transient emotions which arise in course of maintaining, developing, and reinforcing the basic emotions. For example, if basic emotion is love then joy in union and anguish in separation will be accompanying ancillary emotions (Saxena, 2002).

Sattvic bhavas, the spontaneous organic manifestations of emotions that spring from *Sattva* (natural state), testify that emotions are experienced in body, mind, and consciousness. Different emotions have same *sattvic bhavas*; for example tears and perspiration manifest during the experience of both shame and fear. *Sattvika* are classified as follows:

1. Inactivity (*stambha*)I is inhibition of all action due to obstructed consciousness displayed in fear, wonder, despair, deep affection, or pride by less emotionally mature people.
2. Perspiration (*sveda*) is experienced in fatigue, fear, shame, anger, or pleasure.
3. Hair-raising (*romanc*) is owing to anger, joy, wonder, and fear.
4. Change in voice (*svarbheda*) is caused due to anger, self-abasement, fear, joy and exhilaration.
5. Trembling (*vepathu*).
6. Color change (*vaivarnya*) of facial skin like reddening, glowing, pallor, dullness is in anger, fear, exhilaration, or embarrassment.
7. Shedding of tears (*Asru*) is during excessive joy, fear, fatigue, wrath, dejection, grief, and jealousy.
8. Insensibility (*pralaya*) is loss of consciousness and complete cessation of mental functions, due to extreme grief and joy. (Sinha, 1958)

Tables 13.1 to 13.4 show the etiological progression of constructive and destructive emotions based on the Rasa-Guna (R-G) theory of emotions.

Table 13.1	Constructive Emotions (*Rasa*): Love (*Rati*), Parental Affection (*Vatsalya*) and Serenity (*Shanta*)		
Permanent Disposition— *Sthayi bhava*	Erotic love— *Sringar rasa*	Parental affection— *Vatsalya rasa*	Serenity—*Shanta rasa*
Potential Determinant cause— *Alambana vibhava*	Two young unattached male and female/Lovers	Offspring/ Children	Spiritual knowledge and practices; ego free
Excitatory cause—*Uddipana vibhava*	Moonlit night, scent, garden, dressing up, spring season, being alone	Children's, growth, and achievements	Fasts, meditation, prayer, moral observances, cleanliness, austerities, etc.
Ensuing Cause— *Anubhava* and *Satvikka bhava*	Looking at each other, staring, sidelong glances, trembling, sweating, touching, deep breathing, etc.	Embracing, stroking, shedding tears, bristling with joy, gazing	Self-abasement, contentment, immobility
Accompanying and Transitory emotions— *Vyabhichari bhava*	Joy, nervousness, jealousy, desire, attachment, etc.	Apprehension, tenderness, joy, pride, jealousy	Equanimity, goodwill, controlled, blissful self abiding, sensitive, empathy, embracing, aversion of sense objects
Guna dominance and impact on consciousness	*Satwic*—positive on self and other; development blooming of consciousness (*vikasa*)	*Satwic*—positive on self; could be harmful to others	*Satwic*—melting of consciousness (*dhuti*)

Managing Constructive and Destructive Emotions

It is normal to experience both constructive and destructive emotions; but when negative emotions stabilize as permanent mood states and bring about undesirable personality changes we become dysfunctional. Neurobiological

Table 13.2	Destructive Emotions (*Rasa*): Grief (*Shoka*), Fear (*Bhaya*), and Disgust (*Jugupsa*)		
Permanent Disposition— *Sthayi bhava*	**Grief—***Shoka/Karuna rasa*	Fear—*Bhaya rasa*	Disgust *Jugupsa rasa*
Potential Determinant cause— *Alambana vibhava*	Death, Loss, Danger	Dreadful objects and events	Rotting, filthy, unclean flesh, blood, etc.
Excitatory cause—*Uddipana vibhava*	Loss of objects; attainment of undesirable objects	Sounds of animals; appearance of objects of fear, being alone in an empty house, cremation ground, captivity, committing an offence, disobedience	Sight, hearing, touching, smelling of all that is disagreeable and loathsome
Ensuing Cause *Anubhava and Satvikka bhava*	Shedding tears, lamentation, pallor, sighing, lapse of memory, loss of consciousness	Trembling perplexity, epilepsy, immobility, horripilate, dryness of mouth, stuttering	Shrinking of the body, narrowing of mouth, covering nose ears, eyes, vomiting, spitting, perspiration, horripilation
Accompanying and Transitory emotions—*Vyabhichari bhava*	Self despise misery, dejection, sickness, fatigue, sorrow	Terror, languor, dejection, sinking feeling, anxiety, stupor	Stupor, sickness, dejection, misery, apprehension, sorrow
Guna Dominance and Impact on consciousness	*Rajasic—Tamasic* Agitation and obstruction of consciousness (*kshobha* and *viksepa*) Potentially harmful to self and others	*Tamasic—*Agitation of consciousness (*kshobha*) Potentially harmful to self and others	*Tamasic—*Agitation of consciousness (*kshobha*) Potentially harmful to self and others

researches on emotions have shown that brain tends to respond to emotion inducing stimuli in ways that it has become used to doing during past experiences. This predictability is due to emotional entrainment—a condition that makes stimulus information be funneled to places in brain which

Table 13.3	Constructive Emotions (*Rasa*): Wonder (*Adhabhuta*) and Mirth (*Hasya*)	
Permanent Disposition *Sthayi bhava*	**WONDER**—*Adhabuta rasa*	MIRTH—*Hasya rasa*
Potential Determinant cause—*Alambana vibhava*	Extraordinary objects, events, people beyond limits of common experience, strangeness	Unnatural, distorted appearance and behavior and situations
Excitatory cause— *Uddipana vibhava*	Sight of heavenly beings, attainment of rare objects, sight of magical feats, captivating beauty, sensations	Wearing awkward clothes, making sounds, imitating, misfit with ways of a place
Ensuing Cause *Anubhava* and *Satvikka bhava*	Opening eyes wide, unblinking, cries of joy, trembling, horripilate, perspiration, shedding tears	Throbbing of nose and lips, clapping, dilation of eyes, laughter, etc.
Accompanying and Transitory emotions *Vyabhichari bhava*	Joy, contentment, pride, eagerness, excitement, etc.	Indolence, fatigue, embarrassment, wonder, crying, joy, energy, envy
Guna dominance *and Impact on consciousness*	*Satwic*—transformation (*visarga*) and expansion (*vistar*) of the consciousness. Positive on self and others	*Satwic*—unfolding (*vicar*) and blooming (*vikas*) of consciousness. Positive on self

were associated with a similar stimulus in an earlier emotion arousing episode (Lewis, 2000), and like a self-fulfilling prophecy we experience the same emotions we had experienced earlier even when the trigger stimulus has changed. That is, we will be angry in future because we have chosen to be angry in the past. Indian knowledge tradition call these habit tendencies (with roots in our past behavior patterns) variously as *vasana* or *sanskar* (Iyengar, 2005) which predispose behavior by overriding cognitive and rational considerations (Sinha, 2003). Researchers have established beyond doubt that negative emotions have a destructive effect on human capacities like decision-making and cognitive function and in periods of stress the power of negative emotions overpower the beneficial effects of positive emotions. Based on Rasa-Guna

Table 13.4	Constructive and Destructive Emotions (*Rasa*): Heroism (*Veera*) and Anger (*Raudra*)	
Permanent Disposition— *Sthayi bhava*	**HEROIC**—*Veera rasa: dana vira (generous); yuddha vira; (courageous); dayavira (compassionate); dharmavira (virtous)*	**ANGER**—*Raudra rasa*
Potential Determinant cause—*Alambana vibhava*	Energy; knowledge of dharma; enemy; prowess	Enemy, prowess, vindictiveness. Absence of knowledge of dharma
Excitatory cause— *Uddipana vibhava*	Acts of wrong, challenge, difficulty and inspiration	Attack, abuse, acts of wrong, challenge, and difficulty
Ensuing Cause *Anubhava* and *Satvikka bhava*	Perseverance, exertion, excitement, delusion, wonder	Exertion, excitement, delusion, vituperation, striking
Accompanying and Transitory emotions— *Vyabhichari bhava*	Contentment, pride, intoxication, fierceness,	Contentment, pride, intoxication, jealousy, fierceness, cruelty
Guna dominance and Impact on consciousness	*Satwic* and *Rajasic* Expansion of consciousness (*vistar* and *vigrah*); Face glowing and shining; Positive on self	*Rajasic* and *Tamasic* Obstruction of consciousness (*viksep*). Face and eyes red. Negative impact on self and others

(R-G) model of emotions a two pronged strategy is suggested to manage constructive and destructive emotions which can be used by lay individuals, as well as experts like psychologists, counselors, and psychiatrists. In the first stage of managing emotions it is important to understand the scope of impact the target emotion has on self and others and in the second stage an action plan to break habit tendencies that predispose individuals from experiencing destructive emotions more frequently than constructive emotions is to be executed.

With respect to scope of impact of emotions both Western and Eastern philosophies agree that while emotions have an adaptive role to play, they also have an ethical function outside the self. It is posited that primary appraisal of an emotion arousing situation is followed by secondary appraisals about consequences with respect to desirable or undesirable impact of one's actions on others and society. Notions of personal, social, and divine good are some aspects of secondary appraisals that individuals engage in and even though these may be socially constructed; suffice is to say, in all societies desired behavior are those that benefit both individual and society alike. From this viewpoint the value we attach to different emotions will depend on the functional–ethical impact of actions that proceed from the experienced emotion. For instance, the initial physiological arousal alerts on several possibilities like: continue the present course of action, give consideration to appropriateness and consequences of actions, and finally even consider a new course of action. These are indicators of moral reasoning triggered by first arousal of emotions and subsequent monitoring, regulation, and expression of emotions which may vary both cross-culturally and historically within cultures and which are indication about moral appropriateness about behavior (Armon-Jones 1986; Frijda and Mesquita 1994; Bilimoria 1995; Keltner & Haidt 1999).

The dialogue between Arjuna and Krishna in Bhagavad Gita, analyzed by Kathryn Ann Johnson (2007), explains the role of emotions in shaping human conduct along three types of moral reasoning: ethic of autonomy, ethic of community, and ethic of divinity (Shweder et al., 1997) that address three types of human goals, namely, personal well-being, community order, and cosmic order. The author says that physiological affect tends to trigger concern for personal well-being and corresponds to Shweder et al.'s ethic of autonomy. According to Nicolas Epley and Eugene M. Caruso (2004), this kind of ethics is egocentric determined by emotions, where the protagonist believes that self-interested outcomes are morally justifiable. In the epic Mahabharata, Arjuna exhibits physiological symptoms of fear and grief at the onset of the battle of Kurukshetra when he realizes that it is his teachers, elders, and brothers who he will kill in war. As a result his limbs are weak and trembling, his bow slips from his hands, mouth is parched and there are goose pimples and mental agitation (BG 1: 29–31). These *sattvikas* (described in R-G model) are the organic manifestations of emotional arousal which are powerful enough to make Arjuna want to abandon his weapons and flee from battle ground, an action by which Arjuna hopes to avert the possibility of incurring sin of killing near and dear ones and suffering pain thereof. Krishna, his friend and counselor, through systematic arguments, mentors Arjuna into controlling his initial emotions which have subordinated his judgment about the right course of action to adopt in the situation that is confronting him. Steadily he cultivates in Arjuna the sense of social ethics that is suppressed and which emphasizes duty to others more than self interest. The crux of Krishna's counsel and enshrined as *Samkhya* philosophy in Bhagavad Gita is that ontology and yoga are complementary system of mental discipline and self-control (Flood 1996, 235). Through yoga one gains control of consciousness by overcoming dualism inherent in body, mind, intellect (of which emotions are a major part), and this helps to align the divided small self with the unity of macro larger self (creation). All actions emanating from the consciousness of this unity are considered ethical.

According to Bilimoria (1995, 2004), emotions are afflictions (*klesas*), leading to intellectual disorders that are unfavorably linked to action (*karma*), and these are like attachments (manifest as pleasurable emotions), aversions (manifest as negative emotions). Krishna is the great teacher who reasons for controlling these afflictions, saying that Arjuna is of warrior caste, a man who must control passion and fight to uphold social order, lest this violation of community ethic becomes detrimental to the cosmic order and also earn him contempt from others. Finally Gita progresses in its poetic exhortation to Arjuna to transform his attitude towards the ethics of divinity whereby in the light of knowledge and devotion to cosmic order he be filled with joy and enthusiasm to do what he eventually must. In the parlance of *Guna* theory, Krishna raises Arjuna from the inertia and stupor of *Tamas* to the consciousness of *kshatriya* (warrior) ego, which is *Rajas*, to finally the elevated ground of *Satwa* from where Arjuna is revitalized and filled with energy of wonder and heroism (*Adhabhuta* and *Veera rasa*) and is capable of fighting a long battle of 18 days with nondiminishing valor, while maintaining the ethics of battle. In Mahabharata, even Yudhisthira who is the most virtuous of the five Pandavas speaks a lie during the battle breaking the ethics of war because of which Dronacharya unfairly dies, but not once does Arjuna default on ethics. (Sinha, 2009). When we subordinate *Rajasic* and *Tamasic guna* and elevate *Satwic guna* through yoga and lifestyle changes the management of destructive emotions becomes easy. Table 13.5 lists diet behaviors and value orientation associated with three *guna* which can be used to map ones existing *guna* profile and bring suitable changes in diet, lifestyle and values. Increase in *satwic guna* and reduction of *rajasic* and *tamasic guna* is likely to enhance the tendency to experience constructive emotions more than destructive emotions in the individual.

The second part of strategy to manage destructive emotions involves breaking habit tendencies that underlie emotions. According to R-G theory, there are several stimulus triggers in the arousal of a particular emotion that appear in an order which lead to progressive intensification of relevant emotion. While it is difficult to eradicate a potential determinant cause (*alambana vibhava*) of an emotion, it is easier to work on excitatory causes (*uddipana vibhava*) and Tables 13.1–13.4 chart the etiology of both constructive and destructive emotions, which can be used to locate intersection points in the progression of an emotion and block causal triggers much before they begin affecting the

Table 13.5 Diet Behaviors, and Value Orientation associated with *Gunas*

	SATWIC	*RAJASIC*	*TAMASIC*
Food	Fresh fruits and vegetables eaten raw, steamed, and boiled; less spices; regular food habits; and small portions of food	Rich, spicy pungent food. Regular, but can over eat	Stale dead food (meat); alcohol; excess carbohydrates. Irregular and tend to over eat
Purity	Cares about bathing and body hygiene, is sexually pure	Likes to dress with lotions and cosmetics Pleasure seeking	Untidy, unclean, Indiscriminating regarding sex
Speech	Temperate and sweet	Extreme—can be both too sweet and abusive	Uncontrolled— foul
Life Style Values	Win–winHigh aspiration but non materialistic; Simple and transparent; Controlled and inward looking; Seeks holistic fulfillment; Can abstain easily from sensual gratification; Can sacrifice simply; Internally driven; and Selfless fullness	Win–LoseHigh aspiration and materialistic Passionate; Aggrandizing and outward looking; Seeks sensual gratification; Sacrifices with sense of martyrdom or heroism; Ego driven and Power seeking	Lose–LoseLow aspiration (blind) Insensitive and emotionally blunt; Mechanical and-Indiscriminate; Narrow focus in sense gratification; Delusion driven
Deference	Unconditional faith, meditates, prays for well-being of all Reads scriptures, performs social work, Attends religious discourses	Conditional faith likes rituals and prays for self-gains.	Nondiscerning, mechanical and ritualistic and can pray for the harm of others

consciousness. A useful illustration of this is present in the epic Mahabharata where cousins Kauravas and Pandavas are enemies due to certain unalterable historical reasons and these causes of enmity fall in the category of *alambana vibhava* (they cannot be changed). But when the Kauravas are invited by the Pandavas to participate in the *Rajasuya Yajna* (an event that celebrates and establishes the supremacy of a king among all others); the display of enormous wealth, prowess, and social power act like excitatory cause (*uddipana vibhava*) and fans the emotion of anger and jealousy in Duryodhana, the chief Kuarava prince. Recognizing the onset of emotions (*anubhava*) and observing the attendant organic symptoms *sattvika bhava* and by timely withdrawal (turtle-like) the full onset of negative emotions can be stopped half way through the trajectory. This never happened in case of Duryodhana as his mentor and uncle Sakuni and close friend Karna would excite and fan destructive emotions in every situation, often even out of proportion. Regular practice (*abhyasa*) of this turtle behavior over a period of time weaken and erase old habits (*vasanas* and *sanskar*)—the deep tracks in the brain enabling management of constructive and destructive emotions. Yoga offers a number of techniques that help in dealing with experiences of full blown negative emotions like anger, grief, fear, or disgust where you become a witness to emotions without involvement while the emotion episode plays out and is drained.

According to Bhagavad Gita, consciousness can be understood as the mind (*manas*) which is the agency through which we make sense of our world. The senses are channels through which mind is fed with inputs about outside world and this makes the mind externalized, cluttered and opaque, thus losing its ability to be transparent and creative. Yoga helps the mind to free itself from this sensual onslaught and become quiescent, pointed, and illumined and *Pranayama*, the fourth step of Patanjal's AstangaYoga, is a powerful technique in this inward journey. The *Sudarshan Kriya* is a variation of *pranayama* developed by Sri Sri Ravi Shankar of The Art of living Foundation that is regularly used in hospitals (NIMHANS and AIIMS) to treat clinical depression. BKS Iyengar (2005), a Yoga expert in his book *Light of Life* explains that breath and mind are same and when we regulate breath we regulate our mind. He says breath is the vehicle of consciousness and by slow and measured observation of breath, we learn to turn away the attention from outside sensory objects to towards the inner calm (*prajna*). The suffic *ayama* means stretching, extension, expand, and restrain breath which controls and stills the mind, freeing, and unhooking the energy stuck in tracts (*vasanas*); and bend inwards to heightened awareness. *Pratyahara* the fifth level of Astanga Yoga comes into play at this point stilling centering, and emptying the mind. Iyengar says *prana* carries awareness (*citta*) and through yogic breathing techniques, which are essentially meditative in their origin, one can transform the consciousness. Inhalation of breath (*puruka*), retention after breathing (*antara kumbhaka*), exhalation (*rechaka*), and retention after exhalation (*bahaya kumbhaka*), each has a separate function that rejuvenates, cleanses, and revitalize the mind and body. The yoga guru adds that inhalation of breath should be long, deep, rhythmic, and slow because you are taking in vital nourishment; and by retaining breath you allow *prana* to circulate, distribute, and assimilate in all the organs of the body and rejuvenate them. By exhalation the toxin (physical and mental) carried in the breath are thrown out and finally by pausing after the out breath all stresses are purged and the mind is silent and tranquil. B. K. S. Iyengar says that the technique of echo exhalation (exhale slowly and fully, then pause, and then exhale again) demonstrates that there is always a residual breath that remains and should be evicted as it carries toxic memory (negative emotions) and the ego out of the self.

The Rasa-Guna model has implications to treat borderline psychiatric patients with affective disorder where teams including psychologists, counselors, social workers, and psychiatrist can analyze the trigger stimuli (*vibhava*) in a patient's life in regard to destructive emotions and arrange suitable interventions aimed to break their habit tendencies. Hospitalization no doubt brings about the radical change in life of patients but interventions can be planned around the local environment where patient lives so that rehabilitation issues do not arise once the patient is cured. The Hindi film *Do Ankhen Baarah Haath* (directed by V. Shantaram, 1954) is a good example of such an intervention, where criminals filled with destructive emotions like anger, vindictiveness, and frustration are allowed to live in a farm with a mentor rather than be jailed; and over a period of time all the criminals are reformed to the extent that their *Tamasic guna* have been transformed to *Satwic guna*.

Conclusion and Direction for Future Research

Human psyche is fundamentally nonmaterial though it coexists with the material body and physical ecosystem and human emotions exemplify this fact. Emotions are the co-dynamics of brain, body, and mind rooted in the visceral physiology, anchored in the mind, with the brain coordinating the relationship between the two. Emotions are not just sensations that trigger cognitions and motivational states leading to actions, but also have a profound ethical dimension to them. The Indian psycho-spiritual frameworks of human existence encompass the material and nonmaterial aspect of human beings, their relationship with ecosystems and the harmony between them is divine cosmic order. From deep agony to unlimited bliss, emotions are the radar through which human beings navigate through life, and both well-being and ill-being is reflected by emotions we experience. Emotions are not chaotic and random nor primordial that human "victims" have to suffer, but are to be cultivated and developed in organized way as explained by the Rasa-Guna theory and substantiated by contemporary studies on emotions.

Indian perspectives are holistic; for instance, the *Panch Kosh* model (Taiitterya Upanishad) conceives human being as a continuum of different energy states (*kosha*) ranging from gross to subtle that interweave and interpenetrate. This means from the food we eat, to what we think and do and the environment that surrounds us will impact us as a whole. The philosophy of Gita assumes an underlying ground unity amidst the diversity we see in creation, implying that all individual level actions have broader social and even cosmic-level impact. Therefore, the ethics of individual autonomy is low order ethics because it serves one, compared to ethics of cosmic order that serves all. The eastern perspective is bottom-up and not vice versa as methods and techniques of Yoga meant for the development of human consciousness emphasize taking small regular steps through which one can incrementally raise the consciousness so that it is capable of taking giant leaps later. The summum bonum of life is *Sat Chit Anand*—the default state of all existence which includes both cognition and affect. *Sat* is what exists (truth), *Chit* is knowledge and awareness of what is, and *Anand* is bliss experienced thereof.

With respect to future research the R-G model is offered for application to validate its propositions. Organizations can design stress-free work environment based on the model and organizational effectiveness can be evaluated. The notion of learning organizations can be revisited to create emotionally intelligent work environment which are also ethical. Institutions dealing with psychological health and which rely dominantly on Western medicine may like to design intervention along the lines of Rasa-Guna theory of emotion. Also, research can be done to assess the effect of different types of *pranayama* with respect to dealing with specific constructive and destructive emotions. It may also be useful and interesting to see which causes of emotions (*vibhava*) are potential and excitatory causes for different emotion cross culturally. The model makes important contribution to theories of emotions with a strong application orientation, an aspect that is in line with Indian knowledge traditions that do not believe in any inherent dichotomy, but unity between the mundane and profound concerns of human life.

References

Ackerman, B.P. Abe, J.A. & Izard, C.E. (1998). Differential emotions theory and emotional development: Mindful of modularity. In M.F. Mascolo and S. Griffin (Eds), *What develops in emotional development?* (pp. 85–106). New York: Plenum.

Armon J.C. (1986). Social function of emotion. In R. Harre (Ed.), *The Social construction of emotions* (pp. 57–82). New York: Basil Blackwell.

Averill, J.R. (1980). A constructionist view of emotion. In R. Plutchik & H. Kellerman (Eds), *Emotion: Theory, research, and experience* (Volume 1, pp. 305–40). New York: Academic Press.

Bhal, K.T. & Debnath, N. (2006). Conceptualizing and measuring gunas: Predictors of workplace ethics of Indian professional. *International Journal of Crosscultural Management*, 6(2), 169–88.

Baral, B.D. & Das, J.P. (2004). What is indigenous to India and what is shared? In R.J. Sternberg (Ed.), *International handbook of intelligence* (pp. 270–301). Cambridge: Cambridge University Press.

Bilimoria, P. (1995). Ethics of emotion: Some Indian reflections. In J. Joel Marks and R.T. Ames (Eds), *Emotions in Asian thought: A dialogue in comparative philosophy* (pp. 65–85). Albany, NY: State University of New York Press.

———— (2004). Perturbations of desire: Emotions disarming morality in the Great Song of the *Mahabharata*. In R.C. Solomon (Ed.), *Thinking about feeling: Contemporary philosophers on emotions* (pp. 214–30). New York: Oxford University Press.

Bradburn, N.M. (1969). *The structure of psychological wellbeing*. Chicago: Aldine.

Chakrabarti, A. (2002). Disgust and the ugly in Indian aesthetics. In *La Pluralit'a Estetica: Lasciti e irradiazioni oltre il Novecento, Associazione Italiana Studi di Estetica, Annali 2000–2001* (p. 352). Torino: Trauben.

Camras, L.A. (1992.). Expressive development and basic emotions. *Cognition and Emotions*, 6, 269–84.

Canon, W.B. (1927). The James-Lange theory of emotions: A critical examination and alternative theory. *American Journal of Psychology*, 39, 106–24.

Cloninger, C.R., Svrakie, N.M. & Svrakie, D.M. (1997). Role of personality self organizations in development of mental order and disorder. *Development and Psychopathology, 9*, 881–906.

Clynes, M. (1978). *Sentics: The touch of emotion*. New York: Doubleday Anchor.

Damasio, A.R. (1994). *Descartes' error: Emotion, reason, and the human brain*. New York: Grosset–Putnam Co.

Damasio, A. (1999). *The feeling of what happens*. NY: Harcourt, Brace & Company.

Das, J.P. (1994). Eastern views of intelligence. In R.J. Sternberg (Ed.), *Encyclopedia of human intelligence* (pp. 387–91). New York: Macmillan.

———— (2008). Planning and decision making: Beware of emotions and illusions. *Journal of Entrepreneurship, 17*(1).

Davidson, R.J. (2000). The functional neuro—Anatomy of affective style. In R.D. Lane & L. Nadfekll (Eds), *Cognitive neuroscience of emotion* (pp. 371–88). New York: Oxford University Press.

Derryberry, D. & Rothbart, M.K. (1997). Reactive and effortless processes in the organization of temperament. *Development and Psychopathology, 9*, 633–52.

Ekman, Paul (1982). *Emotion in the human face*. Cambridge: Cambridge

———— (1992). Are there basic emotions? *Psychological Review, 99*, 550–53.

Ellsworth, P.C. & Scherer, K.R. (2003). Appraisal processes in emotion. In R.J. Davidson, H. Goldsmith, & K.R. Scherer (Eds), *Handbook of the affective sciences* (pp. 572–95). New York: Oxford University Press.

Epley, N. & Eugene M.C. (2004). Egocentric ethics. *Social Justice Research, 17.2* (June), 171–87.

Flood, G. (1996). *An introduction to Hinduism.* Cambridge: Cambridge University Press.

Fogel, A. (1993). *Developing through relationships: Origins of communication self and culture.* Chicago: University of Chicago press.

Freeman, W.J. (1995). *Societies of brains.* Hilldale, NJ: Erlbaum.

Frijda, N.H. (1986). *The emotions.* Cambridge: Cambridge University Press.

Frijda, N.H. & Mesquita, B. (1994). The social roles and functions of emotions. In S. Kitayama & H.R. Markus (Eds), *Emotion and culture: Empirical studies of mutual influence* (pp. 51–87). Washington, DC: American Psychological Association.

———— (1998). The analysis of emotions: Dimensions of variations. In M.F. Mocolo & S. Griffen (Eds), *What develops in emotional development* (pp. 273–95). New York: Plenum.

Gergen, K.J. (1985). Social pragmatics and the origins of psychological discourse. In K.J. Gergen & K.E. Davis (Eds), *The social construction of the person* (pp. 111–27). New York: Springer (Verlag).

Goleman, D. (1988). *The meditative mind.* New York: Tracer/Putnam.

Gray, J.A. (1982). *The neuropsychology of anxiety.* New York: Oxford University Press.

Guenther, H.V. (1974). *Philosophy and psychology in the abhidharma.* Delhi: Motilal Banarsidas.

Harre R. & Finaly-Jones, R. (1986). Emotion talk across times. In R. Harre (Ed.), *The social construction of emotions* (pp. 220–33). Oxford: Basil Blackwell.

Harre, R. & Gillet, G. (1994). *The discursive mind.* CA, Thousand Oaks: SAGE.

Haviland, J.M. & Kalbaugh, P. (1993). Emotion and identity processes. In M. Lewis & J. Haviland(Eds), *The handbook of emotion* (pp. 327–38). New York: Guildford.

Herzberg, F., Mausner, B, & Snyderman, B. (1959). *The motivation to work.* New York: Wiley.

Higgens, K.M. (2007). An alchemy of emotions: Rasa and aesthetic breakthrough. In S. Feagin (Ed.), *Global theories of the arts and aesthetics* (pp. 44–54). New York: Wiley Blackwell.

Iyengar, B.K.S. (2005). *Light on life.* London: Rodale.

Izard, C.E. (1971). *The face of emotion.* New York: Appleton Century Croft.

Jain, U. (2002). An Indian perspective on emotions. In G. Misra & A.K. Mohanty (Eds), *Perspectives on indigenous psychology* (pp. 281–91). New Delhi: Concept Publishing.

Johnson, K.A. (2007). The social construction of emotions in the Bhagavad Gita: Locating ethics in a redacted text. *Journal of Religious Ethics, Inc.,* 35 (4), 655–79.

Keltner, D. & Haidt, J. (1999). Social functions of emotions at four levels of analysis. *Cognition and Emotion, 13*(5), 505–21.

Lange, C.G. & James, W. (1922). *The emotions.* Baltimore, Md: Williams and Wilkins.

Lang, P.J., Bradley, M.M., & Cuthbert, B.N. (1998). Emotions, motivation and anxiety: Brain mechanism and psychophysiology. *Biological Psychiatry, 44,* 1248–63.

Lazarus, R.S. (1984). On the primacy of cognition. *American Psychologist, 39,* 124–29.

———— (1991). *Emotion and adaptation.* New York: Oxford University Press.

Le Doux, J. (1996). *The emotional brain: The mysterious underpinning of emotional life.* New York: Simon & Schuster.

Levenson, R.W., Ekman, P., Heider, K., & Wallace, V.F. (1992). Emotion and autonomic nervous system activity in the Minangkabau of West Sumatra. *Journal of Personality and Social Psychology 62,* 972–88.

Lewis, M.D. (1995). Cognition—emotions feedback and the self organizations of development paths. *Human Development, 38,* 72–102.

Lewis, M.D. (2000). Emotional self-organization at three time scales. In M.D. Lewis & I. Granic (Eds), *Emotional development and self organization: Dynamic system approaches to emotional development* (pp. 15–36). UK: Cambridge University Press.

Magai, C. & Nusbaum, B. (1996). Personality change in adulthood: Dynamic systems, emotions and transformed self. In C Magai & S.H. McFadden (Eds), *Handbook of emotion, adult development and aging* (pp. 403–20). San Diego, CA: Academic Press.

Malenka, R.C., Hamblin, M.W., & Barchas, J.D. (1989). Biochemical hypotheses of affective disorder and anxiety. In G.J. Seigal, B.W. Agranoff, R.W. Albors, & P.B. Molinoff (Eds), *Basic neurochemistry: Molecular cellular and medical aspects* (Fourth edition). New York: Raven Press.

Menon, U. & Shweder, R.A. (1994). Kali's tongue: Cultural psychology and power of emotion shame in Orissa. In S. Kitayama & H.R. Markus (Eds), *Emotion and culture*. Washington, DC: American Psychological Association.

Mishra, S.R. (1964). *Theory of Rasa in Indian drama*. Chhatarpur: Vindhyachal Prakashan.

Osgood C.E., Suci, G.J., & Tannenbaum, P.H. (1957). *The measurement of Meaning*. Urabana: University of Illinois Press.

Pande, G.C. (1990). *Foundations of Indian culture* (Volume 1). Delhi: Motilal Banarsidas Publishers.

Panksepp, J. (1998). *Affective neuro science: The foundation of human and animal emotions*. New York: Oxford University press.

Paranjpe, A.C. & Bhatt, G.S. (1997) Emotion: A perspective from the Indian tradition. In H.S.R. Kao & D. Sinha (Eds), *Asian perspectives in psychology*. New Delhi: SAGE.

Paranjpe, A.C. (1998). *Self and identity in modern psychology and Indian thought*. New York: Plenum Press.

——— (2009). In defense of an Indian approach to psychology of emotions. *Psychological Studies*, *54*, 3–22.

Parkinson, B. (2004). Auditing emotions: What should we count? *Social Science Information*, *43*(4), 633–45.

Radhakrishnan, S. & Moore, C.A. (1957). *A sourcebook in Indian philosophy*. Princeton, NJ: Princeton University Press.

Rozin, P., Lowery, L., Imada, S., & Haidt, J. (1999). The CAD triad hypothesis: A mapping between three moral emotions (contempt, anger, disgust) and three moral codes (community, autonomy, divinity). *Journal of Personality and Social Psychology*, *76*(4), 574–86.

Roseman, I.J., Spindel, M.S, & Jose, P.E. (1990). Appraisal of emotions eliciting events: Testing a theory of discrete emotions. *Journal of Personality and Social Psychology*, *67*, 37–47.

Rozin, P. & Cohen, A.B. (2003). High frequency of facial expressions corresponding to confusion, concentration, and worry in an analysis of naturally occurring facial expressions of Americans. *Emotions*, *3*, 68–75.

Russell, J.A. and Carroll, J.M. (1999). On the bipolarity of positive and negative affect. *Psychological Bulletin*, *125*, 3–30.

Saxena, S.K. (2002). The Rasa theory: Its meaning and relevance. *Sangeet Natak*, *XXXVII*(2). Sangeet Natak Academy.

Schacter, S., & Singer, J.E. (1962). Cognitive, social, and psychological determinants of emotional state. *Psychological Review 69*, 379–99.

Scherer, K.R. (1997). The role of culture in emotions—antecedent appraisal. *Journal of Personality and Social Psychology 73*(5), 902–22.

Scherer, K.R. & Wallbott, H.G. (1994). Evidence for universality and cultural variation of differential emotions response patterning. *Journal of Personality and Social Psychology* 66(2), 310–28.

Scherer, K.R. (2000). Emotions as episodes of subsystem synchronization driven by nonlinear appraisal processes. In M.D. Lewis and I. Granic (Eds), *Emotion, development, and self-organization: Dynamic systems approaches to emotional development* (pp. 70–99). New York and Cambridge: Cambridge University Press.

———— (2005). What are emotions? And can they be measured? *Social Science Information, 44*, 695. SAGE.

Schore, A.N. (1997). Early organization of the linear right brain and development of a predisposition to psychiatric disorders. *Development and Psycho patholog, 9*, 595–631.

Shweder, R.A. & Haidt, J. (2000). The cultural psychology of the emotions: Ancient and new. In M. Lewis & J.M. Haviland-Jones (Eds), *Handbook of emotions* (Second edition, pp. 397–414). New York: Guidford Press.

Shweder, R.A., Much, N.C., Mahapatra, M., & Park, L. (1997). The 'big three' of morality (autonomy, community, divinity) and the 'big three' explanations of suffering. In A.M. Brandt & P. Rozin (Eds), *Morality and health* (pp. 119–69). New York: Routledge.

Sinha, J. (1958). *Indian psychology* (2 volumes, Second edition). Calcutta.

Sinha, M. (2003). Empowerment—The way of Vedanta. In A.K. Singh & D. Chauhan (Eds), *Developing leaders, teams and organizations* (pp. 155–76). New Delhi: Excel Books.

———— (2005). Values alignment scale and collective intelligence of organizations. In S.K. Tuteja (Ed.), *Management Mosaic* (pp. 45–72). New Delhi: Excel Books.

———— (2009). Leadership ethos derived from Vedic thought: The heroes of Mahabharata. Presented at Inaugural Conference of the Indian Academy of Management (IAOM), December 28–30, 2009. XLRI, Jamshedpur.

Sinha M. and Pathak, S. (2007). Values alignment scale (VAS): A psychometric inventory based on the Svabhava—Guna theory from the Bhagavad-Gita. In S. Sengupta & D. Fields (Eds), *Integrating spirituality and organizational leadership* (pp. 605–14). Macmillan. New Delhi.

Teasdale, J.D. & Barnard, P.J. (1993). *Affect, cognition and change: Remodeling of depressive thought.* Hilldale: Erlbaum.

Tomkins, S.S. (1984). Affect theory. In K.R. Scherer and P. Ekman (Eds), *Approaches to emotion* (pp. 163–96). Hillsdale, NJ: Erlbaum.

Watson, D., Weise, D., Vaidya, J., & Tellegen, A. (1999). The two general activation systems of affect: Structural findings, evolutionary considerations and psychobiological evidence. *Journal of Personality and Social Psychology, 76*, 820–38.

Wise R.A. & Hoffman D.C. (1992). Localization of drug reward mechanism by intracranial injections. *Synapse, 10*, 247–63.

Zajonc, R.B. (1980). Feeling and thinking: Preferences need no inferences. *American Psychologist, 2*, 151–76.

Zautra, A.J., Berkhof, J., & Nicholson, N.A. (2002). Changes in affect interrelations as a function of stress events. *Cognition and Emotions, 16*, 309–18.

Zautra, A.J. (2003). *Emotions stress and health.* New York: Oxford University Press.

14

Vipassana Meditation Reduces Stress and Strain: An Empirical Study

D. Gopalakrishna

Abstract

Buddhist principles are time-tested universal laws provides lasting solutions to the problems of mankind. Buddhist meditation techniques are highly effective in dealing with the problems of stress, strain, and conflict in contemporary business world. The research study is aimed at deeper analysis of Buddhist meditation with special reference to Vipassana meditation and its effect on executives and nonexecutives. Now there has been notable increase in recent years of Vipassana applications by a much wider, greater interest than ever before.

Keywords: Buddhism, stress, strain, vipassana Meditation, personal effectiveness, professional effectiveness

Introduction

Questions are asked as to how the Buddhism can be related to modern management. This can be answered in two ways. One is the work done with spirituality and full devotion will lead to perfection, increasing efficiency, productivity, reducing the stress and strain. Spirituality and the work go together in Buddhism. Spiritual health and material well-being are not enemies; they are natural allies. Another way of answering the question is through understanding the triple gem—the *Buddha*, the *Dhamma*, and the *Sangha*.

Buddha

Shinichi (1997) described that *Buddha* the great visionary with compassion preached the *Dhamma*—the universal laws and moral precepts and formulated the *Sangha* to establish peace and harmony in the society. The *Sangha* is a democratic organization, consisting of lay people *Upāsakas* (laymen), *Upāsikās* (laywomen), *Bhikkhus* (monks), and *Bhikkhunis* (nuns). They held full and frequent assemblies. They met in concord, rose in concord and carried on business in concord. The laypeople voluntarily follow the precepts—the *Sīlas,* and monks voluntarily follow more than 227 precepts and work for the welfare of the society. Both lay people and monks develop mutual respect, sharing, caring, follow the precepts for better understanding and harmonious living.

As can be seen from the above, the roots of the modern organization are in the *Buddhist Sangha*. The modern organizations function on the principles of sharing and caring as guided in the *Buddhist Sangha* which was established more than 2500 years ago. This way the correlation can be established easily, as Buddha focused on team work for achieving the goals.

Shinichi (1997) described the work one does for living is an important part of Buddhist thinking. The Buddha recognized this by highlighting "livelihood" as one of the components of the Eight-fold path or the way to live a Buddhist life. The Buddhist attitude to work is exemplified by the story of Chinese Zen monk *Pai-chang* (749–814 BC). When the master had become rather elderly, his disciples became concerned for his health and hid the tools he used for working in the fields so that he would not need to exert physically. When *Pai-chang* discovered this, he told his disciples that his Buddhist training was far from complete and he could not depend on other people to work for his food. With the words *A day without work is a day without food,* he refused to eat until his disciples had returned his tools. So the work itself is a way of life, putting Buddhism into practice. The question of right livelihood is not just a question of right income; it is a question of right living. It is clear action.

Buddhism

Buddhism is a treasure house of scientific knowledge which stultifies blind beliefs and develops scientific temperament, finds solution to the problems confronting the mankind. Buddha suggests that nothing should be accepted without inquiry. Like a scientist, he guided the people to test and accept the truth if it benefits one and all. In *Kālāma Sutta*, Buddha said: *When you know for yourselves—these things are moral, these things are blameless, these things are praised by the wise, when performed and undertaken, conduce to well-being and happiness—then do you live and act accordingly.*

Shinichi (1997) regarded Buddhism as a science of mind. Buddha lays much emphasis on the mind and purification of the mind. This he declares that there is no world without mind. By mind the world is led, by mind the world is moved. And all good and bad things exist in the world because of the mind. Therefore, Buddha suggests training the mind: "The trained mind gives one the best: what neither mother, nor father, nor any other relative can, does a well-trained mind do; it elevates oneself. Among all the forces, the force of the (purified) mind is the most potent and powerful."

Stephen (1989) observed the basic principles of Buddhism—four noble truths are not dry philosophy but it is a scientific, experiential exposition of our "existence" which is unsatisfactory—*Dukkha*. Since this evolving process is unsatisfactory Buddha suggests that it should be managed through developmental process of eight-fold path. All mental and bodily sufferings such as birth, ageing, disease, death, association with unloved, disassociation from the loved, not getting what one wants[1] are ordinary forms of *Dukkha*—Suffering; Un-satisfactoriness—the conflict.

If we want to understand what Buddhism teaches us about building affinity and living in harmony with others, we must first understand the four great all embracing virtues. The Buddha teaches that for us to realize our true capacity of connecting with and serving our fellow citizens, we have to first build a good rapport and the four virtues are tools to that end. The four virtues are: giving, speaking with kind words, conducting oneself for the benefit of others, and adapting oneself to others.

His holiness the Dalai Lama states that as human beings we all have the potential to be happy and compassionate, and also have the potential to be miserable and harmful to others. The potential for all these things is present within each of us. If we want to be happy, then the important thing is to try to promote the positive and useful aspects in each of us and try to reduce the negative.

BUSINESS MANAGEMENT

Shinichi (1997) stated that Buddhism embraces all human activities much less the economic activity. Buddhist attitude towards worldly activity and commerce are based on the idea, the true happiness involves the integration of both spiritual and material wealth. Combining Buddhist or spiritual dimension with material comfort must become priority if people are to have a balanced approach in their lives, in which spiritual happiness is as important as material happiness. The Buddha became a spiritual seeker because he was concerned with how to be free from sufferings. In that he tried to deliver people from suffering and give them the happiness, his path might be called "the path of happiness."

Management is an art of getting things done by and through the people. It is the positive behavior of the people which transform the inputs into value-added outputs. Through purification and positive development of mind, the organizations can be built and managed.

Organization is an arena of conflict and tensions, caused due to scarce resources. Desires are unlimited, while allocating the scarce resources, naturally tension and stress is created. Slight imbalance in the structure, certainly disturbs the equanimity leading to stress and strain, which naturally affects the productivity and profitability of the organization.

Robbins (2002) explained that stress is associated with constraints and demands. Stress is a dynamic condition in which an individual is confronted with an opportunity, constraint or demand related to what he or she desires and for which the outcome is perceived to be both uncertain and important.

Shinichi (1997) illustrated that the modern psychologist suggest that, at the individual level, there is a need to reduce stress by doing physical exercise, relaxation training, expanding the social support network, and the like. The general orientation has been to attain happiness by increasing wealth so that one can get more of what one desires.

Anyway these techniques to some extent may temporarily reduce the stress and strain but do not effectively deal the problems at the root level. The causes of the problem have to be identified in order to get lasting solution that is, "The Tranquil Mind" so necessary in this endless distraction. Although our minds are usually far from tranquil, being able to access this psychological state may be extremely helpful for clear business decisions.

BUDDHIST MEDITATION

The Buddhist meditation techniques taught by Buddha are more effective in finding solution to the modern day stress and strain in the organizations. It gives people a taste of the power a concentrated and calm mind generates, evoking feelings of kindness, generosity, goodwill, love, and forgiveness. It strikes a deep chord in many people and cultivates strong positive emotions within ourselves and to let go of ill will and resentment. Meditation forms the very heart and core of Buddha's teaching. Meditation simply means purification of the mind. It is a mental exercise for man's inner sense of development. The word meditation means *Bhāvanā* which literally means development of "Mind Culture."

Although there are forty objects of meditation, only three are significantly and universally practiced by all types of personalities: (*a*) *Ānāpānasati* (mindfulness of breathing), (*b*) *Vipassana* (insight meditation), and (*c*) *Brahmavihāra* (four sublime states of mind).

ĀNĀPĀNASATI (MINDFULNESS OF BREATHING)

Ven Nyanaponika Thera (1996) believed that it is a very important technique used to develop concentration of the mind which brings peace and harmony. It is a simple way to the initial states of concentration used either as a prelude to other exercises or as a practice in its own right.

VIPASSANA (INSIGHT MEDITATION)

William, (1987) described that *Vipassana* is a Pali word which means insight; of seeing things as they really are. It is a technique that purifies the mind, which helps us to overcome negative qualities of anger, hatred, greed, and selfishness largely through self-observation and introspection. The technique is systematic and dispassionate observation of sensation within oneself. Roop (1997) stated that *Vipassana* helps to gain control over mind and thus develop equanimity. *Vipassana* has reduced instances of confrontation, where conflict arises unnecessarily. After all *Vipassana* makes happy individuals, makes a happy organization. One can't separate *samatha* and *vipassana*. Samatha is tranquillity, vipassana is contemplation. In order to contemplate, one must be tranquil, and in order to be tranquil, one must contemplate to know the mind. Wanting to separate them would be like picking up a log of wood in the middle and wanting only one end of the log to come up. Both of its ends must come up at the same time ultimate is both cannot separate.

Gunjan (2011) shows the importance of *Vipassana* and its reflections on the new science has reflected on the importance of Vipassana and its applications in different social settings. As Dr P.L. Dhar, a former Professor of mechanical engineering, IIT, Delhi, who introduced Vipassana to IIT Students, observed that Vipassana techniques of meditation are very close to science of emotions and feelings.

measures to improve the performance and reduce the stress and conflicts of executives and nonexecutives in the modern organization.

Method

SAMPLING

In order to draw logical and reasonable conclusions, the researcher has selected 100 respondents who have attended at least one ten-day Vipassana meditation residential course and working in private, public sector manufacturing and service sectors.

MEASURES

The primary data was collected using structured questionnaire, to study the impact of *Vipassana* on executives and nonexecutives covering 42 variables (qualities) grouped onto three categories as (*a*) personal effectiveness, (*b*) interpersonal effectiveness, (*c*) professional effectiveness.

The data has been gathered on (using Likert Scale) five-point scale for both positive and negative qualities. The rating for the positive qualities are marked as "low," "marginally low," "average," "marginally high," "high" and its corresponding scales used are 1, 2, 3, 4, and 5. The same pattern is followed for negative qualities by assigning the rating in reverse order 5, 4, 3, 2, and 1. For the positive qualities ascending order indicates the improvement/increase in the qualities and for negative qualities the reversing order is followed for reduction/decrease in the negative qualities. This effect is studied using various statistical tools, such as frequency, percentage, mean, standard deviation, and so on. Detailed analysis has been made on the said three factors of personal effectiveness, the result of discussions and findings are narrated in the following:

Findings

IMPACT OF VIPASSANA MEDITATION ON PERSONAL EFFECTIVENESS

The growth of personal effectiveness depends on the reduction of negative qualities and development of positive qualities. In the personal effectiveness,

25 variables were identified for the study. Out of 25 variables, 15 are positive variables and the ten are negative variables. The study conclusively proved that all the ten negative variables/qualities have reduced substantially and conversely all the fifteen positive variables have increased to a great extent. The findings of personal effectiveness are discussed as follows:

1. *Stress, personal health, and calmness*: Heavy work causes stress, and disturbs peace and affects health. Majority of the respondents have expressed that there is a sharp reduction in stress (mean 3.7), while there is high improvement in the health condition (mean 3.8), leading to calmness (mean 3.8).

2. *Greed, anger, fear, and frustration*: Greed is the root cause of all problems, when desires are not fulfilled; it results in fear, frustration, anger, affecting the individual health. The study shows that there is a high reduction in the negative qualities of fear (mean 3.6), frustration (mean 3.7), greed (mean 3.7), and anger (mean 3.6).

3. *Generosity, tolerance, self-confidence, and discipline*: While there is reduction in negative qualities, naturally meditation develops positive qualities of generosity (mean 3.9), tolerance (mean 3.9), self-confidence (mean 4), and discipline (mean 3.9) which improves both mental and physical health.

4. *Hatred, Prejudice, Revenge, and Arrogance*: Hatred, prejudice, revenge, arrogance, creates rivalry, affects the relationship which is harmful to the individual growth. The study suggests that there is a sharp reduction in these negative qualities of hatred (mean 3.6), anger (mean 3.6), prejudice (mean 3.6), revenge (mean 3.6), and arrogance (mean 3.7).

5. *Compassion, forgiveness, humility, equanimity, and loving kindness*: When there is a reduction in the negative qualities, naturally the positive qualities, such compassion (mean 3.9), forgiveness (mean 4), humility (mean 4), equanimity (mean 4), and loving kindness (mean 4.1) have developed to high degree as the study indicates. This positive development improves the interpersonal relationship and performance.

6. *Ego*: "Ego" is the root cause of all conflicts, sufferings, which affects the individual, team and organizational growth. All the respondents have expressed that there is a significant reduction in ego (mean 3.7).

7. *Creativity, will power, sense of gratitude, and ability to learn*: When the ego is reduced naturally creativity (mean 3.9), will power (mean 4.0),

learning ability (mean 3.9), and sense of gratitude (mean 4) develops as revealed by the study. This brings about individual growth.

8. *Buddhist practice is clearly a subjective first person phenomenon*: There has been on-again-off-again interest in the therapeutic uses of meditation for the last three decades—since a small circle of psychotherapists first became aware of (and themselves tried) meditation practice. But there has also been notable increase in recent years of these applications by a much wider slice of psychotherapists-far greater interest than ever before.

Impact of Vipassana Meditation on Interpersonal Effectiveness

When there is a reduction in negative qualities and consequent development of positive qualities, the interpersonal effectiveness increases which naturally improves the interpersonal relations. To study the interpersonal effectiveness, ten variables are identified. Out of which two are negative, and eight are positive variables. The results proved a sharp reduction in negative qualities and high development of positive qualities. They are briefly discussed as follows:

1. *Conflicts*: Conflicts disturb the relations and affect the team work. All the respondents have expressed reduction in conflicts (mean 3.6) which removes discord.

2. *Domestic happiness, patience with others, trust in others, communication with others, and team spirit*: The study revealed that, when conflicts are reduced, the peace is established, leading to improved interpersonal relations, which in turn, develops domestic happiness (mean 3.9), patience with others (mean 4.0), team spirit (mean 3.8), and communication (mean 4.0). The harmonious relations strengthen team work, increases the effectiveness and efficiency.

3. *Jealousy*: Jealousy creates enmity—hating others' prosperity. Jealousy disturbs the relationship. The study suggests a sharp reduction in jealousy (mean 3.7).

4. *Sympathetic joy, trust in others, accommodating others' views, and coordination*: When the jealousy is reduced naturally one shares the joy at others' success (mean 3.9), developing trust (mean 3.7), cooperation (mean 4) while accommodating others' views (mean 3.7). The positive development of interpersonal relations in turn develops the professional effectiveness.

Table 14.1 Impact of Vipassana Meditation on Personal Effectiveness (a) Positive Personal Qualities

SL. No.	Personal Effectiveness (a) Positive personal qualities	No. Responses/N-Value	Sample or Actual Mean ($\bar{x}$)	Standard Deviation/SD	Propositions (Assumptions) Null $H_0(\bar{x})=3=\mu$	Propositions (Assumptions) Alternative $H_1(\bar{x})>3$	Degree of Freedom (N-1)	Z-Value as per Table	Critical Value/Limits (CV): Or $H_0 \pm Z$ (SD÷√n) Upper Limit (UL) H_0+Z (SD÷√n)	Lower Limit (LL) H_0-Z (SD÷√n)	Actual Facts (i.e., Actual Location of $\bar{x}$ under normal curve's critical limits)	Accepted Propositions
1	Personal Health	100	3.8	0.86	$\bar{X}=3$	$\bar{X}>3$	99	1.98	3.1703	2.8297	$\bar{X}>$ UL	H_1
2	Calmness	100	3.8	0.93	$\bar{X}=3$	$\bar{X}>3$	99	1.98	3.1844	2.8159	$\bar{X}>$ UL	H_1
3	Tolerance	100	3.9	0.83	$\bar{X}=3$	$\bar{X}>3$	99	1.98	3.1643	2.8357	$\bar{X}>$ UL	H_1
4	Generosity	100	3.9	0.87	$\bar{X}=3$	$\bar{X}>3$	99	1.98	3.1723	2.8277	$\bar{X}>$ UL	H_1
5	Self Confidence	100	4.0	0.87	$\bar{X}=3$	$\bar{X}>3$	99	1.98	3.1723	2.8277	$\bar{X}>$ UL	H_1
6	Discipline	100	3.9	0.87	$\bar{X}=3$	$\bar{X}>3$	99	1.98	3.1723	2.8277	$\bar{X}>$ UL	H_1
7	Compassion	100	3.9	0.87	$\bar{X}=3$	$\bar{X}>3$	99	1.98	3.1723	2.8277	$\bar{X}>$ UL	H_1
8	Forgiveness	100	4.1	0.91	$\bar{X}=3$	$\bar{X}>3$	99	1.98	3.1801	2.8198	$\bar{X}>$ UL	H_1
9	Humility	100	4.0	0.92	$\bar{X}=3$	$\bar{X}>3$	99	1.98	3.1801	2.8198	$\bar{X}>$ UL	H_1
10	Equanimity	100	4.0	0.83	$\bar{X}=3$	$\bar{X}>3$	99	1.98	3.1643	2.8357	$\bar{X}>$ UL	H_1

(Table 14.1 Continued)

(Table 14.1 Continued)

Sl. No.	Personal Effectiveness (a) Positive personal qualities	No. Responses/N-Value	Sample or Actual Mean ($\bar{x}$)	Standard Deviation/SD	Propositions (Assumptions) Null $H_0(\bar{x})=3=\mu$	Propositions (Assumptions) Alternative $H_1(\bar{x})>3$	Degree of Freedom (N-1)	Z-Value as per Table	Critical Value/Limits (CV): Or $H_0 \pm Z$ (SD÷√n) Upper Limit (UL) H_0+Z (SD÷√n)	Lower Limit (LL) H_0-Z (SD÷√n)	Actual Facts (i.e., Actual Location of $\bar{x}$ under normal curve's critical limits)	Accepted Propositions
11	Creativity	100	3.9	0.98	$\bar{X}=3$	$\bar{X}>3$	99	1.98	3.1940	2.8060	$\bar{X}>$ UL	H_1
12	Will Power	100	4.0	0.88	$\bar{X}=3$	$\bar{X}>3$	99	1.98	3.1742	2.8257	$\bar{X}>$ UL	H_1
13	Loving Kindness	100	4.1	0.95	$\bar{X}=3$	$\bar{X}>3$	99	1.98	3.1881	2.8119	$\bar{X}>$ UL	H_1
14	Sense of gratitude	100	4.0	0.95	$\bar{X}=3$	$\bar{X}>3$	99	1.98	3.1881	2.8119	$\bar{X}>$ UL	H_1
15	Ability to learn	100	3.9	0.90	$\bar{X}=3$	$\bar{X}>3$	99	1.98	3.1782	2.8218	$\bar{X}>$ UL	H_1

Source: Field Investigation.

Note: The table in detail explains the increase in all 15 positive qualities with mean, standard deviation, Z-Value, etc.
The null Hypothesis was formulated as H_0, which was rejected and alternative hypothesis H_1 accepted as there is increase in positive qualities.

Table 14.2 Impact of Vipassana Meditation on Personal Effectiveness (b) Negative Personal Qualities

Sl. No.	Personal Effectiveness (b) Negative personal qualities	No. Responses/N-Value	Sample or Actual Mean (x̄)	Standard Deviation/SD	Propositions (Assumptions) Null $H_0(\bar{x})=3=\mu$	Propositions (Assumptions) Alternative $H_1(\bar{x})>3$	Degree of Freedom (N-1)	Z-Value as per Table	Critical Value/Limits (CV): Or $H_0 \pm Z$ (SD÷√n) Upper Limit (UL) H_0+Z (SD÷√n)	Lower Limit (LL) H_0-Z (SD÷√n)	Actual Facts (i.e., Actual Location of x under normal curve's critical limits)	Accepted Propositions
1	Stress and Strain	100	3.7	0.93	X̄ =3	X̄ > 3	99	1.98	3.1841	2.8157	X̄ > UL	H_1
2	Fear	100	3.6	1.06	X̄ =3	X̄ > 3	99	1.98	3.2098	2.7202	X̄ > UL	H_1
3	Frustration	100	3.7	1.03	X̄ =3	X̄ > 3	99	1.98	3.2039	2.7961	X̄ > UL	H_1
4	Greed	100	3.7	1.06	X̄ =3	X̄ > 3	99	1.98	3.2039	2.7961	X̄ > UL	H_1
5	Anger	100	3.6	0.97	X̄ =3	X̄ > 3	99	1.98	3.1921	2.8079	X̄ > UL	H_1
6	Hatred	100	3.6	0.96	X̄ =3	X̄ > 3	99	1.98	3.1900	2.8100	X̄ > UL	H_1
7	Prejudice	100	3.6	0.99	X̄ =3	X̄ > 3	99	1.98	3.1960	2.8040	X̄ > UL	H_1
8	Revenge	100	3.6	1.23	X̄ =3	X̄ > 3	99	1.98	3.2435	2.7565	X̄ > UL	H_1
9	Arrogance	100	3.7	1.18	X̄ =3	X̄ > 3	99	1.98	3.2337	2.7663	X̄ > UL	H_1
10	Ego	100	3.7	1.08	X̄ =3	X̄ > 3	99	1.98	3.2138	2.7861	X̄ > UL	H_1

Source: Field Investigation.

Note: The table in detail explains the decrease in all 10 negative qualities with Mean, Standard Deviation, Z-Value, etc.
The null Hypothesis was formulated as H_0, which was rejected and alternative hypothesis H_1 accepted as there is reduction of negative qualities.

Table 14.3 Impact of Vipassana Meditation on Personal Effectiveness (a) Positive Interpersonal Qualities

Sl. No.	Interpersonal Effectiveness (a) Positive Interpersonal Qualities	No. Responses/N-Value	Sample or Actual Mean ($\bar{x}$)	Standard Deviation/SD	Propositions (Assumptions) Null $H_0(\bar{x})=3=\mu$	Propositions (Assumptions) Alternative $H_1(\bar{x})>3$	Degree of Freedom (N-1)	Z-Value as per Table	Critical Value/Limits (CV): Or $H_0 \pm Z\,(SD \div \sqrt{n})$ Upper Limit (UL) $H_0+Z\,(SD \div \sqrt{n})$	Critical Value/Limits (CV): Or $H_0 \pm Z\,(SD \div \sqrt{n})$ Lower Limit (LL) $H_0-Z\,(SD \div \sqrt{n})$	Actual Facts (i.e., Actual Location of $\bar{x}$ under normal curve's critical limits)	Accepted Propositions
1	Domestic Happiness	100	3.9	0.87	$\bar{X}=3$	$\bar{X}>3$	99	1.98	3.1723	2.8277	$\bar{X}>UL$	H_1
2	Patience with others	100	4.0	0.82	$\bar{X}=3$	$\bar{X}>3$	99	1.98	3.1624	2.8376	$\bar{X}>UL$	H_1
3	Team spirit	100	3.8	0.85	$\bar{X}=3$	$\bar{X}>3$	99	1.98	3.1683	2.8317	$\bar{X}>UL$	H_1
4	Trust in others	100	3.7	0.94	$\bar{X}=3$	$\bar{X}>3$	99	1.98	3.1862	2.8138	$\bar{X}>UL$	H_1
5	Accommodating others view	100	3.7	0.91	$\bar{X}=3$	$\bar{X}>3$	99	1.98	3.1802	2.8108	$\bar{X}>UL$	H_1
6	Sympathetic joy	100	3.9	0.90	$\bar{X}=3$	$\bar{X}>3$	99	1.98	3.1782	2.8218	$\bar{X}>UL$	H_1
7	Communication with others	100	4.0	0.80	$\bar{X}=3$	$\bar{X}>3$	99	1.98	3.1584	2.8416	$\bar{X}>UL$	H_1
8	Coordination	100	4.0	0.81	$\bar{X}=3$	$\bar{X}>3$	99	1.98	3.1604	2.8396	$\bar{X}>UL$	H_1

Source: Field Investigation.

Note: The table in detail explains the increase in all positive qualities of interpersonal relationships with Mean, Standard Deviation, Z-Value, etc. The null Hypothesis was formulated as H_0, which was rejected and alternative Hypothesis H_1 accepted as there is increase in positive qualities.

Table 14.4 Impact of Vipassana Meditation on Interpersonal Effectiveness (b) Negative Interpersonal Qualities

Sl. No.	Interpersonal Effectiveness (b) Negative Interpersonal Qualities	No. Responses/N-Value	Sample or Actual Mean ($\bar{x}$)	Standard Deviation/SD	Propositions (Assumptions) Null $H_0(\bar{x})=3=\mu$	Propositions (Assumptions) Alternative $H_1(\bar{x})>3$	Degree of Freedom (N-1)	Z-Value as per Table	Critical Value/Limits (CV): Or $H0 \pm Z (SD \div \sqrt{n})$: Upper Limit (UL) $H_0+Z (SD\div\sqrt{n})$	Lower Limit (LL) $H_0-Z (SD\div\sqrt{n})$	Actual Facts (i.e., Actual Location of $\bar{x}$ under normal curve's critical limits)	Accepted Propositions
1	Jealousy	100	3.7	1.12	$\bar{X}=3$	$\bar{X}>3$	99	1.98	3.2276	2.7784	$\bar{X}>UL$	H_1
2	Interpersonal conflict	100	3.6	0.82	$\bar{X}=3$	$\bar{X}>3$	99	1.98	3.1999	2.8001	$\bar{X}>UL$	H_1

Source: Field Investigation.

Note: The table in detail explains, the decrease in two negative qualities with Mean, Standard Deviation, Z-Value, etc.
The null Hypothesis was formulated as H_0, which was rejected and alternative Hypothesis H_1 accepted as there is reduction in negative qualities.

IMPACT OF VIPASSANA MEDITATION ON PROFESSIONAL EFFECTIVENESS

Professional effectiveness depends on the positive development of individual qualities, leading to harmonious interpersonal relations. All the respondents have expressed, that all the seven components of professional effectiveness have developed to high degree leading to organizational effectiveness/growth.

1. *Job satisfaction, productivity, sense of responsibility*: The study suggests that the meditation has developed/improved the job satisfaction (mean 4.0), productivity (mean 4), and sense of responsibility (mean 4.1) to high degree.
2. *Self motivation, commitment to work, performance at work, and concentration*: The study also suggests that the self motivation (mean 4.1), commitment to work (mean 4.2) performance (mean 4.1) and concentration (mean 4.1) have increased to a great extent after meditation. This is very much essential for the growth of organization. Growth is the essence of corporate life and stagnancy is the death.

SCHEMATIC MODEL

The critical analysis has thrown more light on various factors, such as increasing the positive qualities, reducing the negative qualities leading to high degree of development of personal effectiveness and interpersonal effectiveness, consequently the development of professional effectiveness. A schematic model showing the structural impact of *Vipassana* on the relationship among personal effectiveness, interpersonal effectiveness and consequently the professional effectiveness is presented in Figure 14.1.

This schematic model is the by-product of the critical analysis of the *Vipassana*. It portrays the responses which *Vipassana* meditation gives out through direct and indirect routes. The most direct response of the meditation can be felt on professional effectiveness, whereas its indirect route is through increase in positive qualities and decrease in negative qualities, in order to ensure personal effectiveness, interpersonal effectiveness, and consequently on professional effectiveness performance factors. It should be emphasized that the reduction of negative qualities and increase in positive qualities would be simultaneous, resulting in the sum total of effectiveness.

Table 14.5 Descriptive Statistics and Statistical Test of x̄ of Responses of 100 Respondents on the Impact of Vipassana on Professional Effectiveness Factor

Sl. No.	Professional Effectiveness Factor	No. Responses/N-Value	Sample or Actual Mean (x̄)	Standard Deviation/SD	Propositions (Assumptions) Null $H_0(\bar{x})=3=\mu$	Alternative $H_1(\bar{x})>3$	Degree of Freedom (N-1)	Z-Value as per Table	Critical Value/Limits (CV): Or $H_0 \pm Z$ (SD÷√n) Upper Limit (UL) H_0+Z (SD÷√n)	Lower Limit (LL) H_0-Z (SD÷√n)	Actual Facts (i.e., Actual Location of x̄ under normal curve's critical limits)	Accepted Propositions
1	Job satisfaction	100	4.0	0.81	$\bar{X}=3$	$\bar{X}>3$	99	1.98	3.1604	2.8396	$\bar{X}>UL$	H_1
2	Commitment to work	100	4.2	0.73	$\bar{X}=3$	$\bar{X}>3$	99	1.98	3.1445	2.855	$\bar{X}>UL$	H_1
3	Performance at work	100	4.1	0.69	$\bar{X}=3$	$\bar{X}>3$	99	1.98	3.1366	2.8634	$\bar{X}>UL$	H_1
4	Sense of responsibility	100	4.1	0.79	$\bar{X}=3$	$\bar{X}>3$	99	1.98	3.1564	2.8436	$\bar{X}>UL$	H_1
5	Productivity	100	4.0	0.90	$\bar{X}=3$	$\bar{X}>3$	99	1.98	3.1782	2.8218	$\bar{X}>UL$	H_1
6	Self motivation	100	4.1	0.79	$\bar{X}=3$	$\bar{X}>3$	99	1.98	3.1564	2.8456	$\bar{X}>UL$	H_1
7	Concentration	100	4.1	0.68	$\bar{X}=3$	$\bar{X}>3$	99	1.98	3.1346	2.8654	$\bar{X}>UL$	H_1

Source: Field Investigation.

Note: The table in detail explains improvement in performance variables with Mean, Standard Deviation, Z-Value, etc. The null hypothesis was formulated as H_0 which was rejected and alternate hypothesis H_1 accepted as there is improvement in the professional performance variables.

| Figure 14.1 | A Schematic Model Showing Impact of Vipassana Meditation on Personal Effectiveness, Interpersonal Effectiveness, and Professional Effectiveness of Managers |

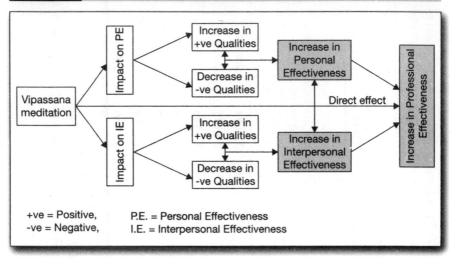

+ve = Positive,
-ve = Negative,

P.E. = Personal Effectiveness
I.E. = Interpersonal Effectiveness

Source: Authors.

Implications for HRD

The research study has conclusively proved that Buddhist principles and meditation techniques can bring multiple benefits to the corporate world.

- *Vipassana* meditation can be used as a powerful tool to teach and develop executives and non-executives which improves health, productivity, reducing stress, and strain and conflicts.
- *Vipassana* meditation can be considered as effective orientation, socialization program for new employees to develop positive attitude to adapt to new culture.
- Employees can be deputed to attend ten days residential meditation course on paid leave with travel and maintanance allowance. This develops the positive mind, improves health, increasing the productivity, efficiency, reducing the expenditure on medical bills and other costs. *Vipassana* can also be used as a de-addiction program. It has been proved in many cases that people who have undergone *Vipassana* have given up addictions to alcohol, smoking, etc.

- Most of the companies give training to their employees to develop interpersonal skills through FIRO-B, Transactional Analysis, Johari window, sensitivity training, and so on. In addition to these, Vipassana technique can be used as an effective tool to develop interpersonal relations with lasting effect with minimum cost.
- The other meditation techniques such as *Ānāpānā* (awareness of breathing) and *Mettā Bhāvanā* (loving kindness) meditation can also be practiced for ten minutes each before and after conducting meetings/deliberations which creates positive environment and gives effective results.
- Team building principles are very well embedded in Buddhist Sangha, which can be adopted to build effective teams in the organization. Buddhist principles constitute the enabling and curing mechanism to introduce a system of shared values in the modern organization.

Conclusion

The growing economic desires for achieving more materialistic needs in the modern organization are creating more stress and strain all over the world, suggest the fact that our understanding of human system, as embodied in management theory, is still far from providing solutions to certain recurring and basic problems.

Although the management concept to some extent provides solutions to human problems, it does not provide concrete solutions in establishing peace and harmony within, which is the key to achieve higher productivity and profitability.

Buddhist "Middle Path" shows the way towards achieving "equanimity" of maintaining both material as well as spiritual progress through time tested concepts and meditation techniques. Meditation simply means purification of the mind, which is mental exercise for man's inner development. *Ānāpānā* (awareness of breathing) meditation develops concentration. Vipassana is an insight meditation purifies the mind and achieves the inner calmness. Vipassana helps meditators to abstain from unwholesome actions and inspires them to perform wholesome actions. Vipassana helps meditators lead happier, more peaceful, and harmonious lives; Vipassana helps one develop a positive attitude towards life. *Mettā Bhāvanā* (loving kindness meditation) develops good will fosters harmonious relations.

Our study leads us to conclude that the Buddhist principles and meditation techniques are scientific universal laws which can be applied to solve the problems, conflicts, of individuals, teams in the organization and society.

References

Anadamaitreya, B. (1993). *Buddhism: Lectures and essays*. Sri Lanka: Samayawardhana.

Bodhi, B. (1999). A comprehensive manual of abhidhamma. Kandy, Sri Lanka: Buddhist Publication Society.

Bapat, P.V. (1987). *2500 years of Buddhism*. India: Publications Division, Ministry of Information and Broadcasting.

Dhamma, G. (1994). *A tree in a forest: A collection of Ajahn Chah's similes*. Chungli, Taiwan: Yuan Kuang Publishing House.

Dhammananda, K. (1994). *Treasure of the Dhamma* (Malaysian edition). Buddhist Missionary Society.

Dhammananda, K. (2007). *How to develop happiness in daily living*. Sasana Abhiwurdhi Wardhana Society.

Gunjan, S (2011). Awake and awake: Those who practice vipassana vouch for its ability to he distress and concentration. *The Week-Health*, 46–50.

Hasmukh, Adhi, Nagendra, H.R., & Mahadevan, B. (2010). Impact of adoption of Yoga way of life on the emotional intelligence of managers. *IIMB Management Review*.

Jon, K.Z. (1990). *Full catastrophe living: Using the wisdom of your body and mind to face stress, pain and illness* (p. 182). New York: Dell Publishing.

John, E.C. (2000). *The quiet mind: A journey through space and mind* (p. 27). New Delhi: New Age Books.

Kirthi, P.S. (1996). *Buddhism and science*. India: Motilal Banarasidas Publications.

Khandwalla, P.N. (2007). *Corporate creativity* (pp. 88–89). India: Tata McGraw-Hill.

Mahathera, P. (1991). *The spectrum of Buddhism*. Taiwan: The Corporate Body of the Buddha Educational Foundation.

Narada, V. (1988). *Buddha & his teachings* (p. 614). Malaysia, Kuala Lumpur: Buddhist Missionary Society (Fourth edition).

Nānamoli, B. (1991). *The path of purification (Visuddhimagga) by Bhadantacariya Buddhaghosa, translated from the Pali*. Kandy, Sri Lanka: Buddhist Publication Society.

Parihar, D.R. (2005). *Impact of Vipassana in government*. Dhamma Giri, Igatpuri: Vipasanna Research Institute.

Roop, J. (1997). *Vipassanā pagoda souvenir* (pp. 22–24). Mumbai, India: Global Vipassanā Foundation.

Robbins, S.P. (2002). *Organisational behaviours*. Prentice Hall, New Delhi: Ninth Updated Edition.

Rinpoche, K.T. (2001). *The essence of Buddhism*. Boston: Shambhala Publication.

Sarao, K.S. (2002). *Buddhism and animal rights*. Taipei: Chung-HWA Institute of Buddist Studies.

Schumacher, E.F. (1993). *Small is beautiful*. London: Vintage Publication.

Shinichi, I. (1997). Putting Buddhism to work: A new approach to management & business. Tokyo: Kodansa International Ltd.

Thera, N. (1996). The heart of Buddhist meditation (pp. 61–62). Sri Lanka: Buddhist Publication Society.

Thero, S.M. (1993). *Treasury of truth*. Singapore: Chief Monk, Singapore Buddhist Meditation Centre.

William, M.H. (1987). *The art of living: Vipassanā meditation as taught by S.N. Goenka* (pp. 90–91). Itagpuri: Vipassanā Research Centre.

15

Methodological Issues in Stress Research: Challenges, Concerns, and Directions

Satish Pandey, Shubhra P. Gaur, and D. M. Pestonjee

Abstract

The topic "stress management" has always been focus of attention for researchers from different disciplines. A number of theories and models for explaining the dynamics of stress and coping behavior have been proposed and discussed critically in the research literature. In this chapter, we attempt to critically discuss paradigm shifts in stress research happening in last few decades, different research approaches being used by researchers, new emerging issues in stress research, and directions for future research.

Keywords: stress research, quantitative vs. qualitative approach, cross-sectional vs. longitudinal studies, measurement issues, multidimensional models, indigenous models of stress, positive stress, quality of stress research

Introduction

The field of stress research has seen rapid growth since the seminal work of Hans Selye *The Stress of Life* was published in 1956, followed by classical contributions by Kahn et al. (1964) on organizational role stress; Lazarus (1966, 1981), Lazarus and Folkman (1984) on coping strategies; McGrath (1976); Beehr and Newman (1978); Cooper (1979); Pareek (1983a, 1983b,1987, 1993) on organizational role stress and role efficacy approach; Edwards (1991, 1992) on P-E fit model and cybernetic theory of stress; Maslach and Jackson (1981) on burnout; Warr (1987, 1990) on employee well-being; Pestonjee (1992) on organizational stress in Indian context; naming a few. Beehr (1995) stated how number of research studies on "occupational stress" published in refereed journals shot up from less than 10 studies per year (before 1974) to 254 studies (1989) and even later maintained average number above 140 studies per year (till 1997). Methodological issues in stress research have been addressed by many researchers in the past (Beehr and Newman, 1978; Kasl, 1978; McGrath, 1982; Glowinkowaski and Cooper, 1985; Kasl, 1986; Kasl, 1987; Frese and Zapf, 1988, Handy, 1988; Harris, 1991; Beehr, 1998, Lazarus, 2000; Cooper, Dewe and O'Driscoll, 2001). Most of dominant issues discussed in those review papers were: objective and subjective measurement of stress and coping variables (Frese and Zapf, 1988), measurement of physiological and psychological variables (Kasl, 1978; McGrawth, 1982; Fried, Rowland, and Ferris, 1984; Fried, 1988), merits and demerits of cross-sectional and longitudinal studies (Frese and Zapf, 1988; Fried et al, 1984; Fried, 1988, Cooper et al., 2001), quantitative and qualitative approaches (Cooper et al. 2001), and relevance of various theoretical models (Frese and Zapf, 1988; Lazarus, 1990; Cooper et al 2001). Beehr (1998) identified most critical issues in stress research: (*a*) confusion in the use of terminology regarding the elements of job stress, (*b*) relatively weak methodology within specific studies, (*c*) the lack of systematic approaches in the research, (*d*) the lack of interdisciplinary approaches, and (*e*) the lack of attention to many elements of the specific facets of stress-coping process (environmental, personal, process, human consequences, organizational consequences, adaptive responses and time). Cooper et al (2001) raised two very fundamental questions relevant to methodological issues in occupational stress research: (*a*) Do current methodologies satisfactorily assess the complex dynamics of stress-coping process? (p. 211) and (*b*) Whose reality are we measuring when measure stress? (p. 218). They also raised the issue of changing work environment and its impact on human-environment interaction in the 21st century and up to what extent our measurement tools are appropriate in the changed job context. In this chapter, we aim to address many such methodological issues of stress research in context of rapidly changing work environment of the 21st century organizations.

Appropriateness of Research Approaches

In the review literature on stress research, the issue of "appropriateness of research approaches" has been raised by many researchers. Cooper et al (2001) expressed the need to introduce significant changes in traditional measurement practices and to the way in which job stress is being conceptualized and investigated. It has been observed that traditional research methods are predominantly based on cross-sectional designs and using self-report questionnaires to assess stressors, strains, and coping mechanisms for not capturing the dynamics of stress-coping process (Spicer, 1997). Bartunek et al. (1993) also questioned traditional research approaches for adopting a narrow interpretation of measurement and expressed the concern over adopting alternative methods of capturing other untapped sources of data. Researchers argued in favor of adopting new advanced research designs, using multiple methods of measurements and different sources of primary data, looking for shift from individual-level assessment to multilevel assessment, development and testing of multidimensional models, and more balanced research approach for reliable and valid results. In this section, we will critically discuss on various research approaches, e.g., quantitative vs. qualitative, cross-sectional vs. longitudinal, positive vs. negative orientation of stress, objective and subjective measurement, individual vs. organization, appropriateness of various research models, applied research on stress management interventions, and quality of research in context of stress research.

QUANTITATIVE VS. QUALITATIVE

It has always been concern for researchers whether quantitative or qualitative methodologies would be more appropriate in understanding the dynamics of stress-coping process. Bhagat and Beehr (1985) raised the issue whether there is a need to search for more vivid and enriched description of processes in qualitative (person-based) as well as quantitative (variable-based) terms. There are many investigators (Spicer 1997, Somerfield 1997, Thoits 1995, Haridas 1983) who have strongly prescribed qualitative methods over quantitative approaches. Somerfield (1997) argued that variable-based methods, though they address fundamental theoretical relationships amongst constructs, may have very limited role to play in exploring the dynamics of the stress process. Haridas (1983) said that as the complexity of theoretical models increases, the measurement of certain aspects of those models might require the use of qualitative methods. Some investigators have used qualitative methods in their studies such as critical incidents interviewing (O'Driscoll and Cooper 1996, 1994; Liu et al., 2007, 2008), semi-structured interviewing (Oakland and Ostell, 1996; Richards et al., 2006), open-ended questions (Erera-Weatherley, 1996, Pandey, 2003), daily diary or panel survey (Thoits, 1995), personal interviews (Srivastava and Broota, 1987, Ashok, 1989; Randall et al., 2007) and focused-group discussion (Harkness et al., 2005; Iwasaki et al., 2006; Gibsons et al., 2008). Qualitative methods are very useful in exploring latent factors related to a particular context where standard psychometric instruments are not so effective in providing enough insight. Researchers, who are interested in person-focused or organization-centered research, have found qualitative methods more appropriate than quantitative ones because of flexibility provided by qualitative methods. These methodological issues raise important concerns for researchers which approach (quantitative or qualitative) could be more appropriate for investigating the stress-coping process.

There are many researchers including Cooper et al (2001), Liu et al (2007, 2008) who have strongly proposed adoption of a "balanced approach" or "the middle ground" between variable-based (quantitative) and person-based (qualitative) approaches. Liu et al (2007, 2008) have successfully demonstrated usage of quantitative–qualitative mixed design in their cross-national study of job stress. Another study by Barley et al (2011) also demonstrated successful usage of mixed design in exploring dynamics of new communication technologies, culture, and stress. Cooper et al (2001) suggested that by using a "balanced approach," researchers might overcome limitations of one approach by strengths of another one. Quantitative and qualitative approaches should not be considered mutually exclusive but complimentary to each other (Morley and Luthans, 1984; Cox et al, 2007). Though most researchers still prefer cross-sectional designs in their researches but longitudinal studies may throw new light on the dynamics of stress-coping process and combination of quantitative and qualitative methods may be very useful for new researchers in exploring new insights in stress research (Randall et al, 2009; Skakon et al, 2010). Disagreements between researchers over the approach to be used can "lead to neglect of common interests and misunderstanding on both sides" (Morley and Luthans, 1984, p. 28). There is a need for a more balanced approach that recognizes the usefulness of data generated by different methods.

CROSS-SECTIONAL VS. LONGITUDINAL STUDIES

It has been observed in most of published review studies that stress research is dominated by cross-sectional researches and very few good longitudinal studies are conducted so far (Fried et al, 1984; Fried, 1988; Frese and Zapf, 1988; Van Der Doef and Maes, 1999; Lazarus, 2000; Cooper et al, 2001; Burke, 2010; Skakon et al, 2010). It has also been observed that in many studies, researchers use cross-sectional design, test their hypotheses and models and at the end recommend longitudinal design as stronger alternative to explain causality between independent and dependent variables. Researchers prefer self-report measures in cross-sectional design because of economy of time, money and efforts. Longitudinal studies need too much patience and investment of time, money and effort. It is very difficult to get sponsors to fund long-term longitudinal research studies which may go for several years ranging from 5–10 years. This could be perhaps the reason that we could not find any longitudinal study in developing/underdeveloped countries. In cross-sectional studies, at least one can reduce costs related to time and can get data from different comparable groups in the shortest possible period, process data, analyze results and get published papers in journals. There are several good longitudinal studies which have used experimental control designs, usage of physiological measures, qualitative approach, mixed designs and multi-wave study approach (Dormann and Zapf, 1999, 2002; De Jonge and Dormann, 2006; Vogt et al, 2008; Chrisopoulos et al 2010). Longitudinal studies provide best opportunity to study impact of time variable on the dynamics of stress-coping process and causal relationships among various variables.

ORIENTATION OF RESEARCH: POSITIVE OR NEGATIVE

In most of research studies, the researchers have used a "reactive" approach to study stress, i.e., they treated stress as "dysfunctional," "negative" or as a reaction to some threatening stimulus in the environment and coping has been interpreted as "a method to master these conditions or adapt to the situation." The concept of "eustress" and "distress" were first proposed by Selye (1956) and later supported by many researchers (Anderson and Arnoult, 1989; Edwards and Cooper, 1988; Pestonjee, 1987; Pestonjee, 1992; Simmons and Nelson, 2001; Nelson and Simmons, 2003; Le Ferve, 2003). However, three dominant theories of stress, P-E fit theory (Edwards et al, 1998), Cybernetic theory (Cummings and Cooper, 1998) and control theory (Spector, 1998) do not seem to be differentiating between eustress and distress (Le Ferve et al, 2003). Nelson and Simmons (2003) suggested that eustress and distress are separate and independents aspects of overall stress response. Le Ferve et al (2003) argued that if eustress and distress are separate constructs then it is also possible that both eustress and distress may occur simultaneously to the same environmental stimuli. Le Ferve et al (2006) supported study of Cavanaugh et al (2000) as a good empirical support to construct of eustress. Kets de Vries (1979) said that each individual needs a moderate amount of stress to be alert and capable of functioning effectively in an organization. Pestonjee (1987) proposed that certain types of stressors are essential for creative managers. Pestonjee (1992) wrote that the organizational context, in which a creative manager operates, might either enhance or mitigate the stresses arising from both traits of the creative person and the creative processes. However, these stresses depend upon whether the person performs in creative or non-creative roles in creative or non-creative organizations (Pestonjee 1992). Snyder (1997) proposed that hope have a positive impact on controlling anxiety and emotions, managing stressful situations and adapting to environmental changes. Luthans (2002) proposed positive OB model that emphasizes on moderating impact of self-efficacy, hope, optimism, subjective well-being and emotional intelligence on stress and coping. Some other researchers (Crant 2000, Aspinwall and Taylor, 1997; Wanberg, 1997; Kinicki and Latack, 1990) also observed in their studies how proactive coping could help individuals in developing a positive self-concept, proactive job behaviors and achieving proactive growth in their careers. Crant (2000) suggested some relevant constructs essentially to be measured in the context of proactive behavior, these are: proactive personality, personal initiative, role breadth self-efficacy and taking charge. Pareek (1987, 1993) also emphasized in his work how role-efficacy based OD interventions can help organizations in developing proactive coping behavior in their employees. McGowan et al (2006) tested eustress-distress model by using structural equation modeling and found that challenge appraisals and task-focused coping were positively associated with eustress, and distress has been found positively associated with threat appraisals and emotion-focused coping; eustress and distress were also found positively and negatively associated with "satisfaction with the outcome of stress process." These researches indicate the need for adopting more "proactive" approach than the "dysfunctional" one in the context of stress and coping. Whereas, Bateman and Crant (1999) cautioned that too much, or misguided proactive behavior can be dysfunctional and counterproductive. Lazarus (2000) argued strongly in his paper that most of current research on stress and coping is quite balanced between positive and negative. Cooper et al (2001) also pointed out that mostly a typical stress study examines predictors (stressors) and outcomes (strain responses) after they have occurred but now there is a strong need to move beyond these post hoc approaches. They also suggested that it is now time to become more innovative, "experimental," and forward-looking in our approaches to research on stress management, rather than continuing solely with "after-the fact" investigation that simply attempt to replicate previous findings concerning the predictors of workplace strains. The debate generated by Cooper and others raises the need to look beyond the "cause-effect" relationship of stress-coping process and to develop a holistic positive context for stress research that is more practical and beneficial for HR practitioners and researchers.

UNIT OF RESEARCH: THE INDIVIDUAL, THE GROUP OR THE ORGANIZATION

Since its inception, the field of stress research has had an individual-level focus. That means how individuals perceive and react to the work environment, and how individual-level differences affect stressor-strain relationships (Beehr and Newman, 1978; Jex, 1998; Katz and Kahn, 1978, Lazarus and Folkman, 1984; McGrath, 1976). Handy (1988) argued that most stress models focus solely on the individual level of analysis and therefore divert attention from serious examination of the social order within organizations. Further, he added that models of work stress might have overemphasized the lack of consensus in organizations and failed to adequately consider issues of power and conflict in the context of individuals' personal stress management. In sum, Handy (1988) suggested that greater attention must be given to the development of methods that explore the social experiences that individuals encounter in their workplaces and the meaning of these experiences for their well-being.

Bliese and Jex (1999) argued while individual-level models have been valuable, it is necessary to understand and model group (i.e., contextual) effects in stress research. Similar views have been expressed by Cox (1997) and Griffiths (1994). In areas, other than occupational stress, such as organizational climate, leadership etc., multi-level analyses have been used by researchers. Some researchers (Bliese and Jex, 1999; Cox, 1997; and Griffiths, 1994) presented occupational stress as a multi-level phenomenon and argued when groups of individuals are exposed to similar environmental factors they often show some degree of non-independence in how they perceive and respond to the environment. This non-independence can be measured, and it affects data analysis and interpretation in several ways (Bliese and Jex, 1999). First, non-independence biases individual-level results if not controlled for (Kreft and De leeuw, 1998); and second, non-independence contributes to non-equivalence between aggregate-level and individual level results (Bliese, 1998). Multi-level analyses (even simple group means) may shed light on relationships that would be missed if one is restricted to individual-level analyses. Simple group-mean analyses may often be the appropriate level of analyses for implementing and evaluating organizational interventions (Moregenstern, 1982; Schwartz, 1994). Multi-level group analyses may provide useful insight in evaluating effectiveness of organizational interventions. Bliese and Jex (1998) also suggested that sometimes even it might not be feasible to implement individual-based interventions and in that situation, the organization might need to design stress management interventions for specific groups. In such situations, multi-level analyses present holistic picture of stress-coping-environment relationship. In his study of 97 teams working on command-and-control simulation through experimental control group design, Ellis (2006) successfully tested hypothesis that acute stress affect negatively mental models and transactive memory and results into poor team performance.

Measurement of Stress and Coping

Self-Report Measures

The literature review of stress-coping research reveals overemphasis on using self-report measures (standardized psychometric questionnaires) and too much dependence on statistical analyses (correlation, multiple regression analysis, factor analysis etc.). In this context, it becomes very important to know: *"Whose reality are we measuring?"* and *"Do our measures actually assess what they purport to?"* (Cooper et al 2001). Cooper et al (2001) also raised this issue that most of frequently-used self-report measures are continually being used by researchers without considering the impact of social and economic change over the last two decades (1980s and 1990s) because they continue to exhibit satisfactory internal reliability. We need to consider, therefore, whether concern over reliability of measures has taken precedence over their relevance to individuals' lives. We also need to consider what interpretation about stressor-strains-coping relationship results from these measures. Do our measures tell us what we want to know and help us in confirming and developing theoretical relationships between constructs (stressors, strains and coping) that may be helpful in developing organizational interventions or they just reveal few statistical inferences. This may result into confounding when instruments that purport to assess one construct (e.g., a stressor) in reality tap into another (e.g., a strain). Researchers may inadvertently introduce confounding into their measurement procedures-for example, instructions to respondents at the beginning of the instrument may be interpreted by respondents differently and confounding may occur. Cooper et al (2001) suggested that existing measures should be evaluated in terms of (a) the content of items, (b) the scoring of responses, and (c) the manner in which internal reliability is established. Cooper et al (2001) also suggested the process how quantitative and qualitative methods could be used in convergence for refining existing measures: (a) reviewing the nature and type of items to be measured; (b) determining the appropriateness of different response categories;

(c) examining the way in which response scales are scored; and (d) evaluating the specificity of the stressor-strain relationship under consideration.

The literature review on refinement of some measures such as Occupational Stress Indicator (Cooper, Sloan and Williams, 1988), Maslach Burnout Inventory (Maslach and Jackson, 1981), COPE Inventory (Carver et al., 1989) sheds light on methodologies adopted by researchers in different context/settings. Most of researchers have used confirmatory factor analysis (LISREL model) such as Evers, Frese and Cooper (2000), Lyne et al. (2000) for Occupational Stress Indicator (OSI), Daniels et al. (1997) for Warr's Measure of affective well-being at work (Warr 1990), Kalliath et al. (2000) for MBI; whereas very few took different path such as multidimensional scaling (Livneh et al., 1996, for COPE Inventory), structural equation modeling (SEM) with multi-group analysis (Van Dierendonck et al., 2001, for MBI). Such revalidation studies over different intervals have helped researchers in continuous refinement of measures and revalidation of theoretical models on which these measures are based.

PHYSIOLOGICAL MEASURES

In their seminal paper, Fried et al (1984) commented on dominance of psychological and behavioral measurements over physiological measures of work stress. They commented further that though there are empirical evidences to suggest a potential relationship between stressful events and physiological variables and physiological indicators might detect a situation of stress among individuals who are not consciously aware of it; but most of stress researchers belonging to organizational behavior stream do not seem to be much interested in physiological measurements of stress (Fried et al, 1988: 343–44). Most of work stress studies have focused on typically three categories of physiological indicators, including: (i) Cardiovascular indicators (heart rate and blood pressure); (ii) Biochemical indicators (levels of uric acid, blood sugar, steroid hormones, cholesterol and catecholamines esp. adrenalin and noradrenaline); and (iii) Gastrointestinal indicators (peptic ulcer). Researchers prefer self-report measures over physiological measures because of administrative convenience. One can administer psychometric questionnaires far easily than taking readings on various physiological measures through sophisticated machines and biomedical tests. Preparing subjects for physiological measurements is also not an easy task. To get reliable data, researcher needs to take multiple measurements on physiological indicators because psychological condition (e.g., resistance, anxiety) of subjects at the time of measurement may also influence physiological measures. Confounding of various physiological variables is also another problem which needs to be controlled through effective experimental designs. In a review of 54 studies on work stress and physiological measures published in the period of 1970–86, Fried et al (1988) found that out of 54 studies, 26 were cross-sectional and only 13 were truly longitudinal in the sense that they examine changes in physiological indicators over a period of several months or years; and very few studies had control group in their experimental designs. Fried et al (1988) suggested further that longitudinal studies which include experimental and control groups, multiple measurements at different times, and use advanced statistical tools could provide better control over confounding factors.

INDIGENOUS VS. "WESTERN IMPORTED" APPROACHES

To make stress research more relevant to a specific national/regional culture (e.g., India/Asia/Africa), researchers need to develop "indigenous models" that try to apply traditional cultural wisdom for explaining psychological environment of modern workplaces. There is also need to develop research methodologies that can help in testing and applying these "indigenous behavioral models" in a scientific manner (Lam and Palsane, 1997; Palsane et al, 1999; Laungani, 1995; Laungani 1999; Laungani, 2007). This is also relevant in the changed context when researchers are focusing more on doing researches that are aimed at improving quality of work life, individuals' life style and their well-being as well as creating "healthy organizations." Laungani (1995, 1996, 2005) cautioned researchers in conducting cross-cultural studies on stress and coping in which most of researchers attempt to do cross-cultural comparisons on the basis of statistics generated by psychological tests developed on the basis of "Western" models which are generally "imported" to "other cultural contexts." Limitations of cross-cultural studies using psychological instruments designed on the basis of "Western" theories and models in "Eastern and other cultural contexts" are also recognized by Spector et al (2004); Burke (2010); and Bhagat et al (2010). Though, instruments can be translated into other languages and adapted to other cultural contexts through proper standardization methods but despite these attempts, deriving "culturally appropriate" interpretations has always been a challenge for researchers. Such kind of imitative research in psychology has been strongly criticized by many scholars of developing countries (Enriquez, 2003; Kakar, 1997; Kim and Berry, 1993; Laungani, 2007; Sinha, 1993; Sinha and Kao, 1997; Zebian et al, 2007; Misra, 2011); and most of them raised their concerns on cultural appropriateness of researches conducted in different cultural environments.

Another important question regarding cultural differences in relation to stress perceptions and coping behavior in different societies, some scholars emphasized on similarities in different urban societies across the world (Ram, 1999). Their daily life experiences, e.g., long hours in commuting, long working hours, hectic lifestyle, less time for family and social life, more health hazards etc. are similar either in UK, US, Japan, India, or any other country. Although cultural differences affect stress perceptions and coping behavior of people but these lifestyle similarities bring some common behavioral patterns in people across different cultures and societies. Researchers need to consider this context very carefully in their interpretations of stress and coping behavior across different groups (Ram, 1999).

Considering the influence of religion on lifestyle of people of developing countries (e.g., India, Pakistan, Srilanka, Bangladesh), this factor needs to be considered while understanding stress-coping-strains process in the context of people belonging to these ethnic populations. Theories and models developed in the West (Europe and America) do not provide holistic framework to understand stress-coping-strain relationship in the context of people of developing countries. Other factors need to be considered, are massive migrations from rural areas to cities, social and economic disparities, education, multi-lingual and multi-ethnic environment within the same country, conflicting religious beliefs and attitudes, and environmental pollution because of unbalanced technological development (Laungani, 1999).

QUALITY OF STRESS RESEARCH: "DEVELOPED" VS. "DEVELOPING" WORLDS

The issue of quality of research in social sciences in developing countries has been raised by many scholars (Laungani, 1999, 2007; Palsane et al, 1999). It is argued that most of research studies conducted in developing countries are "imitative," weak adaptation of western models and not very culturally appropriate. For example, in western countries, instruments like occupational stress indicator (Cooper and 1988), Maslach Burnout Inventory (Maslach and Jackson, 1981) ways of coping checklist (Folkman Sloan, & William Lazarus, 1985), COPE scale (Carver et al, 1989) etc. have been revalidated and revised by several times by researchers. However, in a review of 122 published research studies between 1970–2004, it came as surprise to us why in India, no researcher tried to revalidate frequently used instruments Organizational Role Stress Scale (Pareek, 1983a), ROLE PICS (Pareek, 1983b), Occupational Stress Index (Srivastava and Singh, 1981), Coping Strategies Scale (Srivastava and Singh, 1988), The Coping Checklist (Rao, Subbakrishna and Prabhu, 1989) at anytime but researchers continued to use those instruments as usual for years; though not only work environment but also social environment too has also changed much from 1980s to 1990s and later after 2000. However, some researchers attempted to develop new scales for measurement of stress and burnout (Menon and Akhilesh, 1994; Gaur, 1996; Sharma, 2007). Revalidation of existing psychometric instruments is required periodically if we want to keep updated our instruments as per changing needs of the time. Effective usage of advanced multivariate models and statistical tools like structural equation modeling and multidimensional scaling could be useful in revalidation and improvement of frequently used measures of stress, coping, burnout and related variables. We also could not find any longitudinal study on stress-related variables conducted in India amongst those studies and even later literature review done for this paper; though some good experimental studies were conducted by few scholars on stress management interventions based on yoga, vipasana and meditation for reducing stress, burnout and hypertension (Sahasi, Mohan and Kakar, 1989; Sachdeva, 1994; Venkatesh, 1994; Malathi et al, 2000; Murugesan, Govindrajulu and Behra, 2000; Gopalakrishna, 2002; Gopalakrishna, 2003; Gopalakrishna, 2006; Telles et al, 2004; Adhia, Nagendra and Mahadevan, 2010).

Considering constraints under which researchers are expected to work in developing countries like India, Pakistan, Srilanka and many countries of Africa; very few researchers tried to go for innovation in research designs. We would like to mention here that in a developing country like India, research funds are so scarce that a researcher can hardly think to go for longitudinal studies or Cargi-scale surveys. This resulted into increase in cross-sectional studies focused on different occupational groups, industrial sectors or work settings; but less attention has been paid to revalidation and revision of existing psychometric tools or developing new more effective psychometric measures. Laungani (1999) mentioned few of these factors like: lack of appropriate technological and informational support (e.g., access to international social science databases, lack of appropriate database for searching all social researches done in India, lack of enough funding to support social research by Indian universities and educational institutes, lack of availability of research funds because of poor industry-academia interface. In India, most of university departments and even some specialized research institutes/centers do not have enough infrastructural support and funds to encourage collaboration between international and local faculty. As a result, many studies conducted in Indian context by Indian researchers just produce some vague interpretations of correlations and regressions; rather than critical analysis of prevalent theoretical models and identifying paradigm shifts. Laungani (1999) commented further "*considering these constraints, research on stress may itself become a stressful experience.*" Laungani (1999) raised this issue that researchers from developed countries (particularly from Europe, America and East Asian developed countries) should try to understand social, cultural and economic constraints of researchers of developing countries. There is a strong need to develop cultural sensitivity between researchers of developing and developed countries; and the gap between two "different worlds" needs to be narrowed down and that can be possible only by encouraging collaborative research efforts between researchers of "developed" and "developing" countries. This is the need of the hour if researchers are looking for developing holistic models for understanding stress-coping process in different *contexts*. It is essential for researchers to respect traditions, beliefs and values of other cultures and learn from them while developing theories and models to explain phenomenon like stress and coping (Palsane et al 1999).

Directions for Future Research

The above discussion indicates towards the paradigm shift in stress research in the changed global context of work and organizations. Across the world, researchers have recognized the need to relook into the concept of stress in context of changed realities of work and life; hence shift in research paradigms is inevitable. Issues are numerous and it is also not possible for us to discuss every research issue under the sun in one paper, though we have attempted to cover as many as possible and tried to create a holistic picture of stress research. We have identified some directions of future research which are given below:

DEFINING THEORETICAL CONSTRUCTS AND MODELS

1. Stress should be defined as relational in nature, involving transactions between the person and the environment. The research in this field should progress toward an understanding of the contextual richness of the stress-coping process. (Cooper, 2001, p. 215, 230).
2. Theoretical models of stress share the idea of a process and a sequence of events, identifying in a variety of ways the evaluative processes that best express the relational-transactional nature of work stress (Cooper, 2001: 218).

3. Investigating stress as a transaction places both conceptual and empirical demands that are substantially different from those required when exploring stress from an interactional perspective (Somerfield, 1997).

ADOPTING APPROPRIATE METHODOLOGIES

4. Combination of both quantitative and qualitative methodologies is the need of the hour that may enable researchers to develop research strategies that benefit from the strengths of both types of approaches and that provide more insight into the transactional stress-coping process (Cooper, 2001: 218). Mixed designs could be good alternatives to traditional methods in exploring dynamics of stress, coping, well-being and work-family conflict in "specific cultural contexts" (Liu et al, 2007, 2008; Barley, 2011).

5. Greater attention must be given to the development of methods that explore the social experiences that individuals encounter in their workplaces and the meaning of these experiences for their well-being (Handy, 1988; Cooper, 2001). Researchers may go for more person-centered, daily process designs which include daily diary recordings, narratives, structured interviews, focused group discussions etc. when they investigate stress-coping process (Tennen et al, 2000, p. 626; Dewe, 2003, p. 517; Randall et al, 2007; Hasan et al, 2010; Iwasaki et al, 2006).

6. Given the dynamic nature of stress-coping process, longitudinal studies may be an effective strategy because it provides the opportunity to clarify causal relationships that are otherwise indeterminable through cross-sectional analysis (Kahn and Byosiere, 1992; Van Der Doef and Maes, 1999; Lazarus, 2000; Hasan et al, 2010). Usage of multi-wave design and advanced techniques like structural equation modeling may reveal new discoveries in context of stress-coping process (Dormann and Zapf, 2002).

MEASUREMENT OF STRESSORS, STRAINS AND COPING

7. Existing measures should be evaluated in terms of (a) content of items, (b) scoring of responses, and the manner in which internal reliability is established. (Cooper, 2001: 229).

8. The issue of *measure confounding* needs to be dealt seriously by stress researchers. Confounding occurs when instruments that purport to

assess one construct (e.g., a stressor) in reality tap into another (e.g., strain). Researchers may inadvertently introduce confounding in their measurement procedures. (Cooper, 2001: 229)

9. While considering a range of measurement strategies (e.g., self-ratings; qualitative; physiological, and physical indicators of strain; and peer observations) for their appropriate research designs, researchers must clearly distinguish between the dependent and independent variables and avoid measurement overlap (Dewe, 2000).

MULTIDIMENSIONAL AND CONTEXTUAL MODELS IN STRESS RESEARCH

10. Researchers need to focus on the *context* in which stress-coping process occurs. Each setting or environment offers different stressors that determine the nature of strains being experienced by the individual (Cooper, 2001, p. 246). Misra (1999) raised this issue in the context of theoretical models on stress and burnout how these models developed in Western countries, can be tested empirically on Indian professionals and expressed the need to adopt contextual approach in interpreting concepts like stress, burnout and coping where she suggested use of qualitative methods and longitudinal studies for the future researches.

11. Stress-coping research should adopt a holistic perspective that takes into account the totality of an individual's life space rather than simply assessing one domain (e.g., job stress) in isolation from others (Cooper, 2001: 247). Similar views have been expressed by Agrawal (1999) who suggested that multidimensional investigations might be very useful in understanding individual differences in the context of stress-coping process. She added further that personal profiling may be used as a tool in such research studies and one type of stress should not be seen in isolation but in relation to other types of life stresses (Agrawal, 1999).

12. The researchers should try to incorporate multiple-level analysis in stress research than just individual-level analysis Measuring stress indicators at individual and group level would provide better insights for developing more effective stress management interventions for organizations and a holistic perspective for researchers. Currently available measures are individual-centric and there is strong need to develop group-level measures that may be more relevant in SM interventions and beneficial for the organizations at large (Bliese and Jex, 1999).

RELEVANCE OF STRESS RESEARCH TO ORGANIZATIONS

13. There is a strong need being felt by many researchers to adopt "proactive approach" in stress research (Luthans, 2002; Bliese and Jex, 1999; Cox, 1997; Griffith, 1994; and Pestonjee, 1992).The time has come to think differently from the traditional "cause-effect" relationship between stressors and strains or between stress and coping. Stress researchers need to be driven toward constructing "healthy organizations" (Cooper and Cartwright, 1994) that contribute to individual well-being rather than inducing or exacerbating levels of strain. The value of stress research should be judged by its contribution to the enhancement of individual well-being as well as organizational productivity and effectiveness.

14. To make stress research more relevant to organizations, organizations need to conduct "stress audit" regularly (e.g., once in a year) because it tries to understand organizational reality and tends to combine it with the individual's psychodynamic profile. Researchers now need to adopt a "holistic health perspective" that takes into account physiological, psychological and spiritual dimensions of health, then, it would be possible to create "healthy organizations." (Pestonjee, 1997, p. 252)

15. Regarding research on stress management interventions (SMIs), more evaluation studies on SMIs need to be conducted for testing effectiveness of techniques like meditation, relaxation therapy, biofeedback, hypnosis, cognitive behavior therapy etc. (Sharma, 1999; Dua 1999).

EMERGING ISSUES IN THE CHANGED WORK ENVIRONMENT OF 21ST CENTURY

16. The changing nature of work, workplaces and careers in 21st century has been recognized as the most important issues by researchers (Murphy, 1999; Gowing et al., 1997; Parker and Inkson, 1999; Murphy and Jackson 1999). New realities of the world of work such as globalization, increasing unemployment, highly uncertain work environment, structural and cultural changes in modern organizations, and emerging technologies must be taken into account (Cooper 2001, p.248). Researchers also do need to pay more attention to gender differences in relation to stress perceptions and coping behavior (Sharma, 1999; Agrawal, 1999).

17. The change in economic, social and political environment of the world is likely to see emergence of more culturally diverse organizations in future

where people from different ethnicities/nationalities will be working together across the miles. Hence, there is strong need to conduct more "culturally appropriate" researches in the field of stress management and develop appropriate "indigenous" models relevant to specific cultural groups/settings. We need more cross-cultural research studies focused on relationships among stress, coping, well-being, work-family conflict which could be helpful in developing new "culturally appropriate" models (Spector et al 2006; Burke, 2010; Bhagat et al 2010; Hasan et al 2010).

The authors also feel that there is strong need to conduct more research on stress management interventions particularly in areas of developing interventions for specific target groups, implementing interventions in specific organizations and evaluating interventions in the context of specific professional groups and organizations. For HR practitioners, effectiveness of stress management interventions in achieving certain organizational goals (e.g., enhancing employee motivation, improving organizational climate and team effectiveness) is more important than just understanding the "cause-effect" relationships between stress-coping and stressors-strains. As we have discussed earlier, most researchers still prefer "causal" approach to study stress rather than adopting "evaluative approach" that emphasizes upon measuring effectiveness of stress management interventions. Although, a lot of discussion and debate were conducted over various "causes and effects" of stress but less work is done on implementing stress management interventions in order to enhance employee well-being and organizational effectiveness.

Conclusion

In this chapter, we attempted to address numerous methodological issues in context of changed environment of world of work and changed realities of organizations. We tried to discuss issues related with qualitative vs. quantitative approaches; cross-sectional vs. longitudinal studies; positive vs. negative orientation of stress; unit of analysis-individual, group or organization; self-report measures vs. physiological measures; reliability and validity of existing measures; indigenous vs. western models of stress; multidimensional and contextual models; and quality of research in developing vs. developed countries. It may be possible that despite our best efforts, we might have missed something from this discussion but this debate suggests that while looking towards future research, we should take a pause, look back, understand the present context and then, move ahead with a fresh approach. Innovation in research does not come from the thin air; research process should be aimed to discover realities, not to just confirm pre-conceived assumptions.

References

Adhia, H., Nagendra, & Mahadevan, B. (2010). Impact of adoption of yoga way of life on the reduction of job burnout of managers. *Vikalpa, 35*(2), 21–33.

Agrawal, R. (1999). Should individuals with visual impairment be stressful: Some theoretical and empirical answers. In D.M. Pestonjee, U. Pareek, & R. Agrawal (Eds), *Studies in stress and its management* (pp. 199–217). New Delhi: Oxford & IBH.

Anderson, C.A. & Arnoult, L.H. (1989). An examination of perceived control, humor, irrational beliefs, and positive stress as moderators of the relation between negative stress and health. *Basic and Applied Social Psychology, 10*(2), 101–17.

Ashok, H.S. (1989). Organizational and interpersonal implications of job stress in prison personnel. Unpublished Ph.D. Thesis, Bangalore University, Bangalore.

Aspinwall, L.G. and Taylor, S.E. (1997). A stitch in time: Self-regulation and proactive coping. *Psychological Bulletin, 121*, 417–36.

Bartunek, J.M., Bobko, P.P., & Venkatratnam, N. (1993). Toward innovation and diversity in management research methods. *Academy of Management Journal, 36*, 1362–73.

Bateman, T.S. and Crant, J.M. (1999). Proactive behavior: Meanings, impact, and recommendations. *Business Horizons*, May–June, 63–70.

Barley, S.R.. Meyerson, D.E. & Grodal, S. (2011). E-mail as a source and symbol of stress. *Organization Science, 22*(4), 887–906.

Beehr, T.A. & Newman, J.D. (1978). Job stress, employee health and organizational effectiveness: A facet analysis, model and literature review. *Personnel Psychology, 31*, 665–99.

Beehr, T.A. (1995). *Psychological stress in the workplace.* London: Routledge.

Beehr, T.A. (1998). Research on occupational stress: An unfinished enterprise. *Personnel Psychology, 51*, 835–44.

Bhagat, R.S. and Beer, T.A. (1985). An evaluation summary and recommendations for future research. In T.A. Beehr & R.S. Bhagat (Eds), *Human stress and cognition in organizations: An integrated perspective* (pp. 417–31). New York: John-Wiley.

Bhagat, R., Krishnan, B., Nelson, T.A., Leonard, K.M., Ford, D.L., & Billing, T.K. (2010). Organizational stress, psychological strain, and work outcomes in six national contexts: A closer look at the moderating influences of coping styles and decision latitude. *Cross-Cultural Management: An International Journal, 17*(1), 10–29.

Bliese, P.D. (1998). Groups size, ICC values and group-level correlations: A simulation. *Occupational Research Methods, 1*, 355–73.

Bliese, P.D. and Jex, S.M. (1999). Incorporating multiple levels of analysis into occupational stress research. *Work & Stress, 13*(1), 1–6.

Burke, R. (2010). Workplace stress and well-being across cultures: Research and practice. *Cross-cultural management: An international journal, 17*(1), 5–9.

Carver, C.S., Scheier, M.F., & Weintraub, J.K. (1989). Assessing coping strategies: A theoretically based approach. *Journal of Personality and Social Psychology, 56*(2), 267–83.

Cavanaugh, M.A., Boswell, W.R., Roehling, M.V., & Boudreau, J.W. (2000). An empirical examination of self-reported work stress among U.S. managers. *Journal of Applied Psychology, 85*(1), 65–74.

Chrisopoulos, S., Dollard, M., Winefield, A.H., & Dormann, C. (2010). Increasing the probability of finding an interaction in work stress research: A two-wave longitudinal test of the triple-match principle. *Journal of Occupational and Organizational Psychology*, *83*, 17–37.

Cooper, C.L. & Cartwright, S. (1994). Healthy mind, healthy organization: A proactive approach on occupational stress. *Human Relations*, *47*, 455–71.

Cooper, C.L., Dewe, P.J., & O'Driscoll, M.P. (2001). *Organizational stress: A review and critique of theory, research, and applications*. Thousand Oaks: SAGE.

Cooper, C.L., Sloan, S.J., & Williams, S. (1988). *Occupational stress indicator: Management guide*. Windsor: NFER-Nelson.

Cox, T. (1997). Workplace health promotion. *Work and Stress*, *11*, 1–5.

Cox, T., Karanika, M., Griffiths, A., & Houdmont, J. (2007). Evaluating organizational-level work stress interventions: Beyond traditional methods. *Work & Stress*, *21*(4), 348–62.

Cummings, T.G. & Cooper, C.L. (1998). A cybernetic theory of organizational stress. In C.L. Cooper (Ed.), *Theories of organizational stress* (pp. 101–21). New York: Oxford University Press.

Crant, J.M. (2000). Proactive behavior in organizations. *Journal of Management*, *26*(3), 435–62.

Daniels, K., Brough, P., Guppy, A., Peters-Bean, K.M., & Weatherstone, L. (1997). A note on a modification to Warr's measures of affective well-being at work. *Journal of Occupational and Organizational Psychology*, *70*, 129–38.

Dewe, P. (2000). Measures of coping with stress at work: A review and critique. In P. Dewe, M. Leiter & T. Cox (Eds), *Coping, health and organizations* (pp. 3–28). New York: Taylor & Francis.

Dewe, P. (2003). A closer examination of the patterns when coping with work-related stress: Implications for measurement. *Journal of Occupational and Organizational Psychology*, *75*, 517–24.

de Jonge, J. & Dormann, C. (2006). Stressors, resources, and strains at work: A longitudinal test of the triple-match principle. *Journal of Applied Psychology*, *91*, 1359–74.

Dormann, C. & Zapf, D. (1999). Social support, stressors, and depression: Testing for main and moderating effects with structural equations in a 3-wave longitudinal study. *Journal of Occupational and Organizational Psychology*, *75*, 33–58.

Dormann, C. & Zapf, D. (2002). Social stressors at work, irritation, and depressive symptoms: Accounting for unmeasured third variables in a multi-wave study. *Journal of Occupational and Organizational Psychology*, *75*, 33–58.

Dua, J. (1999). Meditation and its effectiveness. In D.M. Pestonjee, U. Pareek, & R. Agrawal (Eds), *Studies in stress and its management* (pp. 249–65). New Delhi: Oxford & IBH.

Edwards, J.R. (1991). Person-job fit: A conceptual integration, literature review, and methodological critique. In C.L. Cooper & I.T. Robertson (Eds), *International Review of Industrial and Organizational Psychology* (Volume 6, pp. 283–357). New York: Wiley.

Edwards, J.R. (1992). The cybernetic theory of stress, coping and well-being in organizations. *Academy of Management Review*, *17*, 238–74.

Edwards, J.R. and Cooper, C.L. (1988). The impacts of positive psychological states on physical health: a review and theoretical framework. *Social Science and Medicine*, *27*, 1447–59.

Edwards, J.R., Caplan, R.D., & Van Harrison, R. (1998). Person-environment fit theory: Conceptual foundations, empirical evidence, and directions for future research. In C.L. Cooper (Ed.), *Theories of organizational stress* (pp. 28–67). New York: Oxford University Press.

Ellis, Alexksander P. (2006). System breakdown: The role of mental models and transactive memory in the relationship between acute stress and team performance. *Academy of Management Journal, 49*(3), 576–89.

Enriquez, V.G. (2003). Developing a Filipino psychology. In U. Kim & J.W. Berry (Eds), *Indigenous psychologies: Research and experience in cultural context* (pp. 30–43). Thousand Oaks, CA: SAGE.

Erera-Weatherley, P.I. (1996). Coping with stress: Public welfare supervisors doing their best. *Human Relations, 49,* 157–70.

Evers, A., Frese, M., & Cooper, C.L. (2000). Revisions and further developments of the occupational stress indicator: LISREL results from four Dutch studies. *Journal of Occupational and Organizational Psychology, 73*(2), 221–40.

Folkman, S. & Lazarus, R.S. (1985). If it changes it must be a process: A study of emotion and coping during three stages of a college examination. *Journal of Personality and Social Psychology, 48,* 150–70.

Frese, M. & Zapf, D. (1988). Methodological issues in the study of work stress: Objective vs. subjective measurement of work stress and the question of longitudinal studies. In Cooper, C.L. & Payne, R. (Eds), *Causes, coping and consequences of stress and work* (pp. 375-411). Chichester: John Wiley & Sons.

Fried, M., Rolland, K.M., & Ferris, G.R. (1984). The physiological measurement of work stress: A critique. *Personnel Psychology, 37,* 583–615.

Fried, Y. (1988). The future of physiological assessments in work situations. In Cooper, C.L. & Payne, R. (Eds), *Causes, coping and consequences of stress and work* (pp. 343–73). Chichester: John Wiley & Sons.

Gaur, S. (1996). Unpublished Ph.D. Thesis, Allahabad University, Allahabad.

Gibbons C., Dempster M., & Moutray M. (2008). Stress and eustress in nursing students. *Journal of Advanced Nursing, 61*(3), 282–90.

Gowing, M., Kraft, J., & Quick, J. (1997). A conceptual framework for coping with new organizational reality. In M. Growing, J Kraft, and J. Quick (Eds), *The new organizational reality: Downsizing, restructuring and rivitalization* (pp. 259–68). Washington DC: American Psychological Association.

Glowinkowski, S.P. & Cooper, C.L. (1985). Current issues in organizational stress research. *Bulletin of the British psychological society, 38,* 212–16.

Griffiths, A. (1994). Editorial: Musculoskeletal upper-limb disorders and white-collar work in UK. *Work and Stress, 9,* 1–3.

Gopalakrishna, D. (2002). Buddhist meditation—Relives stress and develops interpersonal effectiveness. In U. Pareek, A.O. Gani, S. Ramanaryan, & T.V. Rao (Eds), *Human resource development in Asia: Trends and challenges* (pp. 309–13). New Delhi: Oxford & IBH.

——— (2003). Impact of Buddhist meditation on modern management. In Chiraprapha, T. Akaraborworn, Aahad Osman Gani, & Gary N. McLean (Eds), *Human resource development in Asia: National policy perspectives.* Bangkok, Thailand: National Institute of Development Administration 6/1-10.

——— (2006). *Buddhism and contemporary management (with special reference to Vipassana meditation).* Srilanka: Buddhist Cultural Centre.

Handy, J.A. (1988). Theoretical and methodological problems within occupational stress and burnout research. *Human Relations, 41,* 351–69.

Haridas, T. (1983). Qualitative research in organizational behavior. *Journal of Management Studies, 3,* 301–14.

Harkness, A.M.B., Long, B.C., Bermbach, N., Patterson, K., Jordan, S., & Kahn, H. (2005). Talking about work stress: Discourse analysis and implications for stress interventions. *Work & Stress, 19*(2), 12–136.

Harris, (1991). The utility of the transactional approach for occupational stress research. *Journal of Social Behavior and Personality, 6,* 21–29.

Hasan, Z., Dollard, M.F., & Winefield, A.H. (2010). Work-family conflict in east vs western countries. *Cross-Cultural Management: An International Journal, 17*(1), 30–49.

Iwasaki, Y., Mackay, K.J., & Mactavish, J.B. (2006). Voices from the margins: Stress, active living, and leisure as a contributor to coping with stress. *Leisure Sciences, 28,* 163–80.

Jex, S.M. (1998). *Stress and job performance: Theory, research, and implications for managerial practice.* Thousands Oaks: SAGE.

Kahn, R.L. & Byosiere, P. (1992). Stress in organizations. In M. Dunnette (Ed.), *Handbook of industrial and organizational psychology* (pp. 571–648). Chicago: Rand McNally.

Kahn, R.L., Wolfe, D.M., Quinn, R.P., Snoeck, J.D., & Rosenthal, R.A. (1964). *Organizational stress: Studies and role conflict and role ambiguity.* New York: Wiley.

Kakar, S. (1997). *Culture and psyche: Selected essays.* Delhi: Oxford University Press.

Kalliath, T.J., O'Driscoll, M., Gillespe, D.F., & Bluedorn, A.C. (2000). A test of the Maslach Burnout Inventory in three samples of healthcare professionals. *Work & Stress, 14*(1), 35–50.

Kasl, S.V. (1978). Epidemiological contributions to the study of work stress. In C.L. Cooper & R. Payne (Eds), *Stress at Work* (pp. 3–48). Chichester: John Wiley & Sons.

——— (1986). Stress and disease in the workplace: A methodological commentary on the accumulated evidence. In M.F. Cataldo & Th. J. Coates (Eds), *Health and industry, a behavioral medicine perspective.* New York: John Wiley & Sons.

——— (1987). Methodologies in stress and health: Past difficulties, present dilemmas, future directions. In S.V. Kasl & C.L. Cooper (Eds), *Stress and health: Issues in research methodology.* New York: John Wiley & Sons.

Katz, D. & Kahn, R.L. (1978). *The social psychology of organizations* (2nd Eds). New York: John Coiley.

Kets De Vries, M.F.R. (1979). Organizational stress: A call for management action. *Sloan Management Review, 21*(1), 3–14.

Kim, U. & Berry, J.W. (1993). *Indigenous psychologies: Research and experience in cultural context.* Newbury Park, CA: SAGE.

Kreft, I. & De Leevw, J. (1998). *Introducing multilevel modeling.* London: SAGE Publications.

Kinicki, A.J. & Latack, J.C. (1990). Explication of the construct of coping with involuntary job loss. *Journal of Vocational Behavior, 36,* 339–60.

Lam, D.J. & Palsane, M.N. (1997). Research on stress and coping: Contemporary Asian approaches. In H.S.R. Kao & D.N. Sinha (Eds), *Asian perspectives on psychology* (pp. 265–81). New Delhi: SAGE.

Laungani, P. (1995). Stress in eastern and western cultures. In J. Brebner, E. Greenglass, P. Laungani, & A. O'Roark (Eds), *Stress and emotion* (Volume 15, pp. 17–43). Washington DC: Taylor & Francis.

——— (1996). Research in cross-cultural settings: Ethical considerations. In E. Miao (Ed.), *Cross-cultural encounters.* Proceedings of the 53rd Annual Convention of International Council of Psychologists (pp. 107–36). Taipei, General Innovation Series.

——— (1999). Stress in India and England. In D. M. Pestonjee, U. Pareek and R. Agrawal (Eds), *Studies in Stress and Its Management,* pp. 17–43, Oxford & IBH, New Delhi.

Laungani, P. (2005). Stress, culture and personality. In C. Cooper (Ed.), *Handbook of Stress Medicine and Health* (pp. 209–27). Boca Raton, FL: CRC Press.

Laungani, P.D. (2007). *Understanding cross-cultural psychology.* New Delhi: SAGE (South Asia).

Lazarus, R.S. (1966). *Psychological stress and the coping process.* New York: McGraw Hill.

———— (1981). The stress and coping paradigm. In C. Eisdorfer, D. Cohen, A. Kleinman, & P. Maxim (Eds), *Models for clinical psychopathology* (pp. 177–214). New York: Spectrum.

Lazarus, R.S. & Folkman, S. (1984). *Stress, appraisal, and coping.* New York: Springer.

Lazarus, R.S. (1990). Theory-based stress measurement. *Psychological Inquiry, 1,* 3–12.

———— (2000). Toward better research on stress and coping. *American Psychologist, 55,* 665–73.

Le Fevre, M., Matheny, J., & Kolt, G.S. (2003). Eustress, distress, and interpretation in occupational stress. *Journal of Managerial Psychology, 18*(7), 726–44.

Le Ferve, M. Kolt & Matheny, J. (2006). Eustress, distress and their interpretation in primary and secondary occupational stress interventions: Which comes first? *Journal of Managerial Psychology,* 21(6), 547–65.

Liu, C., Spector, P.E., & Shi, L. (2007). Cross-national job stress: A quantitative and qualitative study. *Journal of Organizational Behavior,* 28(2), 209–39.

———— (2008). Use of both qualitative and quantitative approaches to study job stress in different gender and occupational groups. *Journal of Occupational Health Psychology, 13,* 357–70.

Livneh, H., Livneh, C.L., Maron, S., & Kaplan, J. (1996). A multidimensional approach to the study of the structure of coping with stress. *The Journal of Psychology, 130*(5), 501–12.

Luthans, F. (2002). Proactive organizational behavior: Developing and managing psychological strengths. *Academy of Management Executive, 16*(1), 57–75.

Lyne, K.D., Barret, P.T., Wiiliams, C., & Coaley, K. (2000). A psychometric evaluation of the Occupational Stress Indicator. *Journal of Occupational and Organizational Psychology,* 73(2), 195–220.

Malathi, A., Damodaran, A., Shah, N., Patil, N., & Maratha, S. (2000). Effect of yogic practices on subjective well being. *Indian Journal of Physiological Pharmacology, 44*(2), 202–06.

Maslach, C. and Jackson, S.E. (1981). The measurement of experienced burnout. *Journal of Organizational Behavior,* 2(4), 99–113.

McGowan, J., Gardner, D., & Fletcher, R. (2006). Positive and negative outcomes of occupational stress. *New Zealand Journal of Psychology, 35*(2), 92–98.

McGrath, J.E. (1976). Stress and behavior in organizations. In M.D. Dunnette (Ed.), *Handbook of industrial and organizational psychology.* Chicago: Rand McNally.

———— (1982). Methodological problems in research on stress. In H.W. Krohn & L. Laux (Eds), *Achievement, stress and anxiety.* New York: Mc Graw-Hill.

Menon, N. & Akhilesh, K.B. (1994). Functionally dependent stress among managers: A new perspective. *Journal of Managerial Psychology, 9*(3), 13–22.

Misra, G. (2011). Preface. In Girishwar Misra (Ed.), *Handbook of psychology in India* (pp. xv–xvi). New Delhi: Oxford University Press.

Misra, N. (1999). People in helping professions and occupational stress: A case for job burnout. In D.M. Pestonjee, U. Pareek, & R. Agrawal (Eds), *Studies in stress and its management* (pp. 149–158). New Delhi: Oxford & IBH.

Morgenstern, H. (1982). User of ecological analysis in epidemiological research. *American Journal of Public Health, 72,* 1336–44.

Morley, N.L. & Luthans, F. (1984). An EMIC perspective and ethnoscience methods for organizational research. *Academy of Management Review, 9,* 27–36.

Murphy, K. (1999). The challenge of staffing a potential workplace. In D. Ilgen & E. Pulakos (Eds), *The changing nature of performance: Implications for staffing, motivation and development* (pp. 295–324). San Francisco: Jossey-Bass.

Murphy, K. & Jackson, S. (1999). Managing work role performance: Challenge for twenty-first century organizations and their employees. In D. Ilgen & E. Pulakos (Eds), *The changing nature of performance: Implications for staffing, motivation and development* (pp. 325–65). San Francisco: Jossey-Bass.

Murugesan, R, Govindarajulu, N., & Bera, T.K. (2000). Effect of selected yogic practices on the management of hypertension. *Indian Journal of Physiological Pharmacology, 44,* 207–10.

Nelson, D.L. & Simmons, B.L. (2003). Health psychology and work stress. In, J.C. Quick & L.E. Tetrick (Eds), *Handbook of occupational health psychology.* Washington, DC: American Psychological Association.

Oakland, S. & Ostell, A. (1996). Measuring coping: A review and critique. *Human Relations, 49,* 133–55.

O'Driscoll, M.P. & Cooper, C.L. (1994). Coping with work-related stress: A critique of existing measures and proposal for an alternative methodology. *Journal of Occupational and Organizational Psychology, 67,* 343–54.

———— (1996). A critical incident analysis of stress-coping behaviors at work. *Stress Medicine, 12,* 123–28.

Palsane, M.N, Bhavsar, S.N., Goswami, R.P., & Evans, G.W. (1999). The concept of stress in the Indian tradition. In D.M. Pestonjee, U. Pareek, & R. Agrawal (Eds), *Studies in stress and its management* (pp. 1–15). New Delhi: Oxford & IBH.

Pandey, S.C. (2003). Work stress in advertising professionals of India: A HRD perspective. In C.T. Akaraborworn, A. Osman Gani, & G.N. McLean (Eds), *Human resource development in Asia: National policy perspectives.* Bangkok, Thailand: National Institute of Development Administration, 16/1–8.

Parker, P. & Inkson, K. (1999). New forms of career: The challenge to human resource management. *Asia Pacific Journal of Human Resources, 37,* 76–86.

Pareek, U. (1983a). Organizational role stress. In L.D. Goodstein & J.W. Pfeiffer (Eds), *The 1983 annual for facilitators, trainers and consultants.* San Diego, California: University Associates.

———— (1983b). *Organizational role pics (o) booklet, answer sheet, and manual.* Ahmedabad: Navin Publications.

———— (1987). *Motivating organizational roles: Role efficacy approach.* Jaipur: Rawat Publications.

———— (1993). *Making organizational roles effective.* New Delhi: Tata McGraw Hill.

Pestonjee, D.M. (1987). Executive stress: Should it always be avoided? *Vikalpa, 12*(1), 23–30.

Pestonjee, D.M. (1992). *Stress and coping: The Indian experience.* New Delhi: SAGE Publications.

———— (1997). Executives under stress: Some findings and reflections. In D.M. Pestonjee & U. Pareek (Eds), *Studies in organizational role stress and coping.* Jaipur, New Delhi: Rawat Publications.

Ram, U. (1999). Daily hassles among working mothers: A cross-cultural study. In D.M. Pestonjee, U. Pareek, & R. Agrawal (Eds), *Studies in stress and its management* (pp. 131–38). New Delhi: Oxford & IBH.

Richards, T.A., Oman, D., Hedberg, Thoresen, C.E., & Bowden, J. (2006). A qualitative examination of a spiritually-based intervention and self-management in the workplace. *Nursing Science Quarterly,* 19(3), 231–39.

Randall, R., Cox, T., & Griffiths, A. (2007). Participants' accounts of a stress management intervention. *Human Relations,* 60(8), 1181–1209.

Randall, R., Nielsen,K., & Tvedt, S.D. (2009). The development of five scales to measure employees' appraisals of organizational-level stress management interventions. *Work & Stress,* 23(1), 1–23.

Rao, K., Subbakrishna, D.K., & Prabhu, G.G. (1989). Development of a coping checklist. *Indian Journal of Psychiatry,* 31, 128–33.

Sachdeva, U. (1994). The effect of yogic lifestyle in hypertension. *Homeostasis in Health and Disease,* 35(4–5), 264.

Sahasi, G., Mohan, D., & Kacker, C. (1989). Effectiveness of yogic techniques in the management of anxiety. *Journal of Personality and Clinical Studies,* 5(1), 51–55.

Schwartz, S. (1994). The fallacy of the ecological fallacy, The potential misuse of a concept and the consequences. *American Journal of Public Health,* 84, 819–824.

Seleye, H. (1956). *The stress of life.* New York: McGraw-Hill.

Sharma, R. (2007). Indian model of executive burnout. *Vikalpa,* 32(2), April–June, 23–38.

Sharma, S. (1999). Occupational stress and well-being: Recent findings and further issues. In D.M. Pestonjee, U. Pareek, & R. Agrawal (Eds), *Studies in stress and its management* (pp. 159–68). New Delhi: Oxford & IBH.

Simmons, B.L. & Nelson, D.L. (2001). Eustress at work: The relationship between hope and health in hospital nurses. *Health Care Management Review,* 26, 63–74.

Sinha, D. (1993). Indigenization of psychology in India and its relevance. In Kim, U. & J.W. Berry (Eds), *Indigenous psychologies: Research and experience in cultural context* (pp. 30–43). Thousand Oaks, CA: SAGE Publications.

Sinha, D. & Kao, H.S.R. (1997). The journey to the east: An introduction. In Kao, H.S.R. & Sinha, D. (Eds), *Asian perspectives of psychology* (Volume 19, *Cross-Cultural Research and Methodology Series,* pp. 9–22). New Delhi: SAGE Publications.

Skakon, J., Nielsen, K., Borg, V., & Guzman, J. (2010). Are leaders' well-being, behaviours and style associated with the affective well-being of their employees? A systematic review of three decades of research. *Work & Stress,* 24(2), 107–39.

Synder, C.R. (1997). Hope: An individual motive for social commerce. *Group Dynamics,* 1, 107–18

Somerfield, M.R. (1997). The utility of systems models of stress and coping for applied research. *Journal of Health Psychology,* 2, 133–51.

Spector, P.E. (1998). A control theory of the job stress process. In C.L. Cooper (Ed.), *Theories of organizational stress* (pp. 153–66). New York: Oxford University Press.

Spector, P.E., Cooper, C.L., Poelmans, S., Allen, T.D., O'Driscoll, M., Sanchez, J.I., et al. (2004). A cross-national comparative study of work/family stressors, working hours, and well-being: China and Latin America vs. the Anglo world. *Personnel Psychology,* 57, 119–42.

Spicer, J. (1997). Systems analysis of stress and coping: A testing proposition. *Journal of Health Psychology,* 2, 167–70.

Srivastava, S. & Broota, K.D. (1987). Stress and cancer. *Journal of Personality and Clinical Studies,* 3(2), 89–94.

Srivastava, A.K. & Singh, A.P. (1981). Construction and standardization of an occupational stress index: A pilot study. *Indian Journal of Clinical Psychology,* 5(2), 9–16.

Srivastava, A.K. & Singh, H.S. (1988). Modifying effects of coping strategies on the relation of organizational role stress and mental health. *Psychological Reports, 62,* 1007–09.

Synder, C.R. (1997). Hope: An individual motive for social commerce. *Group Dynamics, 1,* 107–18.

Telles, S., Joshi, M., Dash, M., Raghuraj, P., Naveen, K., & Nagendra, H.R. (2004). An evaluation of the ability to voluntarily reduce the heart rate after a month of *yoga* practice. *Integrative Physiological and Behavioral Science, 39*(2), 119–25.

Tennen, H., Affleck, G., Armeli, S., & Careny, M.A. (2000). A daily process approach to coping. *American Psychologist, 55,* 626–36.

Thoits, P.A. (1995). Stress, coping and social support processes: Where are we? What next? *Journal of Health and Social Behavior,* (extra issue), 53–79.

Van Der Doef, M., & Maes, S. (1999). The job-demand-control (-support) model and psychological well-being: A review of 20 years of empirical research. *Work & Stress, 13*(2), 87–114.

Van Dierendonck, D., Schaufeli, W.B., & Buunk, B.P. (2001). Toward a process model of burnout: Results from a secondary analysis. *European Journal of Work and Organizational Psychology, 10*(1), 41–52.

Venkatesh, S. (1994). A comparative study of *yoga* practitioners and controls on certain psychological variables. *Indian Journal of Clinical Psychology, 21*(1), 22–27.

Vogt, D.S., Rizvi, S.L., Shipherd, J.C., & Resick, P.A. (2010). Longitudinal investigation of reciprocal relationship between stress reactions and hardiness. *Personality and Social Psychology Bulletin, 34*(1), 61–73.

Wanberg, C.R. (1997). Antecedents and outcomes of coping behavior among unemployed and reemployed individuals. *Journal of Applied Psychology, 82,* 731–44.

Warr, P. (1987). *Work, unemployment and mental health.* Oxford, UK: Clarendon Press.

——— (1990). The measurement of well-being and other aspects of mental health. *Journal of Occupational Psychology, 63,* 193–210.

Zebian, S., Alamuddin, R., Maalouf, M., & Chatila, Y. (2007). Developing an appropriate psychology through culturally-sensitive research practices in the arabic-speaking world: A content analysis of psychological research published between 1950 and 2004. *Journal of Cross-Cultural Psychology, 38*(2), 91–122.

16

Epilogue: The Road Ahead

Satish Pandey and D. M. Pestonjee

When the idea of this volume *Stress and Work: Perspectives on Understanding and Managing Stress* (later modified to the present title) came into our minds, we thought of it as a compendium of knowledge generated by some valuable researches recently done by researchers in the Indian context. We believed that such kind of volume could be a ready-to-refer handbook of stress research in hands of researchers from any discipline who wish to know about various perspectives of stress management as a scientific discipline. This volume reflects on the current state of affairs on stress research in the Indian context; whereas it also explores into future directions for innovative research. The final output somewhat approximates our original vision of the volume. We have included many valuable research contributions from different academicians and researchers who belong to Indian culture but are working in different organizational settings, universities, research institutes, and management institutes. The number of essays we wanted to include had to be curtailed and controlled in the light of impositions placed by the publisher with regard to the size of the volume. While concluding on various research papers in this volume, we would like to reflect on a few trends emerging out of those contributions.

It is quite visible in many essays included in this volume that positive psychology school is making an impact. Now, there is sudden spurt in researches focused on positive psychology constructs associated with stress, e.g., happiness, hope, optimism, positive affectivity, life satisfaction, and so on. This is perhaps happening because of a strong wave of happiness research flowing in the Western countries and suddenly everyone is rushing towards happiness. A recent January–February 2012 issue of *Harvard Business Review* reflects on this "Happiness Wave" in the Western world.[1] We need to be cautious here

---

[1] *The Harvard Business Review*, January–February 2012 issue has published a special section "The Happiness Factor" which includes five articles "The Economics of Well-being" (Justin Fox), "The Science Behind the Smile" (An interview with Daniel Gilbert, Professor, Harvard University), "Creating Sustainable Performance" (Gretchen Spreitzer and Christine Porath), "Positive Intelligence" (Shawn Anchor), and "The History of Happiness" (Peter N. Stearns).

because blind orientation towards positive psychology could be as dangerous as obsession to reducing distress and perceiving "stress" as "distress." Lazarus (2003) argued in his paper while criticizing positive psychologists about "negativity" label given by them to stress researches, and commented further that stress-coping research is quite balanced and we should not be feeling too positive about positive psychology approach. Pestonjee (1992) also argued that we should not consider stress as a *foe*, but rather consider it as an inevitable element of our life and learn how to live with it. Positive psychology constructs like happiness, hope, and forgiveness need to be defined in culturally appropriate ways and appropriate research methods should be adopted.

Another important trend, which we have observed in some of the contributions, that there is now a paradigm shift from organization-oriented performance focus to maintaining work-life balance and achieving well-being. Earlier researches were done with the focus that stress (or distress) is not good for performance of individuals and organizations; hence we should try to prevent it and reduce it, so that organizational performance does not suffer. Most of stress theories generated in Western countries, e.g., person–environment fit model, job demands–control–support model, work–family conflict model, preventive stress management model, cybernetic theory, burnout model, etc., are more focused on implementing control in the work environment, job design, workplace management, etc., for increasing organizational productivity and not on improving individual's life and well-being. Now, work-life balance and well-being of employees are coming in focus. Organizations should also shift their focus from their productivity to employee happiness, work-life balance and well-being if they wish to build healthy organizational culture and achieve excellence in the long run.

The chapters included in this volume also reflect towards contextualization of stress research especially in cultural contexts of developing countries like India. Whereas Sharma argued about Indian model of burnout and found in her study that Western conceptualization of burnout as psychological construct is not "culturally appropriate" for a country like India; Rajadhyaksha and Ramadoss also tested Karasek's (1979) job demands–control–support model and Frone, Yardley and Markle's (1997) work–family conflict model in Indian context and found failure of these models to explain stress dynamics in Indian cultural context. In the chapter on methodological issues, we have also argued strongly on cultural appropriateness and contextualization of stress research in different contexts—occupational or social. In future, researchers need to be very careful in understanding and defining their context and contextualize their researches and theories appropriately.

Another trend which could be observed in some of the chapters, is increasing emphasis on spirituality and Indian philosophies, e.g., Buddhism. There are some attempts to establish empirical evidence of testing effectiveness of spirituality-focused stress management techniques in workplace environment. We need more interdisciplinary researches in which neurologists, psychiatrists, clinical and social psychologists, sociologists, anthropologists, and philosophers can work together to combine their strengths for making human life better through relevant scientific researches. Research should be focused on scientific inquiry of reality, not confirmation of preconceived assumptions; and it should be relevant to the society and humanity.

References

Frone, M.R., Yardley, J.K., & Markel, K.S. (1997). Developing and testing an integrative model of the work–family interface. *Journal of Vocational Behavior, 50,* 145–167.

Karasek, R.A. Jr. (1979). Job demands, job decision latitude, and mental strain: Implication for job redesign. *Administrative Science Quarterly, 24,* 285–311.

Lazarus, R.S. (2003b). The Lazarus manifesto for positive psychology and psychology in general. *Psychological Inquiry, 14*(2), 173–89.

Pestonjee, D.M. (1992). *Stress and coping: The Indian experience.* New Delhi: SAGE.

About the Editors and Contributors

Editors

D. M. Pestonjee, PhD, is currently associated with School of Petroleum Management, Pandit Deendayal Petroleum University, Gandhinagar, as GSPL Chair Professor since July 2009. He is also associated with CEPT University, Ahmedabad, as Dean, Faculty of Applied Management. He has served at eminent institutions like IIM, Ahmedabad and Banaras Hindu University. He is a psychologist having PhD in Industrial Psychology from the Aligarh Muslim University and he was conferred the D.Litt. (Honoris Causa) by the Banaras Hindu University in April 2003. In November, 2000, he was conferred the title of Honorary Professor of the Albert Schweitzer International University, Geneva (Switzerland). He was awarded the Albert Schweitzer Medal for Science and Peace in April 2004. He has over four decades of teaching and research experience. Among his better known works are: *Organization Structure and Job Attitudes* (1973), *Behavioral Processes in Organization* (1981), *Second Handbook of Psychological and Social Instruments* (1988), *Third Handbook of Psychological and Social Instruments* (1997), *Studies in Organizational Roles and Stress and Coping* (1997), *Studies in Stress and Its Management* (1999), and the celebrated *Stress and Coping: The Indian Experience* (1992, 2002).

Satish Pandey, PhD, is currently working with School of Petroleum Management (SPM), Pandit Deendayal Petroleum University, Gandhinagar, as Associate Professor in Organizational Behavior and HRM area, since August 2007. He has done PhD in Psychology from Gurukul Kangri Vishwavidyalaya, Haridwar (Uttarakhand), in 1995. He has around 16 years' teaching and research experience at various institutions. Prior to joining SPM, he has worked with reputed institutions like Mudra Institute of

Communications, Ahmedabad (MICA), Nirma Institute of Management, Ahmedabad, Institute of Banking Personnel Selection, Mumbai (IBPS), and Birla Institute of Technology and Science (BITS), Pilani. He has presented papers in national and international academic conferences, and published papers in refereed journals and edited books on topics related to stress management, personality, organizational culture, cross-cultural management, organizational turnaround, organizational learning, and behavior change communication.

Contributors

Cathlyn N. Bennett has completed her Masters from Christ University, Bangalore. She has been awarded the University Grants Commission–Junior Research Fellowship. She is currently pursuing her PhD in the area of Clinical Neuropsychology titled "EEG Neurofeedback Training in Traumatic Brain injury—Clinical, Cognitive, Biochemical and Electrophysiological studies." She has presented several papers at national and international conferences. Her research interests include neuropsychological assessment and rehabilitation of various clinical conditions.

Shubhra P. Gaur, PhD, has a DPhil in Psychology from the University of Allahabad, Allahabad, and has 20 years of research and teaching experience. She has been awarded fellowship from University Grants Commission. She is a Professor at Mudra Institute of Communications Ahmedabad (MICA), India, and has held many key positions in the institute including that of Chairperson, Gender Equality, and Anti–sexual harassment Committee and Editor, *Journal of Creative Communications* (JOCC, SAGE). She has taught at the University of Delhi and has been a visiting faculty at IIM, Ahmedabad; School of Petroleum Management (SPM), Pandit Deendayal Petroleum University (PDPU), Gandhinagar; and Mahatama Gandhi Labour Institute, Ahmedabad. She has several publications in the area of gender issues, psychosocial competence and work-related stress, and interpersonal and internal communication. Her teaching and research interests are personal, interpersonal, group and organizational dynamics, creativity, stress management, and cross-cultural and gender issues at workplace.

D. Gopalakrishna, MBA, MCom, LLB, has received PhD for his thesis entitled "Impact of Buddhism on Modern Management—A Study". He has more than 23 years of corporate experience and he has been working as a faculty member at the Post Graduate – MBA – Department (CBSMS), Bangalore University, the largest university in the Asian region. He has totally 37 years of varied experience His area of research interest includes HRD, Industrial Relations, and Buddhist Philosophy and its application in the areas of contemporary management. He has published a book entitled *Buddhism and Contemporary Management* in Sri Lanka. He has been adjudged as a second-best teacher in Bangalore University. He has lectured at Mahachulalongkornrajavidyalaya University, Bangkok, Thailand which was broadcasted on Thai Radio and BBC World Service, and Chaired Technical sessions at International Conference of Academy of HRD.

Akbar Husain, PhD, is Professor at the Department of Psychology, Faculty of Social Sciences, Aligarh Muslim University, Aligarh (India). He has over 31 years of teaching and research experience. He has authored, co-authored, and edited 24 books. Besides, he has contributed 165 research papers, theoretical articles in the refereed and web of sciences journals, and book chapters. Dr Husain was offered Founding Member of the International Board of the International Transpersonal Association, USA in 2009 and he was also offered Membership of the Nyenrode Spirituality in Business Community, the Netherlands, in 2008. His current areas of research are: Spiritual Psychology, Health Psychology, Counseling Psychology, and Positive Psychology.

Shikha S. Jain is currently working with Mudra Institute of Communications, Ahmedabad (MICA), as Research Assistant in Organizational Behavior area, since April 2011. She has done MSc in Clinical Psychology. Prior to joining MICA, she has worked for state- and national-level research projects which include HIV/AIDS awareness among tribal population in Gujarat and socio-economic consequences of Dedicated Freight Corridor. Her research interests include gender studies, self-perception among pre-adolescents, attitude and perception towards veganism.

Updesh Kumar, PhD, is Scientist 'F' and Head, Mental Health Division at Defence Institute of Psychological Research, DRDO, Ministry of Defence, Delhi. He specializes in the area of mental health, suicidal behavior, and terrorism research. Dr Kumar has edited four quality volumes on *Recent Developments of Psychology*; *Counseling: A Practical Approach*; *Suicidal Behaviour: Assessment of People-at-Risk*; and *Countering Terrorism: Psycho-Social Strategies*. Dr Kumar has authored four manuals on *Suicide and Fratricide: Dynamics and Management*, *Managing Emotions in Daily Life and at Work Place*, *Overcoming Obsolescence and Becoming Creative in R&D Environment*, and *Self-help Techniques in Military Settings*. He also has more than 30 other academic publications. Dr Kumar has been a psychological assessor for eight years for the selection of officers in Indian Armed Forces. He is a certified psychologist by The British Psychological Society. He was conferred DRDO's Best Popular Science Communication Award 2009 by the Defense Minister of India. He has also been the recipient of DRDO Technology Group Award in 2001 and 2009, Professor Manju Thakur Memorial Award 2009 by Indian Academy of Applied Psychology, and Professor N. N. Sen Best Paper Award for the year 2010 by the Indian Association of Clinical Psychologists.

Manas K. Mandal, PhD, is Director of the Defence Institute of Psychological Research, DRDO, Ministry of Defence, Delhi. Born in 1956, Dr Mandal obtained his Postgraduate and Doctorate degrees from Calcutta University in 1979 and 1984, respectively. He has completed his Postdoctoral Research Programme at Delware University (Fulbright Fellow), USA, in 1986–87 and at Waterloo University (Shastri and NSERC Fellow), Canada, in 1993–94. Dr Mandal has been a professor of psychology at Department of Humanities and Social Sciences, Indian Institute of Technology, Kharagpur. He has been a visiting professor at Kyushu University, Japan, in 1997 and 2010–11. In 2003, he was a Fulbright Visiting Lecturer at Harvard University, USA. He has been awarded various Research Fellowships and Scientific Awards such as, International Scientific Exchange Award (Canada), Seymour Kety Grant (USA), DRDO Scientist of the Year 2006 Award (India), Virmani Award (National Medical Association of India), Career Award (India), and Young Scientist Award (Indian Science Congress), etc. Dr Mandal, to his credit, has eight books and more than 100 research papers and book chapters with international publication houses. He has supervised more than 20 doctoral and postdoctoral theses. Dr Mandal has been the President of the National Academy of Psychology (NAOP), India, for the year 2011.

Seema Mehrotra, PhD, is working at the National Institute of Mental Health and Neuro Sciences, Bangalore, as Additional Professor of Clinical Psychology. She is the coordinator of the Positive Psychology unit and a consultant in an adult psychiatry unit at NIMHANS. She served in faculty positions at the Kasturba Medical College (KMC), Manipal before joining NIMHANS in 2002. She completed her MPhil training in Clinical Psychology from NIMHANS and subsequently PhD in Psychology from Nagpur University in 1996. She has 18 years of clinical, teaching, and research experience. She has supervised several research dissertations and theses in the area of positive psychology, published articles in peer reviewed indexed journals, and contributed chapters in books. She is currently undertaking research projects funded by ICMR, ICSSR and CSIR. Her areas of research and practice include positive psychology, mental health promotion, process of adaptation to major life events and emotional regulation.

Vijay Parkash, PhD, is currently working as Scientist 'B' at Defence Institute of Psychological Research, Defence R&D Organization, Delhi. After completing his postgraduation, he was awarded DRDO Research Fellowship and he completed his doctorate in Psychology from Kurukshetra University, Kurukshetra. Health psychology, personality, and psychometrics are the areas of his interest and he has around eight years of research experience. He has also served as a Psychologist at Air Force Selection Board, Dehradun, for around two years. He has been involved in some major research projects related to suicidal behavior and test constructions for personnel selection in armed forces and paramilitary forces. He has been one of the editors of two edited volumes: *Recent Developments in Psychology* and *Counseling: A Practical Approach*. He has to his credit around 15 other academic publications in journals and books.

Ujvala Rajadhyaksha, PhD, is currently Associate Professor at the Department of Business Administration and Economics at Saint Mary's College, Notre Dame, Indiana, USA. Previously she has worked as faculty at Shailesh J. Mehta School of Management at Indian Institute of Technology, Bombay, and at Indian Institute of Management, Calcutta, both in India. She has been visiting faculty at Zhongshan University, PRC, and visiting research scholar at McGill University, Canada, as a recipient of the Shastri Indo-Canadian Fellowship. Ujvala's research interests include work and family issues, gender issues in management, and international and cross-cultural management with a special focus on India. Her research papers in these areas have been nominated for the Carolyn Dexter Award for internationalizing the academy at the Academy of Management conferences. She has published in journals such as *Human Relations, Sex Roles, Journal of Business Ethics, Journal of Management Education*, to name a few.

Jamuna Rajeswaran, PhD, completed her doctorate in Clinical Psychology in 2000. Her specialization is in the area of Clinical Neuropsychology. She joined as faculty at the Department of Clinical Psychology, National Institute of Mental Health and Neuro Sciences (NIMHANS), Bangalore, India, in 2004. Currently she is working as Associate Professor and Head of Clinical Neuropsychology at the Neuropsychology Unit, NIMHANS. She has pioneered the Holistic Neuropsychological Rehabilitation work in India.

She is the first person to introduce the EEG Neurofeedback training in India for various clinical conditions, after obtaining training in Neurofeedback Therapy from the Brain Masters, Cleveland, Ohio, USA. She has guided several MPhil, PhD, Clinical Psychology, MCh Neurosurgery, and MD Psychiatry theses. She is the recipient of the UGC Visiting Faculty Fellowship to Maurities. She has presented papers in several national and international conferences and published articles in national and international journals. She has also written chapters in books.

Kamala Ramadoss, PhD, is an Assistant Professor at Syracuse University's Department of Child and Family Studies since 2008. She holds a PhD in Family Studies from Purdue University. She is a certified family life educator and is the Co-Chair of the Work and Family Focus Group at the National Council on Family Relations, USA. Her research focuses on the links between workplace conditions and family life, particularly support in the workplace and work–life issues. She is the author of numerous papers/articles on work–family issues and she teaches undergraduate- and graduate-level courses on work and family issues at Syracuse University. Previously, Kamala worked at Sardar Patel University, Gujarat, and Punjab Agricultural University, Ludhiana, and continues her research and teaching collaborations with M.S. University of Baroda, Gujarat. She conducts training and consultation in research methods and applied statistics for students and faculty both in the US and in India.

Irfana Rashid is currently pursuing PhD from Aligarh Muslim University (AMU), Aligarh. She got enrolled in doctorate degree on 14 December 2009. She has qualified UGC–NET and UGC–JRF in June 2009. She presented papers in national and international conferences, and published papers in conference proceedings, edited book, and refereed journal on the topic Stress Management.

Fakir Mohan Sahoo, PhD, is a Research Professor in the Xavier Institute of Management, Bhubaneswar, India. He is also a former Professor and Head at the Center of Advanced Study in Psychology, Utkal University, Bhubaneswar, India. He received the Canadian Commonwealth Scholarship and received Doctoral Degree from Queen's University, Kingston, Canada. He was also a visiting Professor in this institution for some time. His research commitments include cross-cultural research and indigenous model of human behavior. His publications include several books on Psychology and Management.

He has received several awards for popularizing psychology, and supervised a large number of MA and MPhil dissertations, and 35 doctoral theses.

Radha R. Sharma, PhD, is a senior Professor, Organisational Behaviour and HRD at Management Development Institute (MDI), India, Raman Munjal Chair Professor and HR Ambassador for India, Academy of Management. She has been a Visiting Professor to International University, Germany, and has taught courses on Intercultural Skills in ESCP–Europe MBA programs. A recipient of four gold medals for academic excellence, Dr Sharma has an Advanced Professional Certification in MBTI from Association of Personality Type, EI certification from EI Learning Systems (USA), and has qualified certificate courses in Corporate Social Responsibility from British Council and New Academy of Business, UK, and the World Bank Institute. She has received certification in participant-centered learning at Harvard Business School, USA. She is recipient of Outstanding Cutting Edge Research Paper Award, 2006, AHRD, (USA); Best Faculty Award: Excellence in Research, 2006 and 2007 at MDI; Outstanding Management Researcher Award, AIMS International (2008). Her research interests are: executive burnout; emotional, social, and cultural intelligence; managerial competencies, leadership, spirituality, diversity, humanism, and CSR. She has published/presented about 100 papers, cases in Rutledge, Palgrave McMillan, Information Age Publishing, Edward Elgar. Her books include: *Change Management and Organisational Transformation* (2012 in press), *Change Management* (2007); *360 Degree Feedback, Competency Mapping and Assessment Centres* (2002); *Organisational Behaviour*, with Steven Mc Shane and Mary Ann Von Glinow (3 editions, 2006, 2008, 2011).

Mala Sinha, PhD, is Associate Professor at Faculty of Management Studies (FMS), University of Delhi. She has obtained PhD in Psychology from University of Allahabad in 1992. Dr Sinha has published several research papers in international journals and books in the area of Work Values, Leadership and Life Skills Education. She is a regular case analyst for *Business World* and many of her analyses have been in Special Collector's Editions of Selected Case Studies by *Business World*. Her researches are primarily focused on Asian perspectives in management, drawing chiefly from scriptural philosophies like Vedanta, Zen Buddhism, and Sufism, and ancient epics like Ramayana and Mahabharata. She is a corporate trainer and consultant to government and multinational organizations and has facilitated workshops for World Bank, WHO, and Confederation of Indian Industries (CII). She has been

Member of Board of Studies to All India Management Association–Centre for Management Education (AIMA–CME), and is life member of International Society for the Study of Work and Organizational Values (ISSWOV), and National HRD Network. Mala Sinha is also a published poet.

Paulomi Sudhir, PhD, is currently working as Associate Professor, at the Department of Clinical Psychology, NIMHANS, Bangalore. Dr Paulomi Sudhir is an alumnus of NIMHANS having completed her MPhil and PhD from NIMHANS. She joined the faculty in 2004. As a consultant at the Behavioural Medicine unit at NIMHANS, she has been contributing to the clinical, training, and research activities of the unit and she specializes in Behavioural and Cognitive Behavioural Therapies for various emotional and stress-related disorders. Dr Paulomi Sudhir has conducted several workshops for training of mental professionals in cognitive behavioral interventions. Her research areas include cognitive behavioral processes and therapies in emotional and stress-related disorders, behavioral medicine, and health psychology and stress management. She has mentored several MPhil dissertations and doctoral theses in her areas of research and has published in national and international journals.

Arathi Taksal is a final year PhD Scholar at the Department of Clinical Psychology, NIMHANS, Bangalore. She joined the Department as an MPhil trainee in the year 2007 and subsequently joined for her PhD program. She has worked in the area of social and neuro-cognition in schizophrenia and is currently pursuing her PhD on an integrated psychological intervention for schizophrenia. She has received intensive training in the area of psychological interventions and in particular individual therapies, family therapy, and cognitive behavioral therapies. She also presented papers at national and international conferences.

Parvaiz Talib, PhD, is currently Professor at Aligarh Muslim University (AMU), Aligarh, UP, as Professor in Business Communication, Stress management, Human Resource and Organization Behavior. He has done PhD in Management from Aligarh Muslim University (UP) in 1999. He successfully completed Faculty Development Program (FDP) from Indian Institute of Management, Ahmedabad. He has a teaching experience of 23 years. He has presented papers in national and international conferences and published papers in refereed journals and edited books on topics related to Stress Management, Strategic Management, and Business Communication.

Ravikesh Tripathi is pursuing his PhD in Clinical Psychology the National Institute of Mental Health and Neuro Sciences, Bangalore, in addition to serving as a research staff in an ongoing project on profiling strengths in Indian youth. He is a qualified clinical psychologist, having completed a two year MPhil training program in Clinical Psychology from NIMHANS, Bangalore. He has served as a clinical psychologist in the same institute for a period of three years. He has authored/co-authored research papers in peer-reviewed indexed journals and has contributed to papers presented in national and international conferences. His areas of interest include neuro-psychology, psychometrics, and positive psychology.

Index